Elements
of
Microeconomics

Second Edition

Elements
of
Microeconomics

Second Edition

Robert S. Main
Charles W. Baird
California State University, Hayward

WEST PUBLISHING COMPANY
St. Paul • New York • Los Angeles • San Francisco

For Jan, Zachary, and Caitlin
For Patti, Eric, and Elizabeth

Photo Credits

Chapter one: Erich Hartmann, Magnum
Chapter two: Virginia State Travel Service
Chapter three: Mike Mazzaschi, Stock, Boston
Chapter four: Hirschfields
Chapter five: Mount Snow Ski Resort Photo by Bob Perry
Chapter six: General Motors Corporation
Chapter seven: Tennessee Valley Authority
Chapter eight: Daniel S. Brody, Stock, Boston
Chapter nine: Oklahoma City Chamber of Commerce
Chapter ten: New York State Department of Commerce
Chapter eleven: Cornell Capa, Magnum
Chapter twelve: Charles L. Farrow
Chapter thirteen: St. Paul Children's Hospital

COPYRIGHT © 1977 By WEST PUBLISHING CO.
COPYRIGHT © 1981 By WEST PUBLISHING CO.
50 West Kellogg Boulevard
P.O. Box 3526
St. Paul, Minnesota 55165

Printed in the United States of America

Library of Congress Cataloging in Publication Data

Main, Robert S.
  Elements of microeconomics.

  Includes index.
  1. Microeconomics. I. Baird, Charles W.,
joint author. II. Title.
HB172.M34 1981 330 80-24717
ISBN 0-8299-0391-7

4th Reprint—1986

Table of Contents

X

xii

Preface to the
Second Edition

In revising this book, we have attempted to retain its distinctive features—
a relatively brief book emphasizing voluntary exchange and the market
process—while strengthening certain areas and introducing new applications. In addition, in response to popular demand we have greatly increased the number of questions following each chapter.

The major changes are as follows:

Chapter 1 contains a rewritten section on efficiency which makes the
concept easier to apply in later chapters. The exchange example in chapter
2 has been expanded and more carefully explained, and two new applications have been added.

The demand chapter is now chapter 3, and it includes new sections
on alternative forms of competition during shortages, and on relative versus absolute prices.

The comparative advantage chapter is now chapter 4, and it has been
completely rewritten. Its new title, "Opportunity Cost and Comparative
Advantage," suggests the general approach we have taken. The Crusoe/
Friday example with its geometry is now an appendix to the chapter. The
chapter itself is a verbal exposition of the principle of comparative advantage based squarely on opportunity cost. The exposition uses such examples as do-it-yourself, the underground economy, the draft, and San
Francisco residential hotels.

Most of the material on profits has been moved to chapter 5. We have added an example of the historical evolution of firms during the industrial revolution to chapter 6.

Chapter 7 includes an expanded treatment of continued possession costs and their role in decision making, as well as new sections on windfall profits, agricultural surpluses in Europe, costs of obtaining oil, and Hayek's approach to relative prices as coordinating devices.

Chapter 9 has more on annuities and sections on saving for the future, as well as a new appendix on inflation and interest rates.

Chapter 10 has a new section on examples of collusion, as well as a revised and expanded section on OPEC, taxi medallions, the effects of licensing, and the political economy of market closure. A new subsection, which explains the two key principles of modern unionism in the United States—exclusive representation and union security—has been added to the discussion of labor unions.

Chapter 11 contains rewritten and expanded sections on quality assurance, brand names, and government regulation.

In chapter 12, the section on government control of externalities has been rewritten and expanded, with improved graphical exposition. The section on aerosol sprays has been replaced by one on pesticides.

Finally, a section on the negative income tax has been added to chapter 13.

We continue to acknowledge with gratitude all of the intellectual debts mentioned in the preface to the first edition. In addition, we should like to thank Daniel R. Blake, California State University, Northridge; Ernest Combs, University of Puget Sound; Peter Gordon, University of Southern California; and Mokhlis Y. Zaki, Northern Michigan University, who provided us with detailed comments on the first edition and suggestions for revision. Also, we should like to single out our friends and colleagues Virgil Salera of California State University, Hayward, and Lester Saft of California State University, Northridge, who took a special interest in the book and provided us with many helpful suggestions for improvement.

Finally, we wish to thank Sandra Anderson for an excellent job in coordinating the typing for this revision, and Peggy Renk for assisting in that regard.

Preface to Instructors— First Edition

In writing this book we have attempted to provide students with an introduction to economics which points out the key features of a voluntary exchange economy and enables them to learn how economists think so that they can more effectively tackle the issues which arise in our economy. The first step in doing this is, we believe, to develop a clear understanding of the concepts of exchange and comparative advantage. This rather unusual approach is very valuable because it is easier to see the pervasive nature of these concepts in later chapters.

The demand chapter, in addition to presenting the usual material, introduces the demand for inputs in order to show the similarities between the two concepts.

The cost chapter utilizes the cost categories (acquisition, possession, and operating) pioneered by Alchian and Allen. The chapter on the firm owes a great deal to the important work by Alchian and Demsetz. And the price-taker versus price-searcher distinction in discussing market structure can also be traced to Alchian and Allen.

The chapter on present values and profits is an attempt to make that difficult and confusing area more comprehensible by showing how the two ideas are related.

The chapters on restrictions on markets, consumerism and advertising, property rights and externalities, and income distribution are attempts to apply the principles learned in the earlier chapters to these important areas of interest.

XVI

The reader of the above brief outline of the book should immediately realize the great debt we owe to Armen A. Alchian and William R. Allen, who raised the level of economic discourse so greatly with their books *University Economics* and *Exchange and Production*. Those books have, more than any others, molded our thinking about the principles course and taught us economics. This book could not have been written without their help.

Some technical features of our book with which instructors should become familiar are the end-of-chapter features: "Points to Remember" (selected listing of important ideas raised in the chapter); "Key Terms" (a glossary of new words and phrases); and the Review Questions (some are fairly mechanical and designed to reinforce ideas developed in the chapters, and some extend the analysis into related new areas). We feel that these can be of significant value in understanding the material.

The entire first draft of this book was written by Main. Baird wrote the final version of Chapter 1 and parts of Chapter 5, and contributed substantially to the revision of the rest of the book. Main would like to thank his teachers, especially Armen Alchian and Jack Hirshleifer of UCLA and Benjamin Rogge of Wabash College. Their influence on his thinking has been very great and is most appreciated. Baird wishes explicitly to thank his former colleagues at UCLA, especially Armen Alchian and William Allen, for all that he learned from them.

The book has utilized many examples and ideas suggested by colleagues, friends, and students. The authors are grateful for all the suggestions received.

The following people read the entire manuscript at one stage or another: William Dickneider, Moorpark College; Donald R. House, Auburn University; Richard Sherman, Ohio State University; Nancy Spillman, Los Angeles Trade Technical College; Richard Tresch, Boston College; and John T. Wenders, University of Arizona. Their comments and constructive criticisms were extremely valuable, and while we did not do all that they wanted us to, the book is clearly better than it would have been without their efforts.

Main wrote the first draft of the book during the summer of 1975 while he and his wife and son were staying with their families in Indiana. He wishes to thank both Claude and Louise Main and Howard and Betty Huesing for providing him with an excellent working environment during that period. He also wishes to express his appreciation for the good humor with which his wife Janet and son Zachary endured the inconveniences which his later work on the project entailed.

Nancy Connolly provided typing services in Indiana and Sandra Anderson, once again, carried the load in California. We are grateful to both for an excellent job. Finally, Clyde Perlee's patience and encouragement as the manuscript passed through the many stages of production, and Merle Holmwood's excellent work as copy editor, contributed significantly to the quality of the final product.

Preface to Students— First Edition

The main topics of this book are the attempts of individuals to cope with the fundamental problem of scarcity, and the social institutions (such as exchange) which attempt to coordinate those attempts. You will find many real-world phenomena, such as the energy crisis, shortages, charity, monopoly and competition, discussed in this book. We hope that you will gain new understanding of and insights into these problems by looking at them from the "economic" point of view.

The book is written to introduce you to the phenomena of exchange and comparative advantage in the first three chapters and then to apply those important concepts throughout the book. We have included many examples of the applications of economic theory throughout the book, as well as many examples which will enable you to apply the theory yourself. There is no mathematics beyond arithmetic and a small amount of simple algebra. However, certain portions of some of the chapters require careful reading. Our experience is that the material is best grasped by reading the numerical examples slowly and following along with paper and pencil. This is especially true of Chapters 2 and 3, as well as some later chapters.

At the end of each chapter are "Points to Remember" and "Key Terms." We should emphasize that these are not intended to be complete lists. They should not be read instead of the chapter, but rather to supplement one's reading of the chapter.

There are also questions at the end of each chapter. These questions serve two purposes. Many of them involve working out numerical examples similar to those in the text so that the concept involved is reinforced. Other questions raise new issues which the student can, we hope, more effectively tackle after having read the chapter material.

If you master the concepts introduced in this book, we think you will be better able to sort out sense from nonsense in discussions of public policy issues. We also think that you will discover that "doing economics" can be fun.

Elements
of
Microeconomics

Second Edition

chapter 1

Getting Started

In any large nation there are millions of independent decision makers. Of course all decisions are made by people, but sometimes people act as decision makers within groups, such as households, firms, and government agencies. Economists call an independent decision-making unit—such as a person acting for himself, a household, a business firm, or a government agency—a *transactor*. It seems, at first glance, that if all these millions of transactors make plans on the basis of their own knowledge and for their own exclusive purposes, not all of these plans can be carried out. For example, if sellers of aluminum make their own plans regarding how much and what kinds of aluminum to make available for sale, and buyers of aluminum make their own plans as to how much and what kinds of aluminum to acquire, it seems likely that the sellers would plan to make available quantities and types that are different from what the buyers plan to buy.

Microeconomics—the subject matter of this book—is the study of how millions of independently made plans can be made to be consistent with each other without any central direction or control. The main coordinating device is changes of prices, so microeconomics is sometimes called *price theory*. The first eight chapters of this book present the fundamentals of price determination. In these chapters we will consider questions of demand (the plans of buyers) and supply (the plans of sellers) and how these plans interact to determine prices and changes in prices.

Chapters 2 and 4 discuss the rudiments of two key economic processes

4

—voluntary exchange and specialization. Chapters 3 and 5 construct the two basic tools of analysis (demand and cost) which permit economists to generalize the principles of voluntary exchange and specialization. Chapter 6 introduces the business firm and considers its essential nature and function, and chapters 7 and 8 discuss decision making within the two different types of business firms—those which take the price of the goods they sell as given (called *price-takers*) and those which have to *choose* the best price to charge (called *price-searchers*).

The remaining chapters of the book—chapters 9 through 13—exposit many of the applications of the principles of microeconomics. In these chapters we will consider such topics as conspiracies to restrict competition, bribery and corruption, charity, labor unions, the consumer movement, advertising, property rights, pollution, education, inheritance, and the distribution of wealth and income. We are convinced that economic analysis can shed light on most of the social and political issues of the 1980s. We think that after you read this book you will agree.

SCARCITY AND COST

A good is something people want some of rather than none of. I would rather have *some* trips to Europe than none. For me, a trip to Europe is a good. I would rather have *no* cigarettes than *some* cigarettes. For me, a cigarette is not a good. A cigarette is, however, a good for some people.

Economic analysis begins with the observation that no matter how things are arranged, not everyone can have as much of every good as he would like. In fact, *no one* has as much of every good as he wants. Economists call this condition *scarcity*. Everyone in every society can name some goods which he would accept more of if they were offered to him free of charge. If we were all isolated, self-sufficient individuals, providing completely for our own wants, the fact of scarcity would be overwhelming. We would all be desperately poor. Through cooperation and specialization we are able to provide more of our wants without working any harder. (This is explained in chapters 2 and 4.) But even with the tremendous expansion in our opportunities which cooperation and specialization bring, we still find that we are not able to obtain as much of everything as we would like. All of us find that if we want to obtain more of some goods, some sacrifice must be made. Some price must be paid. A longer vacation means not getting a new car; a nicer apartment means fewer clothes; time spent at a football game means less time studying economics (time, too, is scarce); more beef in the diet means less bourbon can be consumed; more tax money spent on police services means less tax money to spend on teachers' salaries; more tax money collected means less money can be used to satisfy private wants, and so on.

Let us consider one of these choices more carefully We said that time spent at a football game means less time studying economics. But studying economics is not the only other thing you could do. Three hours at a football game means three hours that cannot be used for *any* other purpose.

You sacrifice three hours at a movie, three hours listening to John Denver, three hours studying English literature, three hours of pleasure driving, and so on. You sacrifice *all* of these things, but you could only do *one* of them if you did not spend the time at the football game. Economists define *cost* as the most highly valued sacrifice incurred when an action is undertaken. (Since cost implies foregoing opportunities, the expression *opportunity cost* is sometimes used to remind the reader of this. The point is sometimes expressed by the phrase "all costs are opportunity costs.") The cost to you of the football game is the alternative use of three hours that you value most highly. If the pleasure drive is your most highly valued alternative, the pleasure drive is your cost of the football game. If studying economics is the most highly valued alternative use of your time, that is the cost you bear when you go to the football game.

This concept of cost can be applied to all resources. If a person works at a certain job (job A), that means that she cannot at the same time work at any other job. The cost of working at job A is the value of the work she could do in her best alternative job. If a factory building is used to produce typewriters, then it cannot be used to produce skates, books, or staplers. To know the cost of using the building to produce typewriters, we must know the value of the benefit which the building would provide in its most highly valued alternative use.

Economists are fond of saying that there is no such thing as a free lunch. What we mean by this is that because most goods are scarce, when one person gets more of a good someone—not necessarily that person—must give up something. Lunches are distributed at a zero price to some schoolchildren, but those lunches are *not* free. Somebody, taxpayers probably, had to give up something in order to make the zero price lunches available to the children. A good is free only if *no one* has to sacrifice anything when someone gets more of it. A good is free, in other words, only if it is not scarce.

SCARCITY VERSUS SHORTAGE

We have said that we are afflicted with scarcity. To determine if a particular good is a scarce good, we ask a hypothetical question: If the price of the good were zero, so that users would pay a zero price for using it and providers would receive a zero price for providing it, would the amount people wanted to use exceed the amount available? If the answer is yes, then the good is scarce. Gasoline is scarce because if its price were zero, people would want to use more than would be made available. The same would be true of most, if not all, other goods. A *shortage* of a good exists if, at the *current* price, the amount people want exceeds the amount available. If the price of gasoline were 10¢ per gallon there would be a shortage; people would want more gasoline than they could get. But if the price of gasoline were $4 per gallon, people would take a lot fewer automobile trips, and sellers of gasoline would be willing to produce a lot more gasoline. In fact, if the price of gasoline were $4 per gallon there would probably be a *surplus* of gasoline. Gasoline would still be scarce because at a zero price people would want more than they could get, but there would be a surplus of gasoline because, at $4 a gallon, people would want less than would be made available.

In the spring of 1979, there was a shortage of gasoline because, at the price sellers were allowed to charge, the amount people wanted was greater than the amount available. The result was lines at gasoline stations.

In the spring of 1980, there was a shortage of funds to lend at federally chartered credit unions. The maximum interest rate that could be charged on loans was 15 percent. At that rate, the amount of money people wanted to borrow was greater than the amount deposited in the credit unions. The result was a long waiting list of loan applicants—in other words, a shortage of loan funds.

Many universities own apartments which they rent to married students. The rents charged for these apartments are invariably lower than the rents for comparable nonuniversity apartments—sometimes $100 per month less. There are invariably long waiting lists of qualified renters seeking to obtain these quarters—a shortage.

WHAT, HOW, FOR WHOM?

Since most goods are scarce, three questions must be answered in any society. If there are insufficient natural resources, time, energy, and ingenuity to produce everything that everybody would like to have produced, *what will be produced? How will these things be produced? For whom will they be produced—in other words, who will get them and how much will they get?* These questions must be addressed in the Soviet Union, in China, in Scandinavia, in the United Kingdom, and in the United States. They must be addressed wherever there is scarcity.

The third question illustrates what economists mean when they say that *scarcity implies competition.* For a given amount produced and made available, when one person receives a larger quantity of a good, someone has to receive a smaller quantity of that good. In a centrally directed economy, competition is based on the ability to influence government decision makers. In an economy where government has no power to answer the basic three questions, competition is based on the ability to produce things that other people are willing to buy. In an economy with a government limited to providing the basic protective services (police, judiciary, and armed forces), a transactor obtains the ability to purchase things by producing some good (an actual commodity or a service) for which other people are willing to pay her. Her ability to acquire goods for herself depends on her ability to compete in serving buyers.

The U.S. economy is characterized by both forms of competition— competition to influence powerful governmental decision makers and competition to satisfy the wants of buyers. Whenever a governmental body has the authority to make decisions regarding the basic three questions, individuals will be tempted to influence these decisions in their own interests. This suggests that one way to reduce the incidence of political corruption is to limit the power given to government personnel. Another (we think more difficult) approach would be to educate people not to act in their own interests.

In an economy with government limited to the basic protective function, the first question, "What will be produced?", is answered as the result of individual transactors trying to get as much purchasing power—ability to purchase goods—for themselves as they can. A acquires lots of money for her own use only if other transactors are willing to purchase voluntarily what she has to sell. Perhaps she sells only her labor services (both mental and physical), and perhaps she sells the services of things that she owns, such as land, buildings, machines, and so on. No matter what she sells she must find buyers. She must, therefore, be very "other directed." She must care very much about what others are willing to buy. The outcome of this striving to find buyers is that what gets produced is precisely what buyers want to have produced.

In a limited government economy the third basic question is answered primarily according to how individuals are capable of identifying and servicing the wants of buyers. Those most capable of doing this are those who have the greatest ability to purchase the goods and services produced. Therefore both the first and the third questions are answered as the result of the competitive striving to get ahead. In a limited government economy the motto is "From each as he chooses, to each as he is chosen."[1] Individuals choose whether and what to sell, but the extent of their success depends on whether buyers voluntarily choose to buy from them.

Of course individuals are never completely able to choose what they wish to sell. Nature has not endowed all individuals with the same mental and physical abilities. Moreover, in a limited government economy, individuals are free to give gifts. A transactor may have a lot to sell today because his father gave him a piece of land or some common stock in the past. In some economies individuals are not permitted to give gifts except to officially approved recipients. We will have more to say on these matters in chapter 13.

In a limited government economy the answer to the second question, "How will goods be produced?", is that they will tend to be produced at the least possible cost. Once sellers think they perceive what buyers are willing to buy they try to make it available. But there is generally more than one way to produce something. Given buyers' attitudes toward the good in question, there is a maximum price that sellers are able to receive from buyers. Sellers, therefore, attempt to produce the good while incurring the least possible cost so that they have as much as possible left over to use for their own purposes.

---

1. This aphorism was suggested by Robert Nozick, *Anarchy, State, and Utopia* (New York: Basic Books, 1974), p. 160. This book is an excellent discussion of the philosophical underpinnings of the limited government society.

8

EFFICIENCY,
INEFFICIENCY,
AND WASTE

One of the most important and most often used concepts in economics is *efficiency*. An *efficient* action is one in which the *benefits* of the action are greater than the *costs*. Recall our discussion of the student a few pages back. If he spent three hours watching football, he had to forego alternatives. We said the benefit that could have been obtained from the *best* of those alternatives represented the *cost* of watching football. Using our definition of efficiency, we would say that it is efficient for the student to watch the football game if the benefits of doing so exceed the costs. An *efficient situation* (or allocation of resources) is one in which all possible efficient *actions* have been taken—that is, one in which all actions for which the benefits are greater than the cost have been taken. When one's resources are allocated efficiently, the only remaining potential actions are inefficient ones—that is, ones for which the benefits are *less than* the cost. If the student has allocated his time efficiently, any reallocation would make him worse off, because it would result in benefits which were less than the costs.

In contrast, an *inefficient allocation of resources* is one from which it is possible to make some *efficient* changes (that is, some changes whose benefits are greater than their costs). Waste accompanies inefficient actions and inefficient allocations of resources. An inefficient action is a wasteful one, and the waste associated with it is the excess of the action's cost over its benefit. An inefficient allocation is also wasteful, and the waste associated with it is the potential excess of benefits over costs which could be obtained if all remaining efficient actions were taken.

How can we apply these notions? Suppose we have decided to produce a certain good or provide a certain service called X. There are many ways to produce X and we want to find the best way. Economists would say the *efficient* way is to produce X at the *least possible cost*. The choice of production technique confronts the decision maker with benefits and costs. Consider production method A. This method entails sacrificed benefits (that is, costs). Resources used to produce X using method A are not then available to produce something else. Now consider alternative method B. If the decision maker chooses to produce by method B, a different set of resources will be required. Some or all of the resources that were required by method A will no longer be used to produce X. They will be used to produce something else. That something else is the *benefit* from switching to method B. But remember that method B entails using resources that would not have been used to produce X if method A had been chosen. The benefits foregone elsewhere due to using method B's resources to produce X are the *cost* of switching to method B. Suppose the benefits that would be foregone elsewhere if method A were used are equivalent to $100, and the benefits that would be foregone elsewhere if method B were used are equivalent to $80. Then we can say two things. First, the benefit of switching from A to B is $20 greater than the cost, so it is efficient to switch. (By contrast it would be *inefficient* to switch from B to A because the cost exceeds the benefit.) Second, the cost of method B ($80) is lower than the cost of method A ($100). If we know that switching from A to B is efficient, we also know that the cost of B is lower than the cost of A. Thus the *efficient* way to produce a *given* good (or benefit) is to produce it at *least cost*. Economists sometimes refer to this application of the notion of efficiency as *least cost efficiency*. Turning this around, we can say that efficient production involves getting the greatest benefit for a specified cost. Are you tempted to say that efficiency means getting the most benefit for the least cost? If so, consider this more concrete illustration of the concept of least cost efficiency (and therefore inefficiency) and waste. Imagine that you have a 200-ft.^{2} lawn to water. The lawn is irregularly shaped, and it is bordered on three sides by pavement. The goal is to keep the lawn green and full. To do this you must water the lawn three times a week. One way to do this is to place the hose sprinkler head first in one section of the lawn and then in another. Each time the hose is placed, the water is turned on with just enough force so that the water falls only on the grass. None runs off onto the pavement. The other way to water the lawn is to ignore the shape of the lawn, place the sprinkler head in the middle of the lawn area, and turn the faucet on full force. This covers all of the lawn with water, but a lot of water falls on the pavement. Which of these alternatives is the more efficient (least costly) one?

If the only cost you consider is the water usage, the first technique is the least costly. No water is lost to the pavement. However, there are other costs to consider. With the first technique you must stay around the area for two hours; with the second technique the job is finished in only one hour. If the monetary value you place on the extra hour of your time is larger than the monetary costs of the water that falls on the pavement, the second technique is the more efficient one.

Notice that the water that falls on the pavement is not referred to as wasted water. It is not wasted if it permits the stated goal to be accomplished with a smaller total cost than could otherwise be attained. Indeed, if you opt for the first technique in order to save water when the monetary value of an hour of your time exceeds the monetary value of the extra water, you are wasting your time. You are behaving inefficiently. Something is wasted only if it is put to a use where the resulting benefit is less than the resulting cost. If you devote the extra hour to lawn-watering, the benefit takes the form of other goods you can buy because you spend less on water. The cost is the benefit foregone because you can't devote that hour to other activities. If the dollar value of the extra time exceeds the dollar value of the extra water, the extra hour would be wasted if used on lawn-watering.

During a drought it is generally considered desirable to consume less water. If the money price of water were allowed to increase during such periods, people would voluntarily choose to consume less water because the monetary value of the water used would increase and, for many people, would exceed the monetary value of time saved (or whatever is saved, perhaps deodorant) when more water is used. Indeed, if the price of water

10

were high enough, many people might choose to let their lawns die. If prices were free to rise and fall in response to changes of the amount of water (and other goods) available, people automatically would be induced to choose efficient ways of accomplishing their goals.

The idea of letting lawns die suggests another way to use the concept of efficiency. In the lawn-watering example, we assume that you are going to water the lawn. Our (efficiency) problem is to find the lowest cost way of doing it. But once we have answered that question, we have another efficiency question: Should the lawn be watered? Using our definition, we would say that it is efficient to water the lawn if the benefit from doing so is greater than the cost. The cost is whatever least cost number we have discovered. As the price of water rises, users who water their lawns will find it efficient to use more time and less water per watering. But the cost per watering will, nevertheless, go up as the price of water rises. (The substitution of time for water makes the cost rise less than it otherwise would, but the cost *does* rise.) As the cost of watering rises, some people will find that it is no longer efficient to water their lawn. For them the cost of watering (even when watering is done in the least cost way) comes to exceed the benefits of watering. Thus the concept of efficiency can be applied to the *mix of goods people produce* as well as to the method by which they are produced. In chapter 2 we shall see that efficiency is also relevant to allocations of goods among transactors.

When considering least cost efficiency, we must weigh one additional factor. For each specified cost there is a maximum benefit that can be derived, but before we can know what the maximum benefit is, we have to know what we have to work with—how much cost we can incur. Talking about a maximum benefit without reference to the amount of cost we can incur is like trying to imagine how far we can go before purchasing gas for our car without knowing how much gas is already in the tank.

Similarly, for each specified benefit there is a least cost way to obtain it. To talk about cutting costs without specifying what you have to accomplish is like discussing how to save on a food budget without first specifying the desired consumption of protein, carbohydrates, minerals, and vitamins. Only when we have some idea of our goals can we talk meaningfully of the least cost (efficient) way to accomplish them. We can either specify the goal and search for the least cost way of attaining it, or we can specify the cost we can incur and search for the most desirable goal that can be attained with that cost. We cannot get the most for the least.

THE METHOD OF ECONOMIC ANALYSIS

Economics has a bad reputation among students. The courses are reputed to be filled with mathematics, graphs, and something called *models* based on unrealistic assumptions which make them good for nothing except to provide employment to teachers of economics. Moreover, economics is never recommended as a way to increase one's grade point average.

You can relax (somewhat) because in this text we use very little mathematics. Most of the important propositions in economics can best be stated in words and illustrated by real-world examples. This is the main approach in the text. However, as you can see merely by leafing through the pages, there are a fair number of graphs. When a graph is used it is because the graph reinforces the verbal discussion and permits you to see readily the effects of changes in the circumstances under discussion. One of the most important functions of economic theory is to see the consequences of such changes of circumstances as new regulations, changes in technology, changes in buyers' tastes, new sources of information, and changes in the prices of things used to produce other things. How these underlying circumstances interact to determine an initial situation (for example, an initial price) and how changes of the underlying circumstances would change the situation (for example, cause price to change) can be discussed verbally. But if the interaction of the most important underlying circumstances as well as any changed circumstances can be depicted graphically, it is not necessary to go through a second verbal analysis to see what the outcome will be. The use of the graph is *efficient* because it reduces the total effort needed to arrive at the conclusions.

Models

A *model* is a simplified representation of some real-world process. It is simplified because it is put together by ignoring many features of the actual process and concentrating on only a few. This means that the model is *abstract*. To abstract means to remove or separate parts of a whole from other parts. In any abstraction it is important to make certain that the features identified as unimportant are in fact unimportant relative to the purpose of the particular analysis under way.

A road map can be considered to be an abstract model. The map represents features of reality that are important to the map users (for example, locations of roads, cities, and bodies of water), and it completely ignores other features of reality that are unimportant (for example, the location of houses, trees, and telephone poles). Moreover, most road maps ignore still other features of reality that could be important to the map users (for example, the location of gasoline stations, restaurants, and motels). The latter are ignored because the *main* purpose of a road map is to show the user how to get from one point to another. In order to accomplish that goal as directly and cheaply as possible, only information most relevant to that goal is included.

An economic model is like a road map. The typical economic model involves humans taking action in response to certain variables. The characteristics of humans are of interest in understanding human action, but some characteristics may be completely uninteresting for the purpose at hand. The height and weight of golfers are not germane to an inquiry into how their decisions to play golf are affected by a change in the price of golf clubs. Thus the height and weight of golfers would be left out of the

12

economic model constructed to consider the effects of such price changes. The extent to which today's generation of golfers had fathers who were also golfers could conceivably be of interest in such an inquiry, but the effect would probably be so small that this factor also would be ignored in the economic model. Only those variables which experience and thought suggest would be of major importance (for example, the price of golf balls and the incomes of golfers) would be explicitly included in the model. The model would abstract from (ignore) the other factors.

Economic models employ assumptions. Sometimes these assumptions are realistic and sometimes not. For example, when an economist discusses the effect of the introduction of a new machine or tool into a production process on the quantity of workers employed, she often assumes that each worker is like every other worker. She does not pay attention to the unique characteristics of individual workers—that is, she abstracts from the reality of those interpersonal differences. Is it legitimate to assume away interpersonal differences of workers in such an analysis? Economists answer this question in a very pragmatic way. The assumption, and the model and analysis based on the assumption, are legitimate if they work. They are not legitimate if they don't work.

What do we mean when we say a model works? We mean only that it brings us to conclusions that are verified by what actually happens. Economic analysis carried out by using models based on assumptions attempts to *predict* what will happen in response to some change that takes place. A model is merely a formalized process of reasoning designed to bring us to conclusions about what will happen before it happens. We say that a model is a good one, and we continue to use it, as long as it permits us to make correct predictions. Models are used before the fact (ex *ante*) to bring us to conclusions that are later (hopefully) verified after the fact (ex *post*).

Economists discard a model only if the predictions that are made while using it are not verified by actual experience or if a new model is devised that permits more accurate predictions. We never discard a model simply because the model is based on unrealistic assumptions, or is too abstract, or is too unreal.

Methodological Individualism

Economic analysis is usually based on *methodological individualism.* That is, our analysis inquires into how people, rather than groups, behave in response to the opportunities that exist. For example, economists think that it is meaningless to talk about how the Department of Energy (DOE) will choose. People make the decisions that determine the official actions of DOE. Moreover, people carry out the actions of DOE. In a very important sense DOE itself never acts; only people who make up DOE act. Economists think that the best way to understand what is done under the name of DOE is to analyze the choices and the actions of the individuals that make up DOE. When we want to predict whether DOE will permit gas stations to stay open on Sundays, we look to the personal and professional goals possessed by and the limitations confronted by the individual or individuals who have the authority to make such a decision.

Marginal Analysis

In analyzing decisions, economists often utilize *marginal analysis*. This means they look at the *additional* (or incremental) benefit and/or cost associated with doing *one more* of something. This enables one conceptually to answer the question of *how much* of an activity to carry out. It is worth it (in other words, efficient) to do one more of something if the additional (that is, marginal) benefit of doing so is greater than the additional (that is, marginal) cost. Decision makers tend to do more of anything as long as the marginal benefit (as they see it) of doing so is greater than the marginal cost (as they see it) of doing so. Efficient decision makers will stop increasing the amount they do of anything when the perceived marginal benefit *equals* the perceived marginal cost. For example, how much time each week should you study economics? If you determine the answer to this question utilizing our notion of efficiency, you should plan to spend an additional hour studying economics only if the benefit you get from that extra hour of study (the marginal benefit of studying economics), exceeds the cost you must bear to study the extra hour (the marginal cost of studying economics). In fact, you should spend more and more time studying economics as long as the marginal/benefit of doing so exceeds the marginal cost of doing so. When you find that, given the amount of time you spend studying economics, if you increase that study time still more the cost you will bear because of the increase will exceed the benefit you will derive because of the increase, you should stop increasing the study time.

POSITIVE AND NORMATIVE STATEMENTS

Some statements made by economists involve the way things are (or were, or will be). Other statements concern the way things ought to be (or ought to have been, or ought to be in the future). The former statements can be tested for accuracy, but the latter statements cannot. The former involve fact, the latter involve opinion. The former are called *positive* statements, and the latter are called *normative* statements.

If you say that the price of gasoline increased in 1973 and in 1974, you make a positive statement. It is positive because it can be tested for accuracy. A statement that the price of gasoline fell in 1973 and in 1974 is also a positive statement. It is positive because it too can be tested. Note that a positive statement does not have to be a true statement. It merely has to be capable of being tested. The statement that the moon is made of green cheese is a positive statement because it can be tested. It is also a false statement because it is refuted by the evidence.

If you say that the price of gasoline increased by too much over the 1973–74 period, you make a normative statement. The statement is neither correct nor incorrect. It is mere opinion. There is no way that the statement can be tested for accuracy. How much of a price increase is "too much"? You will get as many answers to this question as the people you ask.

Normative statements are often the result of a value judgment combined with some positive analysis. A statement that "fair-trade laws in liquor (laws that force all liquor sellers to charge the same high price) are a good thing," is clearly normative. One who utters it could start with the value judgment (opinion) that liquor consumption is bad and should be discouraged. He could then reason as follows: (1) if the price of liquor is higher, less will be consumed; (2) if fair-trade laws are imposed, the price will be higher; (3) therefore, liquor consumption will be reduced by means of fair-trade laws. Notice that the statements are positive because they are capable of being tested.

An economist could explain the step-by-step reasoning involved in statements (1)-(3) to anyone, no matter what his or her normative position on liquor. An owner of a liquor store would be likely to conclude on the basis of the statements that fair-trade laws in liquor are bad. The Women's Christian Temperance Union would come to the opposite conclusion on the basis of the same positive statements.

Reasoning from one positive statement to another is called positive analysis. The end result of positive analysis is a set of positive conclusions. If the positive conclusions are not refuted by actual experience, we regard the positive analysis used to arrive at the conclusions to be a useful economic model. Whether the analyst (or any person) likes or approves of the positive conclusions is up to her. In this text we concentrate on the positive analysis of economic problems. The text is designed to tell you what economics says, not what economists say.

However, a couple of warnings are in order. First, by the very choice of the topics covered, we are exercising some value judgments about what is useful and important. Other economists may well exercise different value judgments in this regard. Second, it is a widely held value judgment among economists that efficiency is good, so when an economist says that a certain policy is efficient or inefficient he (and we) often comes close to saying that the policy is good or bad. The temptation to make this jump should be resisted in order to keep the two types of analyses distinct.

LOOKING AHEAD

In the next chapter we begin our positive analysis. We discuss one of the most basic economic processes—voluntary exchange. This is the process by which goods are allocated, the signals that guide production are generated, and people's incomes and wealth are determined.

POINTS TO REMEMBER

1. Microeconomics is the study of how prices help to coordinate the independently made plans of the many transactors in an economy.

2. A good is something people want some of rather than none of.

3. Scarcity means that not everyone has as much of every good as she wants.

4. A good is scarce if, at a zero price, the amount demanded exceeds the amount made available by nature and other transactors. Most goods are scarce.

5. Scarcity is not the same thing as shortage.

6. The cost of an action is the most highly valued alternative which is sacrificed when the action is taken.

7. The three major questions which must be answered in any economy are: What will be produced? How will these things be produced? For whom will they be produced?

8. An efficient (inefficient) action is one for which the benefit is greater (less) than the cost.

9. An efficient method of production is one which obtains a given benefit at the lowest possible cost (or obtains the greatest benefit from a given specified cost).

10. Efficient production does not entail using the smallest amount of any particular input, but rather minimizing the sum of the costs of all inputs used for a given output.

11. An efficient allocation of resources is one in which it is not possible to take any further efficient actions.

12. The usefulness of an economic model is judged by how closely its predictions conform to the facts, not by how realistic its assumptions are.

13. Economic analysis builds on the behavior of individuals, not groups.

14. Economists often utilize marginal analysis.

KEY TERMS

Cost: The most highly valued sacrifice incurred when an action is undertaken.

Efficient action: An action for which the benefit is greater than the cost.

Efficient allocation: A situation such that the cost of any further action will be greater than its benefit.

Efficient method of production: A method which provides a given benefit at the lowest possible cost or which provides the most benefit for a given cost.

Good: Something which someone wants some of rather than none of.

Marginal analysis: Analysis of the effects of small changes in decision variables. Specifically, an analysis of the marginal benefit and/or marginal cost of a one-unit change in something.

Methodological individualism: An approach which takes the individual as the starting point of analysis. It is a denial of the idea of collective values or preferences, other than as an amalgamation of individual values and preferences.

Microeconomics: The study of the behavior of individual transactors under scarcity, and the coordination of their actions by mechanisms such as prices.

Model: A simplified (abstract) representation of some real-world process.

Normative statement: A statement based, at least in part, on opinion about what ought to be (or ought to have been, or ought to be in the future). It cannot be shown to be true or false.

Positive statement: A statement which can be tested (at least in principle) and shown to be true or false. A statement about the way things are, or were, or will be.

Scarcity: A situation in which not everyone can have as much of everything as she wants.

Shortage: A situation in which the amount of a good wanted at the actual existing price exceeds the amount made available at that price.

Surplus: A situation in which the amount of a good wanted is less than the amount made available at that price.

Transactor: An individual decision-making unit in the economy, such as a household, firm, or government agency.

REVIEW QUESTIONS

1. Are beautiful sunsets a scarce good? Explain.

2. "In these days of high gasoline prices, it is important that cars be more efficient." Comment on this assertion. Could you think of a better way of expressing the sentiment?

3. "There is currently a shortage of low-income housing." What do you think this means? Is the usage of shortage consistent with its economic meaning?

4. "Before the energy crisis of a few years ago, people wasted a lot of

energy by having little or no insulation in their homes, and by having many large windows which allowed heat to escape easily." Comment.

5. "There is no such thing as a free lunch." What do you think this statement means? Is it true by definition, or is it capable of being tested?

6. Which of the following are positive statements? Which are normative? (a) "The Dodgers will win the pennant this year." (b) "Picasso's paintings are beautiful." (c) "The price of beef is too high." (d) "The unemployment rate would be lowered if we reduced unemployment insurance benefits."

7. In the lawn-watering example, suppose method A entails using four hundred gallons of water and spending one and one half hours. Method B uses fourteen hundred gallons of water and requires a half hour of time. Suppose the price of water is .1¢ per gallon, and the value you place on your time is $4 per hour. (a) What does it cost you to water your lawn by method A? By method B? Which is less costly? (b) What is the benefit of switching from A to B? What is the cost of switching? (c) Is it efficient to switch from A to B? (d) Is your answer to (c) consistent with your answers to (a)? (e) Suppose the price of water rises to .5¢ per gallon, while the value you place on your time remains at $4. Reanswer (a)–(d). (f) Suppose the benefit you get from watering the lawn is equivalent to $9. Would you water it if the price of water were .5¢ per gallon? If it were 1¢ per gallon? Explain.

8. Suppose your small factory produces potato chips. You use fifty pounds of peeled potatoes per hour. There are two methods of obtaining them. Method A uses two workers who peel very carefully so that very little edible potato is thrown away. With this method, fifty-four pounds of unpeeled potatoes are required in order to obtain fifty pounds of peeled potatoes. Method B utilizes just one peeler, who works faster (but no harder) and throws away more edible potato. This method requires sixty pounds of unpeeled potatoes to yield fifty pounds of peeled potatoes. If the wage rate is $2 per hour and the price of potatoes is 25¢ per pound, which is the more efficient method? Explain. What if the price of potatoes is 50¢ per pound?

9. "Reducing your speed from 70 mph to 55 mph can be expected to increase your miles per gallon of gasoline by 20 percent. Take this as a fact. Suppose your car would get 25 mpg at 70 mph, and 30 mpg at 55 mph, and that the price of gasoline is $1.50 per gallon. You are contemplating a trip of 770 miles. (a) How much gas would you save if you drove 55 rather than 70? (b) How much longer would the trip take? (c) How high would the monetary value of saving an hour of time have to be in order for the benefit of saving time due to going faster to outweigh the extra cost of using more gasoline? (d) If these two factors were the only considerations, would it be efficient to drive 55 mph if the monetary value you place on saving an hour were $3? (e) There are other benefits to you from driving 55 mph. List some. (f) How much would they have to be per *mile* in order to make it efficient to drive 55 mph?

10. "To minimize fuel use, replace your furnace filters every thirty days." Does this mean that you should change the filters every thirty days?

11. "About 50 percent of the cars on the road need a tuneup. If they all got one, we would use 5 percent less gasoline." (a) What does the first sentence mean? (b) Does the quotation mean that those cars should get a tuneup? (c) Would car owners get more frequent tuneups if the price of gasoline were 50¢ per gallon or $1.50? Express this in terms of the relative *efficiency* of getting a tuneup in the two cases. (d) A tuneup on a four-cylinder car costs less than one on an eight-cylinder car. In light of this, can you explain in terms of efficiency why (aside from the fact that four-cylinder cars get better gas mileage than eight-cylinder cars) drivers would be expected to switch more to four-cylinder engines as the price of gasoline rises?

12. The use of an automatic transmission reduces a car's miles per gallon by as much as 10 percent. Explain why some people would find it efficient to have an automatic transmission if the price of gasoline is 50¢ per gallon, but inefficient if the price is $2 per gallon.

13. The following appeared in an advertisement in the *Wall Street Journal*[2]:

"Each year the Department of Defense drops thousands of sonobuoys [sonar devices to detect submarines] into various oceans. Until we provided our alternative, the sonobuoy batteries they used were made of silver. That made them expensive. And because sonobuoys are not retrievable, it also meant that precious silver was being wasted on the ocean floor. You can guess the rest. Our scientists found a way to make a silver-free battery, using lead instead. Which substantially lowered the cost. And prevented the unnecessary loss of a valuable metal."

(a) Is the new device more efficient than the previous ones? What is your criterion? (b) In your decision making as to which sonobuoy to use, would you consider whether or not it "wasted" silver? (c) Would your answer to (b) be any different if you were charged with making decisions "in the national interest"?

14. "Recycled aluminum requires only one third as much energy to produce as virgin aluminum." (a) Does that mean recycled aluminum is less costly to make? Why isn't more aluminum recycled? (b) What sorts of costs does virgin aluminum have that recycled does not have? What sorts of costs does recycled have that virgin does not? Do these costs depend on what percentage of all aluminum one tries to recycle? (c) Suppose it is less costly, considering all costs, to obtain aluminum through recycling. Might it nevertheless be *efficient* to make some virgin aluminum? Explain.

15. There are two methods of picking the tomatoes in a field. Method A requires one hundred labor-hours and two machine-hours, while Method

2. *Wall Street Journal,* 22 September 1976.

B requires fifty labor-hours and seven machine-hours. (a) Suppose the wage is $3 and the rental price of a machine is $25. Which is the more efficient method of picking the tomatoes? Explain. (b) What if the rental price of a machine were $35? (c) What if method B required only six machine-hours instead of seven (with wage of $3 and machine price of $35)? (d) On what two types of information does the question of efficient production depend in this example?

16. The two schedules show the total amount of benefit obtained by spending various amounts of time playing tennis and studying.

Hours	Tennis Total Benefit	Marginal Benefit	Hours	Studying Total Benefit	Marginal Benefit
1	40		1	30	
2	75		2	45	
3	105		3	58	
4	130		4	69	
5	150		5	77	
6	165		6	83	
7	175		7	86	
8	180		8	87	

(a) Suppose four hours are devoted to each activity. What is the marginal cost of devoting one more hour to tennis? What is the marginal benefit?

(b) Fill in the Marginal Benefit schedules for both activities. Which allocation of the eight hours maximizes the sum of Total Benefit (tennis) + Total Benefit (study)? What is the marginal benefit of an additional hour in each use at that allocation? (c) What does efficiency in the allocation of time mean in this context? How could an inefficient or wasteful situation be diagnosed? Give an example of a wasteful allocation of time between tennis and studying.

chapter 2

Exchange

We mentioned in chapter 1 that the answers to the questions of *what, how,* and *for whom* will goods be produced depends on the system the society uses to establish values. Decisions about whether to produce a certain good depend on what the benefits of such production are and what benefits are foregone elsewhere as a result of deciding on one alternative over others. How are these benefits discovered, and how are decision makers encouraged to take the values into account? Similar issues arise for the *how* and *for whom* problems. In a private property exchange economy prices are very important in directing and coordinating the behavior of transactors. This chapter shows how a given quantity of goods comes to be allocated in such an economy and how the exchange process determines the prices which coordinate activity.

SUBSTITUTION

An important observation which aids in understanding the phenomenon of exchange is that people are willing to make substitutions among goods. That is, every person is willing to give up some of any good in return for additional amounts of other goods. For instance, I may be willing to do with less gasoline if that reduction enables me to get more food, clothing, or entertainment. Likewise, I may be willing to forego some safety in return for enough more comfort (or vice versa). The fact that people do not consume goods in fixed and unchanging proportions, but rather change the proportions in which goods are consumed in response to changed circumstances, is crucial to understanding an exchange economy.

THE CONCEPT OF MARGINAL VALUE

If I am willing to give up some of one good to get more of another, it is not hard to imagine that there is a maximum amount of one good which I would be willing to give up in order to get one more of another good. For example, I might be willing to give up at most three pieces of pizza to get another glass of beer. If I did make that exchange, I would judge myself to be no better and no worse off than I was before. In that case, I would say that "the marginal value I place on a glass of beer is three pieces of pizza," or $MV_B = 3P$. This magnitude is the *marginal value* of beer because we are discussing the amount of pizza I would be willing to give up to get *one* more beer. Note that the marginal value I place on beer is expressed as a certain amount of *some other good* (in this case, pizza) which I would be willing to give up in order to get another beer.

The concept of marginal value is related to the concept of *indifference*. We can express the fact that the marginal value I place on a glass of beer is three pieces of pizza by saying that I would be indifferent between giving up three pieces of pizza in return for one glass of beer and staying where I am. Of course, it follows that if I were offered the opportunity to give up only two pieces of pizza in return for a beer, I would take it. I am no better or worse off giving up three pieces, so giving up only two pieces makes me better off. Giving up four pieces of pizza for a beer would make me *worse* off than I now am.

Suppose I have three beers and eight pieces of pizza. We could say that I have a *bundle* of goods containing those items. Imagine having different bundles of goods, involving different combinations of beer and pizza. (See table 2-1.)

The bundle with three beers and eight pieces of pizza is represented in the first row, labeled Y. The bundle I would have if I gave up three pieces of pizza in return for one beer is shown in the second row, labeled Z. Since I said I am indifferent between giving up three pieces of pizza in return for a beer and staying where I am, I am *indifferent* between bundles Y and Z. The marginal value of beer (to me) is shown by the fact that the one-unit

TABLE 2-1
TWO BUNDLES OF GOODS

Bundle	Beer (glasses)	Pizza (pieces)	
Y	3	8	
Z	4	5	$MV_B = 3P$ per B

change in beers is associated with the three-unit change in pieces of pizza. We can always establish the marginal value of a good by examining two bundles between which a person is indifferent. To get the marginal value of beer, we take the *change in pieces of pizza per one-unit change in beer*, or divide the change in pieces of pizza by the change in beers (change in pizza/change in beer). To get the marginal value of pieces of pizza over the same range, we reverse the process. We divide the change in beers by the change in pieces of pizza to get the change in beers per piece of pizza (change in beer/change in pizza). Thus over this range, the marginal value of pizza (MV_P) is one third beer per piece of pizza (one beer/three pieces of pizza). Thus the marginal value of pizza is the reciprocal of the marginal value of beer.

Notice that the concept of marginal value is developed and expressed entirely in terms of observable behavior of individuals in making choices. The marginal value is not intrinsic to the glass of beer, but rather is an expression of my willingness to give up other goods to get more of it. The marginal value I place on a good does not depend on how much effort was expended in creating the good. I might be willing to give up more pieces of pizza to get (in other words, place a higher marginal value on) a glass of beer than I would to get a luscious dessert which required the work of four chefs for a day. Marginal value is a subjective matter depending on preferences and not determinable by looking at what was involved in producing the good.

DECREASING MARGINAL VALUE

The more a person has of a good, the lower the marginal value he places on that good. It is easy to think of extreme examples which illustrate this principle. The parched prospector stumbling from the desert into an oasis would be willing to give up a great deal for a drink of water. But after a few hours of refreshment, he would offer very little to get one more drink of water. The more he has, the lower the marginal value he places on the good.

One of the implications of this is that the amount I would be willing to pay in order to get one more than I now have of something is always less than the amount I would require in payment to get me to give up one of what I have. Again suppose that I have three glasses of beer and eight pieces of pizza. We already know I would be willing to give up three pieces of pizza to get another beer. I would also be willing to give up one of my three beers in return for additional pizza. How much more pizza would I require? The principle of decreasing marginal value says that the amount would have to be greater than three pieces. The smaller the amount of beer I have, the greater its marginal value to me. If I have bundle Z, I would give up the fourth beer for three pieces of pizza and be no better and no worse off. But having given up the fourth beer, I then place a higher marginal value on beer and would give up another beer only if I were compensated

TABLE 2-2
TWO BUNDLES OF GOODS

Bundle	Beer (glasses)	Pizza (pieces)	
X	2	12	
Y	3	8	$MV_B = 4P$ per B
Z	4	5	$MV_B = 3P$ per B

by more than three pieces of pizza (say *four* pieces of pizza). If the marginal value of the third beer were four pieces of pizza, I would be indifferent between bundles X, Y, and Z in table 2-2. (That is, if I were confronted with the three bundles and asked to choose, I would be unable to and would resort to such things as coin flipping to make a choice.)

Bundle X has two beers and twelve pieces of pizza. In going from bundle Y to bundle X, I am giving up one beer in return for four pieces of pizza. If I am indifferent between bundles X and Y, this establishes the value of beer over that range.

In this case the principle of decreasing marginal value is illustrated in reverse, by showing that the *smaller* the amount of beer, the *higher* its value. Alternatively, we could show that, starting at bundle X (with two beers and twelve pieces of pizza), I am willing to give up four pieces of pizza to get one more beer. Having attained the extra beer (at bundle Y), I would be willing to give up only three more pieces of pizza to get a fourth beer. The value of beer decreases as I get more of it.

THE BASIS FOR EXCHANGE

Note: the following sections involve the use of a numerical example to illustrate the basis for exchange. In order to best understand the points raised, you should follow through the example using pencil and paper. Follow each step and go slowly.

Suppose that Main and Baird have gone on a backpacking trip. They each have been supplied with gorp (a mixture of raisins, nuts, and candy) and dehydrated meat. Main has ten ounces of gorp and eight packages of meat (bundle B) and is indifferent between bundles A, B, and C shown in table 2-3.

Note again that Main actually possesses bundle B. Bundles A and C are bundles he *might* have, but doesn't. They are shown for comparison only. Since Main is indifferent between B and hypothetical bundle A, he would be willing to give up one ounce of gorp if he received five packages of meat in return. Thus, Main's *minimum asking price* for gorp is five meats per gorp. If he received five and one half packages, he would be better off. Would he be willing to accept four and one half packages of meat

TABLE 2-3
BUNDLES BETWEEN WHICH MAIN IS INDIFFERENT

Bundle	Gorp (oz)	Meat (pkgs)
A	9	13
B	10	8
C	11	4

in return for giving up one ounce of gorp? No. That is less than his minimum asking price. It would not be sufficient to compensate him for the loss of his tenth ounce of gorp. Since Main is indifferent between B and hypothetical bundle C, he would be willing to give up at most four packages of meat in order to obtain one more ounce of gorp than he has. Thus, Main's *maximum offer price* for gorp is four meats per gorp. If he were asked to give up only three and one half packages, he would do so and be better off than he now is. Would he be willing to give up (pay) four and one half packages of meat in return for receiving an additional ounce of gorp? No. That price would be higher than his maximum offer price, which is the marginal value he places on additional gorp.

Baird has been given six ounces of gorp and fifteen meats (bundle E) and is indifferent between bundles D, E, and F shown in table 2-4.

Again keep in mind that Baird actually has bundle E. Bundles D and F are bundles he might have, but doesn't. They are shown for comparison only. Since Baird is indifferent between E and hypothetical bundle D, he would be willing to give up one of his six ounces of gorp if he could receive at least two meats in return. Thus, Baird's minimum asking price for gorp is two meats per gorp. If he received two and one half meats in return, he would be better off. Would he be willing to give up one of his six ounces of gorp if he received one and one half meats in return? No. That is less than his minimum asking price. It would not be sufficient to compensate him for the loss of his sixth ounce of gorp. Since Baird is indifferent between E and hypothetical bundle F, he would be willing to give up at most one meat in order to obtain one more ounce of gorp than he has. Thus, Baird's maximum offer price for gorp is one meat per gorp. If he were asked to give up only one half meat, he would do so and be better off than he now is. Would he be willing to give up (pay) one and one half meats in

TABLE 2-4
BUNDLES BETWEEN WHICH BAIRD IS INDIFFERENT

Bundle	Gorp (oz)	Meat (pkgs)
D	5	17
E	6	15
F	7	14

TABLE 2-5
INITIAL HOLDINGS

	Gorp	Meat
Main (bundle B)	10	8
Baird (bundle E)	6	15
Total	16	23

return for having one more ounce of gorp (seven instead of six)? No. That price would be higher than his maximum offer price, which is the marginal value that Baird places on additional gorp.

Notice that since Main's minimum asking price for gorp (five meats per gorp) is greater than his maximum offer price (four meats per gorp), his preferences are consistent with the principle of decreasing marginal value. The more gorp he has, the lower the marginal value he places on it. Similarly, Baird's preferences are also consistent with the principle of decreasing marginal value because his maximum offer price for gorp is only one meat per gorp, while his minimum asking price is two meats per gorp.

Now let us step back and take a look at the situation we have constructed. Both Main and Baird are endowed with initial holdings of gorp and meat (bundle B for Main and bundle E for Baird). Together they hold sixteen ounces of gorp and twenty-three packages of meat (table 2-5). The question we ask is: with no change in the total amounts, is it possible for any reallocation of gorp and meat between Main and Baird to make them both better off? At first blush the answer would seem to be *obviously not!* After all, the "size of the pie" is fixed. If one person is made better off, mustn't the other be made worse off? The answer to this last question is *No.* It *is* possible to make both better off than they currently are, even without changing the size of the pie. This is an almost magical result, so we should be careful to follow the logic to make sure that when the rabbit is pulled out of the hat we know exactly how it was put in. The first question is, how are we going to know whether Main and Baird are better off after the reallocation (exchange) than before? The answer is that we will use information which Main and Baird have already given us.

Remember that Main and Baird both consider gorp and meat to be scarce goods. This means they would prefer more rather than less of both goods. Our previous discussion showed how each would be willing to substitute between the goods. Both Main and Baird would like to have more gorp than they have, and each has a maximum offer price (marginal value of more gorp) which tells the most meat he would be willing to pay in order to get one more gorp. If Main (or Baird) could buy gorp for a price lower than his maximum offer price, he would be better off. Similarly, both would like more meat, and they would be willing to give up some gorp if they could get enough meat in return. Each has a minimum asking price for gorp (marginal value of the last unit) which tells the least amount of meat he would accept in return for giving up one gorp. If Baird (or Main) could sell gorp for more than his minimum asking price, he would be better off.

If you have been reading carefully, you may already have discovered how both Main and Baird can be made better off. To see it, we must keep a few things in mind. First, if one person ends up with more of a good, the other must end up with just that much less of the same good, since there is no change in the total amount of either good. And neither person can end up with more of both goods than he started with, because that would mean that the other would have less of both goods, making him worse off. (We don't want that, since we are trying to see if both can be made *better* off!) So a change which makes both better off must be one where Main gets more of one good and less of the second, while Baird ends up with *less* of the first and *more* of the second. But not all such changes would necessarily make both better off. To see if *any* changes can be mutually beneficial, we must consider the two possible ways in which exchange might proceed. Method 1 is to have Main buy gorp from Baird (and have Main pay Baird some meat). Method 2 is to have Baird buy gorp from Main (and have Baird pay Main some meat). We shall examine both methods.

If the exchange is to be mutually beneficial, the price actually paid for gorp must be *less than* the maximum offer price of the buyer and *greater than* the minimum asking price of the seller. If it is in that range, then both will be better off. Examining method 1, we see that Main's maximum offer price for gorp is four meat per gorp, while Baird's minimum asking price is two meat per gorp. In order for the trade of one gorp to be mutually beneficial, the price must be less than four meats, so as to make Main better off, but greater than two meats, so as to make Baird better off. Any price in that range (such as three meats per gorp) would make *both* better off. The case where Main buys one gorp from Baird at a price of three meats is shown in table 2-6.

As a result of the transaction, Main moves from his initial spot (bundle B) to bundle C′, which contains one more ounce of gorp but three fewer packages of meat than did bundle B. At the same time, Baird moves from his initial spot (bundle E) to bundle D′, which has one *less* ounce of gorp and three more packages of meat than E did. Since the price of three meats

TABLE 2-6
MAIN BUYS ONE OUNCE OF GORP FROM BAIRD
AT A PRICE OF THREE MEATS

	Gorp (Main)	Meat		Gorp (Baird)	Meat
A	9	13	D′	5	18
B	10	8	D	5	17
C	11	4	E	6	15
C′	11	5	F	7	14

for the gorp was less than Main's maximum offer price and greater than Baird's minimum asking price, we know both transactors are better off due to the trade. We see this is another way by looking at table 2-6. We cannot *directly* compare Main's new point (bundle C') with his original one (bundle B) because C' has more gorp but less meat than B does. But we can compare them indirectly. Remember that Main is *indifferent* between his initial bundle (B) and hypothetical bundles A and C. Bundle C' (with eleven of gorp and five of meat) has the same amount of gorp as bundle C, but more meat. So C' must be preferred by Main to C. And since Main is indifferent between B and C, he must prefer C' to B. So we see again that Main has been made better off (according to his own preferences) by the purchase of one gorp for three meats.

Summarizing: Main prefers C' to C, and he is indifferent between C and B. So he prefers C' to B.

Similarly, we can use table 2-6 to convince ourselves that Baird is also better off than he was originally. Baird's new bundle (D') has the same amount of gorp (five) as hypothetical bundle D. But D' has more meat (eighteen versus seventeen). So D' is preferred to D. But Baird would be indifferent between D and his initial bundle E. So he must prefer his postexchange bundle D' to his preexchange bundle E, meaning that Baird has been made better off by the sale of one gorp for three meats.

Summarizing: Baird prefers D' to D, and he is indifferent between D and E. So he prefers D' to E.

So Main and Baird are both better off than before, even though the size of the pie is no larger than before. To see this, look at table 2-7, which shows postexchange holdings by Main and Baird.

There are sixteen ounces of gorp and twenty-three packages of meat between the two transactors, just as before, but the pie *seems* bigger because each transactor prefers his new holdings to his old ones.

We have seen that it is possible for both Main and Baird to be made

TABLE 2-7
POSTEXCHANGE HOLDINGS

	Gorp	Meat
Main (bundle C')	11	5
Baird (bundle D')	5	18
Postexchange Total	16	23

better off by what we have called method 1, whereby Main buys a gorp from Baird. As long as Main pays between two and four meats for the gorp, both will benefit. The source of the gain from trade was that Main's maximum offer price for a gorp (four meats) was greater than Baird's minimum asking price (two meats).

Now let us examine method 2, whereby Baird buys a gorp from Main (and pays Main some meat). (Start again with Main having bundle B and Baird having bundle E.) Could such an exchange be mutually beneficial? As we know, Main is willing to sell an ounce of gorp, as long as he receives at least five meats in return. (If you do not see how we got this number, go back and reread the discussion on Main's minimum asking price.) Similarly, Baird would be willing to buy an ounce of gorp as long as he doesn't have to pay more than one package of meat for it. (Again, check to make sure you can obtain this number yourself.) So Main would be willing to sell gorp, and Baird would be willing to buy it; but Main will not sell gorp to Baird because Baird's maximum offer price (one meat) is less than Main's minimum asking price (five meats). If the price of a gorp were high enough (greater than five meats) to make Main better off, it would make Baird worse off. And if it were low enough (less than one meat) to make Baird better off, it would make Main worse off. So in this example it is not possible to work out a mutually beneficial exchange where Baird buys gorp from Main.

To summarize to this point, the *basis* for exchange is that different people place different marginal values on the same good. *The direction of the exchange is that the person who places the higher marginal value on the good will get more of it, and the person who places the lower marginal value on the good gets less of it. With voluntary exchange goods go toward those who place a higher value on them.* In this example, Main placed a higher marginal value on gorp than Baird did, as evidenced by the fact that his maximum offer price was greater than Baird's minimum asking price. (Who placed a higher marginal value on meat? See question 6 at the end of the chapter.)

CONVERGENCE OF
MARGINAL VALUES
WITH EXCHANGE

Will this process continue until Main has no meat or Baird has no gorp? It could, but it is not likely. The reason lies in the principle of diminishing marginal value. As Main gets more gorp and fewer packages of meat, the marginal value he places on gorp will fall. (Give *two* reasons why.) Similarly, as Baird gets more meat and less gorp, his marginal value on gorp will rise. (Again there are two reasons.) The process of exchange brings the marginal values of the transactors closer together by raising the lower marginal value and lowering the higher marginal value. The process of exchange thus tends to destroy the basis for further exchange. If Main and

Baird could bargain costlessly, they would finally reach a point where they had *equal* marginal values on gorp. That common marginal value would be somewhere between two and four packages of meat per ounce of gorp, and that common marginal value would be indicated by the price at which the last transaction occurred.

EFFICIENCY AND EXCHANGE

In chapter 1, we discussed the concept of efficiency, and stated that an efficient action is one for which the benefits are greater than the costs. Is mutually beneficial exchange efficient? When Main bought an ounce of gorp from Baird in return for three packages of meat, both were made better off. The exchange involved a benefit and a cost for both transactors, but each viewed his benefit as being bigger than his cost. The benefit to Main came from the additional gorp he obtained, and the cost was the three meats he paid. Main's benefit was greater than his cost because the gorp was *equivalent* in his mind to four meats, but he had to pay only three meats. Similarly, Baird's benefit was greater than his cost. His benefit came from the three meats he received from Main and his cost was the foregone gorp. In Baird's mind, the gorp he gave up was *equivalent* to two meats, but he received three from Main. Thus, mutually beneficial exchange involves efficient actions by both transactors.

Similarly, the allocation of goods which exists after all mutually beneficial exchanges have taken place is an *efficient allocation*. Recall that we said an efficient allocation of resources was one where it was impossible to make any changes for which the benefits were greater than the costs. Exchange will tend to proceed until the marginal value (maximum offer price) that one transactor places on a good equals the marginal value (minimum asking price) that the other places on the same good. At that point no further mutually beneficial trade can take place. Any further reallocations would have to make at least one transactor worse off (his benefit would be less than his cost). Thus, any further reallocations would be *inefficient* for at least one transactor. This means that the allocation after all mutually beneficial trades have taken place is efficient. Looking at it another way, if goods are allocated so that the marginal values of transactors are *not* equal (in other words, the maximum offer price of one person is greater than the minimum asking price of another) this is *inefficient* or *wasteful*, because it is possible to arrange transactions which involve benefits greater than costs for both transactors. In the context of exchange, a resource is being *wasted* if it is in the hands of a transactor who places a lower marginal value on it than some other transactor does. Thus any government policy or law which can be shown to result in different transactors' placing different marginal values on a good is thereby shown to be an *inefficient* policy or law. Can you think of any such laws or policies?

COMPARISONS OF ABSOLUTE LIKES AND DISLIKES

It is tempting to conclude, because Main places a *higher marginal value* on gorp than Baird does, that he likes gorp better than Baird does. But we cannot conclude anything of the sort. All we know is that Main is willing to pay more (in terms of meat) to get another ounce of gorp. It could be that Baird dearly loves *both* gorp and meat, while Main is only mildly fond of both. The observed transaction is consistent with this story *or its opposite!* So we cannot infer that either story is true from the evidence of the exchange. In the jargon of economics, we say "it is not legitimate to make interpersonal utility comparisons." Utility is a word once used to denote an objectively measurable index of the well-being of people. It was thought to be meaningfully comparable among people, so that one could say, for example, "Main is better off than Baird is," or "Main likes gorp more than Baird does." Today, economists are more careful in their use of words, realizing that such statements cannot validly be inferred from any behavior. Thus today utility is used to denote the ranking of bundles of goods, as in "Main prefers bundle C' to bundle B, so C' gives more utility than B does."

As a side point, we cannot say who is made happier by the exchange, Main or Baird, since we cannot measure or compare well-being among people. All we can infer is that Main and Baird are better off after the exchange. In the real world we cannot even say quite *this* much. If we see Main hand Baird three packages of meat and Baird hand Main an ounce of gorp, we can presume that they both *expect* to be better off. But information about the characteristics of goods is costly. The meat may be rotten. The gorp may be stale. So either or both parties may in fact regret having made any particular exchange. However, the fact remains that mutually beneficial exchange *is* possible; that people engage in it because they expect to be made better off; and that if it takes place, goods will go from those who place a lower marginal value on them to persons who place a higher marginal value on them; and that marginal values will tend to converge.

COST OF TRANSACTING— A DETERRENT TO EXCHANGE

Suppose Main and Baird did not know one another, but went into the wilderness separately. They might never run across each other, or they might cross paths but be too tired or shy to try to strike a bargain. Or it simply might never occur to them that such a difference in marginal values exists. For any or all of these reasons, potential mutually beneficial exchanges might not occur. We lump all of these barriers to exchange—distance, inertia, ignorance—into the category of costs of transacting. More exchanges would take place if these barriers did not exist; and the higher the barriers, the greater the divergencies in marginal values which will remain after all mutually beneficial exchanges have taken place.

MIDDLEMEN—A METHOD OF REDUCING THE COST OF TRANSACTING

When there are unexploited exchange opportunities, there are opportunities for clever people to gain. In the most fundamental sense, a middleman is a person (or firm) who moves goods from lower-valued uses to higher-valued uses. In our example of Main and Baird, the middleman might be an engaging, friendly person who happens to walk from campsite to campsite striking up conversation. In the course of such conversation, he discovers the disparity in values which we discussed. He offers to do Main "a favor" by bringing him an ounce of gorp for "only" three and one half packages of meat. Main tries to haggle but to no avail. "Take it or leave it," says the middleman. Since he is better off by taking it, Main accepts the deal. The middleman then goes to Baird and offers two and one half packages of meat if Baird will give him an ounce of gorp. Baird is tired and starts to turn over and go to sleep, but the middleman persists. Finally, Baird relents and gives up the ounce of gorp for two and one half packages of meat. The middleman takes a package of meat for himself and gives the ounce of gorp to Main. If the time and effort the middleman invested were not worth more to him than one package of meat, all three are better off. But wouldn't Main and Baird have been better off performing the exchange by themselves, without the middleman taking his cut? Perhaps. They might have happened onto each other and worked out the exchange without the middleman, but they might well have not met or not been astute enough to think of the exchange. There is no law saying that Main and Baird *must* deal with the middleman. If they find that they do better without the middleman, they can simply refuse to do business with him. Middlemen will not survive unless they can perform for a lower price than the transactors themselves could do it.

There are some situations in which middlemen are *not* used in carrying out exchanges. For example, babysitters and grass cutters usually deal directly with the final purchaser of the service. They are not paid by a third party, who in turn makes the contract with the customer. In most cases, however, we buy goods from middlemen, who in turn often buy from other middlemen, who buy from the ultimate sellers of the good.

Some questions arise here. First, why are some exchange processes characterized by no middlemen, while others have one or more layers of middlemen? As suggested above, the answer is: If people are free to choose whether to deal with middlemen, middlemen will survive if, and only if, their costs of performing the services are lower than the costs of the ultimate transactors. (We shall elaborate further on this point in chapter 4, where we discuss comparative advantage and opportunity cost.)

The second question that arises is: Given that a middleman can arrange a given type of exchange at a lower cost than the ultimate consumers can, what determines the price charged to the ultimate consumers and the price paid to the ultimate suppliers? In short, what determines the middleman's cut?

COMPETITION AMONG MIDDLEMEN

If the middleman's cut is larger than his cost of doing business, and if other potential middlemen also have costs which are less than the cut being taken, there is an opportunity for successful undercutting. Suppose the alternatives our middleman had to forego to arrange this exchange had a value to him of only a half package of meat (that is, this was his cost), whereas his cut is one whole package of meat. If there is another potential middleman who also has a cost of a half package of meat for arranging an exchange, then the second will have an interest in undercutting the first. The result will usually be a lower price for the middleman's services. This process of having alternative suppliers offer their services to the same potential customer is the essence of what economists mean by competition.

Middlemen do *not* compete with the ultimate buyers or sellers with whom they deal, but rather with *other middlemen* whose presence constrains the size of the cut they are able to take. When you buy a car from a dealer, it is the presence of *other dealers* with whom you might deal that constrains the amount of markup which the dealer is able to charge. With whom does the ultimate buyer compete then? With *other buyers*. When other potential buyers increase their willingness to pay for a good I want to buy, the price I have to pay goes up. Suppose I am trying to buy a house. I may have information which leads me to believe that the current owner of the house would be willing to sell it for anything over $50,000. I would, let us say, be willing to pay as much as $65,000 if I had to, but I offer $51,000 because that is all that is necessary to get the seller to sell. But if at the same time another potential buyer offers $58,000, I will have to offer more than that or I will not get it. I am not competing with the broker, who will take a certain percentage commission, or even with the seller, but rather with the other potential buyer. Buyers compete against other buyers, sellers compete against other sellers, and middlemen compete against other middlemen.

The original middleman in our example will not be happy about the competition he faces and may try to find ways to prevent it or to limit its scope. In the real world, firms (or middlemen, since all firms are middlemen) often work to restrict access to the market by competitors. Blue Laws (restricting business at night or on Sunday) and licensing are allegedly to protect the public by preventing them from doing business with disreputable or unqualified firms. These firms usually operate under conditions their competitors would rather not meet, or they charge too low a price. In later chapters we shall explore more fully the various types of competition and the methods used by suppliers in attempting to thwart it.

We have purposely constructed our examples until now in such a way that the exchanges are carried out without the use of money. Gorp is traded for meat. In contrast, almost all our daily transactions involve either selling things in exchange for money or using money to buy things. The reason we have chosen to leave out money is to show that, despite appearances, people substitute and exchange one *good* for another *good*. There would be no reason to sell something for money if we did not expect at some time to trade the money for other goods. Once we understand that the underlying reality involves exchange of one kind of good for another kind, we can carry on our analysis in a less cumbersome way by expressing marginal values and prices in dollar terms instead of in terms of other goods. If five apples sell for $1 and three peaches sell for $1 and I am willing to give up *either* five apples *or* three peaches to get an avocado, then it is convenient to say that the marginal value I place on an avocado is $1. This is the convention we shall follow in future discussions of exchange. Such a discussion then focuses on one good, with the other good being a means of buying *any other* good. Thus if Baird owns a bicycle which he would be willing to part with for anything over $20, and Main would be willing to pay up to $30 for such a bicycle, there is a potential gain from trade. If the transaction cost involved in arranging the trade is no greater than $10, Main will buy the bicycle from Baird.

HALF-FARE COUPONS

During part of 1979, United Airlines (and later American Airlines) gave its customers coupons which entitled the bearer to half off the regular price of a later flight on that airline. Not long after the coupons first appeared, customers began exchanging them. Enterprising teenagers met passengers as they left their planes and offered $10 or so for coupons, hoping to resell them later for a profit. Later, some individuals advertised in the *Wall Street Journal* that they would buy coupons for (say) $25 or sell them for (say) $40. Economic theory would lead one to expect some exchanging of coupons. The marginal value that a person would place on a coupon would be the amount he would be willing to pay for some flight minus one half of the normal fare. For example, suppose Mr. Smith would be willing to pay $120 to fly to Phoenix, and the regular fare is $150. With the half-fare coupon, he could get a ticket for $75, so he would be willing to pay $45 (that is, $120 − $75) for the coupon. Suppose Ms. Jones has just returned from a flight and has a coupon. She makes a similar calculation for her favorite destination and decides that the coupon is worth $20 to her. Then Smith and Jones can make a mutually beneficial trade, if it doesn't cost more than $25 to arrange it.

Whether widespread exchanging of coupons would be expected to occur depends on the disparity of marginal use values which holders and potential users place on them, and on the cost of transacting. The greater the former and the smaller the latter, the more exchanges can be expected to take place. In the case of these coupons only about half were ever redeemed, so the costs of transacting must have been substantial, compared to the disparities in values.

CONVERGENCE OF VALUES—ONCE MORE

Earlier we argued that, if Main and Baird were exchanging with each other, the process of exchange would tend to bring their marginal values closer together (make them converge) because the person placing the lower marginal value on gorp (Baird) was giving up gorp, while Main, who placed a higher marginal value on gorp, got more. (The less Baird has of gorp, the more highly he values his marginal ounce of it; and the more gorp Main has, the less highly he values an additional ounce of it.) How does the convergence process work in everyday exchange? As noted, when we buy something, we usually buy from a middleman (say a retail store). Suppose I am buying oranges. If the price is 20¢ per pound, and I place a value of 50¢ on my first pound (that is, I would be willing to pay 50¢ rather than go without that first pound), then I should buy a pound of oranges. (I should if I want to make myself better off.) Suppose that, having bought one pound, I would be willing to pay 30¢ for another pound. Then I should buy that too. Having bought two pounds, suppose my value on a third pound is 22¢. Then I should buy a third pound. If I value a fourth pound at only 15¢, I should stop at three. Note that I adjust my purchases so that the value I place on the last pound is at least as great as the price, but the value I would place on an additional pound is *less* than the price. Thus it is in my interest to stop buying when my marginal value is approximately equal to the price. Other consumers have a similar interest, so we can expect their marginal values to be approximately equal to the price they pay. If we all pay the same price, we will all adjust our purchases so that we all place about the same marginal value on any good. That is, our marginal values converge.

It is because of this tendency for all consumers to adjust their purchases of a commodity so that the marginal value they place on it equals its market price which gives rise to the notion that *the marginal value of a commodity is indicated by its market price*. We shall use this notion later, especially in chapter 8, where we compare the efficiency of various market structures.

"WATER IS LIFE—DON'T WASTE IT"

One of the slogans of the water utilities in California is "Water Is Life— Don't Waste It." Understanding the terms *efficiency* and *waste*, you should be in a position to comment on this notion. First, suppose each person is allocated a certain amount of water to do with as she pleases. Can you specify what it means for any person to allocate her water efficiently among her alternative uses (in other words, avoid waste)? That solution would entail that she allocate water to various uses so that any further reallocation would involve marginal costs greater than marginal benefits. This will be true if the marginal value to her of water in any given use (expressed in dollars) is equal to its marginal value to her in any other use. That common value would be the *value of water* to that user. (Refer to question 16 of chapter 1 for a similar allocation problem.) If all users are given an allotment, each one can be expected to arrive at her own efficient allocation of her water and in the process arrive at a value of water to herself, at the margin. One person's might be 25¢ per hundred gallons, while another's might be 60¢ per hundred gallons. Would this allocation be efficient? There are two levels of answers. At the level of the individual user, the answer is yes—given the person's allotment of water there is no reallocation of her water which would make her better off (that is, involve benefits greater than costs). This is because the value to her of water at the margin is the same in all of *her* uses. But since that common value may be 25¢ for her and 60¢ for someone else, there *is* waste and inefficiency at the *social* level. It is possible to make both of these transactors better off by having the first person sell some water to the second for a price somewhere between 25¢ and 60¢ (say 40¢). The first person gains because she gets more benefit from the other things she could buy with the money than she would from the water. (She would have been willing to sell for anything over 25¢.) On the other hand, the second person would prefer to have the water rather than the money as long as he does not have to pay over 60¢, so he gains from the trade as well. Since the transactors could (in principle) engage in trades which improve their positions, the initial allocation among consumers was inefficient or wasteful.

If we could imagine the outcome of costless exchange between all the transactors in this situation, when all mutually beneficial exchanges had occurred all would place the same value on one hundred gallons of water, at the margin. (See question 26 at the end of the chapter.) (Suppose this common value is 30¢ per hundred gallons.) This outcome is *efficient* because it is not possible to make anyone better off without making someone else worse off—in other words, no more mutually beneficial trades can be made. Each transactor is induced to act efficiently (to forego low-valued uses of water) by the offers of beneficial trade from those who place a higher value on the water.

The same outcome can be achieved by having the water authority establish a *price* of 30¢ per hundred gallons and let each user buy as much as she wants. Each buyer will purchase more water as long as the value she places on it is greater than 30¢, and she will stop when her value equals 30¢. Again the outcome will be efficient because each transactor will buy enough water so that her value is 30¢. Since all place the same value on water, no mutually beneficial trades among users is possible. Since all the water is being used and each user gets as much as she wants at the going price, this price is the *market clearing* price. The market clearing price simultaneously conveys information to each transactor about the value that all the other transactors place on water. It serves the same purpose that the exchange among all the transactors did. It induces the transactors to act efficiently—to economize on water to the *appropriate* extent: not too much or too little. (A question for further thought: Are managers of a publicly owned water utility likely to arrive at this price?)

Now suppose that because of some calamity such as a drought, the amount of water available is smaller than usual. Then at a price of 30¢, more water will be wanted than is available. Suppose the water authority keeps the price at 30¢ but instructs everyone not to waste water. How should a consumer respond to this request? Suppose the user wants to use water efficiently and not waste it. Which uses should she cut out? We already know that she would not use water in any way that was worth less than 30¢ to her, because she still has to pay that amount. But she has no good way of knowing which more valuable uses should be foregone. If the price were set at the new market clearing level, then each transactor would know how much to cut back—she would cut back until her value on water equaled the new (higher) price. The price would then tell each consumer how valuable water is to other users. It would coordinate behavior, promote efficient use, and cause wasteful uses of water to be discontinued. (Remember that wasteful uses are those which have a value to the user less than the market clearing price, and users would voluntarily choose not to engage in them if they had to pay the market clearing price.)

The situation is entirely different if the price is kept below the market clearing level. Not only are transactors not given any positive inducement to consume efficiently, they have no way of knowing *how* highly valued it is and what (formerly efficient) uses have now become wasteful due to their relatively low value. Are uses that are worth 50¢ per hundred gallons wasteful? We cannot know in this kind of environment.

EXCHANGE, PRICES, AND COORDINATION

Exchange is extremely important in understanding a market economy because the prices we see are exchange prices, like the price at which Main and Baird chose to transact. We can now see that these exchanges enable transactors who place different marginal values on a good to benefit from reallocation of goods. The prices that emerge through the exchange process tend to bring the marginal values that different transactors place on a good into equality with each other. Those prices then indicate how highly consumers value goods in comparison with each other. If the price of a pound of almonds is $6 while a pound of walnuts goes for $2, this means that at the margin, people are willing to substitute three pounds of walnuts for a pound of almonds. These prices (and the relative values implicit in them) convey information to potential suppliers. Suppose a supplier is now growing one hundred pounds of walnuts, but with the same resources he could grow fifty pounds of almonds instead. A little arithmetic shows that he could do better growing almonds ($300 in revenue with almonds versus $200 with walnuts). Since the benefit to him of switching to almonds ($300) is greater than the cost ($200), it is efficient for him to switch. If he switched, he would be causing a reduction of two pounds of walnuts for every pound of almonds, but consumers at the margin are willing to forego *three* pounds of walnuts for every pound of almonds. They would prefer such a change in outputs to what they have now. (In other words, such a change in the output mix would be efficient from their point of view as well.) The exchange-determined prices of walnuts and almonds thus guide the producers of almonds and walnuts to produce an output mix that is most in accord with the preferences of the transactors.

SUMMARY

In this chapter we have discussed voluntary exchange, a fundamental process which tends to occur if there are no legal barriers. One result is that goods tend to go to those who place the highest marginal value on them. Another result is that people place a more nearly equal marginal value on a commodity. Indeed, if it were not costly to arrange exchanges, the marginal value for any commodity would be identical for all persons after all exchange opportunities were exhausted. Since exchanges are costly, this equalizing of values process is not complete, but the existence of middlemen more nearly brings it about. This tendency toward a common value among all persons for a given commodity is of crucial importance in a private property exchange economy, because the common values generated by the exchange process are used in making decisions about what and how to produce, and who gets what. The comparison of values of resources in alternative uses guides these decisions.

LOOKING AHEAD

Chapter 3 discusses one of the most important of the economist's tools—demand. The notion of demand for goods incorporates both the ideas of substitution and limited resources, and enables us to understand the factors which determine what goods people consume, how relative preferences for goods reflect themselves in the prices of goods, and how prices coordinate behavior.

POINTS TO REMEMBER

1. Individuals are willing to substitute among goods, that is, put up with a smaller amount of any good in return for sufficiently greater amounts of other goods.

2. The maximum amount a person would be willing to give up of one good (X) in return for getting one more unit of another good (Y) is called the marginal value of the second good (Y). Alternatively, the marginal value of Y can be thought of as the minimum amount of X that the person would require in payment for giving up a unit of Y.

3. The marginal value of a good is not intrinsic to the good, but rather a subjective matter arising out of the preferences and the amounts of goods which the individuals have.

4. The marginal value placed on a good decreases as the person has more of it and increases as he has less of it.

5. The marginal value of a good can (and often does) differ between persons because of differences in tastes or amounts owned.

6. If the marginal value one person places on a good differs from the marginal value that another person places on it, mutually beneficial exchange between the two persons is possible, involving the good in question and some other good.

7. Exchange always goes in the direction in which the person placing the higher marginal value on a good gets more, while the person placing the lower marginal value on the good gives up that good.

8. As exchange proceeds, the values that the two transactors place on any good will converge, because the person giving up the good places a higher marginal value on it (he has less), and the person getting the good places a lower marginal value on it (she has more).

9. Because of ignorance, transportation costs, and other factors, not all mutually beneficial exchanges occur.

10. Middlemen lower the costs of transacting and thus promote more complete exchange. The existence of middlemen serves to make the price lower to buyers and the price higher to the ultimate suppliers.

KEY TERMS

Exchange: The activity whereby one person gives some of one good to another person, in return for which the second person gives some of another good to the first person.

Indifference curve: A locus of points representing combinations of goods between which a transactor is indifferent. (See appendix at end of chapter.)

Marginal value of a good: The maximum amount of another good a person would be willing to give up in order to get one more unit of the good in question. (If she gave up more than this amount she would be worse off after the transaction.) This is the person's maximum offer price. Alternatively, the value of a good is the minimum amount of another good the person would be willing to accept in return for giving up one unit of the good in question. (If she received less than this amount, she would be worse off after the transaction.) This is the person's minimum asking price.

Middleman: A transactor who buys a good from one transactor for reselling to another transactor. Firms are middlemen.

Price: The amount of other goods (often money) which a transactor must pay in order to obtain one unit of a good in exchange.

Utility: A word used to denote the preference for one good or bundle of goods. "Bundle A has more utility for me than bundle B" means "I prefer bundle A to bundle B."

REVIEW QUESTIONS

1. Suppose Terry is indifferent between the following bundles of beer and pizza:

Terry

	Beer (glasses)	Pizza (pieces)
A	2	8
B	3	6
C	4	5

Fran is indifferent between the following bundles of beer and pizza:

Fran

	Beer (glasses)	Pizza (pieces)
D	3	9
E	4	5
F	5	2

Terry currently has three beers and six pieces of pizza, while Fran currently has four beers and five pieces of pizza. (a) Who likes beer more, Fran or Terry? (b) Who places a higher marginal value on beer? (c) Illustrate a mutually beneficial exchange between Terry and Fran.

2. One section of a company finds that it could do the same work it is now doing if it had five more calculators and three fewer typewriters. Another section of the same company finds that it could do the same work it now does if it had three more typewriters and seven fewer calculators. Can you suggest a way to get a larger total output from each section?

3. "Suppose the subjective value I place on a book is 50¢. But if someone has offered me $2 for the book, I will not sell it to you for 75¢, even though your offer exceeds my subjective value. This means that the concept of subjective value is useless in explaining exchange." Is it?

4. If I do not have a garden hose, I would be willing to pay up to $15 to get one. The price is $7, so I buy one. Now that I have one, I would be willing to pay up to $4 to buy a second. Since the price is $7, I do not buy it. Is the marginal value I place on garden hoses equal to their price? How would you modify the statement in the chapter that "consumers adjust their purchases of a commodity so that the value they place on it equals the market price" to handle this situation?

5. In the Main and Baird exchange example, would a price of five meats per gorp result in a mutually beneficial exchange? Explain. What about a price of one and one half per gorp?

6. In the Main and Baird exchange example, Main placed a higher marginal value on gorp than Baird did. Who placed a higher marginal value on meat? In the example, who ended up with more meat? Did both gorp and meat go to the person who placed the higher marginal value on them? Could that be the same person? Why not?

7. Consider the Main and Baird exchange example. (a) After all mutually beneficial changes take place, Main and Baird will both place the same marginal value on an ounce of gorp, and that marginal value will be between two and four packages of meat per ounce of gorp. Why? (b) Suppose that common marginal value turns out to be three meat per gorp. Now suppose another person, Joe, appears on the scene. His offer price of an ounce of gorp is six meat per gorp. What will happen? Who will exchange with whom? When all mutually beneficial exchanges have taken place, what will be the relationship between the marginal values that the three persons place on gorp? Explain.

8. Suppose there were ten people (or one hundred) involved in the Main and Baird example. When all exchanges had taken place, what would be the relationship between the marginal values that all ten (or all one hundred) would place on gorp?

9. In the Main and Baird exchange example, Main's maximum offer price (four meats per gorp) exceeded Baird's minimum asking price (two meats per gorp) by two meats. This difference is called the gain from trade. Since the transaction price was three meats for one gorp, Main and Baird each gained the equivalent of one meat. Suppose the price had been three and one half meats per gorp. What would have been the individual and total gains from trade? Which price is better? What do you mean by better?

10. (a) What would have been the individual and total gains from trade if the transaction price had been three meats, but Main had to devote time valued at one half meat to carrying out the exchange, while Baird had to devote time valued at one quarter meat? (b) Suppose instead that Baird incurred time costs of six tenths of a meat but charged Main three and four tenths meats for the gorp. (Main incurs no time costs.) Would Main and Baird both prefer this? (c) Which of these two arrangements is more likely to emerge? Explain.

11. Suppose that Main and Baird have carried out several exchanges, and that for the last ounce of gorp traded, the price was three meats. Main's maximum offer price was three meats, as was Baird's minimum asking price. (The trade would not make either transactor better off, but neither would it make them worse off, so let us suppose it takes place.) Suppose Main's maximum offer price for one more gorp would be 2.9 meats, and Baird's minimum asking price would be 3.1 meats. (a) Can you see why Main's offer price would have to be less than three and Baird's asking price would have to be greater than three? (b) Could Main and Baird benefit from further exchange? (c) Is it possible for *any* reallocation of gorp and meat to be efficient for *both* Main and Baird? Explain.

12. "Come to the auto auction supermarket of used cars! Buy where the dealers buy and save the middleman's cost." Evaluate.

13. Would exchange ever be possible if all people had exactly the same preferences? Explain.

14. How are middlemen's jobs being "reassigned" if you decide to form a cooperative and buy your fresh vegetables directly from the central produce market in your city?

15. You are bidding at an antique auction. Are you competing with the auctioneer? If not, with whom are you competing and with whom is the auctioneer competing?

16. Why are some items sold on consignment by middlemen, while others are bought from the seller and sold to the buyer?

17. Why isn't there a market for store coupons, just as there was for airline (half-fare) coupons? Would you expect the percentage of these coupons which are redeemed to be higher or lower than for airline coupons?

18. In late 1979, Air West instituted a half-fare coupon program similar to United's. Would you expect a more highly or less highly developed resale market in these coupons than in the United coupons? Would you expect the percentage of these coupons that were redeemed to be larger or smaller than for United's coupons? (Hint: Compare the average length of flight for the two airlines.)

19. Refer to the section on "Exchange, Prices, and Coordination." Suppose growing fifty pounds of almonds required the same amount of land as growing one hundred pounds of walnuts, but the almonds required $60 more in other resources. Would it still be efficient for the grower to switch from walnuts to almonds?

20. (a) In some auctions the auctioneer acts as an agent for the actual seller and collects a fee from the seller. Would you expect this fee to be a fixed amount per item or related to the ultimate sale price? Why? (b) In other cases, the auctioneer purchases goods piecemeal, sells them for whatever he can get, and keeps the difference. Can you explain why some auctions are run one way and some the other?

21. In the chapter we argued that people's substitutions and exchanges are ultimately good for good. If so, why is money one of the items in nearly every transaction?

22. Suppose you live in a rent-controlled apartment. The rent ceiling is $200 per month. You would be willing to give up your right to occupy the apartment (while still paying the landlord $200 per month) for $240 per month. A potential tenant would be willing to pay $300 per month to have your apartment. Is the existing allocation of apartments efficient?

23. Suppose the price of gasoline were controlled at $1 per gallon and that at that price there is a shortage. (Check chapter 1 for the definition of shortage.) To handle the shortage "equitably," the government issues ration coupons which must be used when purchasing gasoline. You receive forty gallons worth of coupons per month. At a price of $1 per gallon, you would like to consume sixty-five gallons per month, and you would be willing to pay $1.50 per gallon for another ten gallons of gas. Another consumer is in a similar situation, except she would be willing to pay $1.20 per gallon. In fact, she would be willing to do without ten of her gallons if she could receive $1.25 per gallon gross (that is, get back her $1 per gallon plus a premium of 25¢ per gallon). Is the existing allocation of gasoline efficient? Explain.

24. Suppose that when user A uses heating oil, he must pay a tax of $5 per barrel, but when user B uses it, no tax is paid. As a seller of heating oil, would you charge a lower price to A than you would to B? Explain. In that case, the price (including tax) will be higher for A than for B. Will this result in an efficient allocation of oil among users? Explain.

25. Suppose that, at the price prevailing for a certain good, the amount people want to buy is greater than the amount forthcoming. Then not every buyer will be able to buy as much as he wants. Not all of them will be able to adjust to the point where the value they place on the commodity equals its price. Will they all place the same value on the commodity? If not, what will tend to happen?

26. Suppose the Big Valley Water District has established a price of $5 per acre-foot of water (the amount necessary to cover one acre of land with one foot of water) to its agricultural users. Farmer Smith can use water on either or both of two crops, W and X. The marginal benefits which the application of successive acre-feet of water would bring to Smith are shown below. Similarly, Farmer Jones can use the water on crops Y or Z.

	Smith			Jones	
Acre – Feet	Marginal Benefit Crop W	Crop X	Acre – Feet	Marginal Benefit Crop Y	Crop Z
1	$10	$8	1	$14	$17
2	9	6	2	12	15
3	8	4	3	10	13
4	7	3	4	8	11
5	6	2	5	6	9½
6	5	1	6	4	7
7	4	½	7	3	4

(a) At a price of $5 per acre-foot, how much water would Smith want? How about Jones? (b) Suppose there is a drought, and only five acre-feet of water are available per farm. The district decides to allocate the water "equitably," so every user gets five acre-feet. How will Smith allocate her water between crops W and X? (Use the concept of efficiency.) How will Jones allocate his five acre-feet? At the margin what would be Smith's maximum offer price for an additional acre-foot of water? Her minimum asking price? What would be Jones' offer and asking price? Is mutually beneficial exchange possible? Who would buy water from whom? How much would be exchanged? In what range would the price for the final unit exchanged lie? (c) In what sense was the original allocation of their five acre-feet by Smith and Jones efficient? In what sense was the allocation between them inefficient? (d) If the district charged a price of $9 per acre-foot, who would consume how much? How does that allocation and price compare with those arrived at through exchange between Smith and Jones?

The Geometry Of Exchange

Most of the discussion of exchange in this chapter has been by means of a numerical example to illustrate the important concepts. This is a perfectly satisfactory way of covering the topic as far as we did. In more advanced courses, exchange and consumer behavior are discussed by means of graphical techniques. These techniques, while more difficult to master than numerical examples, are more powerful tools in that they permit more direct discussion of some topics which would be cumbersome with numerical examples, and once mastered, they are easier to manipulate. This appendix serves as a brief introduction to the basic graphical tool used for discussing exchange—indifference curves.

We mentioned earler that the concept of value is closely related to the idea of *indifference*. The marginal value placed on a commodity can be determined by comparing two bundles of goods between which a person is indifferent. For example, in table 2-3, Main was indifferent between bundles A and B. The difference between the two bundles was that bundle B had one more ounce of gorp and five fewer packages of dehydrated meat than bundle A. Thus Main was indifferent to making a move in which he gave up five meats for one gorp. The marginal *value* of gorp (the maximum amount of meat Main would be willing to give up for an ounce of gorp) was five packages of meat.

We can express the ideas of indifference and marginal value graphically by means of a device called an *indifference curve*—a locus of points (representing bundles of goods) between which a person is indifferent. We can illustrate the concept by using the exchange example we have already discussed. Main's situation is represented in figure 2-1. The diagram contains two axes. Along the horizontal axis, we show various amounts of gorp, starting at zero where the axes intersect and increasing as we move to the right. Along the vertical axis, we show amounts of meat, starting at zero at the intersection and increasing as we go up. We can represent a particular bundle (or combination) of the two goods by starting at the origin (the intersection of the two axes), then moving to the right by the number of ounces of gorp, and moving up by the number of packages of meat. Bundle A is thus nine units to the right of the origin and thirteen units above (shown as A in the diagram). Points in the diagram represent bundles containing some of each good.

Bundles A, B, and C are shown as points in the figure. Since we assumed that Main was indifferent between the three bundles, we have connected the three points with a line, which we call an indifference curve. By so doing, we are saying that Main is also indifferent between *A* and every point on the curve. We have listed the three points merely for convenience.

A few other observations about the indifference curve diagram are in order. Consider point *C'*. This point lies above *C*, meaning that it has more meat than point *C* and the same amount of gorp. Thus, since gorp and meat are both goods, Main must prefer *C'* to *C*. Since he is indifferent between *C* and any *other*

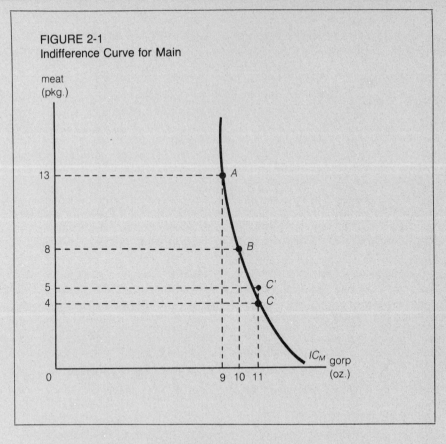

FIGURE 2-1
Indifference Curve for Main

point on IC_M, he prefers C' to all points on the indifference curve. This is merely an example of a more general idea. Any point (bundle) which lies above or to the right of a given indifference curve is preferred to every point (bundle) on that curve.

There must be bundles of goods which are equally as desirable as C'. Thus there must be an indifference curve connecting those points which goes through C'. Of course every point on *that* indifference curve would be preferable to every point on IC_M.

The concept of *decreasing marginal value* is illustrated by the shape of the indifference curve. The marginal value of gorp is the change in meat divided by the change in gorp along an indifference curve

$$\frac{\text{change in } M}{\text{change in } G}$$

but

$$\frac{\text{change in } M}{\text{change in } G}$$

is the *slope* of the indifference curve. For example, the slope from A to B is approximately

$$(\text{minus}) \frac{5}{1} = -5.$$

But 5 meat per ounce of gorp is also the marginal value of gorp. So the marginal value of gorp is the slope of the indifference curve. The assumption that the marginal value Main places on gorp falls as he gets more gorp is shown by the fact that the slope of the indifference curve (ignoring whether it is positive or negative) gets smaller as Main gets more gorp. When a curve gets flatter as we move down and to the right, we say it is *convex to the origin*. Thus the assumption of decreasing marginal value is

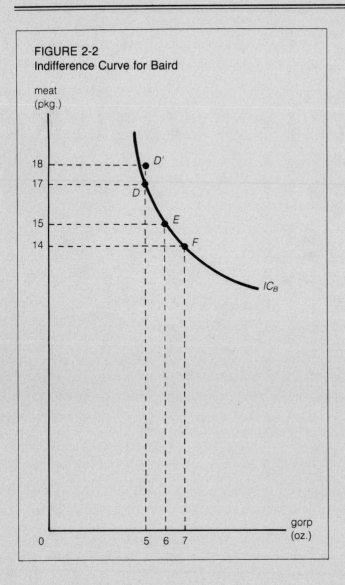

FIGURE 2-2
Indifference Curve for Baird

equivalent to assuming that indifference curves are convex to the origin.

We can construct an indifference curve for Baird just as we did for Main. Points D, E, and F are shown in figure 2-2. The line connecting those points is labeled IC_B. Note that IC_B is convex to the origin just as IC_M was for Main. Again, this merely reflects our assumption that Baird's preferences are consistent with the principles of decreasing value.

Note also that, since both gorp and meat are goods, bundle D' is preferred to

bundle D and every other bundle shown as a point on IC_B.

The exchange we discussed in the chapter can now be illustrated by means of figures 2-1 and 2-2. Recall that we assumed that Main was located at point B, and that Baird was at point E. Main would be willing to move in a southeasterly direction as long as he does not have to give up more than four packages of meat in return for one ounce of gorp. This is Main's maximum offer price for gorp. In order for Main to be able to move south-east, Baird must move northwest (*giving up* gorp in return for meat). He is willing to do so as long as he gets at least two packages of meat in return for giving up an ounce of gorp. This is Baird's minimum asking price for gorp. The exchange illustrated meets the conditions specified for both men, involving a trade of three packages of meat for one ounce of gorp. It is lower than Main's maximum offer price and higher than Baird's minimum asking price. This moves Main to point C', and Baird to point D', points already shown to be preferred to the initial points.

chapter 3

FOR
RENT
6000 SQ FT

NATHAN R MILLER
PROPERTIES LTD.

742-9480

Demand

Is the amount of goods consumed a matter of chance, or custom, or purely biological need? Each of these factors probably plays a role, but there are other influences which warrant examination. The amount of any good that I choose to consume is a function of (depends on) its price, my income, what I think the future price will be, and the prices of other goods. In this chapter we shall discuss each factor having an effect on consumption choices.

THE DEMAND CURVE

One of the most important tools for economists is the demand curve. This construction allows us to isolate one particular influence on the amount of a good people choose to consume, namely, its price. The demand curve is in fact a schedule or curve representing the relationship between the amount of a good that people are ready, willing and able to buy, and its price, holding constant other factors such as income, expected future prices, and prices of other goods. Table 3-1 illustrates a hypothetical demand schedule for a good.

The demand schedule also can be represented in pictorial form as a *curve* (although in this case it is a straight line). (See figure 3-1.) The

TABLE 3-1
HYPOTHETICAL DEMAND SCHEDULE

Price per Unit	Quantity Demand
$10	1
9	2
8	3
7	4
6	5
5	6
4	7
3	8
2	9
1	10

demand curve is an iffy thing. It says that *if* the price were $8 per unit, three units would be demanded. On the other hand, *if* the price were $4 per unit, seven units would be demanded.

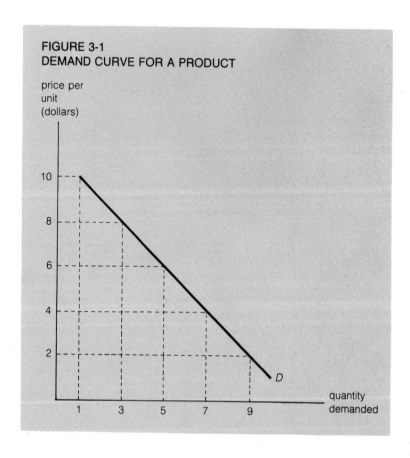

FIGURE 3-1
DEMAND CURVE FOR A PRODUCT

THE FIRST LAW
OF DEMAND

Notice that the demand curve was drawn sloping downward from left to right. This was not accidental. In fact, economists believe that *all* demand curves are downward-sloping. The evidence supporting this proposition is so strong that it has come to be called a *law*, the First Law of Demand. It says that the higher the price of any good, the less people will demand of it (other things equal). This means that if the price of a good goes up, and income, prices of other goods, and expected future prices do not change, less of the good will be demanded.

The First Law of Demand is really just a variation on the idea of substitution. The price of a good represents the dollar equivalent of the amount of other goods which must be sacrificed in order to get one more unit of the good in question. A consumer chooses how much to buy by comparing how much another unit is worth to her (in terms of other goods she is willing to forego) with the amount of other goods she must forego to get the additional unit (the price). If the price of a good rises, the amount of other goods which must be foregone to get each unit is greater, and the point at which the extra unit of good is not worth the price is reached sooner.

If this explanation seems too rational and calculating to be true, the law can be viewed in a slightly different way. Assume that people act this way and see what the implications of that assumption are. The main implication is, of course, that demand curves are downward-sloping. What kind of real-world behavior does that imply? It implies that when fruits and vegetables are in season, the price will be lower. Consumers can be induced to consume the greater amount available only if the price falls. If the Russians buy part of our wheat crop, that reduces the amount available to domestic consumers. A sufficient rise in price will reduce the amount demanded so that it is in conformity with this changed circumstance. If the coffee-producing countries burn 25 percent of their crop, the price will rise in the absence of restrictions on exchange. If the price of gasoline rises, the amount demanded will be smaller. Those implications, and more, are all borne out. We can be fairly confident that the First Law of Demand holds.

The First Law of Demand is a denial of the idea that human needs are fixed and unresponsive to changes in circumstances. One might say, as some U.S. senators have, that we *need* gasoline because people have to drive to work. True enough, but the *need* seems to vary inversely with the price. The higher the price, the less we need. How does this happen? Partly, it is because the types of cars being driven are changing. The number of miles per gallon obtainable is rising. Partly, also, more people are using public transportation. They are doing less sightseeing by car—less pleasure driving. The upshot is that we are consuming less than we would have if the price had not risen, in spite of the fact that people have to drive to work.

54 CETERIS PARIBUS

As noted above, when we draw the demand curve, we are isolating the effect of the price of a good on the quantity demanded. This means we are, for the purpose of analysis, holding constant other factors which might affect the amount people want to consume. The First Law of Demand is then a hypothetical (iffy) statement: *if* the price of a good falls, and *if* the other factors don't change, then the amount of the good demanded will rise. This is often expressed as "a fall in the price of a good increases the quantity demanded, *ceteris paribus*." *Ceteris paribus* is a Latin phrase meaning "other things equal," and is a shorter way of saying that the statement being made isolates the effect of the price change from the effect of the other factors.

A CHANGE IN QUANTITY DEMANDED VERSUS A CHANGE IN DEMAND

The First Law of Demand refers to a movement along the demand curve. The demand curve does not *move* in response to the change in price. The change in price induces a change in the *quantity demanded*. For example, look at figure 3-2(a). Suppose this demand curve represents your demand for steaks. Assume that the price was originally $2.50 per pound, and that as a result you consumed one pound per month. If the price falls (*ceteris paribus*), to $1.50 per pound, you will buy more. Suppose you now buy two pounds per month. This change (illustrated by a movement down the demand curve) is referred to as a change (increase) in quantity demanded.

In contrast to this case, suppose there is a change in one of the other things, so that, at every price, you demand more than before. (Perhaps you get a big pay increase. We shall see later exactly why this might cause you to demand more at every price.) This is called a *change in demand* because the whole curve moves. Examine figure 3-2(b). The new demand curve is labelled *D'*, and the movement is an *increase in demand*. With your new higher demand, you will buy more steak even though its price stays at $2.50 per pound. Suppose your consumption rises to two and a half pounds per month. If the price is $1.50 per pound and you get your raise, then your consumption will rise, say, from two to three and a quarter pounds per month.

So that the reader can know which of these two phenomena is being discussed, it is important to reserve the term *change* (increase or decrease) *in demand* for shifts in the curve, as in 3-2(b).

CHANGE IN DEMAND AND PRICE AT THE SAME TIME

Sometimes a change in demand can be accompanied by a change in price, resulting in a movement along the new demand curve. For example, sup-

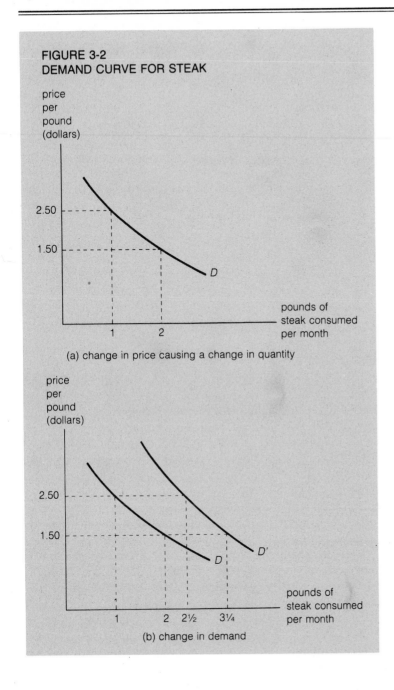

FIGURE 3-2
DEMAND CURVE FOR STEAK

(a) change in price causing a change in quantity

(b) change in demand

pose that, in figure 3-2(b), the price was originally $1.50 per pound, and you had your old, lower salary. Then your demand curve would be D, and you would buy two pounds of steak per month. Now suppose you get your raise, shifting your demand to D,' and at the same time the price rises from $1.50 to $2.50 per pound. You will respond in two counteracting ways. On the one hand, the increased demand means that, had the price stayed at

$1.50, you would have increased your consumption to three and a quarter pounds per month. But the price rises to $2.50 per pound, so you cut consumption from three and a quarter back to two and a half pounds per month. In this example, the higher price does not quite offset the increased demand, so the quantity you consume is larger after the combined change. Does this mean that the First Law of Demand is false since both price and quantity demanded rose? Not at all. The First Law of Demand says only that *along any demand curve*, a higher price means a smaller quantity demanded. And that is exactly what happened. When the price rose from $1.50 to $2.50, the quantity you demanded fell from three and a quarter to two and a half. But in this example, other factors were changing in such a way as to mask the operation of the First Law of Demand.

While a change in demand can be accompanied by (or even cause) a change in price, resulting in a change in quantity demanded, a change in the price of a good does *not* cause the demand curve to shift (change in demand). The change in price merely results in a movement along the curve.

DO PEOPLE "CONSULT" THEIR DEMAND CURVES?

When economists are using demand curves to illustrate a point, they draw a specific curve to make the example concrete. But naturally, it is not possible to know what the demand for any product looks like exactly. The information requirements would be too great. While it would be nice to know the exact shape and location of every demand curve, economists get many benefits out of the demand curve concept without that extra information.

Oftentimes we shall use our numerical examples in such a way as to suggest that consumers "consult" their demand curves in order to decide how much of a good to buy (or whether the value they place on another unit of the good is sufficient to justify buying it). While this procedure is useful, we do not really believe that people "consult" their demand curves in this sense. We construct models which *assume* (unrealistically) that they do because it enables us to derive testable implications in a simple and direct way. It is the *implications* of the theory, not its assumptions, which determine its value as a theory. (At this point, perhaps the reader should reread the section entitled "The Method of Economic Analysis" in chapter 1, in which this point is discussed in somewhat greater detail.) If, by assuming that consumers consult their demand curves, we get implications not in conflict with the facts, then the assumption is warranted. In particular, our theory implies that people will choose to consume less of a good at a higher price. One easy way to generate that implication is to assume that consumers have emblazoned on their brains a downward-sloping demand curve which they consult. When the price rises, they move up the demand curve and consume less. It is this final result (less consumption) following from the price change which is the key feature of the model. Whether or not consumers consult their demand curves, it is sufficient that they act *as if* they did; then the theory is vindicated.

CAUSES OF CHANGES IN DEMAND

Income—Normal and Inferior Goods

For most goods, an increase in income causes demand to increase. This is true of such things as beef, housing, clothing, and many other goods. Since this is the usual or normal case, we call such goods *normal goods*. This is illustrated in figure 3-3. When income is $100 the demand curve is D. When income rises to $150, the demand curve shifts to the right (to D'). At every price, more is demanded than before. For some other goods, called *inferior goods*, the situation is reversed. As income rises, the demand for these goods falls. Figure 3-4 illustrates this point. When income is $100, the demand is given by D. When income rises to $150, the demand shifts to the left. The new demand curve is D'.

Examples of inferior goods include public transportation, navy beans, and probably some brands of margarine. Forty years ago, margarine was an excellent example of an inferior good. It was a good used mostly by poor people, and as their incomes rose, they switched to butter. Today, im-

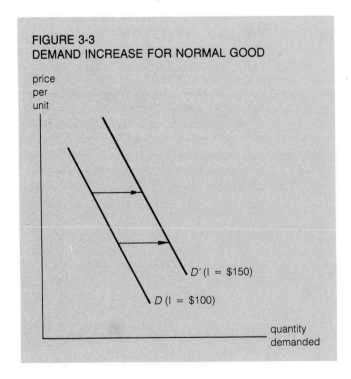

FIGURE 3-3
DEMAND INCREASE FOR NORMAL GOOD

price
per
unit

D' (I = $150)

D (I = $100)

quantity
demanded

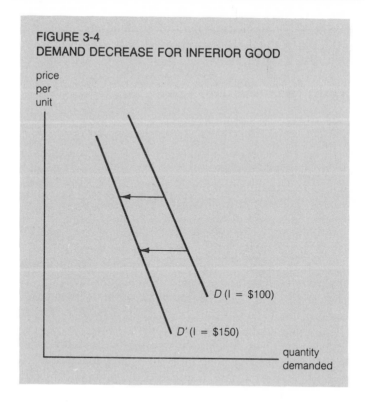

FIGURE 3-4
DEMAND DECREASE FOR INFERIOR GOOD

provements of margarines (such as making them soft and using polyunsaturated fats, resulting in general consumer acceptance) have made many margarines normal goods. What happens now is that as incomes rise, people buy better margarines, rather than moving from margarine to butter. In fact, with the current concern over saturated fats, some corn oil margarines may be considered the "most superior" spreads by many consumers.

Related Goods—Substitutes

When two or more goods are somewhat interchangeable in serving the same want, they are thought of as *substitutes*. Blue Bonnet and Imperial margarine, Fords and Chevrolets, electricity and natural gas, cars and public transportation are all examples of substitutes. Economists define substitutes by the way in which their demands are interrelated. Goods A and B are substitutes if a higher price for A increases the demand for B and vice versa. Thus Blue Bonnet and Imperial are substitutes, because if the price of Blue Bonnet rises, there will be a tendency for consumers to increase their consumption of Imperial at the expense of Blue Bonnet, even if Imperial's price does not change (see figure 3-5). Suppose that the price of Blue Bonnet is originally 60¢ per pound, and the price of Imperial is 75¢. If the price of Blue Bonnet rises to 70¢, some consumers will decide that

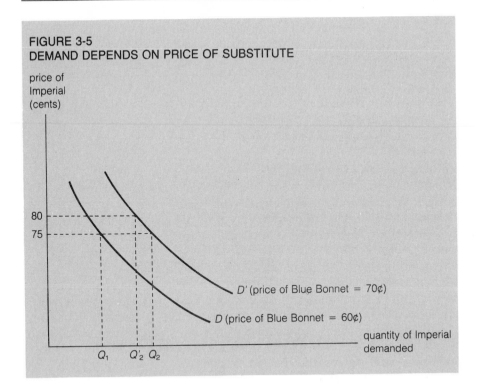

FIGURE 3-5
DEMAND DEPENDS ON PRICE OF SUBSTITUTE

price of
Imperial
(cents)

80

75

D' (price of Blue Bonnet = 70¢)

D (price of Blue Bonnet = 60¢)

quantity of Imperial
demanded

Q_1 Q'_2 Q_2

Imperial is now a better buy. They will switch, even if the price of Imperial
stays at 75¢. Although Imperial is still more expensive than Blue Bonnet,
it is less expensive *relative* to Blue Bonnet than before; thus some substitution will occur.

The higher demand for Imperial may well lead to a higher price (say
80¢). Why? With the increased demand for Imperial, sellers notice that
stocks are being depleted faster than before. They find that they can raise
prices and not lose too many sales. Then two things are happening in the
Imperial market. The demand increases due to the higher price of Blue
Bonnet; this results in the higher price of Imperial, which causes consumers to move up the new higher demand curve. In figure 3-5, the original
situation showed quantity Q_1 of Imperial being bought when it was 75¢ and
Blue Bonnet was 60¢. In response to the rise in Blue Bonnet's price (to 70¢),
the quantity of Imperial rises to Q_2 if the price stays at 75¢. But the higher
demand causes the price of Imperial to rise to 80¢, resulting in a reduction
in quantity from Q_2 to Q'_2.

What does the higher price of Imperial do to the demand for Blue
Bonnet? Since they are substitutes, the demand for Blue Bonnet increases.
We can infer from this that, in the case of substitutes, prices tend to move
together. An increase in beef prices increases the demand and price for
pork, cheese, beans, eggs, and other substitutes. How does this happen?
When there is an increase in beef prices, consumers try to substitute pork,
fish, cheese, beans, and eggs. This substitution appears as an increase in

demand for the beef substitutes. Sellers of these goods find that they are running out more quickly. If they run out of items each week while some buyers still want to buy more, they can increase price (reducing the amount demanded) and still sell all they normally have per week. It is clearly in the interest of sellers to do this, and we can expect them to do it. So prices of all these commodities will tend to move together, although by unequal amounts.

Related Goods—Complements

When two goods are used together in the same consumption activity, we think of them as being complementary—the goods help each other out in satisfying the want in question. Having more of one good makes the other more desirable. The empirical counterpart of this interaction is that when the price of a good falls, the demand for its complement rises. This is illustrated in figure 3-6. When the price of gasoline is 60¢ per gallon the demand for tires is given by D. If the price falls to 40¢, people will drive more and wear out tires faster, so that more tires will be bought at every price. So a decrease in the price of gasoline tends to increase the quantity of both gasoline and tires consumed.

Other examples of complements are golf balls and golf clubs, bread and butter, and stereos and records. Suppose we ban the importation of Japanese stereos. This tends to increase the price of stereos sold in this

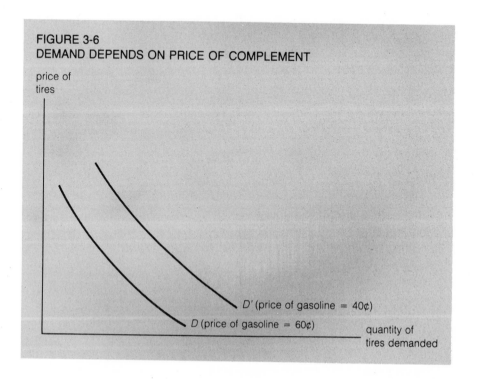

FIGURE 3-6
DEMAND DEPENDS ON PRICE OF COMPLEMENT

price of tires

D' (price of gasoline = 40¢)

D (price of gasoline = 60¢)

quantity of tires demanded

country. The higher price of stereos decreases the demand for records, reducing sales and tending to lower prices.

Expected Future Prices

The price you expect a good to have in the future influences the amount you are willing to buy today. If you expect to pay a higher price in the future, it may pay to stock up on the good. The inconvenience and cost of storing the good in the interim will be more than made up for by the savings you can expect, if the future price is expected to change significantly. This is known as *speculation*, and people often engage in it. In the summer of 1975 there were rumors that the sugar beet crop would be smaller than usual, thus triggering another rise in prices, and the shelves in some supermarkets were emptied by speculating consumers.

A couple of interesting things happen when expected future prices change. Suppose that today we change our opinion and think that sugar prices will be higher in two months. Two things may happen: first, the price of sugar may rise sooner—say in one week. The general belief that future prices will be higher tends to make the price go up today as people speculate by stocking up. Second, the quantity purchased may rise in the face of a somewhat higher price. This would happen if people thought the price was going to rise still further. (See figure 3-7.) Suppose the price of sugar is originally 20¢ per pound and you expect the future price to be 30¢

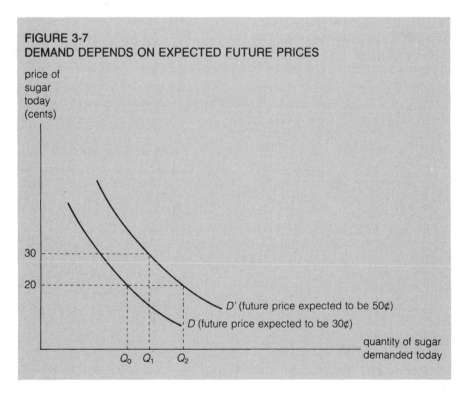

FIGURE 3-7
DEMAND DEPENDS ON EXPECTED FUTURE PRICES

price of sugar today (cents)

30

20

D' (future price expected to be 50¢)

D (future price expected to be 30¢)

quantity of sugar demanded today

Q_0 Q_1 Q_2

per pound. Then you would buy amount Q_0 of sugar. Now suppose your beliefs about the future change, and you now think the future price will be 50¢. If the price were to stay temporarily at 20¢, you would buy Q_2. If the price rises today to 30¢, you would buy Q_1. In the example shown, this is still larger than your original purchase of Q_0. If we look only at the quantity bought at the prescare 20¢ price and the quantity bought at 30¢, we might mistakenly think that people buy more as the price rises. But the change in expectations has changed the demand. If the price had remained at 20¢, even more would have been bought. Given the new expectations, less is bought at 30¢ than would have been bought at 20¢.

Tastes

Another factor in determining the amount of a good demanded is *tastes*. When we can't explain consumption by means of the other factors mentioned above, we use *tastes* to explain it. Thus we say that sales of tortillas and hot chilis will be greater in Mexican neighborhoods than in Anglo neighborhoods. There is no particular relationship between this phenomenon and income or the prices of other goods, so we attributed it to tastes. Tastes are for the most part not inborn. People learn what things to like partly through family upbringing and other social interactions, as well as schooling. Tastes can also be influenced by advertising. We leave the discussion of this topic for chapter 11.

ECONOMIC ANALYSIS, MULTIPLE CAUSATION, AND CETERIS PARIBUS

Economists generally refrain from trying to explain why any particular event happens. For example, suppose Smith chooses to take a certain job (job A). It is usually futile to ask *the* reason for that choice. A questionnaire might obtain answers such as, "I like the pay," or "The working conditions are good," or "It is close to where I live." A reasonable guess is that *all* these factors and more play roles in determining the choice, so it is not helpful to ask for *one* reason for it. How does an economist approach the problem of analyzing job choice? He or she constructs a *model* of the choice of occupation which states the factors which, on the basis of intuition, introspection, or familiarity with the situation, seem reasonable to include. Using logical relationships, empirical relationships observed elsewhere, and assumptions, the investigator conducts conceptual experiments to attempt to determine what these assumptions and logical relationships imply. The experiments are *ceteris paribus* experiments. In our job choice example, one asks, "If the pay at job A increases, holding working conditions, distance from home, and wages in other potential jobs unchanged, would the person be more or less likely to take job A?" Similar predictions emerge when other conceptual experiments are performed. The predictions that result are all *ceteris paribus* predictions about the effect of a change in some factor which influences the choice. In order to study its usefulness, one would then use statistical techniques to see whether these predictions hold up in a sample of a large number of workers. (We do not try to predict any particular worker's choice, but rather the general trends of behavior of the group.) Our analysis of the various factors which determine the quantity demanded of a good is an example of this sort of process at work.

DEMAND AND MARGINAL VALUE

There are two ways of looking at the demand curve. The first has been discussed; the demand curve tells the amount demanded at each price. "You give me a price and I'll give you a quantity." For example, figure 3-8 shows a hypothetical demand for oranges. Along the demand curve, we see that at a price of 30¢, three oranges are consumed; at a price of 20¢, four are consumed. This is perfectly acceptable, and for many purposes it is the handiest way to view a problem. But there is another, equivalent way to look at the demand curve. This approach views the curve as a schedule expressing the *marginal value* a consumer places on the commodity—that is, the amount she would be willing to pay to have one more unit. "You give me a quantity and I'll tell you how much I would be willing to pay for one more unit." The height of the demand curve expresses the *marginal* value. For example, in figure 3-8, when the consumer is consuming two oranges per week, she would be willing to pay 30¢ to consume a third orange per week. If the price were 30¢, she would choose three oranges. We can see this by starting at the point when the consumer has *no* oranges. At that point she would be willing to pay 50¢ to have one orange per week. Since the price is only 30¢, she will buy an orange. Since she has one, she would be willing to pay 40¢ to get a second orange. Since the price is 30¢, she will buy a second orange. Having two oranges, she would be willing to pay 30¢ for a third orange. Since the price is 30¢, she will buy it. Will she buy a fourth orange? No. Her demand (marginal value) curve tells us that she would be willing to pay up to 20¢ for a fourth orange but not 30¢. So if the price is 30¢, she will buy three oranges. At a price of 30¢, she would be better off consuming three oranges than any amount greater or smaller than three. She does the best she can by just *reaching* the demand curve, rather than being to its right or left.

The First Law of Demand says that demand curves are downward-sloping. We can now see that this is equivalent to saying that the marginal value a person places on a good decreases as she has more of it. Thus the First Law of Demand is a variant of the principle of diminishing marginal value which we introduced in chapter 2.

DEMAND AND EXCHANGE

Viewing the demand curve as a marginal value curve gives us a different perspective on some problems. For example, we can analyze exchange by

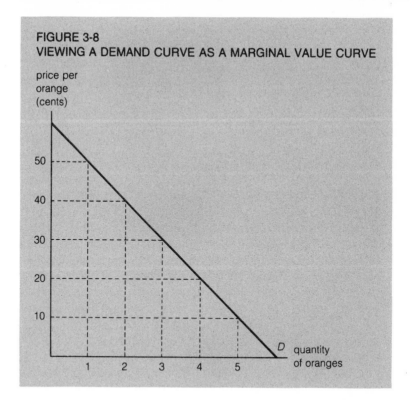

FIGURE 3-8
VIEWING A DEMAND CURVE AS A MARGINAL VALUE CURVE

means of demand. Suppose two people have the same demand for oranges (figure 3-8). Suppose person A has five, while person B has only one. Notice that their marginal values differ. Person B would be willing to pay up to 40¢ to get a second orange. (That is her maximum offer price.) How much would person A require in payment? His demand schedule says that to get his fifth orange he would have been willing to pay 10¢. So presumably he would *give up* the fifth orange if offered *more than* 10¢ for it. (So 10¢ is his minimum asking price.) Any price between 10¢ and 40¢ would be mutually agreeable, so we can presume that A and B will exchange, with A giving up the orange for say 35¢. Now A has four oranges, and B has two. Are any more mutually beneficial exchanges possible? B would be willing to pay up to 30¢ to get a third orange, while A would sell for anything more than 20¢. Again there is room for a bargain. Suppose the price is 28¢. After this exchange, each has three oranges. No further mutually beneficial exchanges are possible. B would like a fourth orange but is willing to pay only up to 20¢ for it. A would sell his third orange but only if he can receive more than 30¢. So no more deals can be made.

This illustrates that problems involving differences in values and exchange can be analyzed by means of the demand curve (when viewed as a marginal value curve). In chapter 12 we will expand this to analyze problems of efficiency in pollution control.

CONSUMER "SURPLUS"

We can utilize the device of the demand curve as a marginal value curve to analyze another interesting concept. We almost never pay as much for a good as we would be willing to pay. A man on the desert might consider a glass of water a bargain at $1.00. We illustrate a less extreme example in figure 3-8. There the person is willing to pay 50¢ to have one orange per week rather than none. If the price is actually 30¢, we say she gets 20¢ of consumer surplus on the first orange. The schedule says she values a second orange at 40¢. If the price is 30¢, she gets another 10¢ of consumer surplus. Since her marginal value is 30¢ for the third orange, she gets no additional surplus on it. Her total consumer surplus at a price of 30¢ is thus 30¢. The total value that she places on having three units rather than none is $1.20 (the sum of the marginal values she places on the three units—50¢ for the first, 40¢ for the second, and 30¢ for the third). But she is required to pay only 90¢ (30¢ for each unit). The difference is a dollar measure of the benefit she gets from being able to buy as many oranges as she wants for 30¢ each. We can see the idea graphically in figure 3-9. The total value the consumer places on the three units of the good is the vertically lined area in figure 3-9(a).

But she is actually required to pay only the amount represented by the horizontally lined area in 3-9(b). The difference, the unlined triangle in 3-9(b), is consumer surplus. We shall use this concept again in chapter 8, where we discuss the pricing behavior of firms. In this section you will note that the word *surplus* has a meaning quite different from its usual meaning. The next section introduces the more common meaning of *surplus* and its companion word, *shortage*.

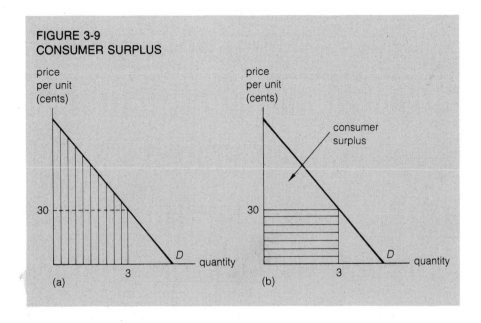

FIGURE 3-9
CONSUMER SURPLUS

66 SHORTAGES, SURPLUSES, AND THE EQUILIBRIUM PRICE

We often hear the words *shortage* and *surplus* applied to situations in which there is an unusually meager or a plentiful amount of a good available. In fact, some go so far as to say that a shortage exists when we have less than we need, and a surplus exists when we have more than we need. As we discovered above, however, *need* is a slippery word. Our needs seem to change as the price of the good changes. Indeed one purpose of using the idea of the demand curve is to make clear this notion of variability in needs.

When economists use the words *shortage* and *surplus*, they keep the variability of needs in mind and define the concepts in terms of the difference between the *amount demanded* and the *amount available*. Since the amount demanded (and usually the amount available) depends on the price, the existence of a shortage or a surplus depends on what price is charged. With a given fixed amount available and an unchanging demand curve, we can either have a shortage or a surplus, or neither, depending on the price charged. If the price is so low that the amount demanded is *greater* than the amount available, there is a shortage. If the price is so high that the amount demanded is *less* than the amount available, we have a surplus. At some intermediate price, the amount demanded will equal the amount available, and we will have *equilibrium*, which means that everyone is able to buy as much as he wants of the good at the existing price. This is shown in figure 3-10. The equilibrium price is shown as price P_E. It is the price which tends to prevail in the market if there are no restrictions on the price which can be charged. If the price is above P_E, a surplus develops, and the amount people want to sell is greater than the amount people want to buy. This puts downward pressure on the price because the unsatisfied sellers will tend to lower prices rather than not sell. As the price falls, the quantity demanded rises, thus reducing the surplus. At price P_E, the surplus is eliminated, and all buyers and sellers can buy and sell as much as they want. At prices below P_E, a shortage develops. This means that some buyers aren't able to buy as much as they want. Sellers could sell more than they have at this price, so if they raised the price some, they could still sell all they have. Thus the price rises. As the price rises, less is demanded, and the shortage is reduced. At price P_E, the shortage is eliminated, and all sellers and buyers are again satisfied. Price P_E is sometimes called the *market-clearing* price because it is the price at which the amount demanded exactly equals the amount available. It is also sometimes called the *coordinating* price, since buyers respond to it by making purchase plans that are consistent with available supply. Note that the coordinating price could never be known ahead of time. It emerges out of the actions of each independent actor as he uses his own knowledge, tastes, preferences, and opportunities to formulate his actions in response to whatever price exists. If the existing price is either higher or lower than P_E, the sum of the independent actions will not be consistent with the

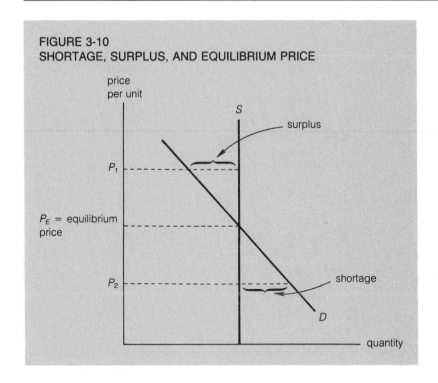

FIGURE 3-10
SHORTAGE, SURPLUS, AND EQUILIBRIUM PRICE

available supply, and that results in changes of the price. No initial authority could gather all of the relevant knowledge, which exists in bits in individual minds, and process it in order to determine the coordinating price.

The statement that the price in a market tends to move to P_E is very similar to the statements we made in chapter 2 and earlier in this chapter about the tendency of all persons in an economy to place the same value on a commodity after exchange opportunities have been exhausted. When we say a shortage exists, it is another way of saying that the unsatisfied buyers place a higher value on the commodity than other persons do. This disparity in values will tend to result in a reallocation of the good away from those persons with the lower value (those who were satisfied with what they had at the low price), and toward those with a higher value (those who wanted more than they had at the low price). This kind of reallocation results in a higher price, and eliminates the shortage.

When there is a surplus, a similar process operates to lower the price. In this case, the unsatisfied sellers (those who can't sell all they want to sell at the current price) place a lower value on the good than the buyers (and the satisfied sellers) do. This disparity tends to result in a reallocation of goods away from the unsatisfied sellers toward the buyers, but only at a lower price.

There are some situations in which the supply curve can usefully be thought of as vertical, meaning that no change in price will cause any change in the amount available. But usually the amount available depends

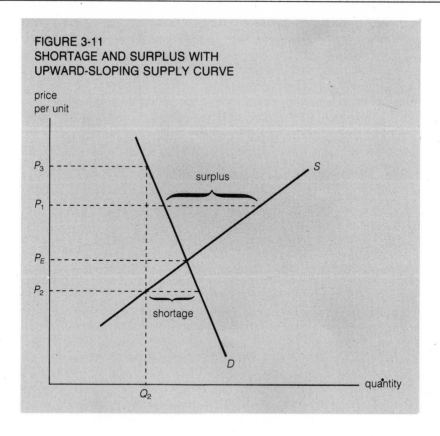

FIGURE 3-11
SHORTAGE AND SURPLUS WITH
UPWARD-SLOPING SUPPLY CURVE

on the price. The higher the price, the more that is made available. This proposition is very similar to our statement with regard to demand. There we said that the lower the price of a good, the more consumers will want. Here we are saying that the more we reward people for doing something (such as supplying a certain good), the more they will do. A low price rewards a consumer for consuming more, and a high price rewards a supplier for supplying more. In both cases, the greater the reward, the more that is done. (Chapter 7 has more detail on this.)

The idea that more is supplied when the price is higher can be expressed graphically by making the supply curve upward-sloping, as in figure 3-11. Here we see that there are now two reasons for a surplus if the price is above P_E, and a shortage if the price is below P_E. At P_1, the quantity supplied exceeds the quantity demanded, both because the quantity demanded decreases when price rises above P_E and because the quantity supplied increases when price is above P_E. Again, the surplus tends to result in a fall in price, which reduces the quantity supplied while increasing the quantity demanded, thus eliminating the surplus. A price below P_E results in a shortage because quantity supplied falls at the lower price, as well as because quantity demanded increases. The price rise eliminates the shortage by reversing these two situations.

The positively sloped supply curve, together with the negatively sloped demand curve, indicates that price movements coordinate the plans and actions of two independent groups of actors. Buyers' plans and actions change as prices change, and so too do the plans and actions of sellers. If price is less than the market-clearing price, the plans and actions of buyers result in more of the good wanted than sellers are willing to make available. Sellers notice that there are a lot of unsatisfied buyers, and they recognize that there will still be many (although fewer) buyers even if the price increases. Sellers therefore increase the price. At the higher price sellers' plans and actions are altered (they plan to sell more), and buyers' plans and actions are altered (some decide not to acquire any, and others decide to acquire less). In this way the gap between what is wanted and what is made available is progressively narrowed until the price reaches a level that causes buyers and sellers to make and execute mutually consistent plans.

If price is greater than the market-clearing price, sellers will plan to sell more than buyers will plan to buy. While some sellers may sell all they want, others sell a lot less than they had planned, and still others may not sell any at all. Disappointed sellers are thus induced to lower their asking prices. At lower prices sellers' plans are altered (they plan to sell less than before), and buyers' plans are altered (they plan to acquire more than before). Again, the gap between what is wanted and what is made available narrows until the price reaches a level that causes buyers and sellers to make and execute mutually consistent plans.

Each of the buyers and each of the sellers uses her own knowledge about her own unique circumstances of time and place to make her own individual plans. The knowledge that is used in this process exists nowhere in its entirety for any central authority to process in the determination of the market-clearing price. The only way that all of the relevant knowledge can be used is if each individual, who possesses her own portion of the total knowledge, is allowed to make and act on her individual plans. Any price that is determined by authority must necessarily be based on less information than a market-determined price; therefore, an authority-determined price will not indicate demand and supply conditions as accurately as a market-determined price.

The upward-sloping supply curve also allows us to understand a common fallacy. If the price is at P_2, resulting in a shortage, some observers might overestimate the price rise necessary to eliminate the shortage because they concentrate only on demand. If the amount supplied did not increase from Q_2 in response to a higher price, then the price would have to rise all the way to P_3 to eliminate the shortage. But if, as shown, the amount supplied increases as price increases, then only the rather modest rise to P_E is required to eliminate the shortage.

One of the implications of this analysis is that there will not be a prolonged shortage or surplus of a good unless some outside restriction is placed on the price at which the good can be exchanged.

A look at the evidence shows that every example of a prolonged shortage or surplus was accompanied by some government price regulation. In the 1950s and 1960s, the price of wheat was artificially raised by government policy. The result was a surplus of wheat. The rents on apartments in New York have been controlled since World War II; the shortage is apparent for all to see. The shortage of natural gas is directly traceable to price control by the Federal Power Commission. In 1976 there was a water shortage in much of California. It was widely thought that the reason for the shortage was the drought which hit the state that year. But the shortage could have been eliminated if the price of water had been raised in the affected areas. The drought was the cause of the increased *scarcity* of water, but when price failed to rise, increased scarcity was converted into a shortage.

Similarly there were shortages of gasoline in 1973–74 and in 1979 in some parts of the country. As in the case of the drought, there was a reduction in the amount available largely because of external factors, but the *shortage* occurred because the price of gasoline was not allowed to adjust fully and rapidly to the temporary increase in scarcity.

SHORTAGES AND "MINDING YOUR OWN BUSINESS"

If you want to convert sensible people who are minding their own business into a bunch of nosy, carping nags, force the price of a good below its equilibrium level. Suddenly everyone becomes concerned with how other people are consuming their good. In 1976, due to the natural gas shortage, the California Public Utilities Commission took it upon itself to determine what was a reasonable use for natural gas. They decided that heating swimming pools was not a reasonable use. As a result, swimming pool owners besieged the Commission with requests for exceptions. Wouldn't it be reasonable to have a heated pool, they asked, if my doctor prescribed it? One can imagine the kind of behavior which such a ruling would induce. The point is that when a shortage is created, the consumption patterns of other people suddenly become very important to us. If the price were high enough to avert the shortage, we would be concerned only to the point of commenting, "If he wants to throw his money away like that, let him," if at all. The market-clearing price of a good is the good's true scarcity value. If one is willing to pay that price, then how the good is used is purely a private matter.

SHORTAGES AND ALTERNATIVE FORMS OF COMPETITION

If the price of a good is kept below the market-clearing level, potential users want more than is available, so some method other than price must be used to decide who gets how much of the good. Various methods of discriminating, or rules for competing, have been known to emerge in the presence of shortages. In 1973–74 and in 1979, the gasoline shortages resulted in lines at the gas stations. Those who were more willing to wait in line a long time or drive around to find an open station were able to obtain more gasoline. Those who were friends of a dealer were often told when to get gasoline without waiting in line.

The dealers discriminated in favor of their friends and against strangers. The dealers might have a preference for dealing with their friends at other times as well, but in the absence of a shortage, a dealer will find that being surly or unhelpful to other customers is costly—he sells less than he otherwise would. But when there is a shortage, a dealer can sell all he has even if he is not nice to some customers. It is less costly to him to discriminate against customers with whom he would rather not deal, so he discriminates more. (This is an application of the First Law of Demand.)

When rent control is imposed, the tendency of owners to use nonprice means of selecting tenants increases. Suppose owners prefer to have single tenants or adult couples rather than families at any given rent. They may believe (rightly or wrongly) that adults do less damage to the apartments and are easier to have as tenants. Or they may not like children. But owners are willing to substitute among goods. They are willing to give up the ease, serenity, and stability of having adult tenants if they are offered a sufficient premium in rent by a family. In the absence of any controls on rents, some owners will be paid enough of a premium to induce them to rent to families. But if rent is controlled below the market-clearing price, potential tenants (such as families) who have characteristics the owners do not like are not able to offer a premium over tenants with more preferred character-istics. Thus the owners, faced with the choice of a more preferred and a less preferred tenant at the same rent, will tend to discriminate more than before against those (such as families) to whom they would rather not rent. The city of San Francisco provides an example of this phenomenon. A rent-control ordinance went into effect in 1979. By early 1980 there had been an enormous increase in complaints by families charging discrimina-tion on obtaining rental units. There were no complaints of discrimination against families in *purchasing* condominiums or houses, where price con-trols were absent.

RESPONSIVENESS—
ELASTICITY OF DEMAND

It is certainly helpful to know that demand curves are downward-sloping. This fact by itself provides us with a good deal of information about what to expect when changes occur. But sometimes it is useful to know *how responsive* the quantity demanded is to changes in the price. We know that the demand for gasoline is downward-sloping, but will the quantity de-manded fall a little or a lot if the price doubles?

Clearly a measure of responsiveness would be helpful—but which measure? One possible measure is the *slope*. When we move down a demand curve there is a certain change in quantity demanded associated

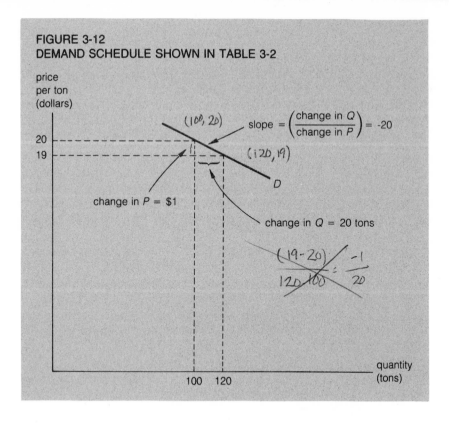

FIGURE 3-12
DEMAND SCHEDULE SHOWN IN TABLE 3-2

with each change in the price. We refer to the ratio of the change in Q divided by the change in P along the demand curve as the slope of the demand curve. Slope is

$$\frac{\text{change in } Q}{\text{change in } P}.$$

(Normally we think of slope as being the change along the vertical axis divided by the change along the horizontal axis, but the terminology we are using is acceptable in this instance.) The difficulty with this measure is that the size of the number depends critically on the units used to measure quantity and price. For example, suppose we are talking about the demand for steel, and we find the two points on the demand schedule shown in table 3-2 and figure 3-12.

With the price specified in dollars per ton and the quantity specified in tons, the slope

$$\frac{\text{change in } Q}{\text{change in } P}$$

equals -20. But if we change the units on the price to yen per ton, then

TABLE 3-2
DEMAND FOR STEEL

P (dollars/ton)	Q (tons)
20	100
19	120

(assuming an exchange rate of 300 yen/dollar) the two points would be as shown in table 3-3, and figure 3-13 and the slope,

$$\frac{\text{change in } Q}{\text{change in } P}, \quad \text{would be} \quad \frac{-20}{300} = \frac{-1}{15}.$$

TABLE 3-3
DEMAND FOR STEEL

P (yen/ton)	Q (tons)
6000	100
5700	120

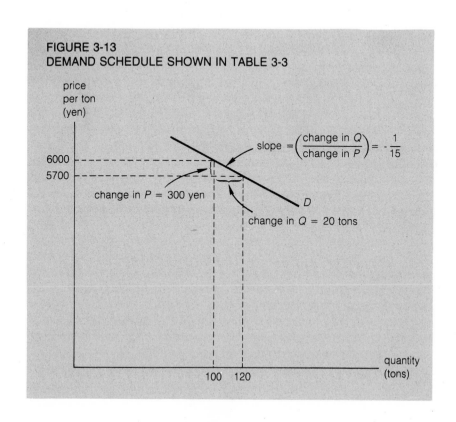

FIGURE 3-13
DEMAND SCHEDULE SHOWN IN TABLE 3-3

The two demand curves tell us exactly the same information, but the slopes are entirely different simply because of the change in units. We could get still another slope by changing the units to metric tons instead of U.S. tons.

Clearly, slope is an unsatisfactory measure of responsiveness. Consequently, economists have borrowed a measure from the mathematicians. The measure is called elasticity, and it does not have the problems that slope has because it is *free of units*. This is done by taking the ratio of the *percentage* change in quantity and the *percentage* change in price as the measure of elasticity:

$$\text{elasticity} = \frac{\% \text{ change in } Q}{\% \text{ change in } P}$$

Using this measure we see that we will get the same answer regardless of what units are used. The percentage change in price from $20 to $19 is the same as from 6000 to 5700 yen (about 5 percent, and whatever units we use to measure quantity, the percentage change from the first point to the second will always be the same (about 20 percent). Thus whatever units we use, we will always get the same answer for the elasticity, about

$$4 = \frac{20\%}{5\%}$$

How do we know how to interpret the elasticity numbers we calculate? It turns out that (if we take the absolute values of the changes—in other words, leave the minus signs off whenever they occur) elasticity can range from zero to infinity. We divide that range into three segments. If the elasticity falls between zero and one, we call it relatively *inelastic*. If it is greater than one, we call it relatively *elastic*, and if it equals one, we call it unitary-elastic. If elasticity is greater than one, this means that the percentage change in quantity is *greater than* the percentage change in price. For example, if along a certain demand curve, a 10 percent change in price resulted in a 20 percent change in quantity, the demand would be relatively *elastic* (two) over that range. If, on the other hand, a 40 percent change in price resulted in only a 5 percent change in quantity, the demand would be relatively *inelastic* (one eighth).

COMPARING ELASTICITIES OF DIFFERENT DEMAND CURVES

Examine figure 3-14. Which of these two demand curves is more elastic at any price? They are parallel, so they have the same slope, but they do *not* have the same elasticity. Suppose the price was initially 10 and

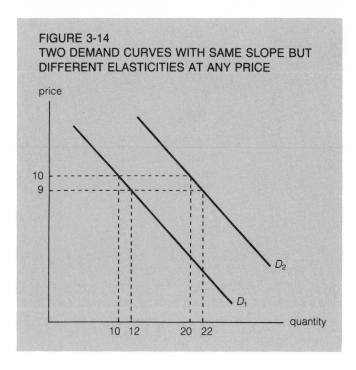

FIGURE 3-14
TWO DEMAND CURVES WITH SAME SLOPE BUT
DIFFERENT ELASTICITIES AT ANY PRICE

that it fell to 9. The quantity on D_1 would rise from 10 to 12, and on D_2 the quantity would rise from 20 to 22. (In both cases the slope

$$\frac{\text{change in } Q}{\text{change in } P}$$

is -2.) The *percentage* change in price is about 10 percent for both demand curves. But the percentage change in quantity is about 20 percent for D_1, while it is only about 10 percent for D_2. Thus, in this price range, D_1 has an elasticity of about two, while D_2 has an elasticity of about one. D_1 is more elastic than D_2. This information is summarized in table 3-4.

Now consider the case shown in figure 3-15. Here D_1 and D_2 intersect at price $20 and quantity 10. If the price were to fall from $20 to $19 along D_1, the elasticity would be about two (the price falls by about 5 percent and the quantity rises from 10 to 11, about 10 percent). Along D_2 the same 5 percent fall in price results in an increase in quantity of about 20 percent

TABLE 3-4
CALCULATION OF ELASTICITIES FOR FIGURE 3-14

		D_1	D_2
elasticity $=$	$\dfrac{\% \text{ change in } Q}{\% \text{ change in } P} =$	$\dfrac{20\%}{10\%} = 2$	$\dfrac{10\%}{10\%} = 1$

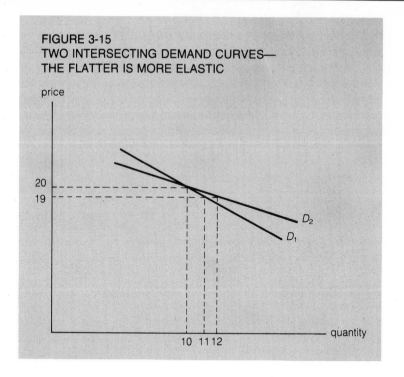

FIGURE 3-15
TWO INTERSECTING DEMAND CURVES—
THE FLATTER IS MORE ELASTIC

TABLE 3-5
CALCULATION OF ELASTICITIES FOR FIGURE 3-15

	D_1	D_2
Elasticity $= \dfrac{\text{\% change in } Q}{\text{\% change in } P} =$	$\dfrac{10\%}{5\%} = 2$	$\dfrac{20\%}{5\%} = 4$

(from 10 to 12), giving an elasticity of about four. In this case of two intersecting demand curves, the flatter is more elastic. (The result is summarized in table 3-5.) Although we can't go into a detailed proof of it here, there is one basic rule in comparing elasticities of straight line demand curves: The one with the smaller intercept along the price axis is more elastic at each price. Following this rule, we would say that in figure 3-14 D_1 is more elastic at each price than D_2, and our calculation suggests this to be correct. Likewise, in figure 3-15, the rule says that D_2 is more elastic than D_1 at each price (since D_2 has the smaller P-intercept), and our calculations also support this result.

What determines the elasticity of demand for a commodity? Basically, it is the ease with which other commodities can be substituted. A good with many close substitutes will have an elastic demand, while one with few substitutes will have a less elastic demand (lower elasticity). For example, margarine will have a more elastic demand than food as a whole, and the demand for Mazola margarine will be more elastic than the demand for margarine. The elasticity of the demand for Mazola margarine sold at Safeway will be still greater, and the elasticity of the demand for Mazola at the Safeway store in your neighborhood will be even greater. In each case there are more and better substitutes than the case before, so responsiveness to a change in price (elasticity) will be greater. Substitution is easier and cheaper when more time is allowed for the substitution. Thus we would expect demand curves to be more elastic in the long run than in the short run. (This point will be discussed more completely later in the chapter.)

ELASTICITY AND
CHANGES IN RECEIPTS

One of the ways in which elasticity is most useful is in predicting the effect which a change in the price of a good will have on the total amount spent on the good. If the price of a good rises, the quantity demanded will fall because of the First Law of Demand. But if the percentage reduction in quantity is smaller than the percentage increased in price (meaning that demand is inelastic), the total amount spent will rise nevertheless. Suppose a 40 percent increase in price results in a 10 percent fall in quantity (elasticity = $\frac{1}{4}$). Then total revenue (TR) of sellers (total amount spent by buyers) will rise. We can see this by noting that the original revenue was equal to the original price multiplied by the original quantity ($P_oQ_o = TR_o$). The new revenue will be ($1.4P_o$) times ($0.9Q_o$), which equals $1.26TR_o$ (greater than TR_o). As long as the percentage change in quantity is less than the percentage change in price, price rises will increase total revenue and price decreases will decrease total revenue. Price and total revenue go in the same direction when demand is inelastic. On the other hand, when demand is elastic, the percentage change in quantity will be larger than the percentage change in price, so that price rises result in *smaller* total revenue, and price reductions result in higher total revenue. Price and total revenue move in opposite directions. For example, if price rises by 10 percent and that causes a 30 percent reduction in quantity demanded (elasticity = 3), the new revenue would be ($1.1P_o$) times ($0.7Q_o$), which equals $0.77P_oQ_o$ or $0.77TR_o$ (less than TR_o).[1]

These relationships help explain why, in the spring of 1975, there were some corn farmers who tried to get their fellow farmers to pledge a 10 percent reduction in plantings for that year. The demand for corn is relatively inelastic. In fact, it was estimated that a 10 percent reduction in the corn crop would cause the price of corn to rise by about 50 percent. Revenue from the corn crop (the amount spent by consumers) would be about 35 percent larger (work this result out for yourself) if the crop were 10 percent smaller, a seemingly paradoxical result which is made more comprehensible by the notion of elasticity.

---

1. See question 8 at the end of the chapter for a more refined method of calculating elasticity.

LONG-RUN VERSUS SHORT-RUN ELASTICITY—THE SECOND LAW OF DEMAND

We have made a good deal of use of the First Law of Demand, that demand curves are downward-sloping. Now it is time to take note of another important relationship: Demand curves are more elastic in the long run than they are in the short run. Another way of saying this is that the response to any price change does not happen immediately. The adjustment is greater, the longer the time period considered. There are two basic reasons for this. First, price changes are not always fully known immediately by everyone. If you don't know the price has changed, you can't very well adjust to it. Second, generally it does not pay to make a complete adjustment to the changed price immediately.

To see how this idea works, let us look at the change in the price of gasoline which occurred during 1979. That period saw the average price of gasoline rise from about 70¢ per gallon to about $1.20 per gallon. Suppose that one day the price of gasoline is 70¢ per gallon and the next morning we wake up to find that it is $1.20 per gallon, and that it is expected to remain at that level in the foreseeable future. Suppose that gasoline consumption before the price increase was 50 million gallons per day. What kind of reduction would we expect one day after the price increase? Probably very little. After all, on that short notice, there is little we can do easily to change habits. People must continue to drive to work, and other uses are not subject to immediate change. A few people might cut out a little pleasure driving, but the rate of use would fall very little, perhaps from 50 million to 49.9 million gallons per day.

If we suppose this to be true we can draw what might be called the "one-day demand curve." It is constructed by recording the initial price and rate of consumption, then raising the price, waiting one day, and recording the new rate of consumption. If we connect these two points, we get the one-day demand curve (see figure 3-16).

If we look at the rate of consumption again after one month, we will probably see a smaller rate of consumption than we did after one day. Why? Because over the period of a month some changes in consumption patterns could conveniently be made by some people. For example, before the price increase, there were some people for whom public transportation or a car pool was a good substitute for driving to work, but at the former low price of gasoline, the savings in gasoline were not worth the inconvenience and other problems of the alternatives. However, at $1.20 per gallon, it is now worthwhile for some people to use public transportation or a car pool. In addition, during the month, some people may examine their pleasure driving habits and decide that some of it is expendable. The upshot is that the "one-month demand curve" will be more elastic than the one-day demand curve. We obtain this demand curve by plotting the original price and rate of consumption (70¢ per gallon and 50 million gallons per day), then plotting the new price and the rate of consumption

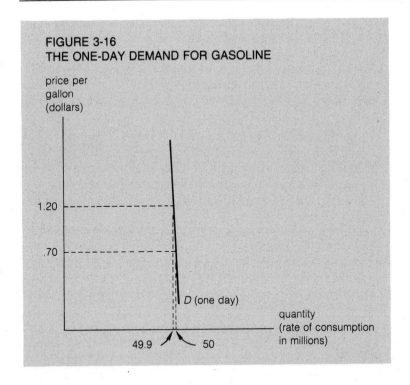

FIGURE 3-16
THE ONE-DAY DEMAND FOR GASOLINE

after one month. Suppose that is $1.20 per gallon and 48 million gallons per day. By connecting these two points, we get the one-month demand curve.

The one-month demand curve is more elastic (responsive) than the one-day demand curve, because the percentage change in quantity is greater, given the same percentage change in price (about 4 percent versus about 0.2 percent for the one-day demand). This is shown in figure 3-17. The one-year demand is still more elastic, because after one year, there will be more substantial adjustments in consumption. By that time there is a noticeable change in the makeup of the stock of automobiles. If 10 percent of the cars are replaced every year, and if the gasoline consumption rate of the new cars is decreased by 20 percent, then there is a 2 percent reduction in the rate of gasoline use even if there are no changes in driving habits. But we expect more changes in driving habits. Some people will move closer to their work. More people will use public transit and car pools, and some recreational driving will be further reduced. Instead of taking a vacation which involves a lot of driving, some people will fly, while others will stay longer at a spot not so far from home.

After five years, the rate of consumption is substantially lowered. Complete redesign of cars to permit lower gasoline consumption is possible over that period of time, and perhaps 50 percent of the cars on the road will get more miles per gallon. The effects of having high gasoline prices over a long period on driving and car-ownership patterns can be seen in Europe, where taxes of $1.50 per gallon and more have made gasoline very expensive for years: cars with high gasoline consumption rates are very rare.

The upshot is that the effect of a price change on consumption will be much greater after time has allowed easier adjustment than it will be immediately after the price change.

There are other factors that might affect the response to a dramatic price change. In the case of the gasoline price increase, the biggest of these forces was the exhortation by political and other leaders to conserve. This served to reduce consumption immediately. The patriotic feelings of many people caused them to forego consumption. One feature of this kind of reduction, however, is that its impact gets smaller as time passes. Patriotically reducing one's consumption gets to be stale after a while and people gradually slip back into their old habits.

While the effect of the Second Law of Demand in reducing consumption gets stronger as time passes, the effect of exhortation gets weaker. The two effects can work in opposite directions on consumption. The slacking off of patriotic fervor can result in *increasing* consumption at the same time the Second Law of Demand is *reducing* consumption further.

Another factor we should consider is income. Gasoline is a normal good, which means that its consumption tends to rise as income rises, holding price constant. When price and income both rise, the two effects

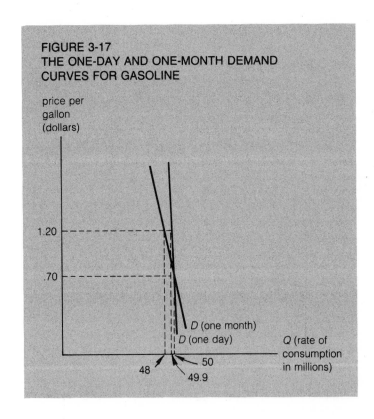

FIGURE 3-17
THE ONE-DAY AND ONE-MONTH DEMAND
CURVES FOR GASOLINE

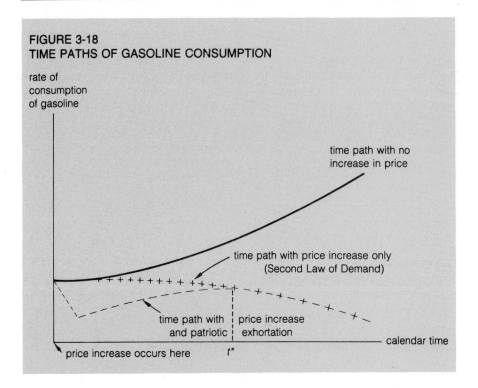

FIGURE 3-18
TIME PATHS OF GASOLINE CONSUMPTION

are going in opposite directions. Thus the reduction in consumption will not be as great as it would be if income were not rising.

The combined effect of all three factors (the income growth, the higher price, and the patriotic exhortation) is shown in figure 3-18. In the early stages, the patriotic response and its ebbing dominate the picture. As time passes, the effect of the higher price, operating almost imperceptibly, gets stronger and stronger. The top curve ("time path with no increase in price") rises because gasoline is a normal good and income can be expected to rise. The second curve ("time path with price increase only") shows a gradually larger reduction in consumption relative to the path with no price increase. The third curve ("time path with price increase and patriotic exhortation") shows a big reduction at first, then a diminishing impact of exhortation as time passes. By time t^*, the effect of exhortation has diminished to nothing, and the third curve shows only the working of the Second Law of Demand.

A NOTE ON
RELATIVE PRICES

When we examine the effect of price changes on behavior we must look at the changes in *relative* prices. If the price of gasoline rises less quickly than prices in general, then its relative price has actually *fallen*. For example, in the year from January 1976 to January 1977, the average price of regular gasoline rose 3.6 percent (from $0.5865 to $0.6065), while prices in general rose 5.2 percent. Thus the price of gasoline was going *down* relative to the average of other prices, so that the amount of other goods that had to be forsaken when one bought a gallon of gasoline was getting smaller. Economic theory says that in this circumstance, people will buy *more* gasoline, *ceteris paribus*. (Gasoline consumption rose by 4 percent in 1976.) Over the period from January 1974 through June 1978, the price of gasoline rose by 45 percent, from $0.4482 to $0.6504. During that same period, the Consumer Price Index rose 40 percent. Thus gasoline prices rose only about five percentage points faster than prices in general over this period. This, in conjunction with the fact that the demand was increasing due to increases in real income and population, helps explain why U.S. gasoline consumption rose by 8.7 percent from 1973 to 1978.

DEMAND FOR PRODUCTIVE INPUTS

Just as there are demand curves for the products we consume, it is useful to talk about the demand for inputs used to produce those goods. What are the inputs? We classify them broadly into the categories of labor, capital, and raw materials. Actually, of course, each of these categories encompasses a wide variety of different inputs, and it is only to simplify matters that we talk about *labor* as though it were homogeneous.

What determines the location of the demand curve for an input? Partly, it is the demand for the product or products it helps to produce. Consequently, the demand for inputs is sometimes called *derived demand*, because the demand is derived from the demand for the final product. Clearly, if there were an increased demand for intricate blown glass, there would be an increased demand for glassblowers. And if the demand for riding horses increased, so would the (derived) demand for blacksmiths. But this is not the whole story. The demand for any particular input also depends on the *productivity* of the input. By productivity we mean the additional output obtainable when one more unit of the input is employed.

For a given price of output, the greater the additional output obtainable by using one more unit of the input, the greater the demand for that input. Let's see how this notion of productivity works. What is the maximum amount an employer is willing to pay in order to use some additional input, for example, an additional hour of labor services? First, we need to know how much additional output is produced when the additional labor is used. Then we need to know how much additional revenue we get by *selling* that additional output. Finally, we have to subtract from this gross benefit the additional cost of such items as electricity and raw materials, which using the additional labor would occasion. This net amount is the value the firm places on having the additional amount of labor.

The demand for an input also depends on the price and availability of substitutes. The lower the price of substitute inputs, the lower the demand for an input. If a low-cost machine comes on the scene which can form horseshoes as well as a blacksmith, it will lower the demand for blacksmiths.

LAWS OF DEMAND
FOR INPUTS

As with demand curves for final products, the two fundamental laws of demand apply to inputs. Demand curves for inputs are downward-sloping. The higher the price of input, the less demanded. This is true because firms tend to switch to substitutes when an input gets more expensive and because physical output changes as more of any input is used. To see how this latter effect might operate, let's construct a simplified example to illustrate the principle. As in chapter 2, the student would be well advised to go slowly through this material and follow the arithmetic with the aid of pencil and paper.

Suppose a broom factory hires ten equally skilled and equally diligent workers. The daily output of the factory is 480 brooms. That averages out to 48 brooms per worker. In order to know the value of the tenth worker (the amount the firm would be willing to pay in order to have ten rather than nine) we must know how much the output would fall if only nine were working. It is plausible to assume that the nine could make up some of the lost output by rearranging their job assignments, so that 450 brooms could be produced with nine workers. Average output per worker has risen from 48 to 50, and total output has fallen by 30 (from 480 to 450). Thus, whatever those 30 extra brooms could be sold for (minus the cost of such things as raw materials) represents the value to the firm of a tenth worker. It also is the *net revenue loss* to the firm when it employs ten workers and any one of them quits.

What would be the value of a ninth worker? In other words, what would be the net revenue loss to the firm should it employ nine workers and any one of them quits? It would almost certainly be greater than the value of a tenth worker, because it is more difficult for eight than for nine to compensate for the loss of one. When eight work instead of nine, total output would be (for example) 408 instead of 450. This means that each of eight workers produces 51 instead of the 50 that each of nine workers produces. Each of the remaining eight workers produces one more broom, but the 50 brooms produced by the worker who quit are not produced. The end result is a decrease of 42 brooms. The value of a ninth worker (that is, the net revenue lost if one of nine workers quits) is the amount of money these 42 brooms could be sold for, minus the extra money for energy and raw materials that is not paid because the 42 brooms are not produced.

When ten workers are working and one quits, broom production falls by 30; and when nine workers are working and one quits, broom production falls by 42. The change in output experienced when the number of workers changes by one unit is called the *marginal product of labor*. Our

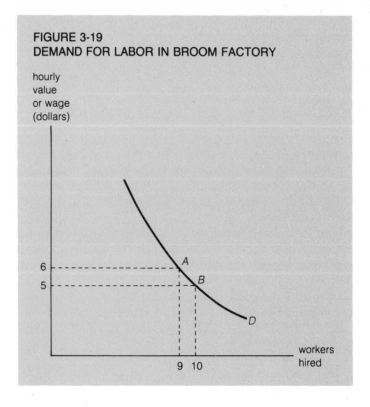

FIGURE 3-19
DEMAND FOR LABOR IN BROOM FACTORY

example illustrates the proposition that the marginal product of labor declines as the number of workers increases. (Remember that we are keeping the amount of machinery and tools constant.) This proposition is referred to as the law of diminishing (marginal) returns, and it is one of the factors which accounts for the downward-sloping demand curve for labor.

Let us consider this example more carefully with the aid of a table and a diagram. Up to now, in order to make the relationships more plausible, we have discussed *decreases* in the amount of labor used. For most purposes, however, it is best to imagine *increases* in labor. When the number of workers increases from eight to nine, the output increases by 42 brooms. Suppose brooms sell for $5 apiece. Then the firm gets $210 in increased revenue. But suppose that producing the extra 42 brooms requires the use of $162 worth of extra raw materials and energy. Then the net increase in revenue which the firm gets from hiring the ninth worker is $210 minus $162, or $48 per day, or $6 per hour. This information is shown in the first row of table 3-6, and illustrated in figure 3-19 by point A. It shows that the height of the demand curve for labor is $6 when there are nine workers. The (net) value of the ninth worker is $6 per hour.

If the firm were to consider hiring a tenth worker, what would happen? The addition of one more worker results in an increase in output of 30 brooms per day. (A tenth worker adds less than a ninth did due to

TABLE 3-6
VALUE OF A WORKER IN BROOM FACTORY

(1)	(2)	(3) Col.1 × Col.2	(4) Change in Col.3	(5) Col.4 × $5	(6)	(7) Col.5 − Col.6	(8) Col.7 ÷ 8hrs.
8	51	408	42	$210	$162	$48	$6
9	50	450	30	$150	$110	$40	$5
10	48	480					

(1) Number of workers
(2) Output of brooms per worker per day
(3) Total broom output per day
(4) Increased output due to using one more worker (and associated raw materials)
(5) Value of the increased output [equals Col.4 × price of output]

(6) Dollar cost of the associated extra raw materials used with the increased labor
(7) Net increase in revenue due to using one more worker
(8) Hourly net increase in revenue due to using one more worker

diminishing marginal returns.) At $5 per broom, this adds $150 to the firm's revenue. Suppose the extra raw material and energy use associated with this increase is $110. Then the net increase in revenue to the firm from hiring ten workers instead of nine is $150 minus $110, or $40 ($5 per hour). This is shown in the bottom row of table 4-6, and at point B of figure 3-19, where the (net) value of the tenth worker is shown as $5 per hour.

If the hourly wage is $6, the employer is not willing to hire more than nine workers, because the value of a tenth worker is only $5 per hour. If the wage is $5 per hour, ten workers are employed. An increase of the wage to $6 per hour means that one worker will be laid off. The downward-sloping line that connects points A and B is the demand for labor curve. Its downward slope illustrates the First Law of Demand as it applies to productive inputs such as labor.

The Second Law of Demand also applies to inputs. Oftentimes the production process used by a firm results in rather fixed proportions of inputs. This means that a certain type of machinery is designed to be used with a certain number of workers, and the number would not change much even if there were a drastic change in the wage rate. But, although the amount of labor may be fixed given the machinery used and the setup of the plant, those things can change. If wage rates go up, there is an incentive to change the type of machinery used and to choose a type which utilizes less labor, even though the machinery is more expensive. Machinery in effect can be substituted for labor. The use of more machinery (or more complex machinery which takes over more tasks from labor) will be worthwhile if the extra machinery costs are more than offset by reduced labor cost. A substitution of machinery for labor which wouldn't be worthwhile at a wage rate of $4 per hour, might be worthwhile if the wage were $5 per hour. Since such changes in machinery are not worth doing instantaneously, the response to price changes is delayed. This is the operation of the Second Law of Demand.

86

AUTOMATION AND THE
SECOND LAW OF DEMAND

Our discussion of the Second Law of Demand enables us to look at the phenomenon of automation in a different light. People talk about automation occurring when a new production process that uses less labor is installed. Usually such changes in the method of production appear to be spontaneous. That is, it appears that someone almost accidentally discovers a new labor-saving process, and it seems to come to the firm out of the blue. But in fact, most of what goes by the name of automation is not spontaneous but rather *induced*. That is, the high wage rate provides a signal which says "the labor we are using has a very high value in alternative uses (that is why we have to pay such a high wage rate). If someone can provide a way of reducing our use of this labor, we (the firms) will be willing to pay for it." Because the higher wage does not bring forth an immediate response, it appears that the jobs are being automated out of existence by some dark, uncontrollable force. In fact, in many cases, it is the Second Law of Demand operating, giving a delayed response to the higher wage.

A case in point is the automated checkout systems now being introduced in supermarkets. The systems will not, of course, replace all labor in the markets, but they will eliminate the labor involved in stamping prices on items to a large extent. At wage rates that prevailed ten years ago for grocery employees, the system probably would not be worthwhile. But at current wage rates, it appears that it may be efficient, in the sense of reducing the cost of providing the service that consumers want. Thus it is not an autonomous monster which springs out of nowhere, but rather a response to changing costs of labor in supermarkets.

Another example is the automation at the telephone company. AT&T recently installed a system whereby many long distance calls, which formerly had to be dialed by the operator (such as collect calls and credit card calls), can now be dialed by the caller. This substitution of machinery for labor (which will reduce the number of long distance operators below what it would have otherwise been) could be called automation, but it certainly is not spontaneous. The technology for performing such tasks has existed for a long time. It simply would not have been worthwhile to install the system while lower wage rates for telephone operators were in effect.

MINIMUM WAGE LAWS
AND THE FIRST LAW
OF DEMAND

Minimum wage laws specify a floor, below which wages in certain occupations cannot go. The laws are supported by individuals who feel genuine concern for the plight of the poor, as well as by groups whose interests are not so altruistic. At first glance it is hard to see why anyone would oppose such a law; after all, we would all like to see that poor people become less poor. But on closer examination, we can see that passing a law which says that a worker can't be paid less than $3.10 per hour does not guarantee that he will be paid $3.10. The true minimum wage is zero, and imposing a legal minimum wage above the wage that would otherwise prevail will result in fewer people being hired. The remainder are no longer employed in the covered sector. This is a simple application of the First Law of Demand: at a higher wage, fewer are hired.

As a related issue we might ask, what groups would selfishly support such a law? To answer this question, we return to the idea of substitutes. If two types of labor are substitutes and the wage rate for one goes up, the *demand* for the other type will increase. Skilled and unskilled workers (also older and younger workers) are substitutes. They can be used somewhat interchangeably to get the same work done. But the higher the wage for unskilled workers, the greater the demand for skilled workers. Consequently, skilled workers, and some unions, would find minimum wage laws in their own interest, *not* because their wage is below the proposed minimum but because the law would raise wages of substitute forms of labor and thereby increase the demand for their services.

LOOKING AHEAD

We shall see in chapter 4 that opportunity costs are influenced by the prices of alternative goods that resources can produce, and that the process of voluntary exchange in markets tends to select the lowest cost producers of goods to engage in their production.

POINTS TO REMEMBER

1. The amounts of goods people consume depend on the prices of goods, income, and expected future prices, as well as tastes and chance.

2. The First Law of Demand states that the higher (lower) the price of a good, the less (more) of it will be demanded, *ceteris paribus*.

3. A change in demand (shift in the location of the demand curve) can be caused by a change in income, changes in prices of substitutes or complements, or a change in expected future prices.

4. The demand for a normal good increases (decreases) when income increases (decreases), while the demand for an inferior good decreases (increases) when income increases (decreases).

5. If two goods are substitutes, an increase (decrease) in the price of one increases (decreases) the demand for the other.

6. If two goods are complements, an increase (decrease) in the price of one decreases (increases) the demand for the other.

7. If the price of a good is expected to rise (fall), the demand for that good will increase (decrease).

8. Consumer surplus is the difference between the maximum amount a consumer would be willing to pay to obtain the quantity of a good she has, and the amount she actually has to pay.

9. A surplus (shortage) exists if, at the going price, the amount people want to buy is less (greater) than the amount available.

10. A surplus (shortage) cannot persist for long in the absence of government intervention because the surplus (shortage) sets in motion forces which lower (raise) the price and eliminate the surplus (shortage).

11. The price elasticity of demand is a measure of the responsiveness of the quantity demanded to the price. It is defined as the percentage change in quantity demanded divided by the percentage change in price.

12. If demand is relatively elastic at the current price, an increase (decrease) in price will decrease (increase) total expenditures by consumers and revenues to sellers. If demand is relatively inelastic at the current price, then an increase (decrease) in price will increase (decrease) total expenditures by consumers and revenues to sellers.

13. If two straight-line demand curves intersect, the flatter will be more elastic at any price.

14. If price increases (decreases), the quantity demanded will fall (rise) by a greater amount in the long run than in the short run. This proposition is referred to as the Second Law of Demand.

15. The demand for inputs (factors of production) depends on the price of the product being produced and on the marginal product of the input.

16. The marginal product of an input is the change in output which results from a one-unit change in the amount of input, holding other inputs constant.

17. The marginal product of an input will eventually decrease as more input is used.

18. The value of an input (the amount that an employer would be willing to pay to have one more unit of the input) equals the marginal product of the input multiplied by the price of the output, minus the cost of the additional inputs (such as raw materials) which must be used when the additional output is produced.

19. The value of an input declines as more of it is employed. Thus the demand for inputs is downward-sloping.

20. The demand for inputs is more elastic in the long run than in the short run.

21. Minimum wage laws tend to result in less employment for low-skill workers, and an increase in demand for (substitutable) high-skill workers.

KEY TERMS

Automation: The substitution of machinery for labor in a production process.

Ceteris paribus: A Latin expression meaning "other things equal." It is what is provisionally assumed in order to talk about such things as the demand curve. In that case, the other things which are held constant are income, prices of other goods, expected future prices, and tastes.

Change in demand: A shift in the location of a demand curve due to a change in income, prices of other goods, expected future prices, or tastes.

Complements: Goods which are related in such a way that an increase (decrease) in the price of one causes the demand for the other to decrease (increase). Such goods usually are used together to perform a given service.

Consumer "surplus": The difference between the maximum total amount which a consumer would be willing to pay to have the quantity of a given good he has (rather than do without it entirely) and the actual total amount he pays for that quantity of the good.

Demand curve: A diagrammatic representation of the relationship between the quantity of a good which is demanded and its price (*ceteris paribus*).

Demand schedule: A tabular representation of the relationship between the amount of a good which is demanded and its price (*ceteris paribus*).

Derived demand: The notion that the demand for such things as inputs into the production process depends on (is derived from) the demand for the final product and the prices of other inputs.

Elastic: Characteristic of a demand curve in the range where its elasticity is greater than one.

Elasticity of demand: (Price elasticity of demand.) A measure of the responsiveness of the quantity demanded to changes in price. It is calculated by taking the ratio of the percentage change in quantity to the percentage change in price which caused that change in quantity.

First Law of Demand: The assertion that the relationship between the price of a good and the quantity demanded is negative, that is, that demand curves are downward-sloping.

Inelastic: Characteristic of a demand curve in the range where its elasticity is less than one.

Inferior good: A good for which the demand decreases (increases) as income increases (decreases).

Minimum wage law: A law which specifies that, in certain industries, no employed person may legally be paid less than a certain amount, called the minimum wage. Of course, an unemployed person receives a zero wage.

Normal good: A good for which the demand increases (decreases) as income increases (decreases).

Second Law of Demand: The assertion that demand curves are more elastic in the long run than in the short run.

Substitutes: Goods which are related in such a way that an increase (decrease) in the price of one causes the demand for the other to increase (decrease). Such goods usually can be used somewhat interchangeably to perform the same services.

Unitary elastic: Characteristic of a demand curve in the range where its elasticity equals one.

REVIEW QUESTIONS

1. "An increase in supply lowers price, but the lower price increases demand, and the increased demand causes the price to go back up again; so an increase in supply will not lower the price." What is wrong with this statement?

2. List five ways in which a rise in gasoline prices might change people's behavior in regard to consumption of gasoline.

3. What are some substitutes for gasoline consumption?

4. What are some goods which are complements to gasoline?

5. In the summer of 1976, after a drought which reduced available water by about 25 percent below normal, the Water District of Marin County (near San Francisco) engaged in several efforts to reduce water consumption in the area. In addition to raising the price by about 25 percent, the District banned the washing of cars and the use of mechanical sprinklers to water lawns, and users were asked to voluntarily conserve water in their homes in various ways. To enforce the restrictions on outside use of water, the District instituted "water patrols," persons whose job it was to report violators (whose water would be temporarily cut off and whose use would be severely restricted in the future).

Can you think of any method of reducing water consumption by 25 percent which would avoid the need for water patrols and restrictions on various uses? What objections would be made to your alternative?

6. Several years ago, there was a sharp increase in the wages paid to elevator operators in Chicago's office buildings. A few months later, office building owners began installing automatic elevators. Would you consider this spontaneous or induced automation?

7. The Southern California Rapid Transit District (RTD), which runs the buses in Los Angeles, raised its basic fare from 25¢ to 35¢ on July 1, 1976.

One month later, ridership had fallen by 7.6 percent. (a) Was the one-month demand curve elastic or inelastic over this price range? (b) What was the effect of the price change on RTD's total revenue? (c) Would you expect the percentage reduction in RTD ridership after one year to be larger or smaller than after one month? Would your answer be different if the price of gasoline rose by a substantial amount over the year?

8. What is the elasticity of the accompanying demand schedule over the range shown?

P	Q
11	9
9	11

Your answer, if you calculated it as shown in the chapter, would be

$$\frac{2/9}{2/11} = \frac{22}{18} = 1\frac{2}{9}(\text{elastic}).$$

But note that total revenue is the same at both prices, which, according to our earlier discussion, means that elasticity is unitary (1). What is wrong? The problem is that when we take fairly large percentage changes in quantity and price, we get a noticeably different percentage change when we use the first price and quantity as a base and when we use the second

$$\frac{2}{9} \text{ versus } \frac{2}{11}.$$

A way around this problem, which also resolves the difficulty about unitary elasticity for such cases, is to use the *average* of the two quantities (ten in this case) and the *average* of the two prices (ten in this case) for the base quantity and price in calculating percentages. Thus the expression for elasticity becomes

$$\frac{\text{change in } Q/\bar{Q}}{\text{change in } P/\bar{P}},$$

where

$$\bar{Q} = \frac{Q_1 + Q_2}{2} \text{ and } \bar{P} = \frac{P_1 + P_2}{2}.$$

In this case, elasticity is

$$\frac{2/10}{2/10} = 1,$$

which is consistent with our other criterion, which states that when total revenue is unchanging, elasticity is unitary.

9. Al, Bill, and Charlie have the following demands for beef, in pounds per month. What is the total demand of the three together? That is, what is the total amount they will buy at each price?

Price	Al	Bill	Charlie	Total
$4.00	.50	1.00	.25	———
3.50	.75	1.25	1.00	———
3.00	1.25	1.35	1.75	———
2.50	1.50	1.45	2.60	———
2.00	1.80	1.85	3.20	———
1.50	2.00	1.95	4.00	———
1.00	3.00	2.00	4.60	———

10. Empirical studies generally have found that public transportation (buses, commuter trains, and so on) is an inferior good. What does this say about the demand for public transportation today versus twenty years ago? Is there any way to get more people to use public transit as income rises?

11. There have been well documented cases in which women and men were doing very similar or identical work, but in which women were paid less than men. Can you think of any reasons why an "equal pay for equal work" law might reduce the number of women employed?

12. Would you be more willing to go out of your way to save 10 percent on the price of *salt* or a car? Why? What implications does this have for the elasticity of demand faced by a given retailer of salt versus cars?

13. Who would be most likely to benefit or be hurt by the imposition of rent control: a family with young children; a member of a racial or ethnic minority; an elderly couple who will stay in one place for a long time; a newcomer to town?

14. If you were able to get your hands on some crude oil (or oil products) and you were convinced that in one month the OPEC (Organization of Petroleum Exporting Countries) would raise the price of crude oil by 15 percent, what effect would that expectation have on your demand to hold oil? If most oil people agreed with your expectation, what would that do to the price of oil *today*?

15. Fill in the blanks in the table, given the following assumptions: The price of the output is $3 per unit; workers work eight hours; for every additional unit of output produced, the cost of extra raw materials and power is $1.

(1)	(2)	(3)	(4)	(5)	(6)	(7)	(8)
1	25	—					
2	20	—	—	—	—	—	—
3	18	—	—	—	—	—	—
4	15	—	—	—	—	—	—
5	13	—	—	—	—	—	—
6	11	—	—	—	—	—	—

(1) Number of workers
(2) Output per worker per day
(3) Total output per day
(4) Increased total output using one more worker (and associated raw materials)
(5) Value of the increased output
(6) Dollar cost of the associated extra raw materials and energy used along with the increased labor
(7) Net increase in revenue due to using one more worker
   (a) How many workers will be hired if the wage is $3.60 per hour? $2.00? $1.40?
   (b) How many workers will lose their jobs if the minimum wage is raised from $2.00 to $3.60?
   (c) Does the First Law of Demand hold in this case?

16. Suppose most apartment owners *wrongly* believe that group A causes them to incur more costs, so they discriminate against people in group A. In the absence of controls on rent, what will happen to the rent paid by group A? How could a nondiscriminating owner make a lot of money? Does discrimination on the basis of incorrect perceptions make apartment owners richer or poorer?

17. Suppose the price of a certain commodity is prevented by law from falling below P_1 and that at P_1 there is a surplus. Would you expect the buyers to engage in more discrimination among sellers on the basis of nonprice characteristics such as terms of payment or quality of service? How would sellers respond to this increased discrimination?

18. Suppose there is a shortage of gasoline and it is being allocated by waiting in line. On the average, a person has to wait thirty minutes to get gasoline. The pump price is $1 per gallon. Both Smith and Jones are waiting to buy ten gallons of gasoline. Smith is a computer programmer who can earn $10 per hour any time he wants to do more work, and he is heading for work right now. Jones is retired. What is the true price per gallon that Smith pays? What is Jones' true price? If Smith's and Jones'

elasticity of demand were the same, who would reduce consumption of gasoline by a larger percentage during the crisis?

19. A law raising the highway speed limit from 55 to 65 mph would (assuming people drove faster than they now do) increase the demand for gasoline for highway use because people would get fewer miles per gallon. Can you think of any other reason the demand for gasoline for highway use would rise with such a change in the law? (Hint: See question 9 in chapter 1.) Assuming people value their time highly, what would the increased speed limit do to the total (time plus gasoline) cost of taking long trips?

20. Some consumer groups and the retail clerks union have lobbied for laws which would require supermarkets to put a price sticker on each item even if they use electronic checkout systems which do not utilize such price markings. (a) How could such laws benefit the unions? (b) How would such laws benefit consumers? (c) How could such laws hurt consumers?

21. Is it useful to ask why a person becomes a criminal? What would be a better approach to understanding and controlling criminal behavior?

22. Suppose the differential between full-serve and self-serve gasoline prices is 4¢ regardless of the price of gasoline. Would you expect a larger proportion of gasoline to be sold self-serve if the prices were 70¢ and 74¢ or $1.20 and $1.24? Explain.

23. Joe and Frank have the following demands for good X.

Joe		Frank	
P	Q_D	P	Q_D
$20	1	$14	1
18	2	13	2
16	3	12	3
14	4	11	4
12	5	10	5
10	6	9	6
8	7	8	7

Joe initially has two and Frank has six. (a) Is mutually beneficial exchange possible? Explain. (b) Assuming no cost of transacting, show how many units will be exchanged and within what range the price might lie for each unit exchanged. (c) For each unit exchanged, specify a price which lies in the range you found, and show the gains to both Joe and Frank from the whole series of exchanges. (d) Now suppose there is a transaction cost of $3 per unit traded. How many units will be traded? What is the range in which the buyers' and seller's prices must lie for each unit exchanged? (e) Answer (c) for the case with $3 transaction cost.

24. Smith has the following demand for good Y.

P	Q
$12	1
11	2
10	3
9	4
8	5
7	6
6	7
5	8
4	9

(a) If the price is $5 per unit, how many units will she buy, and what will her consumer surplus be? (b) What are your answers to (a) if the price is $9 per unit? (c) Suppose Smith were told that the price of Y was $9 but that if she bought any at all she would have to buy nine units. Would she do it? What if the minimum purchase were seven units? Explain.

25. Suppose an insect destroys 20 percent of every grower's apple crop. As a result, the price rises from 25¢ to 50¢ per pound, and the total market value of the crop rises by 60 percent above what it would have been with no crop loss. Has the total value of the crop really increased? Explain.

chapter 4

Opportunity Cost and Comparative Advantage

Why do people hire out for the jobs they do? Is it purely a matter of chance or class privilege? Does one take a job only because he really likes the work? Or is it solely the relative pecuniary reward which determines who does what? In any economy all these factors play a role, but the relative importance of the factors differs among systems. In a private property exchange economy, workers' preferences and relative rewards will loom larger than chance and privilege. Economics is not very good at talking about what determines job preferences of workers, but economics aids in understanding the forces that determine the relative rewards a person can obtain in various occupations. The tools we use are *opportunity cost* and *comparative advantage*.

OPPORTUNITY COST

Professor Smith is considering painting his house. What does it cost to paint it himself? The obvious costs are the amounts paid for paint and brushes. These are *explicit* costs. They involve an outlay of money. A less obvious cost is the professor's *time*. He does not have enough time to do all the things he might like to do. He has to choose which things to do and which not to do. If he allocates some time to painting his house, that time cannot be used any other way. The most highly valued foregone use of his time represents his time cost of painting the house. The best use might be paid employment or leisure. Let us suppose that Smith's best alternative use of his time is to do some book reviewing for a publisher at the rate of $15 per hour. If painting his house will require thirty hours of Smith's time, then the time cost is $450. This is a cost every bit as much as the paint and brushes, but it is an *implicit* cost because it does not involve an outlay of money. Rather it involves the foregoing of an *inflow* of money (the $15 per hour he could have earned reviewing books). If it were summertime and Smith's best alternative were to do some tutoring at $10 per hour, then the time cost of painting the house would be only $300. If his best alternative were tutoring, but it took him forty hours to paint the house, then his time cost would be $400.

From this example we can see that two factors determine Smith's time cost of painting his own house. The first is his productivity as a painter. The more productive he is as a painter (in other words, the faster he can paint the house), the lower his cost of house painting. The second is the amount he could make per hour in his best alternative occupation. The lower that is, the lower his cost of house painting.

We have noted that the cost of using Professor Smith's time to paint his house depends not only on how productive he is at house painting, but on what he can make by selling his labor services in alternative ways. If the amount he can make doing book reviews goes up, his cost of house painting goes up. The amount that *other people* are willing to pay to use his resources (labor services) in other ways determines the cost of using them in this way (house painting). His productivity in house painting determines how many hours of his time are required to paint the house. Multiplying this by the cost per hour gives Smith's cost of painting the house himself.

COMPARATIVE ADVANTAGE

When we talk about *comparative advantage* we are talking about whether one person or resource has a lower cost of doing a certain job than another person or resource. In our house painting example, we want to know whether it is less costly to have Smith paint his own house or hire someone else to do it. Suppose that a professional painter would require twenty hours at a price of $20 per hour, for a cost of $400. If Smith's best alternative is reviewing books at $15 per hour, it is more costly for Smith to spend thirty hours painting the house himself, and the painter has the comparative advantage in painting Smith's house. (The painter's cost is $400, whereas Smith's cost is $450.) If Smith spent the thirty hours reviewing books (earning $450) and spent the $400 to pay the painter, he would be $50 to the good, relative to his position if he painted the house himself. (This discussion ignores taxes.) For a discussion of the effects of taxes, see the section "Fun, Taxes, and the Underground Economy," in this chapter.

It would be *efficient* for Smith to hire the painter to paint the house because his benefit from doing so is greater than his cost.

On the other hand, if Smith's best alternative is to tutor at $10 per hour, he has a comparative advantage in painting his own house because his cost is only $300, which is less than the painter's cost of $400. This case is particularly instructive because Smith has a comparative advantage in painting his own house (that is, he can do it at a lower cost) even though he is less productive at it than the professional painter. (It takes him thirty hours, while the professional can do it in only twenty hours.) Smith has a *comparative* advantage in painting his own house, even though he does not have an *absolute* advantage. Resource A is said to have an absolute advantage (relative to resource B) in some activity if resource A is more productive at the activity than B is. In this case, the painter has the absolute advantage in painting Smith's house, but when Smith can earn only $10 per hour elsewhere, he has the *comparative* advantage over the painter. Using the same reasoning as before, if Smith paints the house himself, he foregoes $300 in revenue from tutoring, but he benefits by saving the $400 he would otherwise have paid to the painter. So he is $100 ahead by doing it himself. It is efficient for Smith to paint the house himself because the benefit of doing so is greater than the cost.

Smith's cost of doing it himself increases as the amount he can earn by spending an hour on something else increases. The same is true for the painter. Suppose a big construction boom hits Smith's city. The demand for painters goes up. The cost of an hour of the painter's time will increase because there will be more alternative employers who will be willing to pay him a lot to paint for them. (The cost to the painter of painting A's house is what the painter could earn painting B's house.) Suppose that at the margin the painter would have to forego a job paying $25 per hour if he took Smith's job. The cost of the painter's painting Smith's house therefore rises from $400 to $500. In this case, Smith would have a comparative advantage in painting his own house even if his alternative were to review books at $15 per hour. (You should check the numbers to make sure you see why this statement is correct.)

DECENTRALIZED COORDINATION

One of the features of the voluntary exchange system is that individuals are induced *by their own self-interest* to do what is efficient from the point of view of the whole economy. If Smith's alternative is to review books for $15 per hour, it is efficient to have the painter do the job, because the cost to the economy (the value of the foregone book reviewing) of having Smith do it is greater than the cost (the value of the foregone other painting) of having the painter do it. Since Smith obtains a net gain of $50 by hiring the painter, his self-interest leads to getting the job done in the most efficient way. Similarly, in the case where Smith's alternative is to work at $10 per hour, his own self-interest leads him to choose the efficient action—painting the house himself. This decentralized coordination, in which no boss tells people what to do, is a key feature of the voluntary exchange (market) economy.

SOME ADDITIONAL EXAMPLES

A few additional examples may serve to help you be more comfortable with the notions of opportunity cost and comparative advantage. In each case, note the importance of the less obvious *implicit* costs. Note also in each case how the outcome that is efficient is brought about by the decentralized self-seeking behavior of the transactors. In one of the cases, the transactors make a mistake about what is in their interest, but the discipline imposed by self-interest and competitive voluntary exchange brings them back into line.

Billy Rose

As a historical example, consider the case of Billy Rose, the Broadway showman. When he was a young man, Rose was trained in shorthand and became extremely proficient at stenography. In fact, at one point he was one of the best stenographers in the world.[1] Later, when he was putting on Broadway shows, he was probably faster at taking shorthand than the stenographers he could have hired. Should he have gone around his office taking shorthand for everyone, or even take his own? Not unless the entertainment value of doing it exceeded the loss in wealth he would have incurred. Why would he be poorer? Suppose that he could take shorthand twice as fast as the usual stenographer, and suppose that one could hire the usual stenographer for two dollars per hour. This means that by doing one hour of shorthand, Rose could have saved four dollars (since he could have done as much as the usual stenographer could in two hours). Would it have been worth it? Not as long as that hour could produce more than four dollars' worth of benefit to him in putting on Broadway shows. Rose's comparative advantage was apparently in putting on the shows, not in taking shorthand.

In deciding whether to do stenography work, Rose found his cost of performing stenography himself (namely, the foregone revenue from not being able to put on as many Broadway shows) was greater than the market price of stenographic services. Thus he chose to buy stenographic services.

This example brings up another point which is useful to remember in connection with comparative advantage. The stenographer was absolutely

---

1. A fascinating discussion of this phase of Rose's life is contained in Earl Conrad, *Billy Rose: Manhattan Primitive* (Cleveland: World Publishing Co., 1968).

worse both at putting on shows and taking shorthand. Nevertheless he had a *comparative* advantage in stenography and was so employed.

General Motors

When General Motors decides whether to make a part or buy it, they are doing the same thing Billy Rose did, but the decision may be a little tougher to make. There are other differences. With Billy Rose the costs of taking his own shorthand were implicit, whereas many of GM's costs in manufacturing its own parts are explicit. That is, GM must pay for wages, raw materials, and machinery. Others are implicit. If they don't use their plant to house the production of this new part, they can use the plant to produce other goods or lease it out. These are implicit costs of GM's producing the part itself, because they involve foregone benefits, even though there are no outlays involved. But whether the costs are implicit or explicit, the "make or buy" decision is ultimately a question of comparative advantage, of whether the firm or person in question has lower costs of performing the given task than someone else, whose cost is represented by the price one must pay to have the task done by others.

Comparative Advantage and Do-It-Yourself

The example of Professor Smith's house serves to remind us that more and more people are engaging in "do-it-yourself" work around the house. The example suggests that certain patterns of do-it-yourself activity will emerge. First, as between two people who are equally skilled at a household job, the one with the lower paying alternative wage will be more likely to do it himself than his higher paid counterpart, because his cost is lower. The poorer man is likely to say he can't afford to pay someone to do it. By this he may mean that the cost (in terms of foregone wages) of doing it himself would be less than the cost of hiring someone. He may also mean that if he had to hire someone to do it, the value of having the job done would be less than the amount he would have to pay. But by the same token, the richer man can say that he can't afford to do it himself. By this he means that the cost (in terms of foregone income) of doing it himself is higher than the cost of hiring someone to do it. The question of whether someone has a comparative advantage in doing it himself depends to a large extent on the alternative value of his time.

Of course, if two people have the same alternative wage rate, the one who is handier (meaning that she can do the job quicker) is more likely to do it herself. Thus productivity is a second consideration in the decision to do it yourself or hire someone to do it.

The third consideration in the same decision is the price the professional charges. The higher the professional's price, the likelier it is that the cost of doing it yourself will be lower than the cost of hiring the professional. (This does not mean it is efficient for you to do it, however, unless the value you place on having the job done is greater than that cost.) If the professional's price is kept artificially high by government regulation, there will be an inducement for some people to do the job themselves even when there are professionals who could (if the government allowed them) do it at less cost. Rates charged by interstate furniture moving companies are kept higher than they would otherwise be by restrictions on entry into the business and by other Interstate Commerce Commission regulations. (For more on this type of regulation, see chapter 10.) As a result, highly paid individuals are induced to rent trucks and move themselves even though there are professional movers who would (if allowed by the regulations) be willing to offer the service at a price lower than the cost these individuals incur in doing it themselves.

Fun, Taxes, and the Underground Economy

If a physician fixes her own car, is she crazy? It is very costly for such an individual to do the work herself because she is foregoing so much income by not working as a doctor for those hours. It is not hard to imagine that the amount she would have to pay a mechanic would be less than the cost of doing it herself. Suppose it takes Dr. Jones five hours to fix her car, and she foregoes $50 per hour by doing so. (Total cost equals $250.) The mechanic would charge (say) $150 for the job. Dr. Jones is $100 poorer by doing it herself. But it is not irrational for Dr. Jones to do the work herself if she enjoys it, and the enjoyment she gets that way is greater than what she could get by spending the lost $100 in the best alternative way. So some highly paid individuals may very well do some do-it-yourself work around the house because they enjoy it. But the higher the wage they thereby forego, the higher the price of this sort of consumption. The First Law of Demand says that as the price rises, they will do less of it.

Another reason some highly paid individuals may do more household work than we might expect is the tax system. Consider our mechanically inclined Dr. Jones. If she works as a doctor for those five hours, instead of fixing her car, she foregoes $250 in *gross* income, but if her marginal tax rate is 50 percent, she only foregoes $125 in *after tax* income. In that case it is actually cheaper for her to do it herself than to hire the mechanic for $150. Because the physician income is taxed, while do-it-yourself "income" is not, her choice is distorted by the tax.

The tax distortion of the do-it-yourself decision would be less powerful if income from doctoring were treated the same way for tax purposes as "income" from do-it-yourself activity. One way people have been making this happen in recent years is by going underground—that is, performing services for each other in ways which do not generate easily taxable income. For example, suppose Dr. Jones agrees to give physical exams to the mechanic's family (total time: three hours) in return for the car repair. Jones incurs an after-tax cost of only $75 (pretax income of $150, minus taxes of $75) to do that. The mechanic would have to pay $150 for the examinations, but since he is in the 40 percent tax bracket, he would have to earn $250 in order to clear that much after taxes. So Dr. Jones is offering to pay the mechanic something which he would have to earn $250 to buy, and the mechanic is offering to sell the service to Dr. Jones for three hours of work, whereas Jones would have to work six hours (earning $300 gross and $150 net after taxes) to earn enough to buy it with cash or five hours to do it herself. Thus both are induced to act according to their true comparative advantages by going underground.

Middlemen

The question of whether to use a middleman is clearly an example of a "make or buy" decision. The middleman provides services of transporting, storing, displaying, and risk bearing. The question is whether someone else can perform those services more cheaply. Not long ago, a group of cattle growers in Kentucky became disgusted with the fact that, while they were receiving a low price for their cattle, consumers were paying a high price for beef. To remedy this situation, the ranchers decided to slaughter, dress, and market their own beef. They set up a small store in the country in which they intended to sell the beef. The goal was to eliminate the middleman so that they could get a higher price for themselves and a lower price for consumers.

What was the result? They may have eliminated the middleman, but his services still had to be performed. Formerly, independent firms slaughtered, dressed, stored, transported, displayed, and sold the beef. Now those jobs were being taken over jointly by the cattle growers and consumers. Consumers, if they wanted to buy from the ranchers, had to transport themselves and the beef farther than they previously did. And the rest of the middleman's jobs were taken over by the ranchers. The venture would be successful only if the lower price the consumers paid more than compensated them for the extra travel and inconvenience, and if the higher price the ranchers received more than covered their costs of providing the middleman's services. In other words, the venture would succeed only if, after adjusting for the new costs incurred by consumers and ranchers, the consumer's price was lower and the rancher's price was higher. And that would be true only if consumers and ranchers could provide the middleman's services more cheaply (at less cost) than the middleman. This was not the case and the venture failed.

Economists would probably have predicted this result, because the presumption is that, if ranchers and consumers were better than the middleman at providing middleman's services, such a change in the organization of the industry would already have happened. But one must be careful not to give too much weight to such reasoning, because it assumes that the least costly way of doing things is always known and in operation —clearly not the case. Often we don't know the best way to do something until some entrepreneur tries it and succeeds. It is the *entrepreneur* who tries alternatives and discovers what works, and it is the imitation of successful entrepreneurs that spreads efficiency throughout the economy. Economists only explain the reasons (such as comparative advantage) for the successes after the fact.

104   COSTS DEPEND ON PRICES

In all of our examples, the cost of using a resource in any one way depends on what it could earn in alternative uses, and what it could earn elsewhere depends in part on the price of things it is capable of producing elsewhere. Consider Professor Smith again. The higher the price of a book review, the more it costs Smith to paint his house. And the more other people are willing to pay to have their houses painted, the higher the cost the professional painter incurs in painting Smith's house.

We often hear that costs determine prices. Our examples have shown that *prices determine costs*. More specifically, the price that others are willing to pay for what a resource can produce elsewhere affects the cost I have to pay to use that resource to produce what I want. The higher that alternative bid, the higher the price the resource owner will charge to let me use it. Resource owners tend to sell or rent their resources to the highest bidder, so if someone else bids more, I must pay more in order to get the use of the resource.

When there was a reduction in the amount of oil available because of the revolution in Iran, this raised my cost of using gasoline. When the Iranian supply was cut off, the customers who could no longer buy from Iran sought oil from other suppliers. Their bids for oil increased the other suppliers' cost of selling to their regular customers. By selling to their regular customers, sellers would be foregoing the higher bids that Iran's former customers were making. Thus sellers raised their prices to all customers. By so doing, oil suppliers allowed Iran's former customers to bid away some of the oil they were formerly selling to others.

A bad grain harvest in South America will increase the cost of raising cattle in the U.S. The reason is that when there is a reduced amount available in South America, sellers find they can still sell all they want at a higher price than before. The higher price causes potential buyers to seek other opportunities to buy grain. One place they can attempt to buy is the U.S. Their offers to buy in the U.S. increase the price which a grain owner can get by selling to someone other than a U.S. cattle rancher. Thus the cost of using it to feed cattle in the U.S. increases. With his cost of feed increased, the cattle rancher will use less and send a smaller amount of beef to market. The price of beef will rise.

When someone found a way to make palatable food out of soybeans (textured soy protein), the cost of raising cattle and corn increased. The cost of cattle increased because the new technology meant new people (textured soy protein processors) were willing to pay for soybeans. This increase in other users' willingness to buy soybeans increased the cost of selling soybeans to farmers for cattle feed. Cattle ranchers had to pay a higher price in order to get soybean-based cattle feed. Thus the cost of raising cattle increased. The higher price of soybeans meant that the cost of growing corn increased because land that is suitable for growing corn is also suitable for soybeans. If a landowner grows corn, he foregoes what he could make growing soybeans. When the price of soybeans went up, the owner of the land had to forego a greater amount than before if he used his land for corn. The cost of growing corn increased, and less corn was grown than would otherwise have been the case.

COST AND THE VOLUNTEER ARMY

The volunteer Army is in trouble. Throughout the period since the draft was ended, the Army has had difficulty meeting its quotas for enlistments. Many units are short of personnel. Furthermore, the people who have joined have lower skill and educational levels than the Army would like. All this has resulted in a renewal of draft registration.

Is it necessary to draft people in order to have a high-quality military force? By now it should be clear that it would be possible to induce whomever we want to join the military if we pay the right price. Everyone is a potential volunteer for the military, but different people have different *supply prices*—that is, the amount necessary to get one person to join will be different from the amount necessary to get another person to join. What determines a person's supply price? Cost in the sense of foregone wages plays an important role. The more a person can earn in civilian life, the higher his supply price to be in the military, *ceteris paribus*. Another factor is the person's evaluation of the nonpecuniary aspects of the Army job versus the civilian job. A person who likes the military life might be willing to join even if he were paid less than he could earn in a civilian job. A person who dislikes military life would require a premium over his civilian wage to get him to join. But whatever skill and educational make-up one would like to see in the military can be obtained by paying recruits a sufficiently high wage—high enough to get the people we want to volunteer.

"But," it might be argued, "if we pay those high wages, the cost of the Army will be too high—certainly much higher than the cost with the draft." Here we must distinguish between *budgetary* cost and *economic* cost. The budgetary cost is clear enough. It is simply the amount that taxpayers must pay. It is the sum of the wages and benefits paid to all military personnel. The economic cost is the sum of all the *incomes foregone* by military personnel because they are not in the civilian labor force. The *budgetary* cost will be higher for a volunteer Army than for a draft Army, but the *economic* cost will be *lower* for a volunteer Army than for a draft Army. Let us see why. Suppose the Army wants 100,000 paratroopers. If it gets them voluntarily, it will have to pay a wage so that exactly 100,000 *satisfactory* volunteers appear. By satisfactory we mean of the right skill level and educational background. (Remember that one of the complaints against the current volunteer Army is that the skill level of recruits is too low.) The wage will have to be high enough to attract *more than* 100,000 volunteers. Then the 100,000 who meet the standards established will be chosen. Let us look at those 100,000 people. Each will have his or her own supply price. Suppose we arrange them in order from the lowest supply price to the highest. This is shown in figure 4-1. The

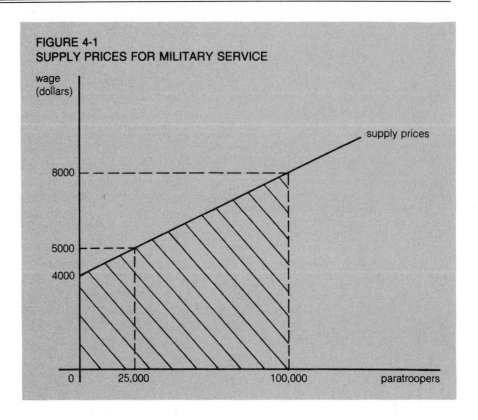

FIGURE 4-1
SUPPLY PRICES FOR MILITARY SERVICE

person whose supply price is lowest is shown on the far left. His supply price is $4000. The supply prices of the other 99,999 volunteers are represented by the height of the supply price line as we move to the right.

Suppose the wage offered is $8000. Then all of the volunteers selected must have a supply price that is less than or equal to $8000, otherwise they would not have volunteered. All persons with a supply price greater than $8000 will refrain from volunteering. The volunteer scheme automatically selects those 100,000 acceptable people who have the lowest supply price. (It is likely, however, that some who volunteer will have a supply price very near $8000, as shown in figure 4-1.) The total budgetary cost of the 100,000 paratroopers is $800 million. The *economic* cost is less than this, however. It is the sum of the supply prices for all 100,000 volunteers, and it is represented by the lined area beneath the supply price line.

Now suppose we obtain 100,000 paratroopers by means of a draft. There is no need for, or advantage from, a draft unless the wage is less than $8000, so let us suppose it is $5000. At a wage of $5000, suppose only 25,000 acceptable people volunteer. We must obtain the other 75,000 through the draft. The budgetary cost of the 100,000 paratroopers is now only $500 million, less than the budgetary cost under the volunteer scheme. But the *economic* cost of the drafted force will be *higher than* the economic cost of the volunteer force because it will not select the same 100,000 people. (Remember, the 100,000 who volunteered at $8000 constituted that group with the lowest supply prices—that is, the lowest opportunity costs. At a wage of $5000 per year, 75,000 of those who would have volunteered at $8000 will not now volunteer. They will join those with supply prices of more than $8000 as potential draftees. But suppose the draft selects randomly from the set of people with acceptable skills who have not volunteered. Then some of the draftees will be from the low-cost group, but some will be from the group with supply prices greater than $8000. Thus, the economic cost (the sum of the supply prices of all those who serve) under the draft will be higher than it would be under the volunteer Army. The draft is therefore a higher cost (less efficient) way of raising whatever kind of Army we want. (But the *distribution* of costs, as well as the total *amount* of cost, is quite different under the two methods. For more on this, see chapter 13.)

OPPORTUNITY COST—SAN FRANCISCO'S RESIDENTIAL HOTELS

An application of the notion of opportunity cost can be found in the plight of the elderly residents of San Francisco's residential hotels. The hotels, mostly located in run-down parts of town, have for many years catered to low-income elderly people, providing room and board for a modest charge. It is reasonable to suppose that the hotel owners have not provided this service out of any great feeling of benevolence, but rather because the net revenue they received in this way (after paying expenses) has been higher than for any other use of the property.

In recent years things have been changing in the part of town where these buildings are located. As San Francisco's tourist and commercial business has expanded, some owners have decided that they could do better by converting their buildings to tourist, rather than residential, hotels, or to office buildings. The usual scenario at first was for the owners to evict the tenants and convert the property to the use they wanted. The owners were accused of being greedy and heartless. It is true that they were greedy, but in fact they were merely acting as the lackeys for the tourists and others who were offering a higher price for the use of the space. (The situation is not different in principle from the socially conscious college professor going on a leave of absence, who decides to rent his house to another professor rather than to a poor student, because the student does not offer to pay as much for it.) With the increased desirability of San Francisco as a tourist spot, the *implicit opportunity cost* of renting to the elderly residents increased. Unless they were willing to pay enough to outbid the tourists, they would have to move elsewhere.

The early attempts at evictions caused some nasty confrontations between the owners and the tenants and their friends. The owners received a lot of bad publicity. This led to a change in tactics. Instead of simply evicting tenants, owners raised rents substantially to reflect the higher *implicit cost* of renting to the residents. Remember, we are not referring to higher maintenance, heating, or food costs. These may have risen as well, but the important cost is the foregone *net income* which could have been earned by converting to another use and catering to other customers. In some cases, enough residential tenants were willing to pay the higher rents to justify keeping the hotels as residential establishments. But for others the tourists and businesses were higher bidders, so those buildings were converted.

Again an outcry arose, charging "rent gouging," since the increases in rents were substantial—much more than could be "justified" by ordinary costs. Partially in response to this outcry, a rent-control ordinance was passed. This ordinance drastically limited increases in rent. The response to this was to attempt even more conversions to tourist hotels or offices, which were not controlled. There was an increase in attempts to convert because, through the rent control, the elderly tenants who were willing to pay enough to outbid the tourists were not allowed to make competing bids sufficient to keep some hotels residential. Thus, the best alternative facing owners was to convert out of the residential sector into the (non–rent controlled) tourist and office sectors.

The increased attempts at conversion brought forth a city-imposed moratorium on conversion of residential units to other uses. In response to this, some owners have allowed their buildings to deteriorate below housing code standards. Then the city condemns the buildings, forcing the tenants to move out, at which point the building can be converted to another use. The result has been that the inevitable reallocation, away from residential users and toward tourists and office users, has continued—in some cases even faster than it would otherwise have occurred—accompanied by much ill feeling, finger-pointing, and social strife.

Are there villains in this piece? The city officials and activists are truly concerned for the welfare of the tenants. Unfortunately, their actions have speeded the demise of the residential hotels, rather than slowing it. What about the owners? They are merely skilled "front men" for the tourists and others who are competing with the old folks for the use of the space. If these people were not willing to pay so much to use the space, the conversions would not be occurring. Is the voluntary exchange price system at fault, then? Taking this out of the hands of the market and having the government make the decisions does not eliminate the problem, which is essentially *scarcity* and the need to decide who will get to use the space. Having the government own the land would merely change the *form* of competition. Those who wished to use the space would have to curry favor with, and act to influence, the city officials charged with deciding on land and property use, instead of making their desires felt by the offers to pay for the use of the property. It is not clear whether the poor elderly tenants or tourists would fare better under such a system, but the government officials would prosper and thrive.

LOOKING AHEAD

This chapter has shown how the decisions of individual transactors are influenced by the abilities and preferences of others. Those abilities and preferences help determine the market prices which individual transactors face. Using those prices in conjunction with knowledge of their own abilities to produce various goods, transactors are able to determine the relative costs to them of taking various actions. The role of prices in inducing transactors to behave in (socially) efficient ways has been emphasized. Prices resulting from unrestricted voluntary exchange convey information which leads to correct decisions. Prices which are distorted by outside forces can no longer serve this informational function.

The next chapter continues our discussion of costs by introducing several different categories of cost. We shall find that some kinds of costs are relevant for certain business decisions, and others are relevant for other decisions.

POINTS TO REMEMBER

1. The (opportunity) cost which a person incurs in performing an action depends on how productively she can perform that action and on what she could earn per hour in her best alternative activity.

2. Between any two persons, firms, or resources, the one with the lower marginal cost of engaging in a given activity has a comparative advantage in that activity, relative to the other person, firm, or resource.

3. A person or firm can have an absolute disadvantage in (be absolutely worse than another person at doing) everything. But he cannot have a higher marginal cost of doing everything. Thus everyone must have a comparative advantage in something.

4. Higher prices offered by alternative users of a resource result in a higher cost of using the resource in any particular way.

5. If persons have private property rights to the goods they produce, then self-interest will induce persons to specialize according to their comparative advantage, thus promoting efficiency.

6. The make or buy decision of households and firms is based largely on comparative advantage. If one has a comparative advantage (lower marginal cost) relative to the market, then one can be richer by making the item in question. In the opposite case, the person can be richer by buying the item in question and producing more of those items in which he has a comparative advantage.

7. The question of whether to use middlemen is a make or buy decision, and thus hinges on comparative advantage (relative costs).

8. The existence of comparative advantage means that by specializing and exchanging, we can have a larger total output than we could with autarky. Thus autarky is inefficient relative to specialization and exchange. (See the appendix.)

KEY TERMS

Absolute advantage: Greater productive capacity. A person has an absolute advantage, relative to another person, in producing a good if he can produce more of it.

Autarky: Self-sufficiency. A system whereby a person or society produces all that it consumes (with no trade).

Comparative advantage: Lower cost. A person (or firm or country) has a comparative advantage in a given activity, relative to another person (or firm or country), if he can produce the activity at a lower cost.

Entrepreneur: A person whose comparative advantage is in seeing discrepancies between the value of a resource in a certain use and its cost to that use (value elsewhere).

Explicit Cost: A cost which entails the outlay of money.

Implicit Cost: A cost which does not involve an outlay of money, but rather the foregoing of an inflow of money or benefit.

Production possibilities curve (PPC): A curve showing the various combinations of goods which can be produced, given the limited resources at the disposal of a person, firm, or economy.

Specialization: Producing more of a good than one consumes.

REVIEW QUESTIONS

1. Attorney Jones can type twice as fast as the average secretary. Should she do her own typing? Explain using the concepts of cost, comparative advantage, and efficiency.

2. Why is it so expensive to have Dr. Michael DeBakey, the renowned surgeon, perform an operation on you? If you answered costs, to which costs are you referring? What is the cost of DeBakey's performing surgery on you?

3. The wages for maids, after allowing for inflation, have risen substantially since the 1930s. Is it because they are more skilled or work harder than they did then? If not, why have their wages risen?

4. The wages of college professors, after allowing for inflation, have fallen in recent years. Are college professors less productive than they were ten years ago?

5. Do some cars have a comparative advantage in going 70 mph, relative to other cars? Explain. Would an increase in the speed limit from 55 to 70 mph be expected to change the types of cars people bought? How?

6. There have been some examples of people who accomplished remarkable feats while in prison (for example, learning to become lawyers, writers, or artists). These same people might not have accomplished these things if they had been on the outside. Can you use the notion of (opportunity) cost to explain this phenomenon?

7. One explanation for the fact that S.A.T. scores have declined since the early 1960s is that students are more affluent and have more things to do. Can you express this in terms of the cost of studying?

8. Suppose Professor Smith calculates that the cost of painting his house himself is $300, whereas the painter will charge $400. But suppose that the quality of the job (in terms of appearance—not duration) is higher if the professional does it. Could it then be efficient for Professor Smith to hire the painter instead of doing it himself? Explain in terms of benefit and cost.

9. Joe can do a given quality of carpentry work twice as fast as Frank. Does that mean Joe has a comparative advantage in carpentry relative to Frank?

10. Land in parts of the coastal regions of California is some of the best farm land in the world. Yet farming has almost disappeared in those regions. Explain, using the concept of comparative advantage.

11. "Land parcel A is better for growing corn than is parcel B." What do you think this means? Does this mean that A should be used to grow corn? Explain.

12. We said that if Professor Smith painted his house, thirty hours worth of book reviewing would be foregone. Can we be sure that the reviews would not be done if Smith did not do them? What sorts of substitutions would likely be made if he painted his house instead of doing the reviewing? Does that mean there would not be any cost to the economy as a whole if Smith painted his house?

13. Japan places very severe restrictions on the importation of oranges. The result is that consumers pay as much as $1 per orange, where the U.S. price is much lower (say, 25¢ each). If the restrictions were eliminated, what would happen to orange prices here and in Japan? Explain. If orange growers charged higher prices here as a result of free trade, could they argue that their *costs* were higher? In what sense?

14. In our example of Professor Smith, the alternatives he faced were always assumed to be jobs for which he would be paid. Another alternative is leisure, by which we mean any other nonpaying activity. Suppose Smith would be willing to forego $20 worth of income in order to enjoy an hour's worth of leisure. What is the *cost* to him of painting his house? What would happen to that cost if Smith unexpectedly inherited a large sum from a long-lost uncle?

15. Dr. Dexter is an orthodontist. Ms. Sharp is an interior decorator and decorating magazine editor. Sharp's son has reasonably straight teeth, but Dexter agrees to straighten them in return for Sharp's services as a decorator of his home. Dexter would ordinarily charge $2000 for the service. Since the teeth are nearly straight, Sharp would only be willing to pay $1200 for the job. Sharp does not ordinarily do individual jobs because she is so busy as an editor, but if she spent the required number of hours, she would normally charge $1800 for what Dexter wants. Dexter could find a very competent but less famous decorator to do it for $1400. (a) If there were no income tax to consider, would Dexter and Sharp trade? Explain. (b) Suppose both are in the 50 percent tax bracket. Explain how (assuming they are able to keep it from the IRS) they could benefit from the trade. (c) Can it thus be said that going underground always promotes efficiency.

16. The *Wall Street Journal*[2] reported that in New York the price of sugar which was to be delivered in May rose amid reports that droughts in India and the USSR would reduce their production of sugar. Do you think buyers from India and the USSR made offers that day in New York? If not, what made the prices go up?

17. In the 1950s and early 1960s certain groups of people, such as students and married men with children, were allowed deferments from the draft. This policy would be expected to increase the number of people in college and the number of marriages and births. In what sense was this wasteful? In what sense did it promote efficiency in selecting military personnel? (Hint: How much would a person with a supply price of $15,000 be willing to pay to avoid being drafted and paid $5000?)

18. One of the criticisms of the volunteer Army is that the number of reserves trained and ready to be inducted into the military during an emergency is too small. Can you think of any way that problem could be remedied without drafting people? How would you answer a person who complained about the high cost of your program?

19. Suppose a potential Army recruit could earn $6000 per year in the private sector and felt that the working conditions there were sufficiently better to require $7000 per year to get him to join the Army. What is the real cost of having him join the Army?

20. Some persons would be willing to work for a lower wage per hour if they could be allowed to work only part-time or have more flexible working hours. Suppose such employment arrangements involve higher bookkeeping supervision and other costs. (a) Would it be "exploitation" of those workers if they were paid less than full-time or rigidly scheduled workers? (b) What would happen to the number of persons hired part-time or on flexible hours if there were a law requiring that they be paid the same as other workers? (c) Suppose it turned out that such arrangements were only slightly more costly for the firms to administer, but resulted in sub-

2. *Wall Street Journal*, 23 April 1980.

stantial savings in wages. What would happen to firms who hired such people? To the number of persons hired that way and their wages as time passed?

21. We said that the price I have to pay to get a good reflects the costs of someone else in producing it. Does that mean that every time a firm's costs increase, it will be able to charge a higher price?

22. "We want to get the best person for the job." Does that mean we want the person who can perform the job best?

23. "The Consumer Cooperative of Berkeley announced yesterday that it had rolled back beef prices by 13 percent. . . . [A spokesman] said that he hoped to recoup some of the money lost in the rollback by buying meat in cheaper carcass loads with the stores doing more of their own butchering. . . ."[3] Does the co-op's line of reasoning make sense?

24. One of the problems the old folks in the residential hotels have faced is that it is difficult to find other accommodations. If you were a landlord, would you be encouraged or discouraged from supplying housing to this group if you knew they were a protected group who could not be evicted if circumstances changed and you decided to rent to someone else?

25. When undeveloped land is being considered for development, the conflicts that arise are often described as pitting conservationists against developers. Do the developers represent only their own interests? If not, whose do they represent? Suggest a better way to cast the conflict.

26. Suppose Joe has been told by his father that he is responsible for mowing the family's lawn. Joe is able to mow the lawn in one hour. Joe can work as a caddy for $4 per hour for as many hours as he wants. Joe's younger brother Frank takes three hours to mow the lawn, but he is too young to caddy. (a) Who is the better (more productive) lawn mower? (b) Who is the more efficient (lower cost) lawn mower? (c) Is there any difference between these two questions? (d) What piece of information would you need to answer (b)?

27. Jim and Sam are neighbors with identical yards. Jim can mow his lawn in one hour and trim it in half an hour. Sam is out of shape and not too coordinated. He can mow his lawn in three hours and trim it in one hour. Can you think of any arrangement Jim and Sam could make so that both would be better off?

28. Al and Bill are brothers. They have just been told by their parents to clean six rooms in their house. Each has been assigned the job of dusting and cleaning the floor in three rooms. It takes Al ten minutes to dust a room and twenty minutes to clean the floor. To clean his assigned three rooms would thus require ninety minutes of his time. Bill is not as coordinated as his older brother. It takes him twenty-five minutes to dust and twenty-

3. *San Francisco Chronicle*, 1 October 1974.

five minutes to scrub each floor. So his three-room assignment would require two and one half hours. Obviously, Al could spend less time if Bill did more rooms, and vice versa; but is there any way that *both* Al and Bill could reduce their work time and still get all six rooms cleaned? Explain.

29. In the previous question, suppose that instead of cleaning his room, Al could be mowing lawns and earning $3 per hour, while Bill could be collecting aluminum cans and earning $1 per hour. What sorts of deals can Al and Bill make? Who will end up doing what? (Hint: What is Al's maximum offer price to have Bill dust one room or clean one floor for him? What is Bill's minimum asking price for a room dusting or floor cleaning?)

30. In question 28, suppose Al required ten minutes for dusting and twenty minutes for floor cleaning, while Bill required twenty-five and fifty minutes, respectively. (a) Would specialization pay? Explain. (b) If these numbers were relevant for question 29, would it pay to exchange? (c) What if Al's lawn mowing still yielded $3 per hour, but Bill's can collecting yielded $1.50 per hour (given the times stated in *this* question)?

31. Suppose Joe and Bill have the production possibility schedules shown below. In autarky, Joe produces and consumes three of X and one of Y, while Bill produces and consumes four of X and two of Y. (See appendix.)

Show that by specializing and exchanging, each can consume more of Y and the same amount of X he is now consuming.

Joe		Bill	
X	Y	X	Y
6	0	8	0
5	1/3	7	1/2
4	2/3	6	1
3	1	5	1 1/2
2	1 1/3	4	2
1	1 2/3	3	2 1/2
0	2	2	3
		1	3 1/2
		0	4

Construct a "community production possibility frontier," which shows the maximum amount of Y that can be produced, given that the two are producing any particular amount of X. If one unit of X is to be produced, who should produce it? If seven units of X are to be produced, who should produce how much?

32. Suppose a third person, Ignacius, entered the island inhabited by

Crusoe and Friday in the text. Ignacius' PPC is represented by the fact that he can produce six fish, or three coconuts, or any linearly interpolated combination. (In isolation, let us suppose, he would produce and consume two fish and two coconuts.) Who will gain and who will lose by the entry of Ignacius into the economy? Why?

In this appendix, we utilize a simplified example to give another perspective on some of the concepts discussed in the chapter. Here we attempt to isolate comparative advantage as a basis for specialization and exchange. In doing so, we necessarily abstract from other aspects of reality in order to expose the essential operating mechanism. Please be patient with the unrealistic nature of the situation described. As mentioned in chapter 1, abstraction is a crucial part of the analysis of any system as complicated as our economy. Again, you are asked to take paper and pencil and follow along with the arithmetic and diagrams.

Robinson Crusoe and Friday inhabit an island. Every day they spend a certain number of hours gathering coconuts and catching fish (the only kinds of food). Neither person has any particular preference for the acts of fishing or coconut gathering. But they both want some fish and coconuts to consume. Both Crusoe and Friday are limited in the amounts of fish they can catch and coconuts they can pick. This limitation is represented by a construction called the production possibilities curve (PPC).

PRODUCTION POSSIBILITIES

In the case of Friday, suppose his

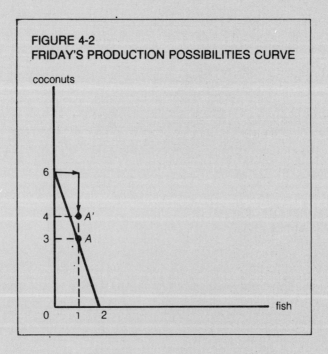

FIGURE 4-2
FRIDAY'S PRODUCTION POSSIBILITIES CURVE

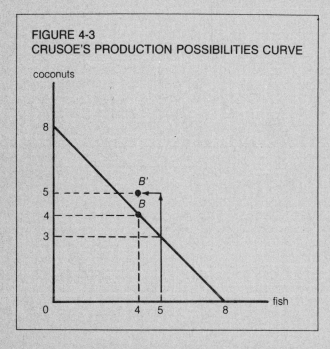

FIGURE 4-3
CRUSOE'S PRODUCTION POSSIBILITIES CURVE

talents and the time he spends working are such that, if he spent the entire work time fishing, he could catch two fish per day. On the other hand, if he spent all his work time picking coconuts, he could pick six coconuts per day. Furthermore, if he spent only the time necessary to catch one fish per day, he would have time left over to pick three coconuts per day. These facts are illustrated in figure 4-2. The vertical axis measures the number of coconuts picked per day, and the horizontal axis measures the number of fish caught per day. The line connecting six on the vertical axis with two on the horizontal axis is Friday's PPC. The line represents both the fact that Friday's productive capacity is limited and the fact that in order to catch an additional fish, he must forego picking three coconuts. Thus three coconuts are Friday's cost of catching a fish.

Similarly, Crusoe is limited in his productive capacity. If he spent all his work time picking coconuts, he could pick eight per day (and catch no fish), but if he spent all day fishing, he could catch eight fish. If Crusoe spends the time

necessary to catch one more fish, he has less time available to pick coconuts and is able to pick one less coconut. Thus, Crusoe's cost of a fish is one coconut. Crusoe's PPC extends from eight on the coconut axis to eight on the fish axis (figure 4-3). Any point on the line, such as four fish and four coconuts, represents a possible combination of fish and coconuts which Crusoe can obtain. But note that Crusoe, by his own labor alone, would not be able to obtain the combination of five coconuts and four fish (point B'). That point is beyond his PPC. Similarly Friday, by his labor alone, would not be able to attain four coconuts and one fish (point A') because that point is beyond his PPC.

AUTARKY
Suppose that initially Friday consumes what he produces and Crusoe does the same. (This is known as *autarky* or self-sufficiency.) Each person would pick the output combination on his PPC that he likes best. Suppose Friday picks the combination of three coconuts and

one fish (point *A*), while Crusoe picks the combination of four of each (point *B*). Production would be as follows:

	Coconuts	Fish
Friday	3	1
Crusoe	4	4
Total	7	5

ABSOLUTE ADVANTAGE

Crusoe's production possibilities are greater than Friday's. Perhaps Crusoe is more skilled, or perhaps he works longer hours or is just luckier. The fact remains that if he spent all his time fishing, he could catch more fish than Friday could. Or if he spent all his time picking coconuts, he could pick more coconuts than Friday could. Thus, Crusoe has an *absolute advantage* in both. He will be richer than Friday in any system which allows him the rights to what he produces.

INEFFICIENCY OF AUTARKY

What we are interested in here, however, is not who is richer, but whether the current production is *efficient*. What do we mean by efficient in this context? According to our definition of efficiency, the output of either good is produced efficiently if it is produced at *least cost*. We know that together, Crusoe and Friday produce seven coconuts (four from Crusoe and three from Friday) and five fish (four from Crusoe and one from Friday). By producing the five fish they are foregoing the opportunity of producing more coconuts. If they hadn't caught any fish, they could have picked fourteen coconuts (eight from Crusoe and six from Friday). So the cost of catching the five fish is seven coconuts. When we ask whether the five fish are being produced efficiently, we really are asking if there is any way to have that many fish while giv-

ing up fewer coconuts, for example, would it be possible to have the same number of fish and have eight or nine coconuts instead of only seven? If so, the current production is inefficient in the sense that the five fish are not being produced at the lowest cost in terms of coconuts. At first glance, it seems that it would *not* be possible to have more coconuts and the same amount of fish because both Friday and Crusoe are working full time. Each is doing the best he can, given the time he allocates to his jobs. But in spite of this, it *is* possible to produce more coconuts along with the five fish. Production *is* inefficient from a social point of view. To see why this is true, we ask if any of the fish are being produced at a higher cost than necessary. If they are, then this is the source of the inefficiency. The one fish that Friday catches comes at the cost of three coconuts which he no longer has time to pick. Is this cost necessary? It is if Friday is to catch a fish. That is what his PPC tells us. But it is not *socially* necessary.

MAKING THE PIE BIGGER

In order for Friday and Crusoe to have a fifth fish between them, they need not rely on Friday. The alternative is to have Crusoe, whose cost is only one coconut per fish, catch the fifth fish along with the other four. If Friday were to forego catching the fish, he could pick three more coconuts. Then if Crusoe produced an extra fish, he would forego only one coconut and the society would be richer —the "pie" to be distributed between Crusoe and Friday would be larger. It would have nine coconuts (six from Friday and three from Crusoe) and the same five fish (all five from Crusoe now). Of course Friday and Crusoe would not move voluntarily to this more efficient outcome if they had to consume what they have produced. (Otherwise, why wouldn't they have done so originally? We assumed that, given that they had to consume what they produced, they were best off at the original points.) However, if Friday were to give Crusoe two of the three extra coconuts he picks in return for the extra fish Crusoe catches, both would be better off, as shown below. The listing shows the new amounts produced; the amounts consumed are in parentheses:

	Coconuts	Fish
Friday	6(4)	0(1)
Crusoe	3(5)	5(4)
Total	9(9)	5(5)

Friday and Crusoe are each consuming as much fish as before but more coconuts. Friday "specializes" in coconut picking. That is, he picks more than he consumes. He now picks six coconuts and sells two to Crusoe, so he consumes four. He consumes bundle A' instead of bundle A (in figure 4-2), which he consumed before specialization and trade. Since he is picking six coconuts, Friday catches no fish, but he gets one fish in return for the two coconuts he sells to Crusoe. So his fish consumption is the same as before. Crusoe specializes in fishing, since he catches five fish while consuming only four. He sells the other one to Friday for two coconuts, leaving him with the same amount of fish as in autarky but more coconuts. He now consumes bundle B' instead of bundle B (in figure 4-3), which he consumed when he didn't specialize or exchange with Friday.

Note that through specialization both Friday and Crusoe are able to consume amounts of fish and coconuts which were unattainable when they were self-sufficient. (A' instead of A for Friday and B' instead or B for Crusoe). The cooperation involved in specialization and exchange makes both parties richer by freeing them from the limits of their own abilities.

Note also that, if the two are permitted to do as they like with what they pro-

duce, their individual self-interest will lead them to do what is efficient; namely, Crusoe will catch more fish and Friday will pick more coconuts. We need not rely on benevolence or "social responsibility" to get the job done. Friday's own (internal) cost of obtaining fish is three coconuts per fish. If he could find a way of obtaining a fish at a lower cost than that, he would be better off. Thus his maximum offer price for a fish is three coconuts. Crusoe's (internal) cost of obtaining fish is only one coconut per fish. He would not be willing to offer more than that in order to buy one. On the other hand, if he were offered a price greater than one coconut for *selling* a fish, he would take it. Since he foregoes only one coconut by producing the extra fish, he is better off if he can produce an extra fish and sell it for more than one coconut. Thus Crusoe's minimum asking price for fish is only one coconut per fish. Since Friday's maximum offer price (equal to his MC_F) is three coconuts, they can mutually benefit by having Friday buy a fish from Crusoe at a price between one and three coconuts. In our example, Friday paid Crusoe two coconuts for the fish. Crusoe had to give up picking one coconut if he devoted the time necessary to catch the extra fish, but since he was paid two coconuts, he ended up consuming the same amount of fish as before, but one more coconut (five coconuts and four fish, instead of four coconuts and four fish).

The other side of this exchange was that Friday bought the fish at a price of two coconuts. By buying the fish instead of catching it himself, Friday was able to devote more time to picking coconuts. He had to pay only two coconuts for the fish he bought. The benefit he obtained from the extra coconut picking was three extra coconuts. Thus he ended up with the same amount of fish, but with one more coconut than under autarky (four coconuts and one fish, instead of three coconuts and one fish).

The basis for their mutually beneficial exchange was that Friday's offer price for fish (three coconuts) was greater than Crusoe's asking price (one coconut). This differential came about because Crusoe had a *lower cost* of catching fish than Friday did. Thus, the two transactors were led *by their own self-interest* to do what was efficient, namely have Crusoe produce the extra fish instead of Friday. If one transactor has a lower marginal cost of doing some-

thing than another does, that automatically creates the basis for an exchange involving specialization, whereby the lower cost producer sells the item to the higher cost producer. In an exchange economy, no one has to tell the transactors to specialize according to their comparative advantage. Their self-interest encourages them *automatically* to do so.

chapter 5

Costs of
Production

In chapters 1 and 4 the concept of cost in relation to efficiency and comparative advantage was discussed. In both instances, emphasis was placed on the idea that cost is an "opportunity" concept. The cost of an action is the value of the best alternative which one foregoes in taking that action. In chapter 4, we learned that costs depend on prices, and that prices are the outcome of the voluntary exchange process. This chapter continues to emphasize these concepts, but concentrates on the fact that the alternatives one foregoes in taking a certain action depend on the circumstances in which one takes the action. For example, the cost of a decision to refrain from producing a certain good depends on whether one is already set up to produce it or not. Furthermore, it is possible to categorize costs according to the decisions to which the costs are relevant. For example, the costs that are relevant in deciding whether to produce a larger or smaller output are different from those that are relevant for deciding whether or not to stay in business.

Another important thing to keep in mind when discussing costs is that firms and persons usually *own* at least some of the inputs they use, and this makes the discussion of costs more complicated than if all inputs were rented—hired on a fee-for-service basis—as labor is.

TYPES OF COSTS

Since not all inputs are rented, costs are not the same as outlays. If I hire labor by the hour, my labor costs are so much per hour. But if I buy a machine now and sell it again in six months, it is not so easy to say what the cost per hour is.

Acquisition Costs

Once we start to think about the fact that many inputs are owned by the users, the question arises as to what cost is incurred when a durable asset, such as a machine or a building, is acquired. The cost is clearly *not* the purchase price. Remember, when we speak of costs, we refer to *foregone* alternatives or opportunities. If we buy an asset and have the ability to resell it immediately for the same amount, we have incurred no cost, because the act of acquiring the asset did not cut us off from any alternative we had *before* we bought the asset. We could, in this (unrealistic) case, return to our previous position. For example, something close to this happens when I buy a bond for $1000 and immediately resell it; I am out only the broker's fee for handling the transactions. However, when I buy a McDonald's Big Mac for $1.25 and take it outside, I am not likely to find anyone who will buy it from me. Thus, the cost of acquiring the asset (the Big Mac) is $1.25, the purchase price. Most assets which provide benefits over time fall somewhere in between these two extremes. If I buy a car, the immediate resale price is a few hundred dollars less than what I pay for it. The difference between the purchase price and the immediate resale price is called the *acquisition cost*. In most cases it is positive but less than the purchase price. The size of the acquisition cost depends on the rarity of the item, as well as how often such items are exchanged. If the asset is a standard item which is heavily traded, such as many financial assets (for example, stocks and bonds), then the acquisition cost is small relative to the value of the asset. But if the item is unique or is seldom traded, then the cost is higher, because it is more difficult to find someone who places as high a value on it as the present owner. Specialized equipment and buildings, such as train stations or tunnels, have very high acquisition costs.

Continued Possession Costs

Another kind of cost is the cost of continuing to possess an asset after it is purchased. Again we want to consider what alternatives we forego when we make a decision to hold onto an asset for a certain time. As an example, consider an airline which has just purchased a DC-10 for $15 million. Suppose that it could be resold immediately for $14 million (the acquisition cost was $1 million). What cost does the airline incur in owning it (not operating it) for a year, given that it is already bought? To answer this, we must know what alternative uses the airline has for the $14 million it could obtain by selling the plane. Suppose that the airline could put the $14 million in another investment which would yield a 10 percent return over a one-year period. Then part of the cost incurred is that $1.4 million in interest the airline foregoes by holding on to the plane. In addition to that, the airline incurs more cost if the plane depreciates over the year. If, after one year, the airline could sell the plane for $12 million, then another $2 million cost will be incurred by holding on to it for a year. If the plane is to be insured, that would be a possession cost, as would any property tax. The possession cost is thus the interest which could have been earned on the *current* resale price (not the purchase price), plus depreciation over the year and taxes and insurance. (Note that the depreciation that we speak of here is true depreciation, not the kind that accountants put in their books. Accounting depreciation is based on formulas which only very roughly approximate the actual decrease in the value of assets over time.)

Operating Costs

We define operating costs as all costs which do not fall into the category of either acquisition or possession costs, including such things as raw materials, labor, utilities, and the rental cost of other inputs. In addition, we include any depreciation occasioned by use and not strictly time-related. An airline's operating costs include outlays for fuel, crew salaries, maintenance and repair, landing fees, and so on. These costs would not be incurred if the airline merely owned the planes but did not operate them.

AVOIDABLE AND UNAVOIDABLE COSTS

We often find ourselves in situations we wish we had avoided. The question sometimes arises as to whether we should "cut our losses" or hold on. Careful analysis can help us to understand similar situations as they are faced by business and society.

Ski Trip

Consider the following example. You have decided to go skiing over a certain weekend. The ski area is two hundred miles from your home. You figure to take about four hours each way. As you start out, you run into a severe snowstorm, which causes a traffic tieup. By the time you reach the halfway point (after four hours of slow driving), you estimate that, given the weather and traffic conditions, it will take another six hours to reach the ski area. Should you continue or not? In order to analyze a situation like this, you must know your alternatives and evaluate them. In this case, there appear to be two choices: (1) go on to the ski area, ski, and return home; or (2) return home immediately.

In order to compare the two, you must know how long it will take to get home if you return immediately (assume three hours), how long it will take to get home after the ski trip (assume the normal time, four hours), and what benefits you will get from the skiing itself. In particular, you must know how many hours of travel to and from the ski area you would be willing to undertake in order to experience the skiing (after taking into account the costs of ski lifts, room and board, and so on).

For this example, suppose that the net benefits of the ski experience are such that, in contemplating this trip, the longest round trip travel time you would have been willing to spend is twelve hours. Recall that your original plan involved an expected travel time of eight hours (four up and four back), so the trip was worthwhile. Now, after four hours of driving, you expect six more hours to get there, plus four more to return after skiing. The total hours you will spend traveling will be fourteen hours, two more than the maximum you were willing to spend and still consider the trip worthwhile. So if you follow option 1, you will be worse off than if you had never started. But that is also true of option 2: you will spend seven hours traveling with no skiing benefit. So you cannot base the decision on whether you will be worse off than if you had never started. That is true for both options. On what basis *can* you make a reasonable choice then? You note that some costs have already been incurred and you can do nothing about them. In this case, the four hours already spent getting this far are "sunk" and irretrievable; no matter what you do, you can't avoid incurring them. As such, then, they are irrelevant for any future decision (as between options 1 and 2, for example). For that matter, you are going to have to spend at least three hours getting home, no matter which alternative you take, so *that* cost is irrelevant for the decision. What we come down to, then, is that option 1 involves spending seven more travel hours than option 2, but option 1 provides the skiing benefits while option 2 doesn't. It is these *additional* costs, as compared with the additional benefits, which are useful for the decision. In this case, the decision should be to go with option 1 because the skiing experience is worth up to twelve hours, and (at this point) to get it, you need to incur only an extra seven hours over what you would incur by going home now (option 2) and getting no skiing benefit.

Of course, the example could have been constructed in such a way as to make option 2 the preferred alternative; but note that, once we have gotten into a project, with some costs sunk, there is a tendency to be (rationally!) locked in, because only the *additional* costs, as compared with the additional benefits, should be considered for the decision to continue the operation. It is often rational to complete or continue projects which should never have been started, because many of the costs are already incurred and are irretrievable (sunk) and therefore irrelevant once we are into the project. Note, however, that when we do our evaluation nearer to the starting point, the alternative of continuing will look worse, because fewer costs will be unavoidable.

It should be clear from the above example that the distinction between sunk (or unavoidable) and avoidable costs is important for purposes of making decisions. How do the cost classifications (acquisition, possession, and operating cost) fit into this framework? Which ones are sunk and which are avoidable? In the case of acquisition costs, the answer depends on when we ask. Acquisition costs are avoidable before we acquire (make or purchase) the asset in question. But once the acquisition has been made, acquisition costs have been incurred and cannot be affected by any future decision; thus they are sunk and irrelevant.

Possession costs are a little more complicated, but the principle is the same. Any decision which does not influence whether an asset will continue to be possessed does not affect or change possession costs. Thus, for that decision, possession costs are sunk and irrelevant.

Airplane

For example, suppose the airline which purchased the DC-10 has decided to keep it for a year and is now trying to decide how much to use it. In particular, the airline is trying to decide whether to use it on a flight that is operated every night. In practice, the decision is likely to involve a choice between the DC-10 and some other plane (say a 707). The decision then comes down to comparing the costs of using each plane with its associated revenue and choosing the one with the greater difference. It will certainly be important for such a decision to be based on a correct and relevant measure of costs. If the airline has already decided to continue owning both planes, the relevant comparison is between the operating costs of the two planes. Suppose the operating cost figures (including extra flight-related depreciation, maintenance, fuel, servicing, labor, and landing fees) are calculated. The cost for the DC-10 is $1500, and the cost for the 707 is $1200.

And suppose that because the DC-10 is newer and larger, it is expected to generate revenues of $2500 per flight versus $2000 per flight for the 707. Then the DC-10 is the better plane to use, because its contribution to covering other costs is greater. The DC-10 generates a revenue of $2500 and has operating costs of $1500, leaving a contribution of $1000. The 707 generates a revenue of $2000 with operating costs of $1200, leaving a contribution of $800. Thus the DC-10 contributes more than the 707 toward defraying other costs. This is summarized in table 5-1.

We can see the importance of looking at only the relevant costs by seeing what would happen if we had used what are called *fully allocated*

TABLE 5-1
COSTS AND REVENUES FOR DC-10 AND 707 (NIGHT FLIGHT)

	DC-10	707
Revenue from flight	$2500	$2000
Operating cost of flight	1500	1200
Net contribution to defraying other costs	$1000	$ 800

costs in making the decision. Fully allocated costs are obtained by taking the total cost of the airplane (including acquisition, possession, and operating costs) and adding some (arbitrary) fraction of the *overhead costs* (management salaries, office costs, and the like), and dividing by, say, the miles the plane flies. Suppose that number comes out to be $15 per mile, and the night flight contemplated is two hundred miles. Then the fully allocated cost of the flight is $3000, and the $2500 revenue does not cover this. Should the flight be cancelled? No, because half of that $3000 is going to be incurred whether this flight takes place or not, and is therefore irrelevant in calculating the costs and benefits of operating this flight. If you think fully allocated costs are too silly to be considered, you should know that governmental agencies, and even some business firms, have in the past incorrectly used this measure of costs to draw inferences about the behavior of firms.[1]

A FURTHER APPLICATION OF THE CONCEPT OF SUNK COST—BART

The San Francisco Bay Area Rapid Transit District (known as BART) is the first entirely new, fixed rail, public transit system in the United States in many years. Voters first approved the concept in the 1950s, and limited service began in the fall of 1972. The system covers about seventy-five miles, including San Francisco, Oakland, and the eastern part of the San Francisco Bay region. The system was quite expensive to build (in the neighborhood of $2 billion—about twice the original estimates) and has been the subject of much controversy since its inception. Some persons have questioned whether any such system is a good investment.

This is not the place to undertake a full discussion of the wisdom of investing in BART. Nevertheless, we can make use of such a system to illustrate the uses of the sunk cost idea. Suppose that BART was an unwise investment—that having seen the costs and benefits, the populace would prefer, all things considered, not to have BART. In other words, suppose the benefits are less than the costs.

Should we then shut down the system? Not necessarily. In order to decide whether to continue to operate, we must know what the avoidable costs are, as compared to the benefits. What will those costs include? They will include possession and operating costs. Acquisition costs should not be considered.

---

1. Are overhead costs possession costs or operating costs? They appear to fall into both categories. The costs of owning the office buildings would seem to be possession cost. But salaries for secretaries and executives and others seem to be operating costs—costs which would not exist if the airline shut down all operations. But they cannot be allocated to any particular operation such as the flight in question.

The Decision to Operate at All

How much of the $2 billion investment was composed of acquisition cost? Another way of asking the same question is, what could we get if we liquidated (sold) the system now? The bridges, tunnels, and tracks have virtually no alternative use. So their salvage value would be very small. The stations could possibly be used as restaurants or something else, which would bring in some revenue from the sale. The cars, although specially designed for the BART system, could perhaps be adapted to another system and sold. All told, if the system were liquidated at this moment, it might bring, optimistically, $100 million. Thus $1.9 billion of the $2 billion purchase price for the system is (sunk) acquisition cost. The annual possession cost would be the interest which could be earned on the $100 million current resale value (at 8 percent, that would be $8 million per year), plus whatever decrease in the resale value would occur per year. In order for it to be worthwhile to continue to operate the system, the annual benefits of operating it must be greater than the sum of the annual possession cost and the operating cost. The ($1.9 billion) acquisition cost is irrelevant for any future decision.

Should the System Operate at Night and on Weekends?

For this decision, *both* the acquisition cost *and* the possession cost are irrelevant. As long as it has been decided to continue the system, only the *extra* costs entailed in operating at night and on weekends must be considered. Costs incurred anyway (acquisition and possession costs) are irrelevant for that decision.

ACQUISITION COSTS AND ORDINARY BUSINESS FIRMS

In the preceding examples, especially that of BART, we have assumed acquisition costs to be very large. Usually, for ordinary business firms, acquisition costs will not be so large. They are large for BART because there is almost no resale market for BART's assets, because the amount of money anyone is willing to pay for public rapid transit services is far less than the operating costs of such systems. BART would never have been built if it had to be financed by private investors. Government, which has the power to force people to turn over money (the power to tax), often undertakes such projects that cannot be paid for except with taxes. In all such cases, the resale markets for the assets are so weak that acquisition costs are large.

But in the more usual case of the ordinary business firm, acquisition cost is very much less important. In that context it merely represents the *transaction costs* incurred in buying and reselling assets. (The acquisition cost represents the cost of finding a seller and negotiating the purchase, plus the cost of finding a buyer and negotiating the sale. The sum of these costs represents how much would be lost if one proceeds from not owning the asset, to owning it, to not owning it again; and this is exactly what acquisition costs are.) Accordingly, in all future discussions of ordinary business firms, we shall ignore acquisition costs, since their inclusion would complicate the analysis without shedding much additional light on it. Operating and possession costs are the principal costs upon which decisions are made.

RELATING COSTS
TO OUTPUT

Thus far we have seen that whether a cost is avoidable depends on the particular decision to be made. Moreover, for any decision the only costs that matter are those which can be avoided. If you are deciding whether to take action A or action B, the only costs that should be considered are those that change as a consequence of the decision. An outlay that has already been made, or an outlay that must be made whether A or B is chosen, is irrelevant to the choice between A or B. This proposition was illustrated by the examples of the ski trip and the airplanes.

It is often useful in attempting to understand the behavior of decision makers in firms to see what happens to avoidable costs as the firm's output rate changes. In any set-up firm, someone must decide whether to continue possession of the plant and equipment. Given the decision to continue possession, someone must decide whether to operate the plant and equipment (whether to produce something). Given the decision to operate, someone must decide how much to produce. The relevant costs for these decisions are continued possession costs and operating costs.

Given a specific quantity of plant and equipment already acquired, there is a fixed amount of continued possession cost. As we saw earlier, this cost equals the interest that could be earned on the money that could be received from the sale of the plant and equipment, plus the decrease in the selling price of the plant and equipment as time goes by (this is pure *time* depreciation, unrelated to the use or wearing out of the plant and equipment), plus the insurance on the plant and equipment, plus any property taxes on the plant and equipment. All of these costs exist whether or not the plant and equipment are actually operated. The total of these costs is the same whether the plant produces zero per week, 100 per week, 200 per week, or 400 per week. Suppose this sum is $1000.

Fixed Costs

In figure 5-1 the *AFC* (average fixed cost) curve depicts what happens to these fixed costs calculated on a per unit basis. If the firm's output rate is 100 per week, continued possession costs per unit (or average fixed costs) are $1000/100 or $10, shown by point *a* on the *AFC* line. If the firm's output rate is 200 per week, average fixed cost is $1000/200 or $5, shown by point

FIGURE 5-1
COSTS AND OUTPUT

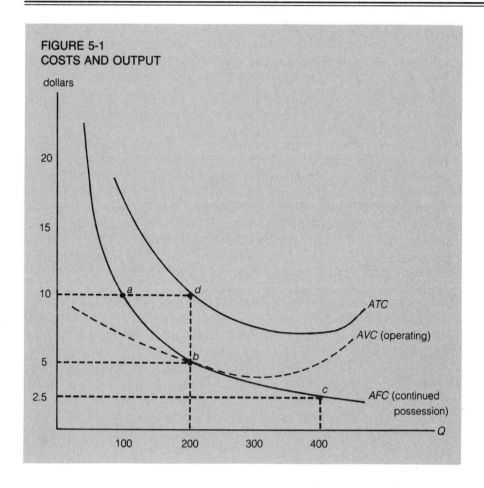

b. If the firm's output rate is 400 per week, the average fixed cost would equal $1000/400 or $2.5, shown by point c. Note that continued possession costs per unit decline as output increases. This is because a fixed amount ($1000) is divided by larger numbers as output increases.

Variable Costs

The AVC (average variable cost) curve depicts what usually happens to operating costs calculated on a per unit basis as output increases. Operating costs are costs incurred if the firm operates; they would not be incurred if the firm did not operate. Operating costs include labor, raw materials, electricity, wear and tear on the plant and equipment, paper and pencils and other office supplies, and so on. No such outlays would be made if the owner shut down the plant. If, when she shuts down the plant, she also gets rid of it, she will not have any continued possession costs either. If she shuts down and continues to own the plant and equipment, her operating costs will be zero, but she will continue to bear the continued possession cost. Note that no matter what she does, she cannot avoid any acquisition cost incurred when she originally bought the plant and equipment; thus acquisition costs do not enter the picture at all.

Operating costs are zero when nothing is produced, and they increase as more is produced. Since operating costs change as the amount of output changes (unlike continued possession costs) they are sometimes called variable costs. Average variable costs are operating costs calculated on a per unit basis.

In figure 5-1 the *AVC* curve first declines as output increases and then rises as output increases. Clearly, when fifty units of output are produced the total of labor, raw materials, and other operating costs will be higher than when only twenty-five units of output are produced. However, there is no reason to think that the total operating costs of producing fifty will be twice the total operating cost of producing twenty-five. It may not be necessary, for example, to double the amount of labor used when production is increased from twenty-five to fifty per week. If four workers were employed when twenty-five were produced, perhaps only five will be employed when fifty are produced. The additional person could conceivably perform services that permit each of the other four to produce more than they did previously. As long as additional workers augment the productivity (amount produced) of the workers already on the job, we would expect average variable costs to fall.

However, as more workers are hired and more output is produced, crowding becomes a problem. There is a fixed amount of plant, machines, and tools. As more people are hired to use the plant, machines, and tools, eventually the productivity of each worker (output per worker) must decline. More is produced when an additional person is hired, but the presence of the additional person reduces the productivity of the other workers. (As long as the amount produced by the additional person exceeds the production lost because the other workers each produce a little less, total output will increase.) Thus at higher outputs, when more workers are used, output per worker falls as more is produced, so operating costs per unit of output (average variable costs) rise.

Although it is possible to rationalize the shape of the *AVC* curve in figure 5-1 by appealing to arguments such as the one used, the important question is: In the real world, do *AVC* curves actually look like that? Fortunately for us, they do. That is, for most actual business firms, when more is produced using a fixed amount of plant, machines, and tools, as well as increasing amounts of labor, materials, and power, operating costs per unit first decline and then rise.

Total Costs

The *ATC* (average total cost) curve in figure 5-1 depicts what happens to average total cost (the total of per unit continued possession costs and per unit operating costs) as output increases. That curve is constructed merely by adding average variable cost to average fixed cost at each output rate. For example, at output equal to 200, average variable cost and average fixed cost both equal $5 (point *b*). Thus average total cost equals $10 (point

TABLE 5-2
AVERAGE FIXED COST, AVERAGE VARIABLE COST, AND AVERAGE
TOTAL COST FOR SELECTED OUTPUTS

Q	AFC	AVC	ATC
25	40.00	9.00	49.00
50	20.00	8.00	28.00
100	10.00	7.00	17.00
200	5.00	5.00	10.00
250	4.00	4.80	8.80
400	2.50	5.00	7.50
425	2.35	5.13	7.48
450	2.22	5.38	7.60

d). Performing this addition at each output rate, we generate the *ATC* curve which, because of the shapes of *AVC* and *AFC* curves, must look like the *ATC* line in figure 5-1. At first, as output increases, average total cost decreases. (Both average fixed cost and average variable cost decline at first.) Later average total cost rises as output increases. (Average variable cost rises and average fixed cost gets so small that it doesn't affect average total cost very much.) These points are shown in more detail in table 5-2. This table shows average fixed cost, average variable cost, and their sum average total cost for several additional output levels. Notice that average fixed cost falls as quantity increases, while average variable cost and average total cost both fall and then rise. The minimum average variable cost is reached at an output of 250, while average total cost does not reach its minimum until output of 425 has been reached.

Average total cost is computed, as we have seen, merely by adding total continued possession cost to total operating cost at each output rate and dividing by the output rate. Like any average, average total cost does not refer to the cost of producing any particular unit of output. It merely apportions total costs equally to all units of output.

Incremental Cost and Marginal Cost

When the decision maker in a firm decides whether to increase (decrease) output he does so by comparing the *addition* to (reduction of) cost that results from the increased (decreased) output and the increase (decrease) of revenue that the firm collects when the additional (reduced) output is sold. *Incremental cost* is defined as the change in cost that is experienced when there is a change in the amount of output produced and sold. If, when five additional units of output are produced and sold, total cost (the sum of continued possession cost and operating cost) increases by $250, we say that the incremental cost of the five units is $250. When we express this increment in cost on a *per unit* of changed output basis, it is called *marginal* cost. Thus the marginal cost is the incremental cost divided by the change in output. In the example above, the marginal cost would be $50 ($250/5).

Note that since marginal and incremental costs refer to how total cost changes, continued possession cost does not affect them. With a fixed amount of plant and equipment, the total of continued possession cost and operating cost changes only if operating cost changes. The source of cost changes, with a fixed amount of plant and equipment, is changes of operating cost. Marginal and incremental costs, in other words, really only tell us how operating (variable) cost changes as output changes.

Marginal cost and average total cost are related in a specific way. Marginal cost is the change in total cost divided by the change in output. Average cost is total cost divided by output. Similarly, your grade point average (gpa) is your total earned grade points divided by the total number of units you have taken. When you take an additional course, your total grade points go up by the number of grade points earned in the new course. For example, if you take a five-unit course and receive an "A" in it, you receive $5 \times 4 = 20$ additional grade points. These are your incremental grade points. Your *marginal* grade point average is the incremental grade points divided by the number of units in the new course: 20/5 = 4. If prior to taking this course you had a 3.1 gpa on the basis of 40 units attempted, the "A" in your new course will clearly raise your overall average as follows: Before you took this course you had attained 124 grade points (3.1 $\times$ 40). After the course, you have 144 grade points and 45 total units attempted, for a new average of 3.2 (that is, 144/45). The higher *marginal* grade point productivity *pulled* up the average. If, instead, you had gotten a "B" in the course, your average would have fallen to 3.089. (You should work out this result for yourself.) If your marginal grade point average for a given term is 3.1 (say, "Bs" in 3 three-unit courses and an "A" in a one-unit course), then the overall grade point average will remain at 3.1. (You should work out this result as well, just to make sure.) The rule for grade point averages is that if the marginal grade point average is above the previous average, the average will rise. If the marginal is less than average, the average will fall. And if the marginal is equal to the previous average, the average will be unchanged. (Note that it is the *marginal* grade point average, not the *incremental grade points*, that is being compared with the previous average in this discussion. In the case where you were assumed to get a "B" in the five-unit course, you earned fifteen *incremental* grade points, well above the previous average. But it is the *marginal* grade point productivity of three which is the relevant comparison.)

The relationship between marginal and average grade points is exactly the same as the relationship between any other marginal and average magnitude. Batting averages, tax rates, and electricity rates all behave according to the same arithmetic law relating marginals and averages. For our purposes, an important relationship is the one between marginal and average *cost*. In figure 5-2 we have redrawn the *ATC* curve from figure 5-1, along with the corresponding marginal cost curve.

Note that as we have drawn the two curves, whenever the marginal cost is below the average total cost, the average is falling. (This happens

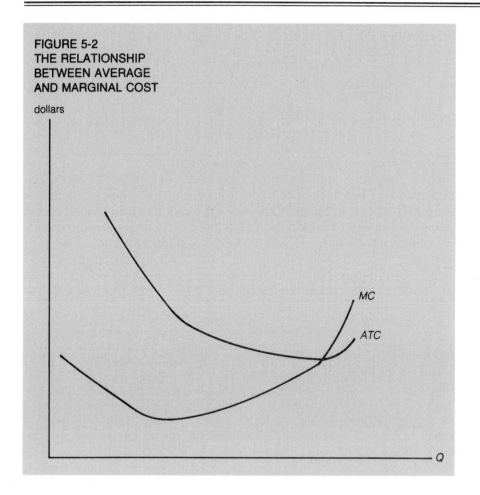

FIGURE 5-2
THE RELATIONSHIP
BETWEEN AVERAGE
AND MARGINAL COST

dollars

even if the marginal cost is increasing.) And whenever the marginal cost is above the average total cost, the average is rising. (This would happen even if, for some reason, marginal cost (MC) were to begin falling after it rose above average total cost.) When the marginal cost is equal to the average total cost, the average is neither rising nor falling—it is at its minimum.

We can see more concretely how marginal cost and average total cost are related by utilizing the numbers from table 5-2, on which figure 5-2 is based. Look at the increment in output from 100 to 200. At output of 100, the average total cost is $17. Thus the total cost is $1700. At output of 200, the average total cost is $10. Thus the total cost is $2000. The incremental cost in going from output of 100 to output of 200 is $300. The *marginal* cost over that range is $3 (the incremental cost of $300 divided by the change in quantity of 100). What this says is that in going from an output of 100 to an output of 200, the extra cost incurred per extra unit produced was only $3.

The total cost per unit at output of 100 was $17, but the extra cost incurred in producing 100 more units was only $3 per unit, so the average total cost at 200 must be less than $17. In fact, as we saw, it is $10.

When we explicitly consider decision making in firms in chapters 7 and 8, we will see how these cost curves can be used to understand the nature of the decisions that must always be considered by firms struggling to prosper in the marketplace.

A More Precise Meaning of Marginal Cost

Often when people talk about marginal cost they refer to the additional cost incurred when output increases by *one unit*. This concept still defines marginal cost as the change in cost divided by the change in quantity, but it specifies that the change in quantity is one unit. If we were trying to draw the smooth curves in figure 5-2, we would first have to estimate the total cost associated with every output from 1 to 450. Then the average total cost at any quantity (say 249) would be the total cost at that point divided by 249, and the marginal cost would be the difference in cost from output 249 to output 250.

ECONOMIC COSTS VERSUS ACCOUNTING COSTS

As we have already seen, careful consideration of cost is an important aspect of decision making. In the remainder of the book, we shall see how the costs we have developed in this chapter are useful for various decisions. For example, if the firm is deciding whether to stay in business, it must consider the total cost of staying in, as compared to the benefit. If it is deciding whether to produce more or less output, it would consider the marginal cost. All this will be spelled out in greater detail in chapters 7 and 8. But for now we should note that in order to make intelligent decisions, the decision maker must consider the *correct* costs. If the measures of costs she uses in arriving at decisions are systematically lower or higher than the *true* costs, then she will make incorrect decisions. Thus for decision-making purposes, it is very important to use conceptually correct measures of costs. As economists, we want to construct useful *models* of the behavior of decision makers. Since it is in the interest of decision makers to consider their true costs, we generally assume in our models that they do so. We assume that the decision maker will choose option A only if the benefits of doing so are greater than the *true* costs as she sees them. Thus when we draw cost curves (ATC, MC, and AVC) as part of our model of the firm's behavior, we assume we are depicting the correct measure of all of the costs.

As we saw in earlier chapters, some of the most important costs for decision-making purposes are *implicit* costs—that is, costs which do not involve an outlay of money, but rather the foregoing of an inflow of money. For example, if a person owns and runs her own business, the cost of the labor services she devotes to the business is an implicit cost, because it involves foregoing income from some other job that she would have had if she were not running the business. Similarly, if she has some of her own money invested in the business, she foregoes the interest the money could earn in a bank, or a bond, or in whatever alternative investment yields the highest rate of interest.

Implicit costs cause problems for two reasons. First, they are hard to pin down. We know that they exist and we assume that decision makers take them into account, but they are not objective in the same way that the amount paid for a raw material is. Since they refer to transactions which might have taken place but did not, they are by their nature more speculative and subject to dispute. For example, we may say that the owner could have earned $20,000 running a similar business, but we cannot really be sure because she is in fact not running the other business. This is troublesome because accountants like to be able to report objective data, and accounting principles are based on the idea that any two skilled accountants looking at the same situation would arrive at approximately the same numbers. For this reason alone, accountants might decide not to record implicit costs on the books. They might reason that since we cannot agree on the size of the implicit costs, we would do better to omit them from our calculation and inform those who read our reports that we have done so.

Another reason implicit costs are troublesome is that, although they are useful for decisions, they may not be useful to those to whom accountants report. Chief among these is the Internal Revenue Service (IRS). The IRS is interested in how much *income* a person made by selling or renting property (including labor services) during the year. Suppose I manage my own business. During a given year I calculate that after paying for hired labor and raw materials and renting my business space, I have $20,000 left over. But since I ran my own business, I had to forego another job which would have paid me $18,000. In that case *I* would say that I made a *profit* of $2000. Another way of saying it is that in that case I would do $2000 better to stay where I am than to go to my best alternative. For *decision* purposes, I should count the $18,000 foregone wages as a cost so that I can tell whether I made the right decision to be in this occupation. (The $2000 profit says that I did.) But the IRS is not interested in whether I did the best I could or not. They want to know how much I made this year *renting my labor services*, and the answer to that is $20,000. The same sort of comment would apply to the implicit cost of the money I put into the business.

For both of these reasons, accountants do not record the implicit costs associated with resources supplied to the business by its owners. This could cause accounting statements to be misleading for some unwary readers. For example, two businesses which were run in exactly the same way would report different costs (and net income) if one owner hired a manager while the other worked as his own manager, or if one owner put his own money into the business while the other borrowed the money from a bank. The owner who hired his manager and borrowed his money would have higher costs (and lower net income) according to the accountant's books, but that is due to the fact that his managerial and interest costs are *explicit* and appear on the books, whereas the other owner's costs are *implicit* and thus not recorded in the books.

Profits—Accounting and Economic

We have said that the accountant's books systematically exclude the implicit costs associated with the resources supplied to the business by its owners. Ignoring those costs, and after subtracting other costs (those associated with purchased or rented inputs) from revenue, the accountant arrives at a figure which we call *net income*. (It is *net* income because the costs of purchased inputs have been subtracted from revenue.) This tells how well the owners did in an absolute sense—how much income the owners of the firm made. As we have said, this is useful to the tax collector and others who want to know how much the owners made. But it is *not* the number we want if we want to know whether the owners put their resources to the *best* (most rewarding) use. For that we want to know whether those resources made more in this activity than they would have in their best alternative use. In other words, for that purpose, we want to subtract as an *implicit cost* what the owners' resources would have been able to make in their best alternative use and calculate a true *net* return over and above the best alternative return. Economists call that net return *profit*. Unfortunately, the net income figure which accountants report is also popularly called *profit*. Since the two concepts are quite different— the one referring to *absolute* income and the other referring to the *excess* income over and above the best alternative—we should have different terms for the different concepts. For the remainder of this book, we shall use the term *profit* to refer to the economist's concept of return over and above the best alternative. Occasionally, to emphasize this meaning, we may call it *economic profit*. When we want to refer to the accountant's concept of return to owners after subtracting the costs of purchased or rented inputs, we shall use the terms *net income* or *accounting profit*.

One feature of our definition which you should keep in mind is that when we say (as we shall) that a firm is "earning zero (economic) profits" or "just breaking even," we do not mean that the firm's owners are doing badly. On the contrary, they may be earning a lot—reporting a high net income and paying a lot of taxes. What we mean is that they are doing just as well as (no better and no worse than) they could do in their best alternative occupation or employment.

Accounting and Economic Costs—Further Distinctions

Another difference between accountants and economists in regard to the treatment of costs is that in making up income statements and balance sheets, accountants tend to look at historical outlays, whereas economists are forward-looking; their emphasis is on decision making, given the alternatives facing the business at the time the decision is to be made. This difference is especially evident in the evaluation of the value of the business' plant and equipment. Recall that the major components of continued possession cost are (1) the interest that could be earned on the money which could be obtained if the asset were sold, and (2) the anticipated decrease in the market value of the asset over the period of time being considered. The first component is an implicit cost. We have already noted that implicit costs are not counted by the accountant. Moreover, the foregone interest cost is based on the *current* market price of the asset. If that price is very low, then the interest foregone due to holding onto the asset will be very low. For example, suppose I buy a machine for $1 million and one year later, due to the appearance of a superior machine, the most I can get for my machine is $200,000. The foregone interest due to holding onto it is based on the $200,000 current value, and the $1 million original purchase price is irrelevant. It is a *sunk* loss and cannot be retrieved. Even if accountants were allowed to count foregone interest as a cost, the rules of accounting make it difficult to write down the value of assets in this way.

The second component of continued possession cost is the anticipated depreciation of the asset in the future period being considered. True depreciation is a real cost of continuing to possess an asset. It represents alternatives foreclosed: If I could sell a machine for $100,000 today, but only $90,000 in one year, then I will forego the opportunity of having that extra $10,000 if I hold onto the asset for a year. For this reason, true anticipated depreciation would be included in the costs which an economist would calculate. Depreciation is also reported as a cost expense by accountants. But the concept as used in financial statements is intimately connected with the calculation of taxable income. As such it is subject to various rules regarding the amount of depreciation which can be claimed in a given year, and these rules have little relationship to the actual decrease in the market value of the asset which is expected to occur. The allowable depreciation might be much higher than true depreciation in the early years, and much lower than true depreciation in later years.

Thus, the costs included in financial statements issued by accountants differ from those which an economist acknowledges in several different ways. The former are backward-looking, while the latter are forward-looking. The former do not include implicit costs, while the latter do. And the former treat depreciation in an arbitrary way, dictated by tax policy, whereas the latter conceive of depreciation as dependent on current and anticipated future *market prices*.

An economist considers two distinct types of depreciation—time depreciation and wear-and-tear depreciation. The former refers to the decrease in the market value of an asset merely because of the passage of time. It has nothing to do with the use of the asset. Time depreciation is included in continued possession costs. Wear-and-tear depreciation is a decline in market value due to the use and wearing-out of the asset. Since this latter kind of depreciation is avoidable simply by not using the asset, even though possession of the asset is maintained, it is included in operating costs. While this distinction is clear analytically, it is very difficult to measure in any actual firm. Accountants simply ignore the distinction.

140   PROFIT VERSUS MARKUP

We have already compared economic profit with accounting profit (net income) and found that both are useful, although we prefer to reserve the word *profit* for the former, since part of accounting profit is not actually excess over and above costs but rather payment for implicit costs. A much more serious confusion arises when people use the word *profit* to describe *markup*—that is, the difference between what one pays for an item and what one sells it for. A store may pay $300 for a TV and sell it for $390, a 30 percent markup, sometimes referred to as a 30 percent profit. This meaning of profit is misleading because it has almost no relation to the economist's meaning of return *over and above costs*. The price paid for the TV is only part of the cost incurred by the dealer, and using the word *profit* to describe the markup presents an entirely different meaning from the one economists (and accountants) have in mind.

LOOKING AHEAD

Chapter 6 deals with the business firm—why there are firms, what types of firms exist, and what types of markets they operate in. Chapter 6 lays the groundwork for the more specific discussions of the various types of markets, which come in chapters 7, 8 and 10.

POINTS TO REMEMBER

1. Costs are not usually the same as outlays because firms often own some of their inputs.

2. Acquisition cost is lower when the item being bought is more standardized and is more frequently traded. It can be avoided only by not acquiring the asset.

3. Continued possession cost is the cost an owner incurs if she decides to continue to own the asset for some specified period of time. It can be avoided by not continuing to possess the asset.

4. Operating costs are all costs other than acquisition and possession costs. They can be avoided by not operating the business, and they may change when output changes.

5. When making a decision, only costs which change if the decision is made are relevant for the decision. In other words, only avoidable costs are of interest.

6. Once a project is begun the avoidable costs are always less than the total cost, so it is often rational to continue and finish projects which should not have been started in the first place.

7. Acquisition costs are generally rather small relative to total costs for ordinary business firms, but they can be very large for government projects because the assets in such projects have very poor alternative uses.

8. For any set-up firm, the avoidable costs are the possession and operating costs.

9. Possession costs can be avoided only by getting out of business, and they do not depend on how much output is being produced, so they are called *fixed costs*.

10. Average fixed cost (AFC), or fixed cost per unit of output, always falls as more output is produced.

11. Operating cost, since it is avoidable by stopping production and since it varies with output, is called *variable cost*.

12. Average variable cost (AVC), or variable cost per unit of output, usually falls and then rises as output rises.

13. The sum of average fixed cost and average variable cost is referred to as average total cost (ATC), or total cost per unit of output.

14. In making decisions, one compares the incremental (increase in) cost due to the decision with the incremental revenue obtained thereby.

15. When the incremental cost is expressed on a per unit basis, it is called *marginal* cost. It is obtained by dividing the incremental cost by the change in output. Possession cost does not enter into the calculation of incremental or marginal cost, since possession cost is fixed with respect to output.

16. If marginal cost is above average variable cost or average total cost, average (variable or total) cost will be rising as output increases. If marginal cost is below average (variable or total) cost, average (variable or total) cost will be falling as output increases.

17. Economic costs differ from accounting costs in that (a) the former are forward-looking, while the latter are based on historical transactions; (b) the former include implicit costs (especially the implicit costs associated with provision of inputs by the owners of the firm), while the latter do not, and (c) the former base depreciation on actual (or anticipated) decreases in the market value of assets, whereas the latter base depreciation on certain formulas having little to do with actual market values.

18. If a firm is receiving revenue greater than the sum of all its costs, it is making an (economic) profit.

19. If a firm is receiving revenue greater than the sum of all of the costs which accountants consider, it is making an accounting profit or positive net revenue.

20. A firm could be making positive net revenue but zero (economic) profit, in which case the owners of the firm are earning exactly as much net income with their resources as they could in their best alternative use.

21. Markup is the difference between the price of output and the cost of some particular purchased input. Therefore, it differs substantially in concept from either economic or accounting profit and is always larger than both.

KEY TERMS

Accounting cost: The costs that accountants are permitted to consider. These differ from economic costs in that they do not include implicit costs and they include depreciation in arbitrary ways.

Accounting profit: The difference between the total revenue a firm obtains and accounting cost.

Acquisition cost: The difference between the purchase price of an asset and its immediate resale price.

Average fixed cost: Fixed cost per unit of output. Fixed cost divided by the quantity produced.

Average total cost: Total cost per unit of output. Total cost divided by the quantity produced.

Average variable cost: Variable cost per unit of output. Variable cost divided by the quantity produced.

Fixed cost: Cost which does not vary with output and which, for certain decisions (such as changes in output while remaining in business), cannot be avoided. For the already set-up firm, fixed cost corresponds to possession cost.

Incremental cost: The change in total cost when the decision maker takes some action (such as increasing the quantity of output produced).

Marginal cost: The change in total cost (or change in variable cost, since fixed cost by definition does not change) per additional unit of output produced. The change in total cost divided by the change in output. More precisely, marginal cost is the change in total cost resulting when there is a change of one unit of output produced.

Markup: The difference between the price of output and the wholesale price of some key input.

Operating cost: Cost other than acquisition and possession cost. This cost is incurred only if the asset is used during the period in question.

Possession cost: The decrease in the resale price of the asset over the period in question, plus the amount of interest which could be earned on the initial resale price, plus any taxes and insurance.

Profit: (economic profit.) The difference between the total revenue the firm obtains and its total costs.

Sunk cost: Cost which has already been incurred and cannot be avoided by taking any further action. Unavoidable cost.

Total cost: The sum of fixed and variable costs.

Variable cost: Cost which varies with output. This corresponds to operating cost.

REVIEW QUESTIONS

1. You have just bought a building to use for your car dealership. There is a large sign used by the previous owner to advertise the name of the business. You could modify the old sign by having your firm's name painted on it for $100. Alternatively, you could buy a new sign with a more pleasing design for $500. Does this mean you should modify the old sign? Under what circumstances might you decide to buy the new sign? (Hint: What about (a) the relative abilities of the signs to attract customers and (b) the resale value of the old sign?)

2. The Alaskan pipeline was built by the companies taking oil out of Alaska, with the expectation that it would be a good investment (that is, that the difference between the price of oil in the "lower 48" and the cost of getting the oil out of the ground and shipping it to market would be great enough, over a period of time, to cover the several billion dollar investment). Suppose that, after the pipeline is built, the price of oil falls to (say) $6 per barrel and that, had that price been anticipated, the pipeline would never have been built. What would you expect to happen to the pipeline? What is the possession cost associated with the pipeline? What was the acquisition cost?

3. Johnny Bench is batting .250 (75 hits in 300 at bats) going into a crucial four-game series. His performance in the four games is shown below. (Fill in the blanks.)

Game	At Bats	Hits	Game Average	Season Average
1	5	2	_____	_____
2	3	1	_____	_____
3	4	0	_____	_____
4	4	1	_____	_____

Which column corresponds to the incremental hits? Which column corresponds to marginal batting productivity? Does this series of numbers behave according to the general rule relating averages and marginals?

4. "When marginal cost is rising, average cost is rising." Explain why this is not true.

5. "When average cost is rising, marginal cost is rising." Can you imagine a case where this would not be true?

6. Fill in the blanks below.

Q	FC	VC	AFC	AVC	ATC		MC
1	10	5	___	___	___		
2	10	7	___	___	___	>	___
3	10	8	___	___	___	>	___
4	10	10	___	___	___	>	___
5	10	14	___	___	___	>	___
6	10	20	___	___	___	>	___
7	10	28	___	___	___	>	___
8	10	38	___	___	___	>	___
9	10	50	___	___	___	>	___
10	10	65	___	___	___	>	___

(a) Do the marginal cost and average variable cost obey the rule of averages and marginals? Do the marginal cost and average total cost? Why do marginal cost and average fixed cost not obey the rule? (b) Why does the lowest value of average variable cost occur at a smaller output than the lowest value of average total cost?

7. Fill in the variable costs and marginal costs (refer to table 5-2).

Q	AFC	VC	AVC	ATC		MC
25	40.00	___	9.00	49.00		
50	20.00	___	8.00	28.00	>	___
100	10.00	___	7.00	17.00	>	___
200	5.00	___	5.00	10.00	>	___
250	4.00	___	4.80	8.80	>	___
400	2.50	___	5.00	7.50	>	___
425	2.35	___	5.13	7.48	>	___
450	2.22	___	5.38	7.60	>	___

8. Suppose a firm finds that the output per worker is related to the number of workers as shown below:

Number of Workers	Output per Worker	Total Output	Labor Cost per Unit of Output
1	10	_____	_____
2	15	_____	_____
3	13	_____	_____
4	11	_____	_____
5	9	_____	_____

(a) Is this relationship consistent with that assumed in this chapter? (b) Assume the wage rate is $10 per worker, and fill in the numbers for the other two columns. (c) As the output per worker rises, what happens to the labor cost per unit of output (approximately equal to average variable cost)? (d) As the output per worker falls, what happens to the labor cost per unit of output?

9. For question 8: (a) How much does the output go up when the second worker is hired? The third? The fourth? The fifth? (b) For the increased output due to hiring the second worker, what is the incremental cost incurred? What is the marginal cost of output over that range? (c) Answer (a) and (b) for the increments in output due to hiring the third, fourth, and fifth workers. (d) Now insert these numbers in a column alongside the average variable cost ("Labor Cost per Unit of Output") column in question 8. Does the relationship between marginal cost and average obey the general rule for average marginal relationships?

10. You are considering starting a boat excursion business on Lake Tahoe. You will have to pay $53,000 for your boat, and you could resell it immediately for $50,000. You estimate that in one year, you could sell it for $46,000 if it were not used during that time. If you did not put the $53,000 into the boat, you could earn 10 percent interest by investing in bonds. Your operating cost per day of operation is $50 (including use-related depreciation, fuel, labor costs, maintenance, and so on). Suppose that one hundred days out of the year you expect to obtain $200/day revenue; another hundred days you expect to get $75/day revenue; the third hundred days you expect to get $20/day revenue; the remaining days you expect to get no revenue. Should you buy the boat and operate it for one year? If you do, how many days per year should you operate it? Explain.

11. For question 10: Suppose that on the basis of the cost and revenue projections we used, you buy the boat. Then, after having bought it, you discover that the revenue you can expect has fallen to $160 per day for the best hundred days, $40 per day on the next hundred days, and $15 per day for the third hundred. Should you keep the boat, or sell it? If you keep it, how many days per year should you operate it? Explain.

12. Suppose you own a house on which you make a certain mortgage payment each month; you also pay property taxes, insurance, water bills, and so on. You have just been transferred to another part of the country for one year. You are considering leasing your house for the year. What is the minimum amount you would accept per month to lease it out? Explain how you would arrive at your answer and what additional information might bear on your decision.

13. Dr. Gums and Dr. Root have just purchased X-ray units for the dental office for $20,000 each. The immediate resale price of each unit is $18,000. Each unit is expected to be salable for $15,000 at the end of one year. Dr. Gums paid cash for his machine, whereas Dr. Root took out a loan. Does this fact influence the size of the continued possession cost for the two dentists?

14. Call a real estate broker and ask what it would cost if you bought a $70,000 house and immediately resold it—that is, what would be the cost of the broker's fee, loan fee, title search, and other fees that must be paid in the purchase of a house? Is this a measure of the acquisition cost for a house?

15. Suppose it was discovered that the BART right of way could, for a cost of $100 million, be paved over with asphalt for use by buses. Would the existence of that alternative increase the cost of maintaining BART as it is? What other information would you need in order to decide whether to convert BART to a bus system?

16. Suppose you recently made a confection which called for one cup of buttermilk. The smallest container of buttermilk you could find was one pint (two cups). Having made it, you have one cup of buttermilk left. You do not like to drink buttermilk, but there is another dessert you could make which would use up your remaining cup. Suppose the pint of buttermilk originally cost 50¢, and the other ingredients in your product and your time cost $2.50. The value you place on the dessert is $2.80. (a) Should you use the buttermilk to make this dessert, or should you throw it out? (b) Would your answer change if the value you placed on the dessert were $2.60? $2.40? (c) If the dessert's value to you were $2.60 and you did not have the buttermilk, how much would you be willing to pay to get it? (d) Is this amount similar to the marginal value that a firm places on labor or some other input? Explain.

17. If your adjusted gross income (AGI) (for a married couple, filing jointly, with no children) were $25,000 in 1979, you would pay $3135 in federal income tax (assuming you took the standard deduction). (a) What is your average rate of tax (that is, the tax as a percentage of your AGI)? (b) If your AGI were $25,100, your tax would rise to $3159. What is the incremental tax? What is the *marginal* rate of tax? What is the new average rate of tax? (c) Does the tax schedule conform to the rule regarding averages and marginals?

18. If your California adjusted gross income (AGI) (for a married couple, filing jointly, with no children) were $25,000 in 1979, you would pay $766 in California state income tax (assuming you took the standard deduction). (a) What is your *average* rate of tax (that is, the tax as a percentage of your AGI)? (b) If your AGI were $25,100, your tax would rise to $773. What is the incremental tax? What is the *marginal* rate of tax? What is the new average rate of tax? (c) Does the tax schedule conform to the rule regarding averages and marginals?

19. Suppose figure 5-2 represents the costs for a firm that is already in business. (a) How high would the price have to be in order to induce that firm to remain in business? (b) Suppose the price is just that high. Would that price be sufficient to induce a new firm to enter the business if the new firm's continued possession and operating costs were identical to those of the firm pictured in figure 5-2? Explain. (c) How much higher would the price have to be to induce the new firm to enter? (d) What is the role of acquisition cost in your answer?

20. Under current (1980) Department of Energy price control rules, the maximum price gasoline retailers are allowed to charge for a gallon of gasoline is an amount equal to the wholesale price (the price the dealer pays the refiner) plus taxes, plus 16¢ per gallon. In newspaper and television reports, the 16¢ is often called the dealer's allowable *profit*. Is it profit? Explain.

21. The *Wall Street Journal* reported that Oregon was offering mortgages to qualified veterans at the interest rate of 5.9 percent, and was "making a profit" on them.[2] This was alleged to be true even though the interest paid on state (tax exempt) bonds, from which the money to make such loans is received, was running at 8 percent or so. The reason was that "most of Oregon's outstanding bonds were sold at interest rates well below the current loan rate (of 5.9 percent). . . . As a result, the composite bond cost is only 5.84 percent, low enough to make a profit on 5.9 percent mortgages."

(a) What do you think of Oregon's notion of cost and profit? (b) If you were a private money lender and had arranged a line of credit for yourself at 5.84 percent at a time when you could lend all you wanted at 13 percent, what would you do? Would that be *gouging* or *profiteering*? What do those terms mean? Would you think that you had a profit if you lent the money at 5.9 percent? (c) Do you think there was a shortage of 5.9 percent mortgages in Oregon in 1980? How do you think the scarce mortgage money was allocated during that period? Do you think that is fairer than letting the customers

2. *Wall Street Journal*, 9 May 1980.

bid up the rate to 12 or 13 percent? (d) If you were the government officials in Oregon, what would you charge and how would you allocate the mortgages?

22. Several years ago, if you had arranged to acquire some crude oil today for a price of $10/barrel, and the current price of crude in transactions made today was $30/barrel, would you consider that you would have made a profit if you sold the oil just obtained for $11? If not, what meaning of cost are you using? Would your accountant report a positive net income for you if you were reporting to the IRS?

chapter 6

The
Firm

Why do firms exist? This question may never have occurred to you. It is almost like asking, "Why are there cities?" One is so taken aback by the question that he hardly knows where to begin. First of all, what do we mean by firms? For our purposes, firms are organizations of people engaged in production. Firms have several outstanding features. After discussing the characteristics of firms, we shall examine the market conditions which various firms face and discuss the meanings of two important words: competition and monopoly.

THE CHARACTERISTICS
OF FIRMS

First, firms are characterized by having owners, managers or bosses, and employees. The owners tell the others what to do. The firm is not simply a collection of individuals working in close proximity, each of whom independently chooses what to do and contracts with others. Rather, there is some central direction, with many actions taken simply because of orders from "the boss." Second, there are many aspects of team action in firms. With teams, it is sometimes difficult to determine the exact contribution of each team member. Moreover, together the team can produce more than the total of what is produced when each member acts separately. A third feature of firms is that the owners (and often the managers) are

ASPECTS OF THE FIRM

1. CENTRAL DIRECTION

2. HARD TO DETERMINE INDIVIDUAL CONTRIBUTION

3. GET MORE DONE AS A TEAM

4. MANAGERS ARE RESIDUAL CLAIMANTS

151

residual claimants to the earnings of the enterprise. The employees are paid directly for their time or output, while the owners get the (positive or negative) difference between what must be paid to suppliers of resources and the revenue collected from customers.

A theory for the existence of firms must deal with each of these features.[1] The basic reason for the existence of firms is that firms reduce the cost of getting things done. But that begs a question. How do they do it? It is conceivable that goods could be produced by means of separate, individually operating people. For example, cars could be produced by having many independent operators perform the separate operations on the parts going into the car—one person would buy pieces of sheet metal and bend them in a certain way, then sell them to another person, who would drill holes in the pieces, and so on. What we want to know is, how can firms reduce costs below what they would be with this type of totally independent organization? Two cost-reducing features of firms are apparent.

Teams, Shirkers, and Monitors

First, team activity is often more productive than individual activity. Two furniture movers lifting together can lift more than the sum of what they can lift separately. Similar examples of the advantage of combining efforts can be found throughout life. But while it is true that a team can produce more than the separate members, there is a problem. It is difficult to measure the contribution of each member to the team output. If a team member decided to "slough off" or "shirk" in his efforts, the resulting fall in output will not be traced directly and completely to him. The loss will thus be shared by all team members. The shirker will not bear the whole cost of his action. Since this is the case, each person tends to shirk more than he would if he bore the whole cost. (This is simply an application of the first Law of Demand. The lower the cost to the shirker, the more he will shirk.) Because of this shirking phenomenon, it pays to have someone monitor the behavior of the members of the team since it is largely by observing a team member's input of effort that one can evaluate his contribution to the team. Then, who should monitor the monitor? This problem can be resolved by giving the monitor a residual claim to earnings, since the more successful he is at monitoring, the greater those residual (leftover) earnings will be. This explains why we have a boss-employee relationship, and why managers often receive a portion of the residual earnings of firms.

As an example, suppose twenty people get together to form a grocery store. The jobs include buying, bookkeeping, and selling. Twenty people getting together to perform those jobs may be able to do better than if each

1. This section draws heavily on the analysis presented in: A. A. Alchian and H. Demsetz, "Production, Information Costs, and Economic Organization," *The American Economic Review* 62 (December 1972): 777-95. The same material is treated at the intermediate level in: C. W. Baird, *Prices and Markets: Microeconomics* (St. Paul: West Publishing Co., 1975).

WHY DO FIRMS EXIST?
1. TEAM PRODUCTION
2. OUTPUT MARKET TRANSACTIONS ARE COSTLY
   (IT'S HARD TO MEASURE INDIVIDUAL OUTPUT)
   VERTICAL INTEGRATION
3. RISKS AND INCENTIVES
   RESIDUAL CLAIMANTS

2/26

worked separately. Suppose the twenty people decide to split the returns according to a formula, based perhaps on what each person could make elsewhere. Now, if the person doing the checkout shirks by being surly with the customers or slow in ringing up purchases, this will cost the team money. Suppose the activity results in reduced net revenue of $100 per week. Then, on the average, *each* member suffers a $5 reduction in net return. The perpetrator bears only one-twentieth (on the average) of the cost of his action. If each person ran his own operation, the shirker would bear the full cost of his action. Thus the shirker will shirk more in the team environment than in a one-man operation. (But, of course, even with less shirking, he could still make less on his own.) This gives rise to the benefits of having a "monitor" or boss, whose job it is to detect and discourage shirking. To encourage the monitor to do his job, the persons involved may agree to being paid some specified amount for performing specified jobs and letting the monitor keep the difference between revenues and outlays. Each person has at least as much interest in shirking as before, but the fact that he may be discovered and fired for too much of it leads him to shirk less than he would in the straight team situation with no monitor.

Specialization in Risk-Bearing

Second, firms are often characterized by specialization in the bearing of risk. The general principle of comparative advantage says that costs are reduced by having the person who has the lowest asking price perform whatever service has to be performed. A person's asking price reflects in part the person's cost of performing the activity (that is, the benefits he would forego if he performed that activity). It may also reflect the person's preferences for engaging in the activity). When we talk about investing in a business, the question of risk immediately arises. The owner of a firm (the residual claimant) inevitably bears risk. Since risk is not something which people desire for its own sake, they must be induced to bear it. The greater the risk involved in an activity, the larger the expected payoff must be in order to get people to take part in it. But different people have different aversions to the risk involved in investing in a company. (Partly this is a reflection of the size of the investment relative to a person's wealth. If your life savings amount to $10,000 and you are asked to invest it in a firm, you may view the investment as much riskier than if your life savings were $100,000 and you were asked to invest $10,000.) In other words, people differ in the expected payoff which they would require to get them to invest in a business (become an owner). The costs will be lower if those with the lowest asking price (least risk aversion) are tapped. Managers of firms are not necessarily those with the comparative advantage in bearing risk. Or, putting it the other way around, those with a willingness to invest in a business may not have a comparative advantage in managing the business. They may prefer to buy that service rather than to do it them-selves. This "separation of ownership from control" may lead to some problems of its own. If the managers own none, or only a small portion, of the firm, then they will be less likely to act as effective monitors. There are tradeoffs involved here. The cost savings in raising capital, which separation of ownership from control brings, must be weighed against the less rigorous management which tends to occur as managers own less of the company.

This can be seen in the context of the example. Suppose the person chosen as the boss or monitor cannot or does not want to put up his own money for the operation. (In other words, his asking price, in terms of expected return on investment, is so high that other alternative sources of funds are preferable.) Then the firm might sell stock to investors who will have no direct hand in the day-to-day operation of the firm. Here is where the comparative advantage in ownership versus management comes in. The fact that the manager is now only a part-owner means that he now has more of an incentive to shirk in his monitoring job, because he bears only a portion of the cost. This leads to the problem of the separation of ownership from control, a topic on which we shall postpone serious discussion until chapter 9, where we introduce "present values" and discounting of future revenues and outlays.

Firms and Exchange

These remarks on the nature of firms cannot do justice to the topic. Our main point here is that firms exist to help facilitate the specialization and exchange processes which are indicated by the preferences of transactors and by the technology of the economy in question. The organization of firms involves the application of those very principles of comparative advantage and exchange we discussed before. They help people put their resources to higher-valued uses.

In chapters 2 and 4, we said that middlemen have a comparative advantage in performing the services of storing, displaying, and transporting goods, as well as in bearing risk. We can see that most middlemen are firms by the definition we have developed here. Furthermore, most of what firms do can be seen to be middleman's services. Middlemen basically perform the entrepreneurial function of moving goods from lower-valued to higher-valued uses. Firms typically try to take a collection of inputs and transform them into goods whose value is greater than the sum of the separate inputs used. Thus firms are formed to try to move resources from lower-valued to higher-valued uses. Thus firms are middlemen.

FACTORIES VERSUS THE "PUTTING OUT" SYSTEM

Some dramatic changes in the way business has been carried out over time can be understood in the light of the theory presented here. An example is the emergence of the factory system and the consequent decline of the "putting out" system of weaving in England in the late eighteenth and early nineteenth centuries. Under the putting out system, production was dispersed in many cottages. For example, weavers would work in their homes; middlemen would bring the thread to a weaver and pick up the finished product after the weaver had done his work; then the product would be sold to final consumers.

When methods of harnessing large power sources (such as falling water) were found, it became possible to do the work of weaving much more rapidly by means of machines connected to the centralized power sources. But this new method of weaving involved *team production*. Several workers might work with the same large machine and cooperate directly in the same productive activity. Under the putting out system it was very easy for an external observer to determine the marginal product of any worker. The middleman simply examined the output to determine whether it was done correctly, and he knew who had done what. In the new system, that determination was more difficult. Thus there was an economic rationale for utilizing a monitor to measure, observe, and organize production. Production in the new system was, in other words, organized in *firms* rather than, as under the putting out system, through separate production and exchange among dispersed individuals.[2]

TYPES OF FIRMS

[handwritten in right margin]
3/3
FORMS OF OWNERSHIP
1. PROPRIETORSHIP
2. PARTNERSHIP
3. CORPORATION
 - LIMITED LIABILITY
 - LEGAL ENTITY
 - DOUBLE TAXATION
 - TRANSFERABLE, DIVISIBLE OWNERSHIP RIGHTS (STOCKS)

There are three major types of profit-seeking firms—proprietorships, partnerships, and corporations. The first two have approximately the same legal status, but they differ in the number of owners. Proprietorships have only one owner, while partnerships have more than one. The important characteristics of proprietorships and partnerships are that the owners (or owner) are liable, to an unlimited extent, for debts or judgments against the business, and that the businesses themselves are not taxed; only the income going to the owners is subject to income taxes. On the other hand, corporations have a different legal status in both respects. The corporation is considered to be a legal "person" and pays taxes on its income before anything is distributed to owners. Thus if a proprietorship and a corporation are identical in every other respect, the corporation and its owners will pay more taxes than the proprietorship. The other feature of the corporation is its provision for limited liability. Although the corporation is fully liable for all of *its* debts, the owners are liable only up to the amount they put into the company. That is, if the company goes bankrupt, they lose what they put into the stock; but their other assets cannot be seized to pay the debts of the corporation. (This is contrary to the case of proprietorships and partnerships.) This limited liability feature is crucial because, although it makes the firm a worse credit risk for any given financial situation, owners are much more willing to put up money; so corporations are able to raise much more money for ventures than proprietorships or partnerships can raise.

2. This example is taken from Alchian and Demsetz, "Production, Information Costs, and Economic Organization."

156

Most of the firms in the U.S. economy are proprietorships, but most of the output comes from corporations. Much of the analysis which follows does not consider the legal status of the firm. Where differences in behavior exist, we shall try to point out how the firm's legal status plays a role.

TYPES OF MARKETS

In everyday accounts of economic events, as well as in the literature of professional economists, two words often appear in describing the market structure which prevails in the selling of commodities. The words are *monopoly* and *competition*. Whenever two words are used as often as these two are, a great many meanings are bound to be attached to them. This is true within the economics profession as well as the popular press. Competition is good and monopoly is bad in the eyes of most people, including economists. But what kinds of behavior are competitive and which are monopolistic? In other words, how do we know whether to call a market competitive or monopolistic?

MEANINGS OF COMPETITION

In everyday language we often use the word competition to denote a striving to get ahead, as in a race. There are connotations of trying to be the first to do something, or do something better than others, as in athletic competition. It is the striving to be first or better than one's *rivals* which conveys the flavor of the word.

While the everyday use of competition emphasizes the striving against rivals, the usual economic meaning of competition emphasizes the *impersonal* nature of the market process whereby, for example, a potential buyer of a commodity solicits "competing" bids. The idea here is that, with a fairly large number of bidders in the game, the bidders will act independently, the bids will reflect the true costs of the operation, and the buyer can choose the lowest-cost producer of the service and get the lowest price.

This general approach has led to an idealization of this impersonal, independent aspect of the competitive process into what is known variously as "perfect" or "pure" competition. This approach examines all of the conditions which ensure that the lowest cost producers supply the good, and that consumers pay the lowest price consistent with the cost, and declares those conditions to constitute perfect (or pure) competition. The conditions are that there be a large number of independent sellers of substantially identical products, and that consumers and suppliers have all relevant information regarding offers to buy and sell by people in the market.

The last condition, complete information, has been attacked as illegiti-

[handwritten margin note:]
CONDITIONS FOR PERFECT (OR PURE) COMPETITION

1. LARGE NUMBER OF INDEPENDENT SELLERS
2. SELLING THE SAME PRODUCT
3. CONSUMERS AND SELLERS ARE AWARE OF ALL OFFERS TO BUY & SELL (CHEAP INFORMATION)

mate by some critics, because it takes one of the *results* of the competitive process and states it as a precondition for competition to exist. The reasoning of the critics goes like this: Information on whose costs and values are what is not given like manna from heaven. It has to be discovered, and the process of transactors' comparing offers *generates* that information as a byproduct. When the competitive exchange process has run its course, that information will be known, but it cannot and should not be assumed as a precondition in order for the process to be deemed competitive.[3]

In a market with a large number of independent sellers of (roughly) identical products (for example, the market for bread and the market for canned vegetables), no individual seller has any significant influence on the market price of the good she is selling. A market in which this is true is called, appropriately enough, a *price-taker's market*. We shall analyze the features and implications of such a market structure in chapter 7. It is a very simplified model of what economists sometimes mean by a *competitive market*.

Although we shall call a price-taker market a competitive market, other types of market arrangement are competitive also. The key feature in these versions is the struggle against rivals. If information is costly, firms won't always know what values consumers would place on various products (especially those not yet produced). Competition then often takes the form of putting out a new product and hoping that consumers place a value on it which is higher than its cost, and that other (competing) firms don't catch on until the firm in question has had a chance to get a little gravy. For example, in the late 1970s in the auto industry, the big guessing game was to decide just how small and how gas saving the consumers wanted their cars to be. The U.S. firms generally lost out because they did not correctly forecast the big increases in gasoline prices that occurred in 1979, and the consequent switch to smaller cars. The result was record losses for U.S. producers and large profits for the Japanese manufacturers. It is the striving by rivals to produce the commodities most highly valued by consumers (relative to cost because that is most profitable) which generates the benefit of competition, as viewed by consumers. This benefit is the consumer's ability to choose among alternative suppliers which are good substitutes for each other. The *results* of this competitive process are similar to those of the simplified price-taker model—namely, that only the goods consumers are willing to pay for survive; that the price paid approaches the cost of production, and that only the lowest-cost producers tend to survive. Thus, while the formal conditions for the price-taker model are not met in the aluminum industry, we can, for some issues, safely use the price-taker model to analyze the aluminum industry, because the predictions of more realistic (and more complicated) models would not be substantially different from those of the price-taker model.

---

3. For a thorough discussion of this view of competition, see F. A. Hayek, "Competition as a Discovery Procedure," in *New Studies in Philosophy, Politics, Economics and the History of Ideas* (Chicago: University of Chicago Press, 1978).

TABLE 6-1
FOUR-FIRM CONCENTRATION RATIOS IN
VARIOUS INDUSTRIES

Industry	Ratio
Motor vehicles	0.93
Tires and inner tubes	0.73
Aircraft production	0.66
Soap and detergents	0.62
Motor vehicle parts	0.61
Electronic computing	0.51
Toilet preparations	0.38
Petroleum refining	0.31
Baking	0.29
Meatpacking plants	0.22
Bottled and canned soft drinks	0.14
Commercial printing	0.04

Source: *Statistical Abstract of the United States* (Washington, D.C.:
Government Printing Office, 1979), pp. 813 – 14.

COMPETITION AND CONCENTRATION

Economists often try to measure the concentration of an industry's output and sales in the hands of a few firms. Although there are many measures of the degree of concentration, one of the most common is the "four-firm concentration ratio," which adds up the output accounted for by the four largest firms in an industry and divides it by the total industry output, giving the fraction of total output accounted for by the top four firms. Some examples of four-firm concentration ratios are given in table 6-1.

Such measures of concentration are sometimes used by careless analysts to give a ranking of the competitiveness of various industries—the higher the concentration ratio, the less competitive. There is some validity to this idea, because the smaller the number of firms, the greater the probability that they will be able to collude successfully to hold prices up.

But it is very misleading to say that a small group of firms (or a highly concentrated industry) is less competitive than a large group. The *form* of competition is quite different at times—more personal and rivalrous with the concentrated industry—but, in the absence of collusion, it is still in every respect competitive, and we do ourselves a disservice to speak otherwise.

MEANINGS OF MONOPOLY

As *competition* has many meanings, so does *monopoly*. The word *monopoly* comes from Greek roots meaning "single seller," a widely used meaning of the word. The difficulty with this definition is that it is so vague as to have almost no content at all. For the term to have meaning, we must know what commodity we are talking about. Take the example of Alcoa prior to the 1940s. Alcoa produced 100 percent of the virgin aluminum produced in the United States. So if we define the commodity as virgin aluminum ingots produced in the United States, Alcoa was a single seller. But other U.S. firms produced recycled aluminum. So if we define the commodity as aluminum ingot production, Alcoa was not a single seller (monopoly). If we define the commodity as "metals," then clearly steel and other metals enter in, and Alcoa is only one of many sellers. If we go further and consider the commodity as building or construction materials, we have to consider wood and plastic in addition to aluminum and other metals, so Alcoa is only one of a very large number of sellers. If we define the commodity broadly enough, no one is a "single seller."

Similarly, if we define the commodity narrowly enough, everyone is a single seller. Although no one cares too much about it, Farmer Jones is the only seller of "Farmer Jones' wheat." So one could interpret Farmer Jones as a monopolist in this sense. A definition which has this much ambiguity in its interpretation is not very useful. In spite of the difficulties, there is something appealing about the "single seller" idea. We shall see later that the appealing feature of this definition can be captured by more precise terms.

Closed Market

An old and useful meaning of *monopoly* refers to restrictions on the entry of new sellers. The first corporations were firms given the exclusive right to deal in certain commodities. Often the monarch would grant a subject the exclusive right to produce and sell salt. In some cases, of course, the exclusive franchise implied by the closed market idea comes close to the single seller idea. But even if there are many sellers, there may be elements of this type of monopoly if there are artificial restrictions on who can enter the market. There are a very large number of examples of this type of behavior: the exclusive franchise of the telephone company; the licensing of doctors, lawyers, teachers, barbers, mechanics, and others; tariffs and quotas in the international sphere. And there seem to be additional proposals every year, such as a recent proposal by some U.S. senators to license oil companies. We shall discuss in chapter 10 the implications of restricted entry on the allocation of resources.

[handwritten margin note:] TYPES OF CLOSED MARKET RESTRICTIONS 1. GRANTING EXCLUSIVE FRANCHISES 2. LICENSING 3. TARIFFS

Price-Searchers

A third meaning of monopoly, and one which probably is used more than any other by economists, refers to a seller who faces a significantly downward-sloping demand curve. We spoke about the *price-taker* firm, a firm which is unable to affect the market price of the commodity it sells and takes the price as given. In contrast, many firms (for example, GM and the telephone company) sell a large enough amount, relative to the market in which they operate, that they can affect the price of the items they sell. Another way of putting it is that this type of firm could raise its price and retain most of its sales. Since this type of firm does not take the price as given, it must choose the *best* price to charge. We refer to it as a *price-searcher firm*. We could also say that it "has some monopoly power"—in other words, it has some power to determine price. Since the word *monopoly* has so many meanings, we shall use the term *price-searcher* rather than *monopolist* to describe the situation in which a firm faces a downward-sloping demand for its product.

WHY PRICE-SEARCHERS?

The question arises as to why there are any markets with price-searchers. A related question is, why are there many firms in some industries and few in others? The answer, in the absence of any restrictions on entry, lies in the concept of "economies of scale." Economies of scale exist when the average cost of the firm's output falls as its scale of operation increases. We are referring here to a concept somewhat different from that encountered in chapter 5, where we discussed the possibility that, with the size of plant and machinery fixed, average cost might fall (up to a point) as the rate of output rose. Here we are talking about the behavior of average cost as output increases by allowing *all* inputs (including plant size and equipment) to change. If average cost falls while output rises within a certain range, economies of scale are said to exist in that range. When the output rate at which average cost begins to rise is reached, we say that economies of scale have been exhausted and further increases in size of operation would encounter *diseconomies* of scale. In any industry, firms will tend to become big enough to take advantage of the economies of scale which exist in producing the good in question, but not so big as to encounter diseconomies of scale. Thus the absolute size of the firm tends to be determined by the extent of economies of scale. Whether a firm is a price-searcher or a price-taker depends on how large the optimal size of the firm is, relative to the "size of the market"—that is, relative to the amount consumers want to buy. If average cost falls until a firm produces one-fourth of the total amount demanded, there will tend to be very few firms in the industry. An example of this situation is the auto industry and the aluminum industry. If average cost falls until output is one ten-thousandth of the total amount demanded, then rises, there will be a great many firms. Examples of these are the production of some agricultural products, such as wheat and corn. If one or a few firms tried to become a large fraction of the industry, they would find that they would have higher costs than, and could be underpriced by, smaller firms. Thus such large firms would tend to die out, and there would be many small firms. One special case of extreme economies of scale involves the situation in which average cost for a single firm would fall even if its output were increased so that it was larger than the total amount demanded by consumers. This case is called "natural monopoly" because the "natural" outcome of the competitive process will be a single firm producing the entire output, for example, the utility companies—telephone, water, and power. This state of affairs gives rise to special problems, discussed more fully in chapter 8.

What determines the extent of economies of scale? We don't know the complete answer to that, but it appears to have something to do with whether the commodity lends itself to standardized, mechanized production of large volume, and with the cost of controlling large enterprises. Some types of production processes apparently run into control problems at lower rates of output than others do.

Another reason for price-searchers is that there are some unique, nonduplicable resources. Examples are usually people, such as Kareem Abdul-Jabbar or Barbra Streisand. Streisand faces a downward-sloping demand for her services because her voice, personality, and talent cannot be duplicated. In fact, no very close substitutes have developed; if there were, she would not be able to raise her fees much above those of the alternatives without losing most of her contracts.

CRITERIA FOR JUDGING MARKET STRUCTURE

It might be useful at this point to summarize some of the points made about types of market organization. There are two basic criteria by which we judge markets. The first is whether there are legal barriers to entry. If they are not substantial (a retailer's license needed to operate in a given city would not be a substantial barrier to entry), we classify the industry as open. If there are substantial barriers to entry (such as the case of medical doctors, where a difficult to obtain license is needed to enter), then we classify the market as closed.

The second criterion is the presence or absence of significant market power, that is, the power to influence the price of the item one sells substantially. If the power exists, the firm is a price-searcher. If it does not exist to any significant degree, the firm is a price-taker.

FOUR CATEGORIES

A firm can be either a price-taker or a price-searcher and can operate either in an open or in a closed market. Thus a firm can fall into four categories: (1) open price-taker; (2) closed price-taker; (3) open price-searcher; (4) closed price-searcher.

Some Gray Areas

Which kinds of firms fall into which categories? There is some room for disagreement because both market power and barriers to entry are a matter of degree. Market power can range all the way from nil (most

[Handwritten margin notes:]

BASIS FOR JUDGING MARKETS

1. ARE THERE SUBSTANTIAL LEGAL BARRIERS TO ENTRY?
   - YES ⇒ CLOSED
   - NO ⇒ OPEN

2. DO YOU HAVE SIGNIFICANT MARKET POWER?
   - YES ⇒ PRICE SEARCHER
   - NO ⇒ PRICE TAKER

farmers) to extremely great (the telephone company). Where is the line to be drawn?

Furthermore, the ability of a firm to profitably raise its price above the level of other firms depends on one's time perspective. A firm which might be able to do so for a week or a month without losing substantial sales might find that, if it tried it for a year, dissemination of information on higher prices, as well as the emergence of other sellers, would greatly reduce its sales. (This is merely the Second Law of Demand in action, making the demand curve more elastic in the long run than in the short run.) Is such a firm able to raise its price successfully? Is it a price-searcher? It depends on one's perspective. We will argue that such a firm would have virtually no market power; thus it would be a price-taker.

Similarly, legal barriers to entry can be trivial (the local retailer's license) or substantial (the franchise of the telephone company, giving it the exclusive right to sell telephone services). Tariffs imposed on the import of foreign goods are a legal barrier to entry. They impose by law costs on foreigners that are higher than those imposed on domestic producers. Tariffs exist on a large number of manufactured products (and similar restrictions apply to many services because of immigration laws), but some are trivial and others are more substantial.

Open Price-Takers

The producers of most agricultural products (corn, soybeans, wheat) fall into this category. Providers of standard auto parts for car manufacturers and similar firms also fit here. Sellers of housing services (apartment building owners) also probably fit here. No apartment owner can raise his rent substantially above the going rate for that quality and keep his tenants for long. What about restaurants? They may fit in here also. Because of the ease of entry and closeness of the substitutes available, restaurants cannot keep the price above standard for long. What about oil refiners? They appear to have little if any influence on the selling price of their products. Perhaps they belong here too.

Closed Price-Takers

This category includes people like President Carter. His much publicized peanut farm can operate only because he has a peanut allotment—a piece of paper that gives him the right to grow peanuts on a specified number of acres. These allotments are licenses to produce, and they are strictly limited in number. In addition, peanut growing benefits from a tariff on imported peanuts. A similar state of affairs exists in tobacco production. Interstate trucking falls into this category, because Interstate Commerce Commission regulations restrict entry by prohibiting operation by any but licensed carriers. Other examples of closed price-takers are such licensed businesses as liquor stores, taxicabs, and doctors. The latter examples represent firms with very little if any long-term market power, although the entry restriction enables them to obtain a higher price for their goods.

Open Price-Searchers

This category includes such industries as auto manufacturing, aluminum production, and some pharmaceuticals, and some big name sports and entertainment figures (such as Jabbar and Streisand).

Closed Price-Searchers

This category includes such firms as the telephone company, the electric company, the gas company, airlines, and railroads, as well as holders of significant patents. The first three are public utilities, often called *natural monopolies*. We shall discuss them in more detail in chapter 8. Until very recently airlines were the beneficiaries of substantial protection, by the Civil Aeronautics Board, from the entry of other firms into the markets where they operated. Similarly, railroads and trucking companies have been protected from competition by Interstate Commerce Commission rules. In recent years, both of these restrictions have been lessened as moves toward "deregulation" have gained wide support. This will be discussed in more detail in chapter 10. For seventeen years after it invented color TV, RCA had the exclusive right to sell it because of a patent. Thus RCA was a closed-market price-searcher.

LOOKING AHEAD

This chapter has discussed the economic rationale for firms and introduced the major types of firms encountered. In discussing firms, the important distinctions are between price-takers and price-searchers on the one hand, and between closed and open markets on the other. The behavior of price-takers and price-searchers will be discussed in chapters 7 and 8, respectively. The importance of closed markets will be discussed in chapter 10.

POINTS TO REMEMBER

1. Firms are organizations of people engaged in production and having: (a) owners, managers, and other employees; (b) aspects of team behavior; (c) owners as residual claimants to the earnings of the firm.

2. Team activity gives rise to a tendency of team members to shirk in their assignments, which in turn gives rise to the monitor, who may be paid by being given rights to the residual earnings of the firm.

3. Firms permit specialization in risk bearing by having owners who are not directly involved in the day-to-day operation of the firm.

4. The three main types of firms are proprietorships, partnerships, and corporations.

5. A major question regarding firms is whether the markets in which they operate are monopolistic or competitive.

6. The term *competition* in economics usually refers to the impersonal market process of exchange in which there are sufficient numbers of buyers and sellers to ensure that the lowest-cost producers supply the good in question and that the consumers pay the lowest price consistent with cost.

7. According to many observers, the conditions which define competition are that: (a) a large number of sellers sell (b) substantially identical products, (c) all buyers and sellers have complete information about the offering prices of other transactors.

8. Some economists have objected to condition (c), arguing that it takes as a precondition to competition one of the results of the competitive process.

9. The basic economic model of competition is based on the assumption that firms are price-takers (face a horizontal demand for their output).

10. The concentration ratio for an industry is sometimes (incorrectly) used as a complete measure of the competitiveness of an industry.

11. There are three basic meanings of *monopoly:* (a) a single seller, (b) restricted entry into the market (closed market), (c) a firm facing a downward-sloping demand curve (price-searcher)—a firm with market power.

12. Meaning (a) is rather ambiguous, but both (b) and (c) convey some useful information.

13. The basic reason for the existence of price-searchers is economies of scale, which cause firms that are large relative to their market to have lower costs per unit of output than smaller firms.

14. Using the criteria of openness of the market and possession of market power, there are four basic categories of firms: (a) open price-takers, (b) closed price-takers, (c) open price-searchers, (d) closed price-searchers.

KEY TERMS

(1) **Competition:** A market structure characterized by having a sufficiently large number of firms producing sufficiently similar products to produce a situation in which the consumers pay the lowest possible price consistent with cost. A process of rivalry among firms which produces these results.

(2) **Concentration ratio:** The ratio of the total amount of output (or assets) accounted for by a particular number of the largest firms in an industry (often four) to the total amount of output (or assets) in the industry.

(3) **Corporation:** A firm with more than one owner, characterized by the

owners' having liability only up to the amount of money they have invested in the firm.

(4) Economies of scale: A situation whereby the cost per unit of output produced by a firm falls as the firm increases in size.

(5) Firm: An organization of people engaged in production, characterized by having: (1) owners (residual claimants) who are sometimes managers, (2) joint production (teamlike production), and (3) a monitor or monitors whose job it is to reduce shirking by the team members.

(6) Monopoly: A firm which is (a) a single seller of the product it produces, or (b) operating in a market where entry is restricted, or (c) a price-searcher firm.

(7) Partnership: A firm with more than one owner, all of whom bear unlimited liability for the debts of the firm.

(8) Price-searcher firm: A firm with market power—that is, power to influence the price of the good it sells. A firm which faces a downward-sloping demand curve.

(9) Price-taker market: A market characterized by having a sufficiently large number of sellers of substantially the same product that each firm takes the price of the product as given. A certain type of competitive market.

(10) Proprietorship: A firm with a single owner who bears unlimited liability for the debts of the firm.

(11) Separation of ownership from control: The phenomenon that occurs when the owners of the firm are not directly involved in its management. This gives rise to problems for the owners in getting the managers to do what the owners want.

REVIEW QUESTIONS

1. One of the roles of the manager of a firm or other enterprise is to act as a monitor to control shirking by other employees. If she owns only a trivial portion of the firm, how can the manager be induced by the owners to be diligent in her monitoring?

2. If the firm is a nonprofit organization, so that there is no concentrated group of owners who can gain by making decisions which increase revenue relative to cost, how is the manager induced to manage well?

3. A legal issue which has arisen in recent years is the question of whether an employer should be permitted to establish dress or grooming codes for employees. Can you give an argument for permitting such codes in for profit firms but not in nonprofit government operations?

4. Can you think of any industries in which firms are typically nonprofit organizations? Employee-owned cooperatives? Profit-seeking firms with employees owning very little of the firm? Does this appear to be random, or is there some order to it? Is there any explanation for it?

5. Would you expect managers to indulge their tastes for discrimination against or for certain groups in hiring and promotion policies to a greater extent if the firm is a profit-seeking or a nonprofit firm?

6. Three differently skilled workers are cooperating to produce output in your plant. Person A is doing job 1; person B is doing job 2; and person C is doing job 3. Could you construct an experiment to enable you to tell what the *marginal product* of each person is? Could you be sure of your answer once you performed the experiment? What factors might throw off your results?

7. As the costs of detecting shirking in a firm increase, would you expect more or less shirking detection to be carried out? As less shirking detection is carried out, would you expect more or less shirking to go on?

8. Tenants who live in apartment buildings with steam (or hot water) heat have never been billed separately for their heat. (Presumably the monthly rent paid covers heat as well as other costs faced by the landlord.) (a) Would you expect tenants to use more heat under this arrangement than under an arrangement whereby each was billed directly for heat used? Explain. (b) Now suppose someone invents a device which allows one to measure the amount of steam or hot water heat used in each apartment. Would that make tenants better or worse off?

9. Suppose a new device is developed which allows your employer to determine at zero cost who is using the photocopying machine for non-business copying. Would that make the typical employee better or worse off?

10. In Yugoslavia, most firms are owned by the employees. The employees share in the earnings that the firm makes in any one year. A worker who stops working for a given firm gives up her claim to a future share of the firm's earnings. (She cannot take her stock with her.) Furthermore, a worker cannot sell her stock (claim on the firm's income) while she still works for the firm. Nor can she put together a large bloc of shares by purchasing them from others. The workers vote to influence the kinds of investment and other decisions the firm makes. Would you expect the firm's decisions to be more concentrated on short-term (quick payoff) projects in this situation as compared with a U.S. corporation? Why?

11. If you own a Kentucky Fried Chicken franchise, is your franchise a separate firm, or are you in effect an employee of the parent company?

12. In most corporations, a large group of stockholders, representing the vast majority of the corporation's shares, do not take part in decisions about how the firm is run. Rather, a small group of managers makes those decisions. (a) Why are there not more corporations in which the majority of shareholders exercise the managers' duties and directly run the affairs of the corporation? What sorts of costs would shareholders have to incur that they do not now incur? What benefits would they get? (b) If large numbers of potential stockholders wanted to hold stock only in companies which allowed them greater control of corporate decisions, how would you expect the rules governing corporations to change over time?

13. Why do you think so many high corporation executives are paid according to formulas which pay them more when the firm's earnings are higher, as verified by independent auditors?

14. The Duncan Yo-Yo Company is reportedly the only company manufacturing yo-yos. Does that mean that Duncan has no competitors? Explain.

15. Do you think the members of the Organization of Petroleum Exporting Countries (OPEC) compete against each other? What is your evidence?

16. According to the *Wall Street Journal*,[4] the United Auto Workers Union "maintains that Japanese importers unfairly have taken advantage of a switch in consumer preferences in favor of small, fuel-efficient vehicles prompted by fuel shortages last year." Do you think the Japanese competed unfairly? If so, to whom were they unfair? Who would have benefitted and who would have been hurt if they had competed "fairly?"

17. It has been argued that limited shareholder liability for corporate debts is a special privilege, justifying special punitive taxes or regulations on corporate behavior. Can you conceive of any situation in which an individual lender and borrower might mutually agree that in case the borrower defaults on the loan, only certain assets could be seized by the lender to serve as repayment? Would that be "limited liability"? Would it justify special taxes or regulations on the borrower?

4.*Wall Street Journal*, 9 May 1980.

chapter 7

Price-
Takers

In chapter 6 we discussed some of the meanings attached to the word *competitive*. We noted that sometimes economists use a particular idealization of an impersonal competitive market made up of independent buyers and sellers. The important feature of this model is that no seller is large enough, relative to the whole market, to have a substantial effect on the market price of the good. Each seller takes the market price as given. The point is not that a seller never expects the market price to change, but that nothing she does *individually* can have any noticable effect on it.

THE DEMAND CURVE OF
THE PRICE-TAKER

When a seller is in this position, what does the demand curve for *her* product look like? As we noted in chapter 4, all demand curves are downward-sloping. Nevertheless, if a firm is small enough, relative to the whole market, the firm's demand curve will appear to be nearly horizontal. How can this happen? Let's use the commodity soybeans as an example. Suppose the demand for soybeans is given by the schedule in table 7-1. Notice that the First Law of Demand holds. As the price falls, the quantity demanded rises. In fact, if we were to calculate the elasticity of the demand curve in this range, we would find that it is relatively *inelastic*.

Suppose 10 million bushels are currently on the market. Our demand

169

TABLE 7-1
MARKET DEMAND FOR SOYBEANS

P (Dollars Per Bushel)	Q (In Millions Of Bushels)
7.00	10
6.50	10.5
6.00	11
5.50	11.5

curve tells us that the price would be $7 per bushel, because that is the price at which the quantity demanded equals 10 million. Farmer Jones has a crop of 1000 bushels which he is considering putting on the market. He wants to know what the demand for his product looks like. If he sells none, the price will be $7 per bushel. If he sells all 1000, the amount on the market will be 10,001,000 bushels, instead of 10,000,000. Interpolating on the demand curve, we see that 1000 is 1/500 as much as half a million, so the price would fall about 1/500 of $.50 or $.001 (one-tenth of a cent), to $6.999. If we plot this demand curve (fig. 7-1), we see that it appears to be almost horizontal; thus the notion of the firm being a price-taker. The market price will be about $7 regardless of what Farmer Jones does. He does not affect the price; he takes it as given. The horizontal demand curve is in a sense an optical illusion. The demand curve which Farmer Jones faces has the same slope as the market demand. While 1000 bushels is a large amount to Farmer Jones, it is a small amount compared to the market as a whole. This is reflected in the fact that, while the market demand is inelastic, the demand confronting Farmer Jones is highly *elastic*. In the neighborhood of $7, a very small percentage change in price is associated with *very large* percentage changes in quantity. Thus the elasticity will be high. (If this is unclear, go back to chapter 3 and review the idea of elasticity.)

MARGINAL REVENUE

Although the price-taker's demand curve only *appears* to be flat, it is useful to simplify the analysis by pretending that the price-taker's demand curve is indeed *perfectly flat*. By doing that we make the discussion of a very important concept much simpler. The concept in question is *marginal revenue.* We have already encountered the word *marginal* when dealing with costs. There and here, a good synonym is *additional*. In particular, *marginal revenue* is the additional revenue obtained when a firm sells one more unit of output. Suppose a firm faces a horizontal demand curve at a price of $7. What is its marginal revenue? Seven dollars. If the price it can sell at is always $7, it will always get $7 more in revenue if it sells one more unit. So if a firm faces a horizontal demand curve, marginal revenue

FIGURE 7-1
DEMAND CURVE FOR A PRICE-TAKER

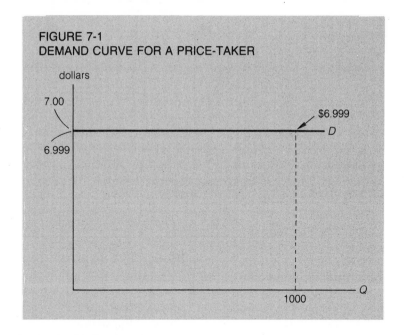

(MR) and the demand are the same thing—both horizontal lines at the level of the given price. (See figure 7-2.) For all firms, it is the marginal revenue, and not the price per se, which is important for determining the best output to produce. In the case of price-takers, there is no difference between price and marginal revenue, but we shall see (in chapter 8) that for price-searcher firms there is a difference, and this difference implies different behavior.

FIGURE 7-2
DEMAND AND MARGINAL REVENUE
FOR A PRICE-TAKER

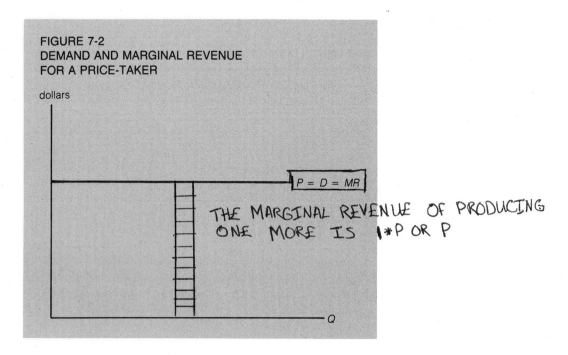

OPTIMAL OUTPUT OF
THE PRICE-TAKER

The demand and marginal revenue curves of the price-taker do not by themselves give us any clue as to how much to produce, or even whether to produce at all. In order to answer those questions we must know the firm's costs. In chapter 5 we examined the cost curves which a firm typically faces. By combining such cost relationships with the price-taker's demand conditions, we can arrive at a framework which enables us to understand what the best (or optimal) output of the firm is.

Examine figure 7-3, in which the cost and demand conditions are both displayed. What is the best output for the firm to produce? The answer depends on what is meant by "best." Most economists probably would say that the best output for the firm to produce would be the profit-maximizing output. This is the output which would make the owners best off; and if the owners decide what goes on, that will be the output chosen. When it comes down to it, the criterion we choose for deciding what output the firm is to produce depends on how well it works. That is, our job as economists is to understand and predict how business firms behave. So we want a theory which predicts well. Consequently, we choose our assumptions with an eye toward the implications to which they lead. We choose the model with best (most accurate) predictions, whatever the assumptions might be. The model which predicts best most times is the one which assumes that firms operate so as to maximize profits.

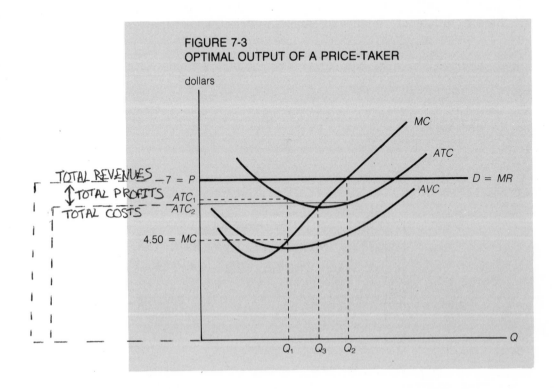

FIGURE 7-3
OPTIMAL OUTPUT OF A PRICE-TAKER

If we start with the assumption of profit maximization, then it is a simple matter to discover the best (most profitable) output. The basic principle is that the firm should (if it wants to maximize profit) increase its output rate as long as doing so increases profit. If an increase in output reduces profits, then it should not be undertaken. The next thing to realize is that if, at a certain quantity (say Q_1), marginal revenue is greater than marginal cost (meaning that the additional revenue obtained by producing and selling an additional unit is greater than the additional cost), then it will pay the firm to produce and sell an additional unit of output per day, because the extra output adds more to daily revenue than to daily cost. The difference between daily revenue and cost will be greater than what it would otherwise have been.

Remember that we define (economic) profit as the difference between total revenue and total cost $(TR - TC)$, where the total cost is the real cost, including correctly calculated implicit costs. Thus the total cost we are using includes the amount which the owner could have earned by working elsewhere and by investing her money elsewhere, in addition to the more usual costs. This means that the profit we are discussing is excess over and above what the owner (or owners) could have earned elsewhere. If, because of an increased output, total revenue goes up by $7 and total cost goes up by $4.50, then profit will have gone up by $2.50. Since we assume that firms are in business to make profits (the more profits the better), our model says that a firm will increase its output above Q_1 if it has the demand and cost curves shown. So the best (profit maximizing) output is greater than Q_1.

How much greater? We now know that as long as marginal revenue is greater than marginal cost, it pays to increase output. Examining figure 7-3, we can see that marginal revenue is greater than marginal cost all the way over to Q_2. For quantities greater than Q_2, marginal revenue is less than marginal cost, so profits would be reduced by increasing Q beyond Q_2. Thus Q_2 is the profit-maximizing output.

We can, by examining figure 7-3, arrive at some useful generalizations. First, note that the firm is making a profit at Q_2—revenue is greater than cost. How do we know this? Revenue is price times quantity. This is represented by the rectangle with height P and width Q_2. Total cost equals average total cost times quantity. This is represented by the rectangle with height ATC_2 and width Q_2. The difference is profit, represented by the rectangle with height $(P - ATC_2)$ and width Q_2.

At first glance you might have thought that output Q_3 in figure 7-3 would be the profit maximizing output, rather than Q_2. After all, average total cost is smaller at Q_3 than it is at Q_2, so profit per unit $(P - ATC)$ is greater at Q_3 than at Q_2. In fact, output Q_3 results in the smallest average total cost of all outputs, so profit per unit is largest at Q_3. But this fact doesn't mean that total profit is largest at Q_3. For larger outputs, all the way up to Q_2, the fall in profit per unit is more than offset by the larger number of units sold, so that total profit grows. The area of the profit rectangle at Q_2 is greater than the area of the profit rectangle we could get at Q_3. While that comparison may be difficult to make unless the diagram is drawn to scale, we can use our earlier logic and know that profit would increase with increases in *quantity* as long as *marginal revenue* is greater than *marginal cost*. Since *marginal revenue* is greater than *marginal cost* at Q_3, profit can be increased above the level obtainable at Q_3.

What if the price were higher than \$7—say \$8? Then the profit maximizing output would be the one where $MC = \$8$. For prices in this range, the best output can always be read right off of the MC curve. The MC curve tells how much would be supplied.

SOME IMPORTANT DECISIONS TO BE MADE

But what about lower prices? How low would the price have to go before the firm would stop producing? Consider figure 7-4. What if the price were P_A? If the firm did the best it could (operating at Q_A, where $MC = MR$), its revenue would be smaller than its total cost. (Revenue would equal the area of the rectangle with height P_A and width Q_A, while total cost would be the area of the rectangle with height ATC_A and width Q_A.) If the owner of the firm expected the price to remain at this level forever, it would do best to get out of business. Why is this so? Remember that costs, as we are conceiving of them, represent the sacrificed opportunities of the alternatives facing the owners of the firm. For example, the continued possession cost (which we are calling *fixed* cost because it does not change as output changes) is based on the current sale value of the firm's plant and equipment. It is the interest foregone when the owner decides to continue possessing the assets rather than selling them and investing the proceeds elsewhere, plus expected time-related depreciation over the period considered. Since it is based on currently available market transactions, this fixed cost is avoidable, just as the variable (operating) cost is. Thus, if the daily revenue one could expect to obtain at quantity Q_A, with price P_A, is \$400, but the daily total cost (operating plus continued possession) at that output is \$600, and if the owners expect this to continue indefinitely, then they would be better off getting out of business immediately, because they would save the \$600 per day in cost and only lose \$400 per day in revenue by getting out.

On the other hand, if the owners expected the price to rise above P_C in the future by enough so that future profits would more than offset the \$200 per day losses that would be incurred by operating now, then it would pay the firm to continue operating at the output Q_A where $MC = MR_A$ (at P_A). As the price rose, output would rise.

Once the owners have decided to stay in business (because they expect price to be substantially above P_C in the future), they have already committed themselves to incurring the continued possession cost. Thus, that cost cannot be avoided by temporarily stopping operations. This means that the only relevant (avoidable) cost to consider in deciding whether or not to operate is the variable (operating) cost. If the revenue that would be ob-

FIGURE 7-4
COST CURVES FACING A PRICE-TAKER FIRM

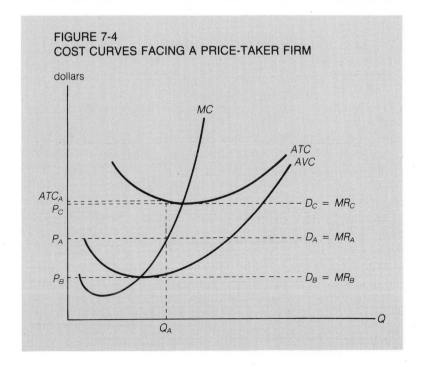

tained by operating is greater than that variable cost, then the firm is better off operating than not operating. For example, suppose that at output Q_A, the variable cost is $150 per day, while revenue is $400 per day and total cost is $600 per day. Since only the variable cost of $150 per day could be avoided by shutting down and since revenue of $400 per day would be lost if they shut down, the owners are $250 per day better off operating than shutting down. (Remember that the owners have already committed themselves to staying in business in hopes of a higher price later, so the continued possession cost will be incurred whether the firm operates or not.) Looking at it the other way around, the incremental revenue from operating is $400, whereas the incremental cost is only $150. Thus, the firm has a $250 per day smaller loss if it operates than if it doesn't.

Suppose the price were below P_B. In that case there would be no output at which the firm could cover even *operating* (variable) costs. If the firm's owner expected that price to last indefinitely, then the best thing to do would be to get out of business. But suppose the owner thought that the price would eventually rise above P_C. Then the best strategy would be for the firm to stay in business, but not operate as long as price is below P_B. *It should not operate because the incremental revenue it would get by operating would be less than the incremental costs it would have to incur in order to operate. For example, suppose that if the firm produces where MR = MC, the variable cost is $100 per day and the revenue at that quantity is $90 per day. The firm's loss would be $10 greater if it operated than if* it did not operate. In other words, by temporarily shutting down, it could save a larger amount by not incurring any variable costs than it would lose by not getting any revenue. When the price rose above P_B, it would again pay the firm to operate (since revenue would again be greater than variable costs), but only if the owner expected the price to eventually rise above P_C. (Otherwise, it would, as noted, be best to sell out and leave the business immediately.)

If the price rose above P_C and were expected to stay above that level for a long time the firms already in the industry would experience economic profits. Then potential entrants with cost curves like those shown would find it worthwhile to enter the industry, because they could expect to make at least as much in this industry as elsewhere.

To summarize the discussion to this point, the owners of the firm can be thought of as facing a three-stage decision problem. First, they must decide whether or not to stay in business. This depends on whether they expect the price to be sufficiently high (above P_C) to cover all costs of being and staying in business. If the decision is negative, that is the end of the story. The assets of the business are sold, and the owners and employees put their resources to their best alternative use. If instead the owners decide that future price prospects justify staying in business, then the second decision to be made is whether or not to operate. Since the decision to stay in business means that the continued possession costs will be incurred whether the firm operates or not, only the variable (operating) costs are relevant for this decision. If the price is above minimum average variable cost (which means that total revenue is greater than variable cost), then the firm should operate; if not, it should temporarily cease operations (while continuing to stay in business). If the owners find that price is above minimum average variable cost, then they must decide what output to produce. As we showed earlier, the best (profit maximizing) output is where $MR = MC$; and since price equals marginal revenue for the price-taker, the best output is found where the marginal cost equals the going price.

PROFIT CONTRIBUTION

We have referred at times to cases where the daily total revenue exceeds the daily variable cost. In those cases, if the firm has decided to stay in business anyway, it will pay to operate rather than shut down. The reason is that the revenue obtained by operating is greater than the *incremental* cost incurred by operating. (Since the firm is staying in business, the continued possession cost will be incurred anyway, so only the variable cost is avoidable with regard to this decision.) The excess of revenue over variable cost is sometimes called *profit contribution*. The notion is that if revenue is greater than variable (operating) cost, the owners will have some revenue left over to help defray fixed (continuing possession) cost. And if revenue is greater than the sum of variable and fixed costs, the remainder is (economic) profit. If revenue is less than variable cost, then there is nothing left over to contribute to defraying fixed cost, so the owners are better off shutting down.

CONTINUED POSSESSION COSTS

An extra complication in trying to decide whether or not to stay in business (but *not* whether or not to operate once one has decided to stay) is the rather tricky nature of fixed (continued possession) costs. Since one of the components of continued possession cost is the interest the owners forego by keeping their money tied up in the firm's assets, that cost depends on the current resale price of the assets (plant and equipment). If that resale price rises, then continued possession cost rises; if the resale price falls, the continued possession cost falls. Thus if other potential owners raised the amount they were willing to pay for your plant and equipment, the profit contribution you would have to generate to justify continuing in business would increase.

The tricky part comes in because there are two classes of potential buyers of your plant and equipment. The first is manufacturers of *other* products. You may have a plant you are using to make rollerskates, but manufacturers of electronic equipment might like to use it. If their offer price goes up, you may decide to sell the plant, even though you are generating a positive profit contribution, because the profit contribution is not enough to cover the new higher continued possession cost. Alternatively, the price of rollerskates might fall, with no change in the offer price by the electronics firms. Your new lower profit contribution might be below the level of fixed cost. If so, you should get out. This is straightforward, and causes no problems. The problems come in analyzing offers from other members of your industry. Suppose much of your plant and equipment is specifically designed for the production of rollerskates, and it would be very costly to modify it for any alternative use. Then the highest bids for sale of your plant are likely to come from other skate manufacturers. Now suppose the price of skates falls. This lowers the profit contribution that you (or *any other* skate manufacturer) can earn from the plant. Since the profit contribution they can earn is lowered, their offer price for your plant will fall as well. But this lowers your fixed (continued possession) cost since one component of the continued possession cost is based on the current resale price of the plant and equipment. Thus as the price of your product falls, your *average total cost* (but not *average variable cost*) may fall enough to make it worthwhile to continue ownership. Of course, if the price of rollerskates falls low enough, a point will be reached where the highest offer price for your plant and equipment will no longer come from other skate makers (even though the plant is specialized) but rather from manufacturers of other goods. Further falls in the price of skates (if they were thought to be permanent) would result in your getting out of business because the profit contribution would have fallen below the fixed (continued possession) cost.

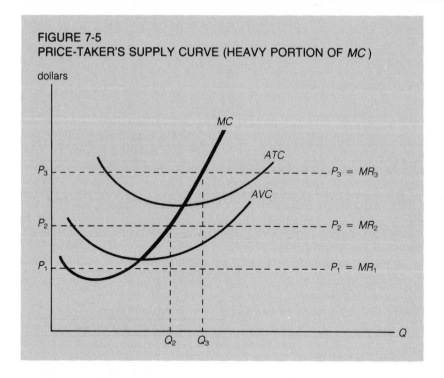

FIGURE 7-5
PRICE-TAKER'S SUPPLY CURVE (HEAVY PORTION OF *MC*)

THE SUPPLY CURVE OF
THE PRICE-TAKER

We can use the points developed above to arrive at the supply curve of the price-taker firm. What is a supply curve? It is a schedule which tells how much a firm will supply at alternative prices. For the price-taker, the amount supplied at any price is given by the MC curve, as long as the firm is operating at all. As we have seen, a firm might produce even if the price is below P_C in figure 7-4, if it thinks price will eventually rise above P_C. But it will not operate if the price is below P_B in figure 7-4, because the revenue would not cover even variable costs, which are surely relevant because they can always be avoided by not operating. So the supply curve can be thought of as the MC curve above minimum average variable cost. This is shown in figure 7-5. If the price is equal to P_3, the quantity supplied by this firm will be Q_3. If the price this price-taker must take is P_2, and if he thinks the price will soon rise enough to cover average total cost, the quantity supplied will be Q_2. If the price is P_1, the quantity supplied will be zero, since that price is not enough to cover even operating costs.

"WINDFALL" PROFITS?

What happens to the firm's profits if price rises? Figure 7-6 shows a price-taker firm's response to an increase in price. If price is originally P_0, the firm would maximize profit by producing output of Q_0. If the price rises to P_1, the firm would make a higher profit even if it continued to produce Q_0. The revenue would be greater by diagonally lined area A, with no change in cost. But the firm could obtain even more profit by increasing output from Q_0 to Q_1, where *marginal cost* equals the new $MR_1 = P_1$. The increase in profit due to the higher output would be the (vertically lined) triangular area B. The incremental revenue the firm would obtain by increasing its output would be P_1 per unit times the extra output ($Q_1 - Q_0$). The incremental cost would be the sum of the marginal costs incurred for the increases in output from Q_0 to Q_1. The difference between the incremental revenue and the incremental cost would be area B. The total increase in profit which the firm obtains due to the higher price is A+B. Politicians are likely to call area A a "windfall." It is the increase in profit which the firm would get simply by "being in the right place at the right time." The firm does not have to produce any more output to get this windfall.

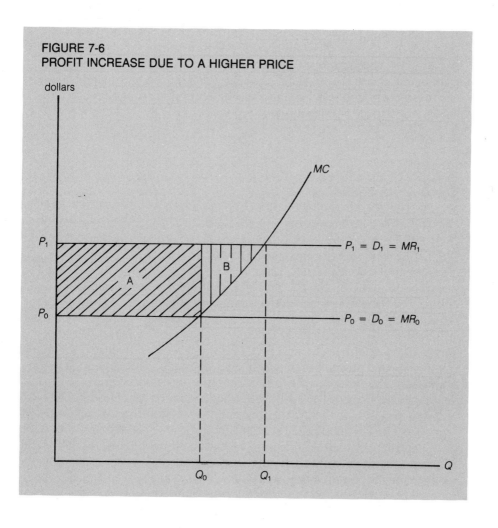

FIGURE 7-6
PROFIT INCREASE DUE TO A HIGHER PRICE

Area B would be viewed more favorably. It is an increase in profit which the firm gets only because it produces more output in response to the higher price. If the firms involved are relatively small in number, and if the amount of money involved is large, public sector entrepreneurs will be tempted to put together a political coalition to tax A and distribute the proceeds among the members of the coalition. The inclination of these government officials would be to exempt B from this windfall profits tax since it occurs as a by-product of the increased output, which benefits constituents. But in practice it is difficult to distinguish between the two types of profit. Thus any attempt to get at A will in practice tax B as well, resulting in reduced incentive to produce more output.

As a final comment, it is not clear that A is, in fact, a windfall. It is a windfall only if receipt of A was not necessary in order to get the firm to supply quantity Q_0. But it is impossible for an outsider to know exactly what price expectations any firm had which led it to invest in the productive capacity which it owns. Being at the right place at the right time is many times a matter of foresight rather than luck; and taxing magnitudes like A will sometimes reduce the return obtained below what would have been necessary to induce suppliers to produce as much as we want. The result is that the knowledge that windfall profits taxes will be imposed will reduce the willingness of entrepreneurs to get involved in businesses which might give rise to such windfalls. The reduced willingness to invest in these areas will mean that less will be produced and prices will be higher than they would otherwise be.

INDUSTRY SUPPLY AND DEMAND

We started our discussion of the price-taker firm by showing how we arrive at the individual firm's demand curve from the industry demand. We now go full circle to show how we arrive at the industry supply curve from the individual firm's supply.

The industry supply is simply the *sum* of the individual firms' supplies. That is, at every price, the amount supplied by the industry is the sum of the amounts supplied by the firms in the industry. Figure 7-7 illustrates how an industry supply curve is obtained when the industry is made up of two firms, A and B. The individual supply curves are given by the relevant portions of the respective *MC* curves. The combined supply curve is a schedule showing the sum of the amounts supplied at any price. For example, at price P_1, only firm A operates, and it supplies Q_1^A. The total amount supplied is thus Q_1^A. At price P_2, firm A supplies Q_2^A, while firm B supplies Q_2^B. The total amount supplied is $Q_2 = Q_2^A + Q_2^B$.

Figure 7-8 illustrates the case of a thousand identical firms. We show the "representative firm's" supply curve in 7-8(a) and the horizontal sum —the industry supply curve—in 7-8(b).

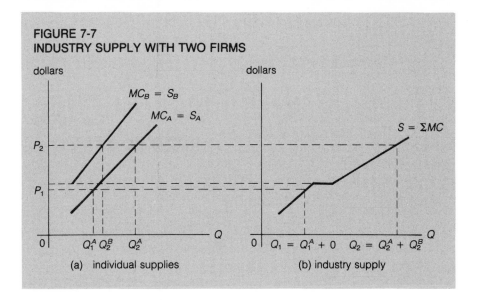

FIGURE 7-7
INDUSTRY SUPPLY WITH TWO FIRMS

(a) individual supplies

(b) industry supply

Note that the scales used to measure output are different in the two parts. A given movement to the right (say one inch) on figure 7-8(b) involves an increase in output that is one thousand times as big as the same movement in 7-8(a). The scale in (a) is a stretched-out version of the scale in (b).

We now have all the tools ncessary to analyze what is loosely called

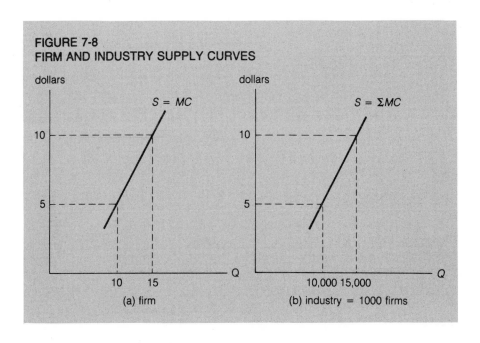

FIGURE 7-8
FIRM AND INDUSTRY SUPPLY CURVES

(a) firm

(b) industry = 1000 firms

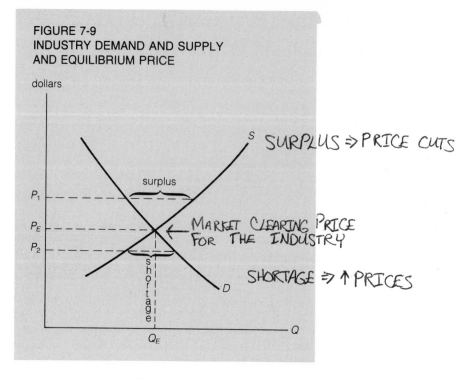

FIGURE 7-9
INDUSTRY DEMAND AND SUPPLY
AND EQUILIBRIUM PRICE

dollars

surplus

S SURPLUS ⇒ PRICE CUTS

P_1

P_E ← MARKET CLEARING PRICE FOR THE INDUSTRY

P_2

shortage

D SHORTAGE ⇒ ↑ PRICES

Q

Q_E

competitive price determination. If we put the industry demand and supply together (see figure 7-9), we see that their intersection determines an equilibrium or market-clearing price in the sense that, if the price is *above* P_E, there will be a surplus, and if it is *below* P_E, there will be a shortage. If the price were *above* P_E (say P_1), some firms would not be able to sell all they want. This would lead to price cuts, because firms would rather sell at a lower price than not sell at all. As one firm cut its price, others would be forced to cut theirs to meet the competition. As the price fell, the amount supplied would be reduced and the amount demanded would rise until the surplus was eliminated at P_E. If the price were *below* P_E (say P_2), then not all consumers would be able to buy as much as they want. This would put sellers in the position of being able to raise the price without losing sales. As the price rose, the amount supplied would increase and the amount demanded would decrease until the shortage was eliminated at P_E.

This result is very similar to the one in chapter 3. Here, as in figure 3-11, we show the supply curve upward-sloping. In chapter 3 we gave a very brief and intuitive explanation for the fact that the supply curve is upward-sloping. Here we note that since the supply curve is the sum of the firms' *MC* curves, the upward slope of the supply curve follows directly from the fact that *marginal cost* increases as more is produced. The assertion that supply curves are upward-sloping (meaning that the higher the price, the more supplied) could be referred to as the *First Law of Supply*.

AGRICULTURAL SURPLUSES IN EUROPE

Agricultural surpluses, once found only in the U.S., are now a part of the European scene. At the prevailing prices for dairy products, producers in the Common Market make 10 to 15 percent more each year than is sold to consumers. How does the surplus occur and why does it continue? The answer is that the government of the Common Market establishes prices above the market-clearing levels and then buys whatever consumers will not buy at that price. In 1979 the Common Market government spent $6.4 billion (one third of its total budget) to buy and store dairy surpluses, and on advertising to convince consumers to buy more. The policy is causing divisions in the European community because the taxes are collected in proportion to total economic activity in all member countries, whereas the benefits tend to go to only a few countries. The United Kingdom, for example, long an importer of much of its food, pays out much more in taxes than its farmers receive in payments for surpluses. On the other hand, France's farmers are recipients of large payments, relative to taxes collected in France.

ELASTICITY OF SUPPLY

Just as we talked about the responsiveness of the *quantity demanded* to changes in price (elasticity of demand), we can talk about the price-responsiveness of the quantity supplied, or *elasticity of supply*. We define the

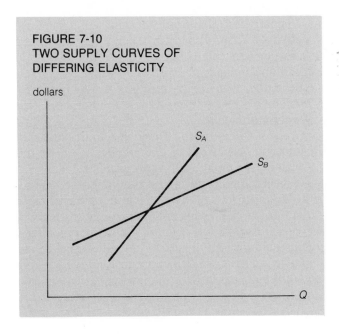

FIGURE 7-10
TWO SUPPLY CURVES OF
DIFFERING ELASTICITY

dollars

S_A

S_B

Q

elasticity of supply in the same way as we did the elasticity of demand, namely, the percentage change in quantity supplied, divided by the percentage change in price:

$$\frac{\% \text{ change in } Qs}{\% \text{ change in } P}$$

Of two intersecting supply curves S_A and S_B in figure 7-10, the flatter one (S_B) is the more elastic or responsive. It responds with a greater percentage change in quantity supplied for any change in price.

LONG-RUN AND SHORT-RUN SUPPLY

If the assertion that supply curves are upward-sloping could be called the First Law of Supply, then the Second Law of Supply says that supply curves are more elastic in the long run than in the short run. That is, in response to a higher (lower) price, there will be some increase (decrease) in the short run, but as time passes, the quantity supplied will increase (decrease) still further. This is illustrated in figure 7-11. At a price of P_0, Q_0 is supplied. If the price were to rise to P_1, the short-run response would be to increase the amount supplied to Q_1. In the long run as existing firms enlarged their plants and new firms entered, the amount that would be supplied at P_1 would rise to Q_1'. The basic reason for this difference between short-run and long-run response is the same as the reason for the Second Law of Demand. That is, it doesn't pay to make one's total response to a change in price immediately. Firms already in the industry may want to expand their plants in response to the higher price. But they won't do it overnight. Rather, they will make plans, design and build the new plant, all of which takes time. Similarly, if the price goes up enough, entrepreneurs may decide they can make money by getting into this industry. But their response, too, will not be immediate.

How long is the long run? It varies among industries. In the roadside fruit stand business, the long run may be only a few months, while for the automobile or steel industries, it is probably several years.

It could well take five years or more for a new automobile company to start in the United States, even if it thought it had a very profitable opportunity. The length of time for a new entrant to appear in the form of a *foreign* supplier would be shorter. This is because the foreign manufacturer is already producing cars and only needs to gear up for sales and service here, rather than starting from scratch to build a manufacturing facility. So the long-run supply of cars to the U.S. market is more elastic and the long run is reached sooner, if we don't have restrictions on the importation of cars.

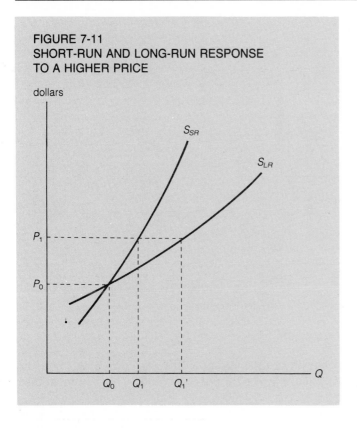

FIGURE 7-11
SHORT-RUN AND LONG-RUN RESPONSE
TO A HIGHER PRICE

WHY ISN'T THE LONG-RUN SUPPLY CURVE HORIZONTAL?

In figure 7-11 we showed the long-run supply as more elastic than the short-run supply, but the long-run supply was not *infinitely* elastic (horizontal). To get at the question of *how elastic* the long-run supply curve is, it is helpful to add demand curves to the supply curves in figure 7-11. This is done in figure 7-12(b). Putting the demand curves in makes it clear that the source of the change in price was an increase in demand (from D_0 to D_1). In the short run, the response to that higher demand is limited to what the existing firms can accomplish with their original plants. The result is that price rises to P_1 and firms in the industry make economic profits, represented by the fact that P_1 is greater than ATC_1. The long-run response to this state of affairs is that new firms enter and firms expand in size. As new firms enter, the short-run supply curve shifts to the right. (Remember that S_{SR} is the horizontal sum of the individual firm supply curves. If there are more firms, the amount supplied at any price will be greater than before—thus a shift to the right in S_{SR}.) As S_{SR} shifts to the right, P falls. If this were all that was happening, entry would continue until the price had fallen back to P_0; because as long as prices were above P_0, it would be

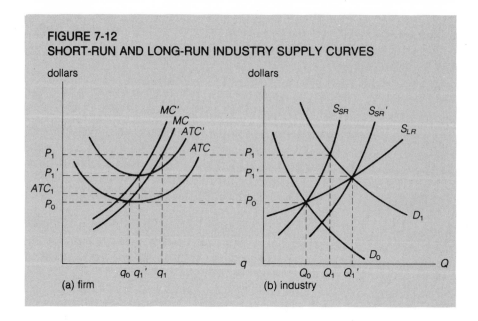

FIGURE 7-12
SHORT-RUN AND LONG-RUN INDUSTRY SUPPLY CURVES

(a) firm

(b) industry

possible to make economic profits, and new firms would enter. (Thus in the long run, price would always be P_0, and S_{LR} would be horizontal at that level.)

But something else is happening. As firms enter the industry and expand, the demand for inputs which the firm uses will go up, and their prices will rise. This causes the cost of doing business to be higher than before.

This phenomenon is shown in figure 7-12(a), in which the MC and ATC have shifted up to MC' and ATC'. Suppose that when a certain number of firms entered, the cost curves shifted as shown, and S_{SR} shifted to S_{SR}'. The price would fall to P_1' (not all the way back to P_0). Given the increased level of costs, the representative firm shown in figure 7-12(a) is just covering costs (it does the best it can at q_1', where $P_1' = MR_1' = MC' = ATC'$), and there is no further incentive for new firms to enter. Since existing firms have no incentive to change their output, and since no more new firms will enter, the output will not change. Thus the price will not change. In particular it will not fall below P_1'. The industry is in a "long-run equilibrium," with no tendency for firms to enter or leave, and the point P_1', Q_1' is a point on the long-run supply curve. In order to get an amount larger than Q_0 produced, the price must be greater than P_0, even in the long run. The S_{LR} is upward-sloping and therefore *not* infinitely elastic.[1]

1. What would the long-run supply curve be like if expansion of the industry *lowered* input prices? Then the ATC and MC curves would shift to below the original ones, and entry would be encouraged until the price fell to the new *lower* minimum ATC value. Thus the long-run supply curve would, in this case, be downward-sloping.

DENIM—AN EXAMPLE OF LONG-RUN ADJUSTMENT

As an example, consider the recent craze for denim clothing. The last few years have seen a big increase in demand. Suppose that the denim manufacturing industry was originally in long-run equilibrium at price P_0 and quantity Q_0, with the typical firm producing at q_0 (in figure 7-12). Now the increase in demand hits. Initially, the denim mills are unable to keep up with demand at the old price, and the temporary shortage causes the price of denim to rise (say to P_1). Those who are geared up for denim make profits. The high profits induce existing firms to expand their capacity and new firms to enter. As the firms order new denim-making machinery, the price of the machinery rises (the market value of already existing machines rises as well). This results in higher costs for all firms in using the machinery. More importantly, since denim is made of cotton, the increased demand for denim increases the demand for, and price of, cotton. Thus major inputs in the production process are more expensive than before, raising (shifting up) the cost curves of all firms. And, while entry lowers the price of denim somewhat, it does not fall back to P_0, but stops at some higher level, such as P_1'. This is because, with the higher costs, firms are no longer making economic profits when price falls to P_1'. Thus there will be no further entry and no change in output from existing firms (since they are already producing where marginal revenue equals marginal cost). Thus the price will not fall any further.

OIL—AN EXAMPLE OF LONG-RUN SUPPLY AND THE HIERARCHY OF COSTS

The petroleum extraction industry in the U.S. shows us another reason for having a long-run supply curve that is upward-sloping. There are many distinct sources from which, and methods by which, petroleum and similar products can be extracted. Some are much more costly than others, and the higher cost sources and processes will come into play only at higher prices. For example, some conventional onshore oil would be developed even if the price were expected to be only $5 per barrel. Some offshore oil would be developed if the price were anything over $10/barrel. Injection of steam into old wells to obtain more oil would be worthwhile as long as the price were greater than (say) $15. Drilling very deep wells in fairly unlikely terrain might be undertaken as long as the price were greater than $20 per barrel. Extraction of oil from tar sands and shale might be feasible as long as the price were at least $30 per barrel. Coal gasification and liquifaction might require a price of $35 per barrel to induce production.

If we combine all of these sources of supply, we obtain an idea of the way U.S. petroleum production would respond to prices in the long run. Figure 7-13 shows how this might look.

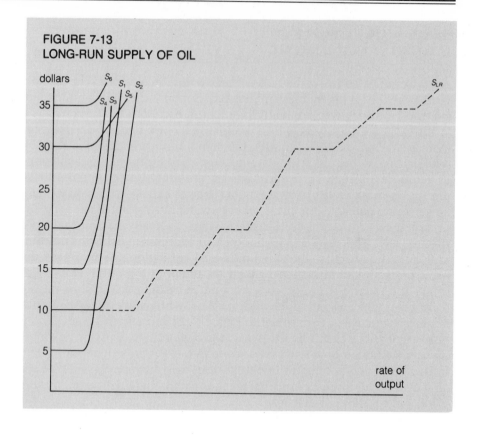

FIGURE 7-13
LONG-RUN SUPPLY OF OIL

CHANGES IN SUPPLY

We should distinguish between a _change in supply_ and a <u>change in the quantity supplied</u>. The former is a shift in the supply curve, while the latter could be a movement along the supply curve caused by a change in price. Figure 7-14 illustrates an increase in supply (a shift to the right in the supply curve). With the original supply curve S^A, the amount supplied at P_1 is Q_1^A, while at P_2, amount Q_2^A is supplied. When supply increases, these amounts increase to Q_1^B and Q_2^B, respectively. Why might such an increase in supply occur?

One reason could be <u>technological improvement,</u> such as the invention of a new machine which makes the good cheaper to produce. The lower the cost of producing the good, the more that will be supplied at any price. Another reason could be a <u>decreased price of an input</u> (decreased opportunity cost of using an input). If the price of soybeans falls, that increases the supply of corn. Why? Because corn and soybeans are substitute ways of using land. If soybean prices fall, the amount which can be earned by using the land for soybeans is lower (the opportunity cost of using it for corn is lower), so more land becomes available for corn growing

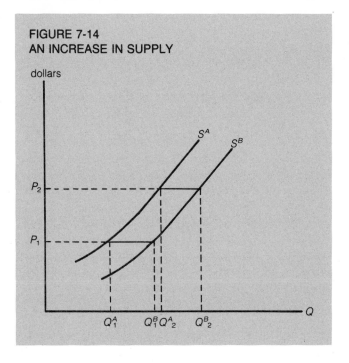

FIGURE 7-14
AN INCREASE IN SUPPLY

at any given corn price—thus an increase in the supply of corn. Similarly, a decrease in the size of the U.S. space program increased the supply of aerospace engineers to other sectors of the economy.

In the same way, an increase in the price (opportunity cost of using) of inputs causes a shift to the left in supply (decrease in supply). The increased use of private security guards in the 1960s and 1970s caused a shift to the left in the supply of personnel to police departments.

ROLE OF PRICES
1. RATIONS THE EXISTING SUPPLY
2. ASSIGNS PRODUCTION

CHANGES IN DEMAND AND SUPPLY

The tools of demand and supply are certainly the most important and useful tools economists have. Indeed when you hear economists talking about issues in microeconomics, virtually everything they say involves the use of supply and demand analysis. What can we do with supply and demand analysis? First of all, it is the filing system or framework into which we cast information about the economy to see if it is logically consistent. For example, suppose you hear that a report has just come out proving that beef causes cancer. You say to your friend, "I think this will cause beef prices to be lower." But your friend says, "No, it *would* lower beef prices, except that in response to that lower beef price, other (skeptical) consumers will increase their consumption of beef, keeping the price from falling, or even raising it." How do you answer your friend? One way

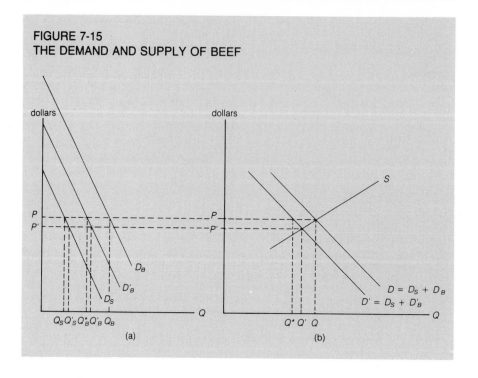

FIGURE 7-15
THE DEMAND AND SUPPLY OF BEEF

is to use supply and demand analysis. One thing this does is to force you to make explicit what you are assuming about people's behavior. In this case, we could translate your initial statement into an assertion that the demand for beef will shift to the left.

Assume there are two groups of beef eaters, those who believe the report and those who are skeptics, denoted by D_B and D_S in figure 7-15(a). The sum of their demands is the total demand for beef. $D = D_B + D_S$ in figure 7-15(b). When the report comes out, the demand by the believers falls (D_B shifts to D_B'), but the demand by the skeptics (D_S) is unchanged, so the total demand falls by the same amount that D_B does, to D'.

The effect of the decreased demand is to lower the price. The reason is that at the old price P, the quantity demanded is now lower than the quantity supplied (Q^* versus Q), so that would be a surplus if price remained at P. As price falls, both the skeptics and the believers consume more than they would have at P, and less is supplied than would have been at P. The price will fall to level P', at which the quantity demanded and the quantity supplied are again equal. Looking at figure 7-15(a), we see that the skeptics are consuming more than before (Q_S' versus Q_S) because of the lower price, and the believers are consuming more than they would have had price remained at level P (Q_B' versus Q_B^*), but less than their original amount (Q_B). The suppliers are supplying less than before and in total the consumers are buying less than before Q' versus Q). This example, in which one group's demand changes while the other's does not, points up the importance of distinguishing between a *change in demand* (due to

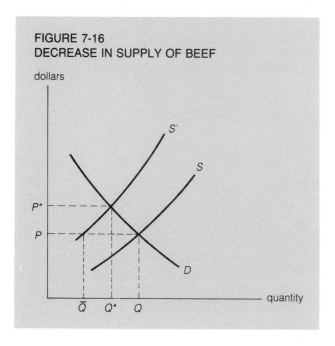

FIGURE 7-16
DECREASE IN SUPPLY OF BEEF

some factor *other than* the price of beef) and a change in the quantity demanded due to change in the price of beef. Both groups increased their quantity demanded *in response to* the lower price, but the lower price was *caused by* the believers' reduced demand. We can simplify the analysis of this problem by looking only at figure 7-15(b). It tells the story very simply: The announcement causes a decrease in demand (and no change in supply). The result is a lower price and a smaller quantity.

Another use for supply and demand analysis, then, is to make predictions about the effects of changes in circumstances. We have seen that a decrease in demand results in a lower price and a lower quantity. An increase in demand would have exactly opposite effects (higher price and quantity). What if there were a corn crop failure in Europe? What would that do to the price of corn and the quantity of beef? The reduced crop size would raise the price of corn the world over. (Why?) The higher price of corn would make cattle feeding and raising less profitable, so less beef would be supplied at any price. This translates into a shift to the left in the supply of beef (see figure 7-16). With the demand (curve) unchanged but a decrease in supply, there would be a shortage if the price remained at its initial level. (Quantity demanded equals Q but quantity supplied equals $\bar{Q}$.) The temporary shortage causes price to rise, increasing the quantity supplied and decreasing the quantity demanded until they are equal at Q^*. The result of the reduced supply is thus to reduce quantity below its original level (Q^* versus Q) and raise price (P^* versus P). An increased supply would have an opposite effect (lower *price* and higher *quantity*).

Suppose now that the European corn crop failure and the cancer

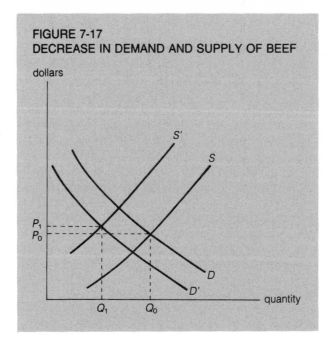

FIGURE 7-17
DECREASE IN DEMAND AND SUPPLY OF BEEF

announcements come at the same time. What would happen to beef prices and quantity? The decreased demand tends to reduce both *price* and *quantity*, while the decreased supply tends to increase *price* and reduce *quantity*. Both tend to reduce *quantity*, so apparently *quantity* will fall. But one tends to raise *price*, while the other causes *price* to fall, so the effect on *price* is unclear. We can see this very easily with the aid of the supply and demand diagram (fig. 7-17). From the diagram, we can see that *quantity* definitely falls, but that the effect on *price* depends on the relative shifts of demand and supply. (One thing is certain, however: cattle ranchers will be very unhappy. Many will go bankrupt, and others will have to trim their herds.)

There are other possible combinations of changes in demand and supply, and you should work out for yourself the consequences of, for example, an increase in supply and a decrease in demand. Thinking in terms of supply and demand is a skill which will provide benefits in terms of more careful analysis.

DEMAND AND SUPPLY
AND THE COORDINATION
OF ECONOMIC ACTIVITIES

The example discussed in the previous section illustrates the notion that the competitive voluntary exchange system coordinates the activities of the many individual transactors by means of prices. We have seen that a change in demand or supply conditions tends to lead to a change in the coordinating (market-clearing) price. Specifically, if one group of consumers reduces its demand, the competitive process tends to reallocate goods away from those transactors and toward others. The means by which this reallocation takes place is a change in the price. The price falls because there is a surplus at the old price. As the price falls, consumers are induced to buy more than they otherwise would and suppliers to supply less than they otherwise would. The price falls to the extent necessary so that every seller can sell as much as he wants at the new going price and every buyer can buy as much as she wants at that price.

By drawing our diagrams we give the impression that we can predict the exact extent to which a price can be expected to fall in such a case. But in fact the information necessary to discover the change in price is not known by any one person. It is dispersed among the many transactors in the marketplace, and the extent of necessary price change is made known only by the action of the buyers and sellers in trying to adjust to the new circumstances. Our diagrams help illuminate the kinds of adjustments which must be made. For example, we know that those whose demand has decreased will end up buying less than before, while those whose demand has not changed will buy more, and that the total amount produced will fall. But just exactly who will change her consumption or production how much is something we cannot know unless we know precisely the shape and slope of their individual demand and supply curves. But we as outsiders cannot know these because they are only revealed bit by bit as transactors respond to changes in circumstances, and the whole curve may change in the time between the collection of one bit of information and the next. Thus we can *understand how* the market adjusts even if we cannot always predict the exact extent of change in price and quantity.

SUPPLY AND DEMAND
AND PRICE-TAKERS

We have seen that supply and demand analysis flows directly from the study of price-takers markets. Does this mean that supply and demand can *only* be used to describe price-takers? No. If we are careful, we can also use it to analyze price-searcher markets in certain cases. For very broad questions, the implications of the two market types are similar. An increased in demand will generally result in higher *quantity* and *price* regardless of the market type. Similarly, changes in supply conditions have approximately the same effect regardless of market type. Care must be used, however, because there are certain situations in which the implications of the two market types are not the same. This applies most importantly to questions about *efficiency*. Chapter 8 will explore some of these differences.

LOOKING AHEAD

In this chapter we have examined the behavior of price-taker firms and industries. We have seen that the price-taker model leads directly to supply and demand analysis, a very powerful tool. In chapter 8 we move on to analyze the behavior of firms with some market power—price-searcher firms. We shall inquire into the factors which constrain their behavior, and examine the forms of competition in markets where there are price-searchers.

POINTS TO REMEMBER

1. The demand curve facing the price-taker firm is virtually horizontal because the firm is very small relative to the market it serves.

2. The marginal revenue curve for the price-taker firm is identical to its demand curve, if we assume the demand curve is literally flat ($P = MR$).

3. The profit-maximizing output for the price-taker is where *marginal revenue* (equal to *price*) is equal to *marginal cost*.

4. If price is expected to remain below average total cost (including possession cost) for the foreseeable future, then the price-taker firm should get out of business; but if the price is expected to eventually rise above average total cost the firm should continue to operate, as long as price remains above average variable cost.

5. The supply curve of the price-taker firm is its *MC* curve in the range where it lies above *average variable cost*.

6. The supply curve of the price-taker industry is the horizontal sum of the individual firm supply curves.

7. The assertion that the quantity supplied increases as the price of the good increases may be referred to as the First Law of Supply.

8. The equilibrium price in a price-taker market is the price at which the quantity demanded equals the quantity supplied (denoted by the intersection of the industry demand and supply curves).

9. Supply curves are more elastic in the long run than in the short run (Second Law of Supply).

10. Long-run supply curves are generally not horizontal because, as the industry expands, it bids up the prices of inputs which it uses, thus raising the costs of the firms in the industry. Since costs per unit are higher, price must be higher if larger amounts of output are to be produced.

11. A change in supply (shift in the supply curve) can be caused by a change in the prices of inputs or by technological change.

Elasticity of supply: The ratio of the percentage change in the quantity supplied to the percentage change in the price of the product.

First Law of Supply: The assertion that the higher the price, the more that will be supplied. The assertion that supply curves are upward-sloping.

Industry supply curve: The horizontal sum of the individual firm supply curves.

Long-run equilibrium: A situation in which the firm is maximizing profits, but at which zero economic profit is being earned. In a price-taker industry it is characterized by having quantity demanded equal quantity supplied, but with zero economic profits. There is no tendency for firms to enter or leave an industry which is in long-run equilibrium.

Price-taker firm's supply curve: The MC curve in the range where it lies above the AVC curve.

Profit contribution: The difference between the revenue that a firm receives and its variable (operating) cost. Profit contribution is available to defray fixed (continued possession) cost, and any left over after paying these costs is economic profit.

Profit-maximizing output: The output at which the extra revenue a firm earns by selling one more unit of output is just offset by the extra cost which must be incurred to produce that extra output ($MR = MC$). For a price-taker, this means that $P = MC$, since $P = MR$ for the price-taker.

Second Law of Supply: The assertion that supply curves are more elastic in the long run than in the short run.

REVIEW QUESTIONS

1. For the accompanying demand curve, calculate the marginal revenue on a per unit basis over the range shown.

P	Q	MR
10	1000	
		$>$
9.98	2000	

2. Does a firm maximize profit by producing where marginal cost equals the going price or marginal revenue? If the two (price and marginal revenue) differed, which would the profit-maximizing firm equate to marginal cost?

3. Refer to the cost data for question 6 of chapter 5. What would be the profit-maximizing output if price were $10? How much profit would be earned at that point?

4. For the previous question, suppose the price is $3. What output should the firm produce if it expects the price to remain at $3? What if the firm expects the price to rise to $10 in the near future?

5. For the previous question, what output should the firm produce if the price is $2.25? What should the firm do if the owners expect the price to rise to $10 in the near future? If they expect price to rise only to $4 and remain there? Explain.

6. For the firm in question 3, would your optimal output change if the fixed cost were $20 instead of $10? Explain. What would happen if your fixed (continued possession) cost increased to $50 because someone made a very attractive offer to buy your plant from you? Explain.

7. In the section "Some Important Decisions to Be Made," the firm was confronted with a price $P_A = MR_A$ (see figure 7-4). At the output where $MR_A = MC$ (output Q_A), the firm was confronted with $600 per day in total costs, of which $150 were variable (operating) and $450 were fixed (continued possession). When the firm's owners expected price eventually to rise above P_C, they decided to stay in business. If the firm operated at Q_A, it would lose $200 per day ($600 − $400). How much would it lose per day if it did not operate? Using this approach, is the firm better off operating or not operating, given that it has decided to remain in business? Is your answer the same as the one in the chapter? Explain.

8. Consider the firm in the section "Some Important Decisions to Be Made." Suppose that instead of owning the firm's assets outright, the owners had borrowed the money to buy them. Would any of its decisions be changed? Explain.

9. (a) Fill in the blanks in the accompanying table of costs for a price-taker firm.

Q	AFC	VC	AVC	MC	ATC
1	15	3	3	3	18
2	7.5	5	2.5	2	10
3	5	7.2	2.4	2.2	—
4	3.75	—	2.5	2.8	6.25
5	3	14	—	4	5.8
6	—	19	3.17	5	5.67
7	2.14	26	3.71	—	5.85
8	1.88	34	4.25	8	6.13
9	1.67	45	5	11	6.67
10	1.5	60	6	15	7.5

(b) How much would the firm produce if the price were $7.50? How much profit would it make? (c) Would the firm stay in business (continue to own its assets) if the price were $4.25 and the owners expected it to remain at that level? What would they do if the price were $4.25 now but they expected it to rise soon to $7.50? How much profit (or loss) would they make if they operated with a price of $4.25? How much loss would they incur if they shut down operations but continued to own the assets? (d) What would the owners do if the price were $2.30, but was expected to rise to $7.50 soon? How much loss would the owners make if they operated in the interim? How much loss would they incur if they shut down operations but continued to own the assets in anticipation of the higher price? If the price rises gradually over time, at what level of price should they begin operating?

10. For question 9: (a) How much would the firm produce if the owners were in business just to cover their costs (a nonprofit firm) and the price were $6.13? Compare that output with the profit-maximizing output at that price. (b) What value do consumers place on the extra output produced under the nonprofit operation? What is the value in alternative uses of the extra resources needed to produce the extra output? (c) Does nonprofit operation make the total amount of goods available in the economy bigger or smaller?

11. The price of a cord of Vermont firewood rose from about $30 in 1973 to about $80–$90 in 1980. Do you think the price would have risen more or less if the price of oil had not increased dramatically over that period? Why? Do you think the owners of the forests from which the firewood comes made a windfall profit? Why isn't there a firewood windfall profits tax?

12. The oil windfall profits tax taxes the difference between the price a U.S. crude oil producer receives and a specified benchmark price. The benchmark was $15 in 1979, and will be adjusted upward each year by the rate of inflation. Does this tax only the windfall as we defined it in the chapter, or does it also reduce the incentive to produce more oil? Explain. Would you expect the tax to increase or decrease the use of foreign oil?

13. In many industries there are some firms which begin operating only when the price is higher than normal. Do they cause the price to be higher or lower than it would otherwise be? Explain.

14. Suppose there is some land (type A) that would be used for cattle raising if the price per pound of beef were 25¢. Other land (type B) would not be used for this purpose unless the price per pound of beef were 50¢; and still other land (type C) would not be used unless the price were $1 per pound of beef. (a) Why are types B and C not used for cattle raising when the price of beef is only 35¢? Are those types of land necessarily *less productive* at cattle raising than type A land? What else might explain the fact that a high price is necessary to get them into the cattle market? Sketch a long-run supply of cattle (similar to figure 7-12 for oil) incorporating the information in this question. (b) Suppose now that the demand for beef is such that the price is 90¢ per pound. Which kinds of land will be used? Why? (c) Now suppose there is a substantial increase in demand for beef, but that type C land is prevented from being used. Show the new equilibrium price. (d) What would happen if the (high cost) type C land were now used? Would the price rise or fall? How can it be that the presence of the higher cost producers results in a lower price?

15. Suppose you are a price-taker and there is an increase in the amount of theft of your inventory, thus raising your costs of doing business. Will you be able to charge a higher price than before?

16. "In a price-taker industry, when all firms are operating at their profit-maximizing output, they all have the same level of marginal cost." Explain.

17. Suppose you are operating in a price-taker industry, but the price is currently above the market-clearing level. What does this mean as far as the ability of sellers to sell all they want or buyers to buy all they want? Is your demand curve horizontal (that is, could you gain sales by lowering your price)?

18. Suppose you operate a business in an industry which is in long-run equilibrium. Now suppose there is an increase in the demand for the product. What happens to the cost of using machinery designed to produce the product? Does it make any difference whether you own your own machinery or not?

19. Every resource used by a firm has an alternative use outside the industry in question. The return a resource gets in its current use will tend to be as high or higher than what it could get in its best alternative use; otherwise the resource would go to the other use. (a) Suppose it were the case that, with some looking, every resource (labor, machinery, land) being used by industry A could be used in an alternative occupation in which it would earn exactly as much as it is now earning. How would the (long-run) supply curve for industry A's product look? (b) Alternatively, how would the long-run supply curve for industry A's product look if all the resource suppliers found that (even with substantial search) the best alternative occupation they could find would pay less than they were earning in A (although for some, what they could make in their best alternative was closer to what they could make in A than it was for others)?

20. In the 1970s there was a big influx of population and tourists into San Francisco's Chinatown. During this period there were many cases of merchants who lost their leases because their rent was doubled or tripled in one year and they could not afford to pay the higher rent. (a) What do you suppose happened to the store space when the old tenants left? Could the building owners legitimately say that their cost of renting the store space had doubled or tripled? Explain. (b) Would the same sorts of changes in usage of store space have taken place if the original tenants had owned the

property? Explain by discussing the effects of the tourist and population increase on the continued possession cost of an owner.

21. Consider the following statement which appeared in a high school government text[2]:

> The price is determined by the market place and the operation of the *law of supply and demand*. Under the law of supply and demand, as the demand for a product goes up, as people want more of a certain product, the price tends to go up. But as the price increases, the demand tends to go down. This decrease in demand tends to lower prices, and lowered prices again tend to increase demand. Supply and demand vary with increase and decrease of prices. Eventually, supply and demand balance, creating a market price.

(a) How would you describe the determination of the market-clearing price using supply and demand? (b) How would you rewrite the author's statement regarding the effect of an increase in demand? (c) Do you think the author has carefully distinguished in his mind between a change in demand and a change in quantity demanded due to a change in price? (d) Cite evidence from the quotation.

22. "If there is an increase in demand, the price rises, but the higher price decreases demand and increases the supply, thus reducing the price back to its original level." Explain what is wrong with this statement and correctly state the effect of an increase in demand.

23. "If there is an increase in supply, this will lower price, but the lower price will increase demand and decrease supply, resulting in an increase in price back to the initial level." Explain what is wrong with this statement and correctly state the effect of an increase in supply.

24. The following is a paraphrase of a statement by a national news reporter[3]:

> Currently, gasoline inventories are at their highest level ever. One might think that this would lead to lower prices for gasoline. But according to oil industry spokesmen, this is not the case. You see, a lower price would lead to an increase in demand for vacation and other summer driving, leading to an increase in price.

(a) Why were gasoline inventories so high in the spring of 1980? (b) What do you think of the reasoning the reporter attributes to the "oil industry spokesmen"? (c) Did the price of gasoline fall (or rise less than prices in general) in the summer of 1980?

25. What will happen to the price and quantity of fish if, at the same time, the government announces that eating fish is a good way to avoid getting cancer, and if the Interior Department begins a program of subsidies to

2. S. E. Dimond and E. F. Pflieger, *Our American Government* (Philadelphia: J. B. Lippincott Co., 1973), p. 608.
3. Dan Rather, CBS Radio, May 1980.

firms which engage in fish farming (controlled raising and harvesting of fish)? How would your answer change if the government's report had been the opposite?

26. Suppose we conceive of the demand for gasoline as being composed of a demand for use on long-distance driving (D_L) and a demand for other uses (D_O). (a) What happens to D_L if a 55 mph speed limit is imposed? Does this affect D_O? (b) Given an upward-sloping supply curve of gasoline, what would be the effect of the law on the price of gasoline? On the total quantity of gasoline consumed? On the quantity consumed on long-distance driving? On the quantity consumed for other purposes?

27. Suppose there is a technological improvement in the production of eggs. Will the price fall by a larger percentage if demand is elastic or inelastic?

28. Suppose there is an increase in the demand for eggs. Will the price rise by a larger percentage if the elasticity of supply is 0.5 or 2?

29. What would happen to the effective (market-revealed) demand for marijuana if it were made legal? What would happen to the market price and quantity sold?

30. In October of 1976, while campaigning in Texas, President Ford announced that he was imposing a system of quotas on the importation of beef from Argentina and Australia. What effect would that action have on the supply (curve) of beef for the United States? What would be the effect on the price of beef in the United States? In Argentina?

chapter 8

Price-
Searchers

Firms which face a downward-sloping demand curve for their product are said to possess "market power" or "monopoly power," meaning that they are large enough in relation to their market to have some influence on the price of their products. As noted in chapter 6, a firm facing a downward-sloping demand curve is called a price-searcher.

In contrast to price-takers, price-searchers have a pricing problem. They must choose the best price and quantity. What determines the best position for the price-searcher? We shall find that the basic criterion for choosing the best price and quantity is the same as that used by price-takers to find the best quantity, but the results are not identical.

CONDITIONS FOR THE EXISTENCE OF PRICE SEARCHERS

1. Differences in tastes and products
2. Costly Information
3. Locational Advantages
4. Few Sellers (economies of scale)

DEMAND AND MARGINAL REVENUE

The concept of *marginal revenue (MR)* was introduced in the discussion on price-takers. It refers to the extra revenue the firm gets by selling one more unit of output. For price-takers, price and marginal revenue are the same, since price is unaffected by the quantity the firm sells. If the price is $8, regardless of how many the firm sells, the additional revenue from selling one more unit marginal revenue will be $8. This equality of price and marginal revenue does not hold for price-searchers, and this discrepancy is the source of the differences in behavior in the two types of markets. How does the discrepancy come about? If a price-searcher finds that in order to sell one more unit of output, he must charge a price of $7, why isn't his extra revenue from selling the extra unit $7? To see why, let's examine a hypothetical demand schedule facing a price-searcher. Let us concentrate on the price and quantity columns for now (see table 8-1 and figure 8-1). Suppose the firm is currently charging $8 per unit. Then the demand schedule says the firm can sell three units per week. If it wants to sell four units per week instead of three, the demand curve says that the firm must lower the price (on all units to all customers) to $7. Then, two things happen: the firm gains something and loses something. It gains the $7 because it sells the extra unit for $7. But it loses $3 because the three units which *could have been* sold for $8 are now selling for $7. (The firm lowered the price on *all* units from $8 to $7.) If we subtract the loss from the gain ($7 − $3), we get the additional revenue from selling one more unit (MR = $4). Marginal revenue is less than the price charged for the extra unit ($4 versus $7). The reason is that the price-searcher faces a downward-sloping demand curve. He must lower the price in order to sell an extra unit of output. (The price-taker does not have this problem. Since he can sell all he wants at the "going" price, he does not need to lower his price in order to sell an additional unit, and there is no loss component to subtract from the price. Thus the price equals marginal revenue.

If we try the same experiment at different points on the demand curve, we will always get a similar result. *Marginal revenue is less than price.* In fact, *marginal revenue* could even be *negative!* For example, suppose the firm is currently charging a price of $5 (the demand curve implies sales of six units). The firm considers lowering the price enough to sell one more unit. That would mean a price of $4 (quantity seven). What is *marginal revenue?* The gain is $4 (the new price), but the loss is $6 (due to the $1 decrease in price on each of the six units which could be sold at $5). So marginal revenue is − $2. Revenue *falls* when the extra unit is sold!

To get another angle on what *marginal revenue* is, look at the total revenue (TR) column of table 8-1. *Total revenue* is simply price times quantity. Since *marginal revenue* is the change in *total revenue* for a one-unit increase in quantity sold,

$$\frac{\text{change in } TR}{\text{change in } Q},$$

the *marginal revenue* column shows the difference between successive *total revenues.* Looking at figure 8-1, *total revenue* for any price is represented by the area of a rectangle with height equal to P and width equal to Q. In comparing the *total revenues* for P = 8 and for P = 7, the difference between the two rectangles is that the second one has the right-hand "gain" column which the first doesn't have, and the first has the upper "loss" area which the second doesn't have. The difference in *total revenues* (that is, *marginal revenue*) is thus equal to gain minus loss just as before.

TABLE 8-1
DEMAND SCEDULE
FOR PRICE-SEARCH

P	Q	TR	MR
$10	1	10	—
9	2	18	8
8	3	24	6
7	4	28	4
6	5	30	2
5	6	30	0
4	7	28	−2
3	8	24	−4
2	9	18	−6
1	10	10	−8

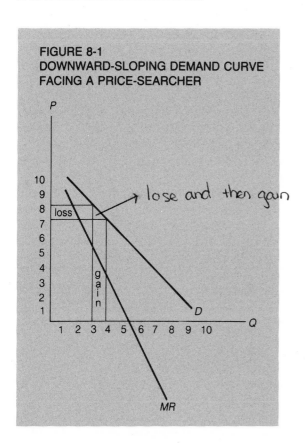

FIGURE 8-1
DOWNWARD-SLOPING DEMAND CURVE
FACING A PRICE-SEARCHER

Marginal revenue always lies below the demand curve when the demand curve is downward-sloping, because the loss component exists. The farther we go to the right along the demand curve, the farther *marginal revenue* is below *demand*. This is because the loss component is larger.

Remember that the loss component equals the quantity sold (at the old price) times the change in price. The farther down the demand curve we go, the larger the quantity and, therefore, the larger the loss component and the greater the difference between *price* (or *demand*) and *marginal revenue*.

A simple rule to remember in constructing the *MR* curve in relation to any straight line demand curve is that the *MR* curve should be drawn so as to bisect any horizontal line drawn from the price axis to the demand curve. In particular, the *MR* curve crosses the quantity axis at a *Q* which is one half as great as that at which the demand curve crosses it.

INCREMENTAL REVENUE
AND MARGINAL REVENUE

The notion of the change in revenue due to selling one more unit of a good may seem far removed from real-world decisions. If General Motors decided to produce one more Chevette, the effect on the price of Chevettes would be insignificant. Nevertheless, the notion of marginal revenue, and the distinction between marginal revenue and price are still very important to GM. To see how we would adapt the notion of marginal revenue to this situation, consider the following hypothetical numbers. Suppose Chevettes are currently selling at the rate of 300,000 per year and that the price per Chevette is $4500. Now suppose that GM's marketing department has estimated that if the price were lowered to $4000, the annual rate of sales would increase from 300,000 per year to 350,000 per year. Should GM lower its price? That depends on whether the incremental revenue (if any) that GM gets due to the higher rate of sales is greater or less than the incremental cost. We will discuss cost a little later in the chapter. For now, let us concentrate on the incremental revenue. At a price of $4500, GM receives revenue at the rate of $1.35 billion per year ($4500 per car times 300,000 cars). If its forecast is correct, it would receive $1.40 billion per year at a price of $4000 per car ($4000 per car times 350,000 cars). The incremental revenue due to selling 350,000 per year at $4000 per car instead of 300,000 per year at $4500 per car is $.05 billion, or $50 million. The extra revenue per extra car is this incremental revenue *divided by* the increase in output (change in TR/change in Q). This is $50 million/50,000 = $1000 per car. We can see that GM's revenue goes up if it lowers the price sufficiently to sell 50,000 more cars, but the extra revenue per extra car—that is, marginal revenue—is only $1000 per car, even though each of those cars sells for $4000. The reason for the discrepancy between price and marginal revenue is the same as it was in our earlier example. If GM wants to sell the extra 50,000 cars, it must charge less than it otherwise would for the 300,000 cars it would be able to sell at $4500. GM gets $200 million revenue from selling the extra 50,000 cars for $4000 each. But it loses $150 million in revenue it could have otherwise obtained from the 300,000 because it is charging $500 less per car than it could have. The (net) change in revenue is $50 million for the 50,000 cars, or $1000 per extra car sold. Unless the marginal cost (extra cost per extra car made) is less than $1000, it will not pay GM to produce and sell the extra cars.

Thus, we see that even when we are dealing with big increments in output, the concept of marginal revenue helps us see more clearly the alternatives the firm faces.

OPTIMAL OUTPUT
AND PRICE

What has been said so far about price-searchers applies regardless of what is assumed about behavior. *Marginal revenue* always lies below the demand curve when it is downward-sloping. Now an assumption must be made about how price-searchers behave. It can be assumed that price-searchers' motivations are the same as those of price-takers. They are in business to make money, and the more the better. In the jargon of economics, they want to maximize profits. There are two reasons for this assumption. First, it is probably correct most of the time. Second, other assumptions which might be made often would not lead to different implications but *would* be much more cumbersome to work with. In more advanced courses you may be introduced to some of the more complicated versions of the theory of the firm.

Once we assume that firms want to maximize profits, what does that tell us about output and price? It rules out certain prices altogether as being inconsistent with profit maximization. Going back to the demand schedule and curve in figure 8-1, we see that any price below $5 is definitely inferior, because revenue is smaller than at $5 and more has to be produced.

We can see how this works by means of an example. Suppose you have contracted to display the next big heavyweight boxing match on closed circuit TV. You have rented the arena and the equipment, and you have paid a fee to the promoters for the TV signal. Your arena has a seating capacity of 2000 equally good seats. (This is a simplifying assumption. What would happen if it were relaxed? The problem would be much more complicated, but no more helpful in terms of insight.) You estimate the demand to be that shown in figure 8-2.

What price would you charge? Let's make another simplifying assumption. All your costs (including such things as the costs of ushers and ticket takers, as well as the fee paid to the promoter) are fixed—that is, they do not depend on how many people attend. If you want to make yourself feel good by having people line up to get in, you could charge $1. Then there would be a shortage of seats and scalpers would probably be able to get at least $3 per seat. (Why?) Or you could charge a price which you estimate would just sell out the place—$3. Or you could charge a higher price and have empty seats. Why might you do this? Because the lost revenue is more than made up for by the increased price received from those who do attend. In other words, we are in the range of negative *marginal revenue,* so that *decreases in quantity raise total revenue* (since *increases in quantity lower total revenue).* In fact, if you raised the price

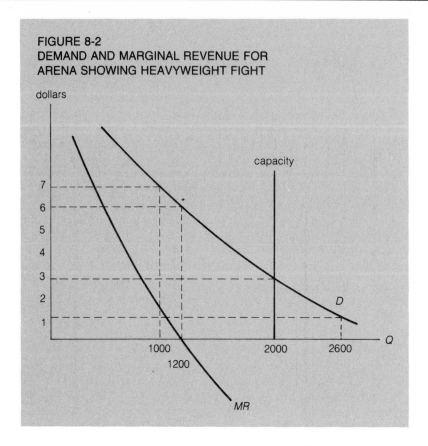

FIGURE 8-2
DEMAND AND MARGINAL REVENUE FOR
ARENA SHOWING HEAVYWEIGHT FIGHT

to $6 per ticket, your revenue would be $7200, as opposed to only $6000 at a price of $3. Further increases in the price would not be worthwhile, since your revenue would be smaller. (For example, a price of $7 would bring only $7000 in revenue.)

What principle is operating here? When costs do not depend on output, the best price to charge is the one where *total* revenue is maximized. That price occurs when *marginal revenue* = 0. As long as *marginal revenue* is greater than zero, an increase in *quantity* (lower price) raises *total revenue*. When *marginal revenue* = 0, no further increases in *total revenue* can be obtained.

There is something *inefficient* about this result. At a price of $6, there are 800 empty seats. If those seats were filled, you wouldn't have to incur any extra cost. And there are people who would be willing to pay for the seats. So why don't you sell them for, say, $3? Suppose that you have put your seats on sale for $6 and have sold 1200; you then say, "OK, now anyone else who wants to buy a ticket can have it for $3." You would sell 800 more tickets for an additional revenue of $2400. Certainly *you* like that, and so do the additional 800 customers. But the first 1200 buyers feel cheated and vow not to get snookered again; and therein lies your problem.

While you would be perfectly happy to charge $6 for the first 1200 customers and $3 for the next 800, you wouldn't be able to get away with it for long. If you tried it again, you would find no takers at $6 and 2000 takers at $3, for a revenue of $6000. Since this is lower than what you get for the single price of $6, you are better off sticking with that if you are selling tickets to events like this on a regular basis.

This brings out a paradoxical result. It is possible for both you *and* the customers to be better off with 2000 (rather than 1200) tickets sold. If 1200 pay $6 and 800 pay $3, the $6 payers are no worse off than they are with the single $6 price, and the $3 payers are better off. But, as we noted, when the two price scheme is tried on a repeated basis, the 1200 potential payers of $6 will tend to wait for you to lower your price so that they pay only $3, reducing your revenue. It is very difficult to identify those who are willing to pay $6 or more and charge them (and only them) the higher price. So the result, in cases where the seller must sell his products on a continuing basis, is often the single (inefficiently high) price.

BRINGING IN COSTS

To make our theory of price-searcher behavior more general, let us consider a situation where the firm's costs depend on how much is produced. We find that the basic principles which guide the price-searcher are the same as for the price-taker, but because she faces a downward-sloping demand curve the price-searcher acts differently.

The situation shown in figure 8-3 is one possible outcome. If we ask what the best (profit maximizing) price is, the answer is the same as for the price-taker: where $MR = MC$. The firm should increase output as long as the extra revenue it gets from doing so (*marginal revenue*) is greater than the extra cost (*marginal cost*). The $MR = MC$ point is the boundary between *profitable* increases in quantity (where $MR > MC$) and *unprofitable* increases (where $MR < MC$). If the firm is to maximize profit it must exploit all profitable increases in quantity, but not stray into the range where increases in quantity reduce profit.

A few observations about this outcome are in order. First, notice that the price charged (P^*) is greater than the *marginal cost* at that point (MC^*). This follows directly from the fact that for the price-searcher, price is greater than marginal revenue, and that to maximize profit, the firm should produce where $MR = MC$. This discrepancy between price and marginal cost results in an inefficiency which we shall discuss later in greater detail.

Recalling our discussion of elasticity in chapter 3, we can relate elasticity to the optimal output of the price-searcher. Recall from our discussion that a way of distinguishing between the elastic and inelastic ranges of the demand curve is that, in the elastic range, a decrease in price (resulting in an increased quantity sold) *increases* total expenditure (total revenue to the seller), while in the inelastic range, a decrease in price (and increase in *quantity*) results in a *lower* total revenue. We can relate

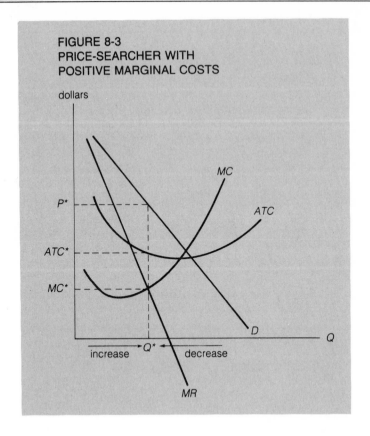

FIGURE 8-3
PRICE-SEARCHER WITH
POSITIVE MARGINAL COSTS

these facts to the concept of marginal revenue. If an increased *quantity* leads to an *increase in total revenue, then marginal revenue is positive. If an increase in quantity results in a lower total revenue, then marginal revenue is negative.* Thus we have the following relationships: when $E > 1$ (elastic), $MR > 0$; when $E < 1$ (inelastic), $MR < 0$; when $E = 1$ (unitary), $MR = 0$. Graphically, it comes out as in figure 8-4.

Since the firm wants to produce where $MR = MC$, and since *marginal cost* will never be negative, the profit-maximizing firm will always be operating where *marginal revenue* is greater than or equal to zero, meaning that the demand (for his product) will be elastic in the range where the price-searcher operates, as long as *marginal cost* is greater than zero.

Note also that the profit-maximizing price and output need not occur where *average total cost* is minimized. It would be only coincidental for that output to be the most profitable one.

The output may involve positive, negative, or zero economic profits. Examine figure 8-3 again. The profit-maximizing output is Q^*. If the firm wants to sell Q^*, the demand curve says that it must charge price P^*. Total revenue will be P^* times Q^*, represented by the rectangle with height P^* and width Q^*. What are total costs at output Q^*? To get this we note that *average* total cost (total cost per unit) is ATC^* when output is Q^*. Then

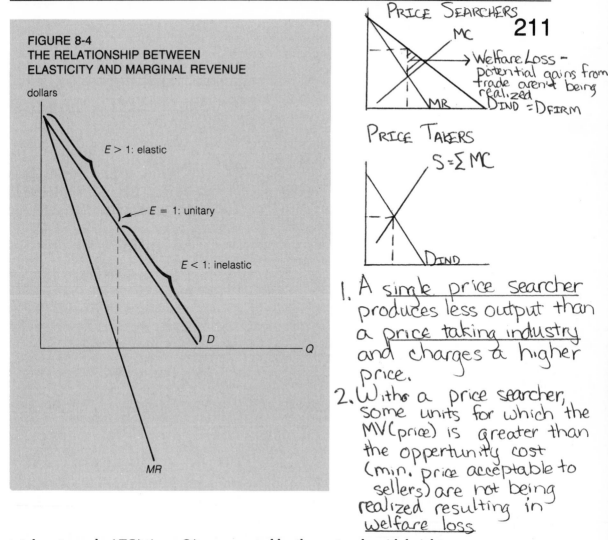

FIGURE 8-4
THE RELATIONSHIP BETWEEN
ELASTICITY AND MARGINAL REVENUE

dollars

$E > 1$: elastic

$E = 1$: unitary

$E < 1$: inelastic

D

Q

MR

PRICE SEARCHERS

MC **211**

→ Welfare Loss -
potential gains from
trade aren't being
realized
$D_{IND} = D_{FIRM}$

MR

PRICE TAKERS

$S = \sum MC$

D_{IND}

1. A single price searcher produces less output than a price taking industry and charges a higher price.

2. With a price searcher, some units for which the MV (price) is greater than the oppertunity cost (min. price acceptable to sellers) are not being realized resulting in welfare loss

total cost equals ATC^* times Q^*, represented by the rectangle with height ATC^* and width Q^*. Economic profit is TR minus TC, or $(P^* - ATC^*)$ times Q^*, represented by the rectangle with height of P^* minus ATC^* and width of Q^*. Thus the case shown here has positive profit, but being a price-searcher is not a guarantee of economic profits. To see this one need only look at the case of the Chrysler Corporation, which was saved from bankruptcy only by government guarantees of loans.

THE LONG RUN

We noted above that the demand curve might lie above or below the ATC curve, so that the firm could be making profits or losses. That is true in the short run. A firm already in the business may sustain losses without immediately getting out (as we saw in chapters 5 and 7), or receive profits

212

OPEN MARKET PRICE SEARCHER

WITH ENTRY OF NEW FIRMS:

① DEMAND FOR INPUTS RISES
→ INCREASED PRICES FOR INPUTS
→ INCREASED AVERAGE TOTAL COSTS

② THE DEMAND FACING ANY INDIVIDUAL FIRM BECOMES MORE ELASTIC BECAUSE MORE SUBSTITUTES ARE AVAILABLE

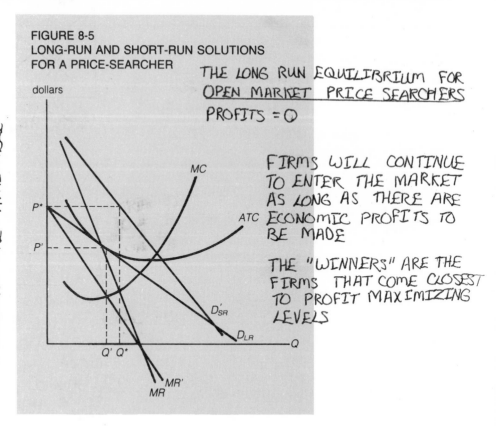

FIGURE 8-5
LONG-RUN AND SHORT-RUN SOLUTIONS
FOR A PRICE-SEARCHER

THE LONG RUN EQUILIBRIUM FOR OPEN MARKET PRICE SEARCHERS

PROFITS = 0

FIRMS WILL CONTINUE TO ENTER THE MARKET AS LONG AS THERE ARE ECONOMIC PROFITS TO BE MADE

THE "WINNERS" ARE THE FIRMS THAT COME CLOSEST TO PROFIT MAXIMIZING LEVELS

without making any immediate increase in the size of its plant. But as time passes, both profits and losses tend to disappear through changes in the size or number of firms, if there are no restrictions on entry or exit. (If there are restrictions on entry, then a profit will not tend to be eroded over time.)

The effect of time and entry on the case in figure 8-3 is shown in figure 8-5. When the opportunity to make a profit by producing a similar good is discovered, new firms enter. Their entry means there are more and better substitutes for the product of our firm. The result is that the demand for our firm's product falls and becomes more elastic. This is shown in figure 8-5 by the shift in demand from D_{SR} to D'_{LR}. This process is in a sense the working out of the Second Law of Demand. One of the things which makes the demand for any product more elastic in the long run than in the short run is the emergence of new substitutes, not merely the rediscovery and increased use of old ones.

Note that there is a tendency for the process to continue until the best that any firm can do is cover its cost (find the price where $P = ATC$). In figure 8-5 we see that D'_{LR} is tangent to ATC at output Q'. For that output, $TR = TC$ (use the technique we described for figure 8-3 to show that this is true); but for any other output, price is less than average total cost, so that the firm would be making a loss. The *best* the firm can do with demand curve D'_{LR} is to just cover all costs. We can confirm that output Q' is the best output by noting that $MR' = MC$ at output Q'. If a price-quantity combination could be found where price is greater than *average total cost*, then it would be profitable for new entry to occur.[1]

Sometimes entry continues until one or more firms find that their demand curve lies *below average total cost* throughout—no output is profitable. Then those firms will tend to leave the industry in the long run. The firm in question might even have been the originator of the idea. The firm which is the first to come up with a new product need not be the lowest-cost producer of it. Once others discover the idea, they may be better at actually producing the good and, by their entry and ability to survive at low prices, may drive out the originator.

[margin note: SURVIVORSHIP PRINCIPLE]

Sometimes firms find themselves in the fortunate position that the cost facing potential new entrants is greater than the cost incurred by existing firms. This could happen, for example, if the firm is able to get laws passed which require only *new* firms to go through certain costly procedures (such as more rigid pollution control standards or more rigorous testing of new products before they can be marketed). When this happens, less entry will occur and the demand curve will probably not shift all the way down to the *average total cost*. We shall more fully discuss the way in which entry barriers affect the operation of a market in chapter 10.

[margin note: LUCK]

PRICE-SEARCHERS WITH COSTLY INFORMATION

We have been treating the price-searcher's choice of price and output as a fairly simple one involving finding the intersection of *marginal revenue* and *marginal cost*. In fact it is not an easy matter to discover the best price. Demand curves (and even cost curves) are not always perfectly known by the firms involved, and without knowledge of these relationships it is not possible to simply pick out the best price. The process is much less precise, sometimes built on guesses or intuition. In fact, many managers may be unfamiliar with the terms marginal revenue and marginal cost. Then what use is our elaborate theorizing? First of all, it tells us what profitable behavior is. Firms which make profits *will* be producing at or near where $MR = MC$ *whether they know it or not*. And firms which, for whatever reason, end up being profitable will be imitated. Those who choose unprofitable price and output combinations will shrink and tend to disappear,

---

1. As was the case for price-takers, entry of new firms tends to result not only in a lower price, but in higher costs per firm. In figure 8-5, this would be reflected in a shift up in *average total cost* and *marginal cost*. The result would be that entry would not be carried as far, and the firm's demand and price would remain somewhat higher in the long-run equilibrium than is shown in figure 8-5.

214

and will not be imitated. Thus there is a tendency for firms to act as the models say they do simply because such behavior is rewarded and tends to survive in the marketplace.

ADMINISTERED PRICES

Some observers of the economic scene have criticized what they view as a situation in which prices are set arbitrarily, and not in accordance with supply and demand. Typical examples are steel, aluminum, automobiles, and other highly concentrated industries. In examining the behavior of price-searchers, we have shed some light on this issue. Note first that it is true that price-searchers have discretion over the price they set because they face a downward-sloping demand curve. But not all prices the price-searcher could charge are equally profitable. Certainly no firm could raise its price forever and increase profits by doing so. No, on the contrary, we note that there is one most profitable price, and that price depends on both the cost and demand conditions the firm faces. We can see this by referring again to figure 8-3. The profit-maximizing price is P^*. The firm could charge a higher or lower price, but it would have a lower profit if it did so. If either demand or marginal cost changes, there will almost always be a change in the profit-maximizing price and output. Even General Motors and U.S. Steel are constrained by their cost and demand conditions, and we have these constraints, not their social conscience, to thank for the fact that their prices are not higher. General Motors could raise prices arbitrarily, but it would do so at the expense of profits.

There are two basic issues in the administered prices controversy. The first is whether firms could arbitrarily raise prices (say when there was a decrease in demand or a fall in costs) and improve their profit situation in so doing. As the above discussion suggests, the answer to that question is no, if the firm was maximizing profits in the situation before the change in cost or demand conditions. The second issue is whether the firms in question are interested in maximizing profits. This is largely an empirical question. If we observe firms raising prices when both their demand and costs have fallen, for example, we could infer that they are not profit-maximizing. If, however, increases in demand or costs tend to result in higher prices, then firms are acting as they would if they were profit-maximizing. We could then reject the administered prices thesis as being empirically false. What is the evidence? There is still some controversy, but there is a good deal of evidence that prices move in the way that profit-maximizing theory predicts.

COMPETITION AS RIVALRY—THE CASE OF DISPOSABLE DIAPERS

In some industries there are so few sellers that each must take into account the reactions of other firms. (This situation is sometimes called _oligopoly_,

---

Handwritten margin notes:

FALLACIES OF PRICE SEARCHING MARKETS

1. PRICES ARE ARBITRARILY SET
   ⇒ prices are constrained by supply and demand

2. CONCENTRATION AND PROFITS
   ⇒ profits are not, necessarily, an indicator of market share

from Greek roots meaning "few sellers." But it is the recognized interdependence rather than the number of firms per se which is important.) In such situations, a complete description of the behavior of the firms in question would require more sophisticated tools to take account of the interactions between the parties. Nevertheless, some general statements can be made about the nature of the interaction. First of all, if the firms act independently (a discussion of firms acting in concert is given in chapter 10), their behavior will be competitive in the sense of rivalry. Often the competition (for the best product or to dominate sales in a given area) takes on aspects of warfare. This personalized feature of the competition is absent from the "large numbers" price-taker case. The two kinds of competition are quite different, although in some respects the outcomes are similar. In a price-takers market, lower-cost firms tend to survive, and higher-cost firms fall by the wayside. Products for which consumers are willing to pay (enough to defray the cost) tend to be produced. Similar results occur when there is more personalized rivalry.

As an example, take a relatively new product—disposable diapers. When Pampers were first introduced, it was not generally known whether consumers were willing to pay the price. Proctor and Gamble (the maker of Pampers) believed they would be successful, but apparently other manufacturers did not. When it became clear that the demand for the product lay above the *ATC* curve, meaning profits for Pampers, other firms decided to get into the game. Kimberly-Clark, makers of Kleenex, made its entry with Kimbies. The existence of a competitor reduced and made more elastic the demand for Pampers, because now there was a better, closer substitute. Each firm tried to convince consumers through advertising that its product was more convenient, and more absorbent and comfortable for the baby. The competition from Kimbies made the price of disposable diapers rise less or fall more than it otherwise would have, and resulted in improvements in the quality of Pampers.

In 1975, Johnson & Johnson decided that it could use its brand name to launch an entry into the fray. Later, the design of Pampers was changed so that they were more absorbent. In 1979, Kimberly-Clark offered a "premium" diaper, with elastic, to prevent leaking. In 1980, Proctor and Gamble responded with a premium brand, in addition to Pampers. As the market for the product grows (through switching consumers from buying cloth diapers to buying disposable diapers—*not* necessarily because of more babies!), it may be that sales of Pampers will continue to grow in absolute size, while falling as a fraction of the total amount sold.

Is this process competition? Most assuredly, although it is direct, subject to rivalry, and personal. Each of the "big three" is keenly aware of just what its rivals are doing in terms of advertising and new products, as well as promotional free distribution (through hospitals, for example). The results are not identical to those of a price-taker's market, but then if there were a hundred or a thousand producers of this product, prices to consumers would not be as low as in this market. There are economies of scale, meaning that the efficient number of firms is small. In that situation, our alternatives are cooperative (known as *collusive*) behavior by the firms, or independent, personalized rivalry, with or without restrictions on entry.

The latter (with free entry) is clearly competitive, and we shall examine the alternative—collusion—in chapter 10.

PRICE DISCRIMINATION

When a seller charges different people different prices for the same good, and when there are no cost differences that can account for the price differences, the seller is practicing "price discrimination." There are many examples of this phenomenon, but there are many others in which casual observation does not enable us to determine whether price discrimination is occurring. Why does price discrimination occur? Under what conditions can a firm successfully engage in price discrimination?

Why do firms engage in price discrimination? It could be because the sellers just don't like some buyers, but much more likely is the presumption that there is something about price discrimination which increases profits. Indeed there are certain circumstances in which price discrimination does increase profits. What are those conditions? First, the firm in question must be a price-searcher. If the firm can't choose the price to charge, it certainly can't charge different prices to different customers for the same product. Second, the seller must be able to identify the groups to which she wants to charge the various prices. And third, the seller must be able to keep the commodity from being resold after she sells it. If a seller charges me $5 and you $50 for the same good, you and I might be tempted to work out a deal whereby I buy the good and sell it to you, thus thwarting the price discriminator.

On what basis would a price discriminator choose to charge her various prices? The answer, very roughly, is that she will attempt to charge a high price to those who will stand still for it, and a lower price to those who won't stand for the higher price. What is the measure of the willingness to stand for a high price? It is the elasticity of demand. If a group of consumers have an inelastic demand, then raising the price will result in only a small percentage decrease in quantity demanded, and an increase in revenue. On the other hand, if another group has an elastic demand, a lower price will result in a large increase in the quantity demanded, resulting in an increase in revenue. Most examples of price discrimination (and all examples of profitable price discrimination) can be explained on this basis.

What are some examples? One of the best has always been the various prices charged by physicians for their services. The usual scheme has been to charge a higher price to those with higher income, because they are likely to have a less elastic demand than poor people. When an attraction (say a movie theater) lets children in for a reduced price or for free, that is price discrimination. The presumption is that people with families have a more elastic demand than childless couples. Youth fares on the airlines was an example of price discrimination. Notice that in all of those cases, it would be difficult or impossible to resell the services.

Many price differentiations are not examples of price discrimination because what seems to be one product is really different products. For example, matinees at movies and plays are not the same commodities as evening performances. The same is true of a nighttime flight as compared to an 8 a.m. flight of an airline, or nighttime use of electricity versus peak hour use. But does the fact that they are different commodities imply that cost is different and that different prices should be charged? The answer is often yes. For example, consider the relatively new practice of *peak load pricing* of electricity. The idea is that the price of electricity should be higher during the peak (heavy use) hours than during the off-peak (light use) hours. Why? The electric utility must build capacity for electricity generation which is great enough to meet the heaviest demand (usually between 4 and 8 p.m.). The consumption during that period causes the capacity to be built. The nighttime use is much smaller and requires much less capacity. In fact, the capacity required by the peak period is just sitting there at night, and the only opportunity cost incurred in using it is the fuel, upkeep, and distribution cost. So the peak load use causes both capacity and operating costs to be incurred, while the off-peak causes only operating costs to be incurred. Thus the off-peak user should be charged less than the peak user.

Similarly, matinees, night flights, and off-hour meals at fancy restaurants should all be priced lower than their peak-hour counterparts, on the basis of efficiency and cost considerations. Does that mean that all such variations in price are efficient? No. The sellers of those services are also price-searchers who can prevent resale, so there *may* also be price discrimination involved in this. It is not possible to tell by casual observation, but the price differentiation does not *in itself* prove price discrimination in these cases.

MULTIPART PRICING

Price discrimination is one way in which different prices may be charged for the same commodity—namely charging a different price to different customers. Another way is to charge different prices to the *same* customer. This is called *multipart pricing*.

Suppose you are a price-searcher who knows the demand curves of individual customers very well. In particular, suppose that one of your customers has the demand curve shown in figure 8-6. Suppose for simplicity that the marginal cost to you of producing your output is $1 per unit. The MR curve shows the additional revenue you can expect to obtain by selling additional amounts, *assuming you charge a single price for all units sold.* Comparing the *marginal revenue* to the *marginal cost* schedule, we see that your best strategy would be to produce and sell four units at a price of $5 each. Your revenue would be $20, while your cost would be $4, for a profit of $16. You could, however, do better if you were permitted

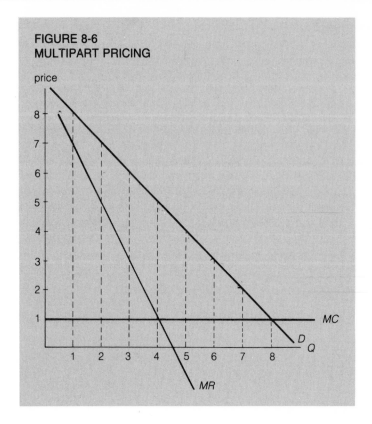

FIGURE 8-6
MULTIPART PRICING

to charge more than one price to the same customer. Suppose, for example, you continued to charge $5 for the first four units sold, and $2 for each additional unit sold. In that case, the customer would, according to his demand curve, buy three more units. (He would buy them because, having already bought four units, he places marginal values of $4, $3, and $2 on the fifth, sixth, and seventh units of output, as shown by his demand curve.) The three extra units sold would add $6 to your revenue and only $3 to your cost, thus raising your profit by $3 (to $19). Would the customer oppose this change in pricing policy? Probably not, because relative to the one-price situation he is better off. (By how much? By $3. He gets a net gain of $2 on the fifth unit, since he valued it at $4 and had to pay only $2, and a net gain of $1 on the sixth unit, since he valued it at $3 and had to pay only $2.) Furthermore, the ability to charge multiple prices, by carrying exchange farther, permits this market arrangement to more closely approach the efficient outcome where the price the customer pays (for the last unit he buys) is equal to the marginal cost of producing the product. (Recall that price-searchers charging a single price always fall short of that output because they produce (as you did originally) where $MR = MC$, and that price is greater than *marginal revenue*, and thus greater than *marginal cost*.)

Could you do even better than this? If you knew the demand curve as well as we are assuming, you could. You could give the customer the following price list: "First unit, $8; second unit, $7; third unit, $6; fourth unit, $5; fifth unit, $4; sixth unit, $3; seventh unit, $2; eighth unit, $1." Your total revenue would be $8 + 7 + 6 + 5 + 4 + 3 + 2 + 1 = \$36$, and the total cost would be $8, for a profit of $28. There is no pricing policy which would give you a larger profit. The customer would buy the eight units because he places a value at least as high as the price he is asked to pay on each succeeding unit. In this case the ideal of the price (for the last unit bought) equalling the marginal cost is met (not just approached), so the result is efficient in the sense that all mutually beneficial exchanges have taken place. But it is not a result the customer is likely to approve of. He gets no net benefit out of dealing with you, since you have extracted the maximum amount he was willing to pay for each succeeding unit. You have obtained all the gains from trade. He would prefer the single price of $5 (and definitely the two-price policy of $5 and $2) to this scheme, even though both are inefficient in regard to carrying out all mutually beneficial exchanges.

An equivalent method of pricing would be for you to charge the customer a $28 ($7 + $6 + $5 + $4 + $3 + $2 + $1) "entry fee," and then let him buy as much as he wants for $1 apiece. (Check to see that the total payment by the customer would again be $36, with a $28 profit for you.) Any entry fee less than $28 would provide some benefits for both of you. If you charged an entry fee of between $16 and $22, you would both be better off than you were with the single price of $5. (It must be greater than $16, because that was your profit with the single $5 price. And it must be less than $22, because that would leave only a $6 net gain for the consumer.[2]

To what extent is this type of pricing policy likely to occur? The extreme case, in which the seller extracts all the gains from trade, is very unlikely, because it requires such detailed knowledge of the demand curve by the seller. (Nevertheless, it is useful as a benchmark, or limiting case.) What about two- or three-part pricing structures? In order for such a policy to work, the seller would again (as in the case of price discrimination) have to be able to prevent resale of the commodity. (Otherwise, one customer could buy a large amount at the lowest price and resell to other customers.) Thus it would be expected to be most prevalent in the area of services, which are difficult to resell.

Public utilities (such as electricity and gas) have often used this type of pricing, whereby, for example, a certain price is charged for the first few kilowatt-hours (kwh) of electrical output, and lower prices per kwh are charged for succeeding units. The admission fee approach is often used by the telephone company, golf courses, and amusement parks. Depending on

---

2. He gets $36 total value for the eight units, minus $8 for direct purchase of goods, minus $22 entry fee, yielding a $6 net gain. When you charged the single $5 price, his net gain was $6 ($8 + $7 + $6 + $5 = $26 value, minus $20 in payments to you). So for him to be better off now, your fee would have to be less than $22.

how high the admission fee is, such pricing may be preferred by consumers to pricing in which a single (higher) price is charged per unit of output consumed.

NATURAL MONOPOLY

In chapter 6 we spoke of the reasons for price-searchers. One of the important ones was *economies of scale*—the idea that (up to a point) a large firm can produce goods for a lower cost per unit (*average total cost*) than a smaller firm. Occasionally a situation arises in which a single firm can produce the good in question at a lower cost per unit than any larger number of firms could. The result is that only one firm will survive— natural monopoly. This phenomenon, of extreme economies of scale, is usually associated with what are called *line industries*. Some kind of line is associated with them, such as telephone, electricity, railroad, highway, natural gas pipeline, sewers, and water.

In the kind of natural monopoly that people worry about, two problems arise. They are illustrated in figure 8-7.

The one firm remaining after the competitive process will be a

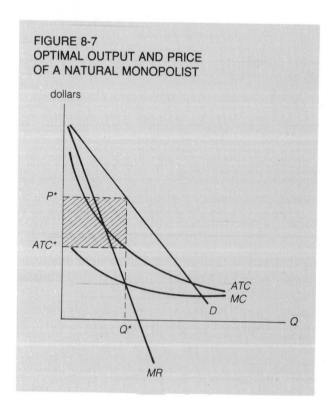

FIGURE 8-7
OPTIMAL OUTPUT AND PRICE
OF A NATURAL MONOPOLIST

monopolist in almost any sense. Entry is unlikely, and there is only one seller. Figure 8-7 shows the cost curves of the single firm remaining after the competitive process. Since it is the only seller, the demand curve it faces is the same as the industry demand. If left to its own devices, the firm would choose the profit-maximizing price of P^* and sell quantity Q^*. As usual, the profit maximizing quantity (Q^*) is the one at which $MR = MC$. In order to sell that quantity the unregulated natural monopolist should charge a price of P^*.

There are two distasteful features of this solution. The first is that, in contrast with the price-taker situation, but in common with other price-searchers, price is greater than marginal cost. What is the problem with this? When price is greater than marginal cost, it means that too little of the good is being produced, in the sense that the value the consumers place on having more of the good is greater than the additional cost of producing more. Whatever price the monopolist sets, consumers will adjust their purchases so that the marginal value they place on the last unit they buy is just equal to the price they must pay for it. Since that price is above marginal cost, the marginal value consumers place on that good is greater than the marginal value consumers place on the goods which would be foregone if more of this good were produced (in other words, the marginal cost.) This is another way of saying that resources are not going to their highest-valued use.

The second problem with the unregulated natural monopoly outcome is that the firm is making economic profits (represented by the shaded area in figure 8-7). In both the price-taker and price-searcher cases, when there is free entry, economic profits tend to be eliminated by the entry process. But with the extreme economies of scale characteristic of natural monopoly, a potential entrant would not enter unless she expected to drive out the firm currently in business. If she were able to do so, then she would be the monopolist, and the problems discussed above would again exist.

Price Equals Marginal Cost

To cope with these two problems economists have proposed two kinds of strategy. To solve the problem of price greater than marginal cost, the solution is to force the monopolist to charge a price equal to marginal cost, as shown in figure 8-8. There are several problems with this solution. An important one is that, since we are in the range where average total cost is falling, marginal cost is less than average total cost, and since $P = MC$, P is less than average total cost, so the firm is operating at a loss. This is illustrated in figure 8-8. The quantity at which $P = MC$ is Q' (with price P' equal to marginal cost MC'). At that quantity, average total cost is ATC'. The loss is represented by the rectangle with height of ATC' minus P' and width of Q'. The loss must be made up somehow, or the monopolist will eventually leave the industry and no new firm will enter. So taxes may have to be levied in order to make up for the loss. Other difficulties are related to the fact that it is difficult for the outside regulatory agency to

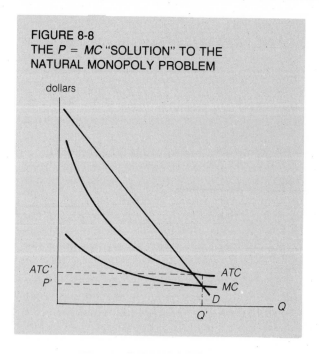

FIGURE 8-8
THE $P = MC$ "SOLUTION" TO THE
NATURAL MONOPOLY PROBLEM

know just what the marginal costs are, or what they would be for a well-run firm. Because of this, there is a tendency for the cost curves to shift up, due to less aggressive management. After all, if the government will supply the difference between costs and revenues, there is little to induce managers to be cost conscious. The solution of setting price equal to marginal cost has its problems.

Price Equals Average Total Cost

The most widely recommended remedy for the problem of price greater than average total cost is that there be direct regulation to force the price down from P^* to $\bar{P}$ equal to $\overline{ATC}$, as shown in figure 8-9. This type of regulation is sometimes called fair return regulation, because if the outcome shown in figure 8-9 is achieved, the firm will be making zero economic profit. This means that the owners will be earning just as much as (but no more than) they could in their best alternative investment. There are two problems with this. First, since average total cost is falling, a price set equal to average total cost will be above marginal cost, although by much less than in the unregulated situation. The other problem is similar to that of the $P = MC$ solution, namely that the regulators have a hard time giving any inducement to the firm's managers to be diligent and innovative. It is apparently true that the management of regulated firms is deficient in these respects, in comparison to unregulated firms, because the managers of the regulated firms have a reduced incentive to cut cost.

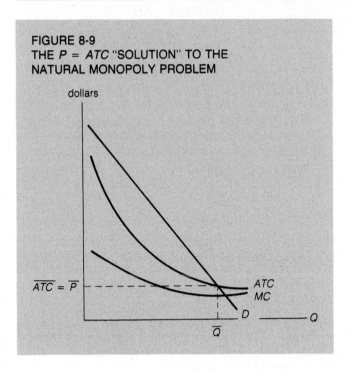

FIGURE 8-9
THE $P = ATC$ "SOLUTION" TO THE
NATURAL MONOPOLY PROBLEM

Other Strategies?

We have seen that it is impossible to solve both deficiencies (*price* greater than *average total cost* and *price* greater than *marginal cost*) of the unregulated natural monopolist at the same time. But even if we settle for solving only one of the problems, there is the problem of the reduced incentive to be innovative and cut costs. Is there any way around this? Perhaps. Recent research has indicated that there may be a way of getting the benefits of $P = ATC$ without having the reduced incentive to be efficient. This method involves what might be called competition *for the* market rather than *in* the market. When we have a natural monopoly, we might *auction off* the right to be the monopolist. But instead of asking for bids of how much firms would be willing to pay to be an unregulated monopolist, we ask for bids in terms of what *prices they would agree to* charge. Then we choose the firm who offers the lowest prices consistent with some specified quality of service.

What would be the result? Each firm would offer a price schedule which permits at least a normal rate of return but underbids the others. If there were a rather large number of bidders (say ten or so), there would be a tendency for the bids to center on the average total cost, so that the winner would just make a normal return. So far the result looks just like the $P = ATC$ solution. But there is a big difference. First, there need be no direct regulation or examination of the operations of the firm. All that is needed is monitoring to make sure the firm is living up to its contract. Second, if the firm finds a way to cut costs, it will get to keep the economic profits it earns thereby (at least until the next auction, when another firm may have discovered the lower-cost secret and force the firm to bid lower). So there is a greatly increased incentive for the firm in question to be well managed. Is this the panacea, then? Maybe not. There are problems with this solution. For example, who owns the fixed plant and equipment? What about collusion among bidders? How easy would it be to monitor quality? It may be that this method has as many flaws as the current ones. But it is worth a closer look.[3]

LOOKING AHEAD

This chapter has attempted to explore some of the special economics of firms facing downward-sloping demand curves—price-searchers. We have seen that for price-searchers in open markets, the motivation of the firm is the same as for price-takers—profits. But the outcome of the search for profits is somewhat different. Often the forms of competition observed are different from those of price-takers. Price discrimination and natural monopoly are two phenomena which are inconsistent with a price-taker's market, but which sometimes occur in price-searcher situations.

Chapter 9 makes our analysis of decisions more complete by showing how outlays and revenues which are expected to occur in the future are handled. A crucial feature of this analysis is the use of the interest rate and discounting. Chapter 9 will also develop the notion of the *normal rate of return* and use this concept to reexamine the concept of profit.

POINTS TO REMEMBER

1. Price-searcher firms are firms which have some market power or monopoly power—that is, those which face a downward-sloping demand curve and must choose the best price to charge.

2. For a price-searcher firm, marginal revenue lies below the demand curve (that is, below price); for a price-taker firm, price and marginal revenue are identical.

3. For a price-searcher firm with only fixed costs, the best price is the one for which marginal revenue equals zero, because this maximizes revenue; and, because cost is constant (all fixed), it maximizes profit.

4. This result is inefficient because there are various conceivable price strategies which could make both the seller and the buyer better off; but these alternatives are generally not feasible, so the firm chooses this price anyway.

3. The interested reader may wish to refer to the original source of this idea, H. Demsetz, "Why Regulate Utilities?" *Journal of Law and Economics* 11 (April 1968): 55–65.

5. If costs vary with output, the price-searcher's best output and price are where marginal revenue equals marginal cost (smaller than if all costs were fixed).

6. A price-searcher firm will never intentionally produce in the inelastic range of its demand curve.

7. If a price-searcher is making economic profits in the short run, new entrants will tend to appear. Their appearance will make the demand curve facing the original firm more elastic and farther to the left.

8. Profitable price discrimination always involves charging a lower price to customers with a more elastic demand and a higher price to customers with a less elastic demand.

9. Not all price differentiations among customers are price discrimination. Sometimes the cost of serving one customer is lower than the cost of serving another.

10. Multipart pricing can conceivably make both seller and buyer better off than charging a single price to a given customer.

11. Natural monopoly usually occurs in line industries, where the economies of serving large numbers of customers are very great.

12. One problem with an unregulated natural monopolist is that price is simultaneously above marginal cost and average total cost.

13. If price for a natural monopolist is set equal to marginal cost, then losses will be incurred because marginal cost is below average total cost. This gives rise to subsidies and consequent reduced incentives to manage effectively.

14. If price for a natural monopolist is set equal to average total cost, then price is still above marginal cost, and since no economic profits can be earned, management incentives are again dulled.

KEY TERMS

Administered price doctrine: The assertion that some firms can and do act arbitrarily to raise prices (as in cases where demand for their product and/or costs fall).

Inefficiency of natural monopolists: The price which the firm charges is greater than the marginal cost of producing additional output.

Multipart pricing: A pricing policy whereby the seller sells different units of the same commodity for different prices to the same buyer. Multipart pricing can only be carried out by a price-searcher who is able to prevent resale of the commodity.

Natural monopoly: An industry in which the natural result of the competitive process is the survival of only one firm. The usual reason for natural monopoly is extreme economies of scale.

Oligopoly: A market setting in which there are few enough sellers for the sellers to take into account the reactions of their rivals to their actions.

Price discrimination: Selling the same commodity for different prices to different customers, or selling different products at prices which do not accurately reflect the differences in marginal costs. It can only be carried out by a price-searcher who is able to prevent resale of the commodity.

REVIEW QUESTIONS

1. In the boxing match example in the chapter, would it pay to put on the show if the total costs you incurred were $6000? What price would you charge? What price would you charge if the costs rose to $7000?

2. In the same example, how might your optimal admission price change if you planned to operate a concession stand at the showing? Suppose the arena owner operates the concession stand. Does he have any interest in what admission price you charge?

3. In the same example, if the arena costs were $6000, but an arena seating only 1200 could be rented for $5500 (full cost), would you choose the smaller arena? What factors would influence your decision? If an arena holding only 1000 people could be obtained for only $5000, would you take it? Why or why not?

4. Suppose the California Peach Board estimates that the crop this year will be 1 million bushels. It also estimates the following demand for peaches:

P(Cents)	Q(Million)
75	0.5
50	0.8
25	1
10	1.12

What should the Peach Board do if it wants to increase revenues to peach sellers?

5. Draw the demand curve for Chevettes in the marginal revenue example in the chapter. On your diagram, label the area corresponding to the gain to General Motors due to selling 50,000 more cars at $4000 each. Label the area corresponding to the loss to GM due to selling the 300,000 cars at

$4000 instead of $4500. If we subtract the second area from the first, what do we get? What name do we give that magnitude? How would we get the marginal revenue of Chevettes over the range from 300,000 to 350,000?

6. In the Chevette example, suppose the model year is already half over when General Motors considers lowering the price. If sales come at a uniform rate, how many could GM expect to sell in the remaining six months if they keep the price at $4500? If they lower it to $4000? Calculate the incremental revenue GM could get by charging $4000 instead of $4500. What is the marginal revenue over that range of output?

7. Suppose that General Motors' marketing department estimates that at a price of $5000 each, 260,000 Chevettes per year would be sold. Suppose also that GM estimates that the marginal cost of Chevettes in the range from 260,000 per year to 300,000 per year is $1400. What should GM do?

8. On April 18, 1980, the *Wall Street Journal* reported that Chrysler Corp. was discontinuing two of the promotional programs it had been using to encourage car sales. The two that were discontinued were free membership in an independent road service club and two years of free scheduled maintenance for buyers of new cars. The reason cited for dropping the promotions was that they didn't receive the "customer response originally expected." Suppose that in the absence of the promotion, Chrysler would sell 40,000 cars per month, and that the promotion costs $200 per car sold. (a) How many dollars worth of additional sales would Chrysler have to make per month in order for Chrysler's revenue to be greater with the promotion than without it? (b) Suppose the average price Chrysler receives per car is $6000 (before deducting the cost of the promotion), and Chrysler estimates that in response to the promotion 1500 additional cars per month are sold. Would Chrysler's revenue (net of promotion) go up? (c) Suppose the marginal cost of a car is $2000 in this range. Would it pay Chrysler to engage in the promotion?

9. Suppose the Alaskan pipeline costs $2 billion more to construct than the builders anticipated. Assuming that the cost overruns have no effect on the capacity of the pipeline to transport oil, would you expect the overrun to have any effect on the price that buyers pay for oil from Alaska? Why? Would your answer change if you thought sellers of Alaskan oil were price-takers rather than price-searchers?

10. Suppose a certain price-searcher has an *MC* curve which is horizontal at a level of $5, and a straight-line demand curve. Now the *MC* curve shifts up to $6. By how much will the firm's optimal price increase?

11. An excursion fare ticket on an airline is one which requires the customer to stay between seven and thirty days at her destination and which cannot be cancelled less than thirty days before the flight. Prices for such tickets are always lower than regular coach tickets. Is this price discrimination?

12. In the boxing match example, is there any way to separate those with a less elastic demand from those with a more elastic demand, so that the former could be charged a lower price? (Hint: What about discount coupons in the newspaper or to clubs?)

13. "With multipart pricing, the more you buy the lower the price." Does this mean that your total bill is lower with a larger quantity than with a smaller quantity? Explain.

14.

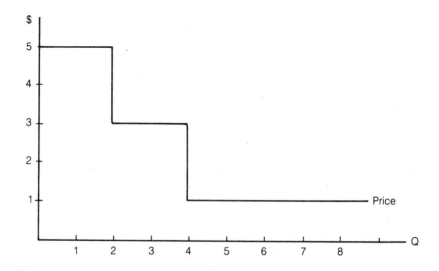

Suppose you are confronted with the multipart pricing schedule shown above (that is, for the first two units you pay $5 each; for the next two units you pay $3 each; and for all remaining units you pay $1 each). What is the *marginal* price you pay for the eighth unit? What is the *average* price you are paying if you buy eight units? Sketch in the average price paid for all quantities between one and eight. How many units of the good would you buy if you were faced with this price schedule? Consider two possible changes in the price schedule you face: (a) pay $5 per unit for the first four units, then $1 per unit thereafter; (b) pay $5 each for the first two, and $3 each for the second two, but $2 each thereafter. Notice that with both new schedules, if you bought eight units, you would pay a total of $24 (or $3 per unit on average). Would you react the same way to these two changes? Explain why or why not.

15. Suppose you are confronted with the following offer: "If you buy one to five copies of our book, you pay $2.50 each. If you buy six or more, you pay only $2.00 apiece. (For example, if you buy ten books, you would pay a total of $20.)" Sketch the marginal and average price schedules for this pricing scheme.

16. Trucks are charged a higher toll to use toll roads and toll bridges than cars are. Is this price discrimination?

17. Why is it that daytime TV show X generates only a fraction of the audience (and advertising revenues) that prime time show Y does, yet Y is cancelled and X stays on the air?

18. The price of a 30-second commercial on the television show "M.A.S.H." was reported in December of 1979 to have been the highest of any regularly scheduled program (over $200,000). Was that because "M.A.S.H." was the most expensive show to produce? If CBS had to pay a higher fee to the producers of "M.A.S.H." to use the show, would they then charge a higher advertising rate? Why might we expect the salaries of the actors to be higher on shows which have higher advertising rates?

19. Suppose a television network makes a contract to a special sports event. The network pays (say) $5 million for the TV rights. Shortly before the event is to take place, the organizers discover that they are short of money and tell the network that they must have an additional $2 million or the event will have to be cancelled. If the network pays the extra $2 million, will it charge a higher advertising rate than it otherwise would have? Explain.

20. Firm X was the only bidder to run the food concession at the state college. Firm X did quite well, because its demand curve lay above its average total cost curve. When the next contract came up, there was another bidder for the contract, but firm X won again (although it had to make a substantially higher bid than before). Will firm X charge higher prices than it would have if it had been the only bidder and been able to bid less?

21. Many public transit systems offer a monthly pass which enables the purchaser to ride an unlimited number of times in a month for no additional charge. What type of pricing is this? Could it be considered to be both multipart pricing *and* price discrimination?

22. In the late 1970s, many electric utilities changed their pricing schemes from declining block (like those in question 14) to increasing block. For example, the Pacific Gas and Electric Company in San Francisco had the following residential rate schedule in May of 1980:

Connnection fee:	$1.75 per mo.
First 240 kwh:	$ .0404 per kwh
Next 240 kwh	$ .06394 per kwh
All over 480 kwh:	$ .08819 per kwh

If you used 100 kwh, what would be the average and marginal prices per kwh in that neighborhood? At 150? At 300? At 500? Sketch the path of marginal and average prices as consumption ranges from zero to 500 kwh per month.

23. Do higher costs always result in a higher price? Can you think of any case in which a higher cost would *not* result in a higher price? Under what circumstances would a higher cost result in a higher price?

24. Draw a diagram illustrating the optimal price and output for a firm whose managers attempt to maximize revenue, subject to the constraint that they earn at least some specified amount of profit. What would happen to price and output if fixed costs rose? Are there any forces at work acting to reduce the extent of this kind of behavior?

25. In 1962, Roger Blough, then Chairman of the Board of the U.S. Steel Corporation, argued that the higher prices his firm was attempting to charge (over President Kennedy's objections) were necessary in order to provide enough revenue for the investments which the company thought it should undertake. Suppose revenue requirements had been still higher. Would that have meant that U.S. Steel would have been able to finance them by charging still higher prices? Suppose U.S. Steel had decided not to invest any more in the near future—would you expect it to charge lower prices? What would the responsible action be? What do you mean by *responsible*?

chapter 9

Present Values and Profits

If you have been thinking carefully about the discussions on behavior of firms in earlier chapters, you may have thought of this criticism: isn't it rather myopic (shortsighted) of firms to make decisions about output rates on the basis of today's demand and cost conditions, when those conditions may change in the future? For example, wouldn't it be silly to buy specialized plant and machinery which was expected to last thirty years if one were producing a good whose demand is expected to fall drastically in two years? This is a valid criticism and points out the "first level of approximation" nature of the specific propositions we have stated so far. To the extent that they ignore the future, those propositions are subject to criticism. In fact, of course, businessmen *do* take the future into account in their decision making. If taking action A will result in extra revenue to the firm in five years, then the rational businessman will compare that amount (after *discounting* it, a process we shall discuss shortly) to the cost of the action to decide if the action results in an increase in net revenue. As you can see, discounting is an important part of the process of taking the future into account. A crucial feature of discounting is its use of the *interest rate*. To build up to discounting, profits, and other topics, we must start with the interest rate.

234 THE INTEREST RATE

When you borrow money, you repay the principal plus interest. The *interest rate* is the amount you pay, per dollar, per year, for the right to borrow the money. The interest rate is thus the price of earlier rather than later availability of money. More generally, the interest rate is the price of earlier rather than later availability of goods. The fact that we usually transact in money merely masks the fact that we are borrowing and repaying real goods and services.

WHY ARE INTEREST RATES POSITIVE?

The fact that the interest rate is a price is helpful in understanding why interest rates are positive. The commodity being exchanged is earlier availability of goods, and this is a scarce commodity. That is, if the interest rate (the price of earlier availability) were zero, more would be demanded than is available—there would be a shortage, tending to bid the price up, as in chapters 2 and 3. This would happen even if the rate of inflation were zero. Why would this be true? Wouldn't there be people who would be willing to supply current purchasing power in return for later purchasing power, with no premium or interest? Yes, there would be, if they had no better alternative. People saving for retirement might well be willing to give up $1000 now for $1000 later in life *if* that were the best deal they could get.[1] But the amount supplied (saved) at a zero rate of interest would be much smaller than the amount demanded (that is, the amount people would like to borrow). The reason is that resources can be *invested* for a positive return. That is, there are ways in which one can, by putting $1000 worth of resources into a certain form, end up with more than $1000 in the future. For example, one might buy a machine for $1000 and rent it out for (say) $136 per year for the next ten years. If you had such an option, you would gladly make a deal with a lender to give you $1000 today, in return for $100 per year for the next ten years. And if you could make such a deal, you would be $36 per year to the good. The point is that there are *many* such

---

1. The reasoning is as follows. Suppose a person was originally considering saving no money over her working life. Then, ignoring welfare and social security, she would have no income when she stopped working. Since people are willing to substitute between present and future consumption, and since this person would, in the absence of saving, have little or no consumption available in the future (retired) period, the marginal value she would place on future goods would be high. She might even be willing to give up $2 worth of current consumption for $1 worth of future consumption, if she had to. The more purchasing power she diverts from the present to the future, the lower the marginal value she places on future consumption. If the rate of interest were zero, that would mean that a person could obtain $1 worth of goods in the future by giving up $1 worth of goods today. Individuals would transfer purchasing power from the present to the future (that is, save) until the marginal value they place on $1 worth of future goods is $1 worth of present goods, which is the price they would have to pay to get $1 worth of future goods.

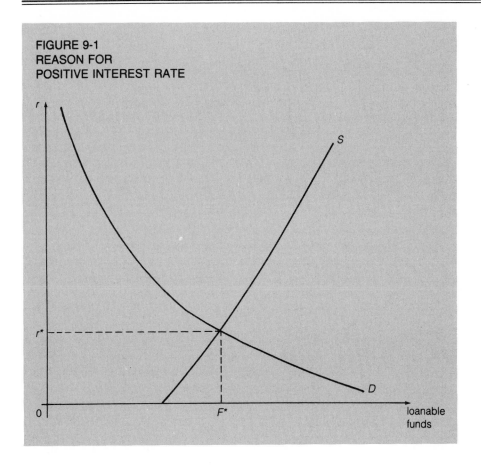

FIGURE 9-1
REASON FOR
POSITIVE INTEREST RATE

options open to people all the time, and the lower the rate of interest, the more of them that look good.

Notice that the amount of current funds people desire to borrow (for investment) obeys the First Law of Demand. The higher the interest rate, the less is demanded. As the interest rate approaches zero, the amount people would want to borrow grows phenomenally. This is because there are many investment projects which would be worth investing in if the interest rate were zero. Investing $1 million in order to get a return of $.01 per year forever would be a good investment at a zero rate of interest. Some projects people would want to borrow money to invest in at or near a zero rate of interest are straightening out all the hills and curves in the railroad tracks to save fuel, more durable goods, or filling in the Gulf of Mexico to make land.

With such a tremendous set of alternative uses for the current resources, it is inconceivable that the price of earlier availability could remain at zero without causing a tremendous shortage of investment funds and a tendency for interest rates to rise to positive levels.

The points we have made are illustrated graphically in figure 9-1. The horizontal axis is labelled "loanable funds." The supply of loanable funds is provided by savers—those who are foregoing current consumption in return for claims to future goods. We show the supply as being upward-sloping—the higher the interest rate, the greater the amount of loanable funds supplied. But we also draw the supply curve intersecting the horizontal axis, meaning that some loanable funds would be supplied even at a zero rate of interest. The demand for loanable funds comes from those who want to invest in capital goods. It is shown as downward-sloping, and the amount demanded grows extremely large as the interest rate approaches zero, as we discussed above. Because of this, it is inconceivable that the rate of interest could remain at zero for a long period of time. The equilibrium (or market-clearing) interest rate in this case is r*.

THE PRESENT VALUE OF A FUTURE AMOUNT

Because interest rates are positive, I am not indifferent between receiving $100 today or $100 in one year. I would always prefer the former, given a positive rate of interest, even if I wanted to consume the money in the future, because I could put the $100 in the bank and take out more than $100 at the end of the year. The question arises, then: What amount today would be equivalent to $100 payable in one year? Clearly the amount would be less than $100, with a positive rate of interest. If my alternative were to invest it at 10 percent, then about $90.91 today would be equivalent to $100 in one year. We can see this by noting the following relationship: If I put $90.91 away today at 10 percent, I will get back the $90.91 plus 10 percent of $90.91:

$$90.91 + (.10)(90.91) = 90.91 + 9.09 = 100.00.$$

Thus the *present value* (the amount I would be willing to pay today) of $100 in one year is $90.91, if my interest rate is 10 percent. We can express this relationship more generally by saying that:

$$P + rP = A_1 \text{ or } P(1 + r) = A_1,$$

where P is the present amount, A_1 is the future amount (paid in one year), and r is the interest rate. If we solve this equation for P (the present value), we obtain:

$$P = \frac{A_1}{1 + r} .$$

$$(1)$$

Suppose the future amount came after *two* years instead of *one*. Suppose, for example, you had $100 and could earn 10 percent compound interest by putting it in a bank. After two years, the $100 would have grown to $121. At the end of the first year, you would have your original $100, plus 10 percent of $100, or $110. At the end of the second year, you would still have your $110, plus 10 percent of that amount ($11), or $121. In general, if one starts with $P, it will grow to A_2 in two years, where $A_2 = P(1 + r) + r [P(1 + r)]$. The first term, $P(1 + r)$, is the amount P grows to after one year, and the second term, $r[P(1 + r)]$, is the interest earned during the second year. This can be rewritten as $A_2 = P(1 + r) (1 + r)$, or $A_2 = P(1 + r)^2$. When we solve this for P, we get

$$P = \frac{A_2}{(1 + r)^2} \cdot$$

(2)

Continuing with our example, if someone offered to pay you $121 two years from now, you would only be willing to give $100 today for that promise (even though you are absolutely certain that it will be repaid), if the interest rate at which you can invest is 10 percent.

This rule can be easily generalized to as many years as one wants. If the future amount comes after t years,

$$P = \frac{A_t}{(1 + r)^t}$$

(3)

is the present value of that future amount.

WHAT DOES THE PRESENT VALUE DEPEND ON?

A couple of common sense rules about how present values work are suggested when we look at equation (3). First, the higher the rate of interest, the smaller the present value of any future amount. We can see this immediately from the algebra by noting that r (the interest rate) appears in the denominator of the fraction. So the larger r is, the smaller the fraction is. This makes perfectly good sense. If your investment opportunity will yield you only 5 percent, the amount which you would have to put away in order for it to grow to $100 in one year would be greater than if your investment opportunity yielded 10 percent. Thus, the amount you would pay today for a promise of $100 in one year would be greater with a 5 percent than with a 10 percent interest rate. So the lower the interest rate, the greater the present value of any future amount.

Rather than laboriously calculating present values each time, we can refer to present value tables, such as table 9-1. This shows the present value of $1, to be paid at the end of from one to one hundred years at various interest rates.

TABLE 9-1
PRESENT VALUE OF A FUTURE DOLLAR AMOUNT

Year	2%	4%	6%	8%	10%	12%	15%	20%
1	.980	.962	.943	.926	.909	.893	.870	.833
2	.961	.925	.890	.857	.826	.797	.756	.694
3	.942	.890	.839	.794	.751	.711	.658	.578
4	.923	.855	.792	.735	.683	.636	.572	.482
5	.906	.832	.747	.681	.620	.567	.497	.402
6	.888	.790	.705	.630	.564	.507	.432	.335
7	.871	.760	.665	.583	.513	.452	.376	.279
8	.854	.731	.627	.540	.466	.404	.326	.233
9	.837	.703	.591	.500	.424	.360	.284	.194
10	.820	.676	.558	.463	.385	.322	.247	.162
11	.804	.650	.526	.429	.350	.287	.215	.134
12	.789	.625	.497	.397	.318	.257	.187	.112
13	.773	.601	.468	.368	.289	.229	.162	.0935
14	.758	.577	.442	.340	.263	.204	.141	.0779
15	.743	.555	.417	.315	.239	.183	.122	.0649
16	.728	.534	.393	.292	.217	.163	.107	.0541
17	.714	.513	.371	.270	.197	.146	.093	.0451
18	.700	.494	.350	.250	.179	.130	.0808	.0376
19	.686	.475	.330	.232	.163	.116	.0703	.0313
20	.673	.456	.311	.215	.148	.104	.0611	.0261
25	.610	.375	.232	.146	.0923	.0588	.0304	.0105
30	.552	.308	.174	.0994	.0573	.0334	.0151	.00421
40	.453	.208	.0972	.0460	.0221	.0107	.00373	.000650
50	.372	.141	.0543	.0213	.00852	.00346	.000922	.000109
100	.138	.0198	.0029	.0004	.00007	.000012	.0000009	.00000012

We can use table 9-1 to find the present value of any amount which comes at some specified future time. First, find the row corresponding to the number of years in the future at which the payment comes (say seven years). Second, find the column corresponding to the appropriate rate of interest (say 12 percent). The entry which lies in that row and column is the present value of $1 coming in the year specified and at the interest rate specified. This number is called the *discount factor* (in this case 0.452). To get the present value of an amount other than $1, multiply the amount times the discount factor. For example, $5 payable in seven years has a present value of $2.26 at 12 percent.

Note that, for any year, the present value is smaller when the interest rate is higher. For example, the present value of $100, to be paid in ten years with an interest rate of 6 percent, is ($100) (.558) = $55.80. But if the interest rate were 10 percent, the present value would be ($100) (.385) = $38.50.

The present value of a given amount of money also depends on when the money is received or paid. The farther into the future, the lower the present value. Again we can see this in equation (3). The denominator expresses one plus the rate of interest, taken to the power t. The larger t is, the larger $(1 + r)^t$ is and the smaller the ratio is. This too is common sense. The farther in the future any amount is, the smaller its present value. At a given rate of interest, the longer the period of time we have to accumulate a specific amount of money, the smaller the amount of money we must begin with. Thus at 10 percent, if we start with $.385, it accumulates to a dollar in ten years (that is, the present value of one dollar received in ten years, at 10 percent interest, is $.385). At the same rate of interest, $.148 accumulates to $1 in twenty years (that is, the present value of one dollar received in twenty years at 10 percent interest is $.148).

The very small size of the present value of an amount which comes after twenty years is an illustration of the power of compound interest. It is the opposite side of the coin to the fact that $1 would grow to a very large amount in twenty years at 10 percent. Table 9-2 shows the calculated future compounded amounts corresponding to an investment of $1 at various interest rates and for various lengths of time. Notice that, for an interest rate (rate of growth) of 10 percent, amounts double about every seven years. This makes it a little easier to see how Japan, which has had a 10 percent annual rate of growth in real income over much of the period since World War II, has become so wealthy so fast.

We can use table 9-2 to find the amount to which any given current amount would grow in a certain number of years at a specified compound interest rate. First, find the row corresponding to the number of years of growth involved (say seventeen years). Second, find the column corresponding to the appropriate interest rate (say 6 percent). The entry corresponding to that row and column is the amount to which $1 would grow in that time at that interest rate (in this case $2.69). To get the future compounded amount to which (say) $5 would grow, multiply $5 by the table entry (the answer is $13.45).

TABLE 9-2
FUTURE COMPOUNDED AMOUNTS (STARTING WITH ONE DOLLAR)

Year	2%	4%	6%	8%	10%	12%	15%	20%
1	1.02	1.04	1.06	1.08	1.10	1.12	1.15	1.20
2	1.04	1.08	1.12	1.17	1.21	1.25	1.32	1.44
3	1.06	1.12	1.19	1.26	1.33	1.40	1.52	1.73
4	1.08	1.17	1.26	1.36	1.46	1.57	1.74	2.07
5	1.10	1.22	1.34	1.47	1.61	1.76	2.01	2.49
6	1.13	1.27	1.41	1.59	1.77	1.97	2.31	2.99
7	1.15	1.32	1.50	1.71	1.94	2.21	2.66	3.58
8	1.17	1.37	1.59	1.85	2.14	2.48	3.05	4.30
9	1.20	1.42	1.68	2.00	2.35	2.77	3.52	5.16
10	1.22	1.48	1.79	2.16	2.59	3.11	4.05	6.19
11	1.24	1.54	1.89	2.33	2.85	3.48	4.66	7.43
12	1.27	1.60	2.01	2.52	3.13	3.90	5.30	8.92
13	1.29	1.67	2.13	2.72	3.45	4.36	6.10	10.7
14	1.32	1.73	2.26	2.94	3.79	4.89	7.00	12.8
15	1.35	1.80	2.39	3.17	4.17	5.47	8.13	15.4
16	1.37	1.87	2.54	3.43	4.59	6.13	9.40	18.5
17	1.40	1.95	2.69	3.70	5.05	6.87	10.6	22.2
18	1.43	2.03	2.85	4.00	5.55	7.70	12.5	26.6
19	1.46	2.11	3.02	4.32	6.11	8.61	14.0	31.9
20	1.49	2.19	3.20	4.66	6.72	9.65	16.1	38.3
25	1.64	2.67	4.29	6.85	10.8	17.0	32.9	95.4
30	1.81	3.24	5.74	10.0	17.4	30.0	66.2	237.
40	2.21	4.80	10.3	21.7	45.3	93.1	267.0	1470.
50	2.69	7.11	18.4	46.9	117.	289.	1080.	9100.
100	7.24	50.50	339.30	2199.76	13,780.6	83,521.	1,166,400.	82,810,000.

ANNUITIES AND PERPETUITIES

To find the present value of a series of future amounts, simply add the present values of the separate amounts together. Thus, the present value of $10 at the end of the first year, $20 at the end of the second year, and $15 at the end of the third year is $9.09 + 16.52 + 11.28 = $36.89 (if the interest rate is 10 percent). Sometimes the future amounts are all equal and come every year for a certain number of years; this is called an *annuity*. So a payment of $10 at the end of each of the next fifteen years is called a fifteen-year annuity of $10 per year. Table 9-3 shows the present values of annuities of $1 per year for various years at various interest rates.

We can use table 9-3 to find the present value of any annual payment coming at the end of the year for any amount of years, starting one year from now. First find the row corresponding to the number of years the payment will be made (say forty years). Second, find the column corresponding to the appropriate interest rate (say 4 percent). The entry for that row and column tells the present value of $1 per year starting one year from now, and continuing for the number of years specified, at the rate of interest specified (in this case $19.80). To get the present value of an amount other than $1, multiply the amount by the table entry. For example, a forty-year annuity of $25 has a present value of ($25) (19.80) = $495 at 4 percent.

A building on which you expect to receive a uniform lease payment for the next thirty years is equivalent to an annuity, and the present value of the annuity (at the appropriate interest rate) represents the amount for which you could sell the lease. For example, if the annual lease payment were $2000, the value of the thirty-year lease would be $18,860 at 10 percent interest. (The table entry for thirty years and 10 percent interest is 9.43, which means that a promise of $1 per year for the next thirty years is worth $9.43 today. Multiplying this by $2000 gives $18,860).

Most bonds are like annuities, with a redemption payment at the end. Suppose you were thinking of buying a bond that matures in five years. At the end of each of those years, you will receive (say) $4 as an interest payment. (The interest payment is usually called a *coupon*, because some bonds actually have small coupons which must be returned in order to receive interest payments.) Suppose the bond has a face value of $100. How much would you be willing to pay for such a bond? It depends on what you could earn elsewhere with equivalent risk. Suppose the current interest rate on an investment of equivalent risk is 8 percent. Then the amount you would be willing to pay for the bond would be the present value of a five-year annuity of $4, plus the present value of a $100 payment coming at the end of five years. From table 9-3 the annuity has a present value of $4 (3.99) = 15.96, and the redemption payment has a present value of $68.10 (from table 9-1), for a total of $84.06. The bond is selling *below par* because the coupon (as a fraction of the face value) is smaller than the interest rate. You would be willing to pay only $84.06 for this bond, because that is all you would have to pay elsewhere (where you

TABLE 9-3
PRESENT VALUE OF ANNUITY OF ONE DOLLAR

Year	2%	4%	6%	8%	10%	12%	15%	20%
1	.98	0.960	0.943	0.926	0.909	0.890	0.870	0.833
2	1.94	1.89	1.83	1.78	1.73	1.69	1.63	1.53
3	2.88	2.78	2.67	2.58	2.48	2.40	2.28	2.11
4	3.81	3.63	3.46	3.31	3.16	3.04	2.86	2.59
5	4.71	4.45	4.21	3.99	3.79	3.60	3.35	2.99
6	5.60	5.24	4.91	4.62	4.35	4.11	3.78	3.33
7	6.47	6.00	5.58	5.21	4.86	4.56	4.16	3.60
8	7.33	6.73	6.20	5.75	5.33	4.97	4.49	3.84
9	8.16	7.44	6.80	6.25	5.75	5.33	4.78	4.03
10	8.98	8.11	7.36	6.71	6.14	5.65	5.02	4.19
11	9.79	8.76	7.88	7.14	6.49	5.94	5.23	4.33
12	10.6	9.39	8.38	7.54	6.81	6.19	5.41	4.44
13	11.3	9.99	8.85	7.90	7.10	6.42	5.65	4.53
14	12.1	10.6	9.29	8.24	7.36	6.63	5.76	4.61
15	12.8	11.1	9.71	8.56	7.60	6.81	5.87	4.68
16	13.6	11.6	10.1	8.85	7.82	6.97	5.96	4.73
17	14.3	12.2	10.4	9.12	8.02	7.12	6.03	4.77
18	15.0	12.7	10.8	9.37	8.20	7.25	6.10	4.81
19	15.7	13.1	11.1	9.60	8.36	7.37	6.17	4.84
20	16.4	13.6	11.4	9.82	8.51	7.47	6.23	4.87
25	19.5	15.6	12.8	10.7	9.08	7.84	6.46	4.95
30	22.4	17.3	13.8	11.3	9.43	8.06	6.57	4.98
40	27.4	19.8	15.0	11.9	9.78	8.24	6.64	5.00
50	31.4	21.5	15.8	12.2	9.91	8.30	6.66	5.00
100	43.1	24.5	16.6	12.5	9.999	8.33	6.66	5.00

could earn your 8 percent) to get the same dollar return; that is, if you put away $84.06 at 8 percent, you could withdraw $4 at the end of each year for five years and still have $100 at the end, precisely as you can with the bond.[2] Thus the most you would be willing to pay for those benefits in the form of the bond would be $84.06.

An annuity which pays forever is called a *perpetuity*. True perpetuities are a rarity—one example is the British *consols* (Consolidated Annuities, issued in 1751 during the reign of George II), which promise a certain payment every year forever. The present value of a perpetuity is not infinite, even though an infinite amount would eventually be paid out. For example, the present value of a perpetuity of $1 per year would be $20 if the interest rate were 5 percent ($PV = 1/.05$). We can see why this is so by noting that, if the interest rate were 5 percent, we could put $20 in the bank and draw out $1 per year forever without ever touching the $20 deposit. Thus we would pay only $20 for a promise of $1 per year forever. In general, the present value of a perpetuity is the annual payment divided by the appropriate interest rate (A/r).

In spite of the fact that there are few genuine perpetuities, the present value formula for perpetuities is handy to know, because it is so simple and because, for long annuities, the present value of a perpetuity is very close to that of the actual annuity. For example, if the interest rate is 5 percent, a fifty-year annuity of $1 has a present value of $18.30, and a perpetuity of $1 has a present value of $20.

ANNUITIES THAT START SEVERAL YEARS IN THE FUTURE

Occasionally we find ourselves involved in a situation in which we could benefit from knowing the present value of an annuity that will start several years in the future. If your employer offers increased pension benefits, or if you plant a tree which will not begin bearing for several years, what is such an asset worth to you? Suppose, for example, we have a tree which will bear fruit annually for ten years, starting five years from today. To see how to calculate the present value, consider figure 9-2, which shows the timing of the payments. As we can see, the payments start five years from today and run through fourteen years from today. By examining the diagram, we can see that the stream described is exactly the same as a four-

2. If you put away $84.06 today, it would grow to $(84.06) (1.08) = 90.78$ in one year. After withdrawing your $4, you would have $86.78. After the second year this would grow to $(86.78) (1.08) = 93.72$. After withdrawing your second $4, you would have $89.72. After the third year this would grow to $(89.72) (1.08) = 96.90$. After withdrawing your third $4, you would have $92.90, which would grow to $(92.90) (1.08) = 100.33$ during the fourth year. After withdrawing your fourth $4, you would have $96.33, which would grow to $(96.33) (1.08) = 104.04$. After withdrawing your fifth $4, you still have $100.04 left (the $.04 is due to rounding error).

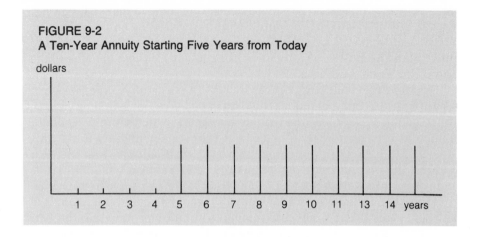

FIGURE 9-2
A Ten-Year Annuity Starting Five Years from Today

teen-year stream starting one year from today minus a four-year stream starting one year from today. If the annual amounts are $100, and the interest rate is 10 percent, the present value is $736 − $316 = $420.

SAVING FOR RETIREMENT

A problem which most of us will face is that of saving for retirement. Suppose a 35-year-old person wanted to save a constant amount each year in order to accumulate a nest egg to consume during her retirement. Suppose, for example, she wants to save $1000 per year, starting one year from today. At that rate, she would make her thirtieth deposit on her sixty-fifth birthday. How much will she have accumulated by that time? The first amount ($A) that she puts away (one year from today) will have twenty-nine years to accumulate interest. It will grow to $A (1 + r)^{29}$. The second payment will accumulate twenty-eight years of compound interest, so it will grow to $A (1 + r)^{28}$, and so on. The thirtieth payment, made on her sixty-fifth birthday, will not accumulate any interest, so it will be simply A. Altogether this will total

$$A (1 + r)^{24} + A (1 + r)^{28} + A (1 + r)^{27} + \ldots + A (1 + r)^{1} + A = FAV,$$

where FAV stands for "future accumulated value". This would be very tedious to calculate; but fortunately we can use the tables we already have to calculate this value. We shall use tables 9-3 and 9-2. First consider table 9-3. Suppose we had a thirty-year annuity whose present value we wished to calculate. That would be a simple matter of finding the proper row and column of table 9-3. But the entries in table 9-3 were calculated by finding the sum

$$\frac{A}{1 + r} + \frac{A}{(1 + r)^2} + \ldots + \frac{A}{(1 + r)^{29}} + \frac{A}{(1 + r)^{30}} = PV.$$

Now this sum is *not* what we want, because it is a present value, rather than a future accumulated value. But if we multiplied that sum by $(1 + r)^{30}$, the expression would become:

$$\frac{A}{(1+r)} \times (1+r)^{30} + \frac{A}{(1+r)^2} \times (1+r)^{30} + \ldots + \frac{A}{(1+r)^{29}} \times (1+r)^{30} +$$

$$\frac{A}{(1+r)^{30}} \times (1+r)^{30} = PV(1+r)^{30} ,$$

or

$$A(1+r)^{29} + A(1+r)^{28} + \ldots + A(1+r) + A = PV \times (1+r)^{30}.$$

The left-hand side of this equation is the same as the expression we got as our future accumulated value. Thus if we could find an easy way to get $(1+r)^{30}$, we could multiply our *present value* number (from table 9-3) by that and get what we want. But table 9-2 can give us $(1+r)^{30}$, since it is a table giving us the future compounded amount which results from putting away $1 today and letting it draw interest for any number of years. So if we multiply the thirty-year entry from table 9-2 by the thirty-year entry from table 9-3, we get what we want.

Getting back to our forward-looking worker, suppose she deposits $1000 per year in the manner specified and earns 6 percent interest. Then the future accumulated value would be $(1000) \times (13.8) \times (5.74) = \$79,212$. This shows the power of compound interest. Even though she only saves a total of $30,000, she accumulates $79,212 because of the interest she earns on the deposits made before her sixty-fifth birthday.

Our saver could then draw $4753 = .06(79,212)$ per year *forever*. If she decided to draw only for twenty years and then take her chances, she could draw $6948 per year. We obtain this by noting that the present value of $1 per year for twenty years at 6 percent is $11.4. So if we had $11.40, we could draw out $1 per year for twenty years. Now $79,212 is 6948 times as big as 11.4 (that is, $79212/11.4 = 6948$), so we could draw out $6948 per year instead of $1 if we had $79,212 instead of $11.40.[3]

RATE OF RETURN

Sometimes you are presented with an option whereby you are asked to pay $P today and receive in return $A per year for n years. Is it a good investment? One way to find out is to calculate the present value of the n-year annuity of $A (at the appropriate rate of interest) and compare it with the price you are being asked to pay. If the calculated present value is larger,

---

3. The problems of accumulation become somewhat trickier if we anticipate inflation. This is discussed in the appendix.

it is a good investment, and you are very lucky to get it at that price. In fact, you would then buy it and, if someone were willing to pay the present value you calculated, you would have made what the securities business calls a *profit*.

An alternative way of seeing whether the option is a good investment is to calculate the *rate of return* (R). The rate of return is calculated by asking, "At what interest rate would the discounted present value of the n-year annuity of $A be equal to the $P I am being asked to pay?" When you have found that interest rate, you have the rate of return on this investment. R is thus defined by the equation

$$P = \frac{A}{(1 + R)} + \frac{A}{(1 + R)^2} + \ldots + \frac{A}{(1 + R)^n} \, . \qquad (4)$$

If the R you obtain by solving that equation is *greater than* the actual interest rate prevailing, it is a good investment. If it is lower, this is a poor investment, because you could get a higher rate of return by investing at the prevailing interest rate.

Suppose you had a chance to buy a machine for $1000 and rent it out for $136 per year for ten years. What is the rate of return implicit in this investment opportunity? One way to find out would be to set up an equation (4) again:

$$1000 = \frac{136}{(1 + R)} + \frac{136}{(1 + R)^2} + \ldots + \frac{136}{(1 + R)^{10}} \, ,$$

and to solve it for R. This is a very cumbersome process. Another way to do it would be to substitute various rates of interest for R and see which one makes the equation hold. It turns out that this works at an interest rate of 6 percent. The present value of $1 per year for ten years at 6 percent is $7.36. The present value of $136 per year for ten years at 6 percent is (7.36)(136) = 1000.96 ($.96 due to rounding error). The rate of return on this investment is 6 percent. Thus at a 6 percent rate of interest, one would be indifferent between purchasing this machine and putting the $1000 in the bank.

THE NORMAL RATE OF RETURN AND THE OPPORTUNITY COST OF INVESTED FUNDS

We have been referring throughout this chapter to "the prevailing interest rate" or "the appropriate rate of interest." It is clear that there is not just one interest rate but many. The biggest determinants of the differentials in interest rates (in the absence of government interference or monopoly in the capital markets) are the risk associated with repayment, and the cost of negotiating, handling, and servicing the loan. Thus one reason personal loans have such a high interest rate is that the costs of negotiating and collecting it are high, relative to the size of the loan. Much of what goes by the name of interest in such loans is not the price of the earlier availability of the money per se; rather, it is the price of arranging the transaction.

We wish to concentrate on these differences in interest rates (or rates of return) as indicating differences in risk. Because people generally wish to avoid risk and must be paid a premium to bear it, the rate of return typically earned (and necessary to attract investors to the industry and away from other uses of their funds) will vary among industries. Very risky industries (such as the auto and possibly the oil industries) will pay a higher rate of return than industries with less risk, such as regulated utilities, because investors will not put funds into the very risky industries unless the differential exists. The rate of return necessary to attract funds to an industry is called the "normal rate of return" for the industry. This is rather difficult to measure because of all the other things going on in the capital markets that prevent our observing it (such as inflation, monetary and fiscal policy, recessions, unusual circumstances in the particular industry), but it is a useful concept, because it enables us to define what economists mean by profit.

The funds invested in any business firm, which are used to buy the buildings, machinery, and other capital goods in the firm, have alternative uses. They could be used to invest in other ventures. In other words, they have an opportunity cost—the return they could earn in an equivalently risky alternative investment.

Sometimes the cost is explicit, as when the owners of a firm pay a bank interest on a loan. Other times it is implicit, as when owners of the firm must decide whether or not to invest their accumulated funds in their business rather than elsewhere. But in both cases a comparison of the return obtainable in this business with those available elsewhere must be made. If an industry does not earn enough to pay the investors, the owners, the bank, or other potential investors as much as they could earn in the alternative, future infusions of funds will not be forthcoming. This is why the rate of return necessary to attract funds to the industry is called the normal rate of return. The industry will not earn above or below that rate of return for long periods, unless there are restrictions on the inflow and outflow of funds. If it earns less, the industry will decline; if it earns more, new firms (and funds) will enter, tending to reduce the return.

ANOTHER LOOK
AT PROFITS

We mentioned in chapter 5 that economic profit is the return the owners of a firm obtain over and above all their costs, including the implicit cost of the funds the owners supply. We can now see that this implicit cost is the normal rate of return for the industry. After subtracting from revenues the costs of labor and materials, depreciation, interest on loans, and taxes, the firm must have some return left over (the normal rate of return) to cover the opportunity cost of the owners' investment. We say *must*. We mean that if that return is not present, the firm will be operating at a loss in the economists' sense. Even though the accountant may report positive net income, the firm will not be earning enough to pay all its continued possession costs. Only if the firm earns *more than* this normal return is it earning an economic profit. For example, suppose the return required to get investors to invest in this industry (the normal rate of return) is 8 percent. Firm A earns 12 percent return this year; then it is earning an economic profit. If it had earned only 6 percent, it would have been operating at a *loss* in the economic sense, because not all costs (including the opportunity cost of the owners' funds) were being covered.

AN ALTERNATIVE APPROACH

While profits are often viewed in this way by economists, there are other ways of looking at the phenomenon and other forms in which profits appear. Sometimes the existence of an opportunity to make a higher-than-normal rate of return shows itself *in the present* in the change in the price of an asset. When it became clear that oil prices were going to rise dramatically in 1973 and 1974 and again in 1979, anyone who owned an oil well or had oil on his land was immediately made richer. The price of the oil rights rose *immediately* to reflect the larger return expected from future oil sales. In fact, the price rose so much that, if an oil well were purchased at the new higher price, the buyer would earn only a normal return. Why? Because at any price below the new higher level, the buyer could make a higher-than-normal return.

Suppose that, given the price of oil you expect to prevail, you think a certain oil well is a steal at its old price of $100,000. So you offer $102,000, hoping to get the well. But others share your optimism, and they offer $110,000. You think that you could earn a higher-than-normal return if you are able to buy it for any price below $300,000, so you up your bid. But the other bidders agree. You are *all* willing to go higher as long as the price is less than $300,000. Because of this, the bids will tend to approach $300,000, with each bidder hoping the others will drop out before that price is reached. But if you all agree, no one will drop out, and the bids will go right up to $300,000. At that price, you just expect to earn a normal rate of return. (You won't bid *above* that amount because then you would get *less than* a normal return—that is, less than you could earn elsewhere in an equally risky investment.) So in spite of the price rise in oil, those who bought oil wells after the new pattern of oil prices was clear *did not* make economic profits. Who did, then? The previous owners. Even though the actual oil was not, and has not yet been sold, they collected the profit, because the future higher difference between operating cost and oil price was capitalized or discounted back to the present in the form of a higher price for the oil *well*.

The higher-than-normal rate of return approach and the change in current price of assets approach are simply two sides of the same coin. The anticipated higher-than-normal return causes the price of assets generating the return to be bid up, thus eliminating any profit (higher-than-normal return) for *future* buyers and conferring a profit on those who owned the assets at the time the new conditions were made known.

Whenever there is a profit in the economic sense, it is caused by a changed perception about the future. If it had been widely known in 1970 that oil prices would rise, prices of oil wells would have gone up *then*, because anyone who could have gotten oil wells at those prices could have made a profit in 1973, when the price rise became generally known. Thus profits (and losses) come about because of *uncertainty* about the future. If there were no uncertainty, there would be no profits in the economic sense.

THE ROLE OF PROFITS

In discussing the role of profits, we should again distinguish between accounting and economic profits. (You may wish to review our discussion of these distinctions in chapter 5.) Accounting profits always include some costs which have not been subtracted from revenue in the calculation. Thus positive accounting profits (sufficient to make revenue cover all costs) are necessary if business firms are to survive for long. Just as firms won't get labor services or materials supplied to them unless they pay as much as these suppliers can get elsewhere (that is, cover labor and materials costs), firms will not be able to get the use of investors' funds unless the investors expect to get at least as much in this investment as elsewhere (that is, unless the opportunity cost of investors' funds is covered). So positive accounting profits are necessary for the survival of business firms. When you hear the Chamber of Commerce talking about the necessity of profits, this is usually what they mean.

What about economic profits? The fundamental role which higher-than-normal returns or profits in the economic sense play is to provide signals to transactors in the economy about where resources are unexpectedly valuable—in other words, where consumers are willing to pay a lot, relative to cost, to have something done. The higher prices for the assets involved in producing those goods encourage people to put more of those assets into operation sooner.

Losses play the same kind of role in reverse. They discourage people from getting into the business involved and reduce the incentive to produce goods which are useful in that industry.

Profits and losses can also signal good or bad ways of organizing production, as well as products which people like or dislike. Firms which have discovered lower-cost ways of doing things will reap profits, thereby encouraging others to imitate them. We can see that profit, as used by economists, is a very useful concept to help in understanding how the economy functions.

250 CAN ECONOMIC PROFITS BE ELIMINATED?

As noted above, the basic source of (economic) profits (and losses) is uncertainty. If everyone always knew exactly what was going to happen (which way and when consumer preferences would change, what natural disasters and what technical changes would occur) there would never be economic profits. If we all knew that five years from now the demand for cars would be such and such, car manufacturers would be able to plan precisely for the demand by building exactly the right plants for exactly the right outputs of exactly the right cars. There would be exactly the correct amount so that there would be neither profits nor losses in the economic sense. It is only because of our ignorance of the future that we will miss this beautiful scenario and that some firms will make profits and others suffer losses.

Since uncertainty is the cause of profits and losses, we cannot simply pass a law and eliminate them. But we can, of course, pass laws which tax them away. Our current law taxes the net income (or accounting profit) of corporations, but as we have noted, this includes some costs as well as profits, so it is not the same as an *economic* profits tax. If a law to tax economic profits and subsidize economic losses were to exist, the first problem to be faced would be the calculation of economic profits. As noted, this would not be an easy task, because we must know what the opportunity cost of capital is in order to subtract it from accounting profits and obtain economic profits.

Second, by taxing away economic profits, we would be reducing the incentive for new investment to occur. As noted, the existence of an opportunity to make higher-than-normal returns tends to bid up the prices of assets (such as building, machinery, and other inputs) in the industry in question. The higher those asset prices are bid up, the more quickly producers of those assets will respond with new assets with which to produce more of the good for which the economic profit exists. Taxing economic profits away, if it could be done, would reduce this incentive to increase production.

The third aspect of such a policy would be that it would reduce the ability to bear risks selectively. If all profits were taxed away (and losses subsidized?), taxpayers as a whole would be reaping the gains or losses from the whims of fortune, whether they wanted to or not. If firm A made an economic profit which was taxed away, taxpayers as a group (rather than the so-called owners) would gain. Whatever amount of government spending they wanted could be obtained with lower taxes (because firm A is paying more). On the other hand, if losses were subsidized by the treasury, taxpayers would lose whenever a firm operated at a loss.[4] If the profits are not taxed, taxpayers do not gain or lose, regardless of the firm's

4. This happens if a business is taken over by the government (as in the case of Amtrak and Conrail) or if loans are guaranteed by the government (as in the cases of Lockheed and Chrysler).

profits or losses. Thus taxpayers are not sharing in the risks of those businesses. This reallocation of risk bearing is not something which can be shown scientifically to be good or bad, but it is an aspect of the issue which bears consideration.

DO THE MANAGERS OF FIRMS DO WHAT THE OWNERS WANT?

In chapter 6 we discussed the rationale of the firm. In that chapter we noted that the potential benefits of team production account for firms. But there is a problem of monitoring the behavior of team members to control and reduce shirking. This gives rise to the manager or boss. We noted that the manager can be induced to monitor team behavior well if he is the owner—the recipient of residual claims. Thus an owner-manager of a firm would be expected to be appropriately diligent in his efforts to monitor team behavior.

We also noted that comparative advantage and specialization in risk bearing and the ease of raising large amounts of money to finance a firm often leads to having owners who don't manage directly and managers who own only a small portion of the company. The large corporation of today typifies this state of affairs.

The question then arises, are managers of large corporations appropriately diligent in their monitoring duties? Since they are not residual claimants to the earnings of the firm, the managers might be expected to be lax. They might not, in other words, do what the *owners* want (which would normally be to produce earnings). After all, if, by their laxity or inept decision making, the firm's earnings were to fall, *they* would not bear the full cost of it, since they have a claim to only a small fraction of the firm's earnings. The First Law of Demand says that the lower the cost to the decision maker of making a poor decision (or managing badly), the more bad decisions and inept management he will undertake.

If there were no institutional features to counteract this tendency, we might expect corporations to be very badly run, and the corporate form of business would be a less attractive form of business enterprise. There are, however, some forces which do counteract the tendency of managers to shirk their duties. These forces are related to the concept of discounting and present values. Suppose you are interested in buying a firm. How will you know how much you are required to pay for it? You will want to know what others are willing to pay for it, because you won't be able to get it for less than the highest of those amounts. How will you find out what that amount is for a given firm? You will look at the price of its stock; suppose there are a million shares and the current price per share is $50. Then you must be prepared to pay at least $50 million for the firm. The price of the common stock of a corporation reflects the value potential investors place on the firm as a going concern. If the corporation owns oil wells, the price of the stock will go up (reflecting a higher present value of the firm itself) whenever investors' expectations of future oil prices go up and vice versa.

Similarly, the price of the stock would be expected to change if there were a change in management. For example, if a sloppy management were replaced by an effective management, the price of the stock, reflecting the present value of the business to potential investors, would be expected to go up and vice versa.

How does this affect the behavior of managers? There are at least two ways in which this can have an effect. First, consider executive stock options. Executives and other employees in firms are often given the right, over some period of time, to buy a specified number of shares of stock in their company at a specified price. If the manager makes a decision or takes other actions which convince investors that the firm is going to be more profitable, the price of the stock will rise; and the executive will be able to make a good buy by being able to buy the stock at the specified level, which is less than the new current price. Giving managers stock options significantly increases their incentive to be good managers.

Another way in which the capitalization of future earnings into stock prices keeps managers in line is through the practice of "raiding" or taking over a firm by outsiders. Suppose you look at a firm and believe that it is being ineffectively managed. This state of affairs is reflected in the low price of its stock. Suppose the firm has a million shares of stock outstanding at $20 per share. You think that by replacing current management with your own people, you can raise the price of the stock to $25. By buying perhaps 10 percent of the stock, you might get enough influence to persuade another 40 percent of the stockholders to go along with you, throw the rascals out, and take control of the company. If the price went up after you took over, you would make $500,000. Many corporate proxy fights, where competing groups of stockholders vie for control of a company, involve just this sort of consideration. Corporate managers are more diligent and alert because of this possibility.

LOOKING AHEAD

Chapter 10 applies the concepts we have developed so far to situations in which there are restrictions on the behavior of firms and consumers, in the form of collusion by firms and restrictions on the entry of firms into industries. Chapter 11 considers consumerism and advertising.

POINTS TO REMEMBER

1. The interest rate is the price of the earlier availability of goods.

2. The interest rate is positive because there are enough good investment opportunities at a zero rate to create a shortage of investment funds at that rate.

3. The present value of a future amount (that is, the amount someone

would pay today to obtain that amount in the future) is equal to the amount one would have to invest, at the going rate of interest, in order to have it grow to the specific future amount:

$$P = \frac{A_t}{(1 + r)^t} .$$

4. The present value of a future amount is smaller, the higher the rate of interest and the farther in the future the amount comes.

5. The present value of an annuity is equal to the sum of the present values of the uniform annual payments in the stream.

6. The present value of a perpetuity is equal to the annual payment divided by the interest rate.

7. The rate of return of an investment project is that interest rate at which the present value of the future returns is equal to the amount of investment required.

8. The normal rate of return in a business is the rate of return which must be earned in order to induce investors to invest there. It is the rate which could be earned on equivalently risky ventures elsewhere in the economy. This return is a cost of doing business (implicit, not explicit).

9. A firm can be said to be earning an economic profit if it is earning a rate of return in excess of the normal rate for that industry, because it is then receiving revenue over and above all costs.

10. Profits of a venture are often reflected in higher prices of the assets associated with the venture. The anticipation of returns higher than costs causes the price of these assets to be bid up to the point where any future buyer receives only a normal return on her investment, when the opportunity cost of the funds she invested in the assets is taken into account.

11. Accounting profits differ from economic profits in that the former do not allow for all of the implicit opportunity costs of a business.

12. Profits provide a reward to those who most quickly and precisely cater to the preferences of consumers and to those who find lower-cost methods of production. Losses punish those who produce products which consumers do not value highly and who use inefficient production techniques.

13. Managers of firms tend to operate more efficiently because it is possible for a relatively small number of outsiders to take over a firm and reap a profit by reorganizing production.

KEY TERMS

Accounting profit: Revenue in excess of accounting costs, which do not include some economic costs.

Annuity: A series of uniform annual payments.

Capital Good: A good which provides benefits over time.

Discount factor: The number by which an amount (or amounts) to be paid in the future is multiplied to obtain the present value of the future amount (or amounts). In the case of a single future amount coming in t years, the discount factor is

$$\frac{1}{(1 + r)^t}.$$

Discount rate: The interest rate (r) which is used in calculating a present value.

Economic profit: A rate of return in excess of the normal rate of return. Revenues greater than the sum of all costs.

Investment: The creation of capital goods. Transforming resources into sources of future rather than present consumption.

Normal rate of return: The rate of return which prospective investors would require to get them to invest in any particular industry. It is equal to the rate of return which could be earned in the best alternative industry with equivalent risk.

Perpetuity: A perpetual annuity.

Present value: The amount which one person would be willing to pay today to obtain the right to a certain amount or series of amounts in the future.

Rate of return: The discount rate at which the present value of the benefits of an investment project equals the investment required.

REVIEW QUESTIONS

1. If the interest rate is 8 percent, what price do you have to pay (in terms of present goods) in order to obtain $1 worth of goods in one year?

2. What is the present value of $350 to be paid in seven years, if the interest rate is 6 percent? 8 percent? 10 percent?

3. What is the present value of a stream of payments of $125 per year for fifty years if the interest rate is 4 percent? 10 percent?

4. What is the present value of an annuity of $10 per year, lasting five years, and starting seven years from today, if the interest rate is 8 percent?

5. How much would you accumulate if you saved $1000 per year (and continually reinvested interest) for thirty years if the interest rate is 4 percent? 10 percent?

6. Your employer, in lieu of a raise, offers to contribute enough so that, when you reach age 65, you will receive $10,000 per year for life. How much is that worth to you today? (What assumptions must you make in order to come up with an answer to this question?)

7. How much could a wage-earner currently earning $15,000 per year expect to receive in Social Security benefits, starting at age 65? How much could he obtain if he invested his Social Security taxes at 5 percent instead of in Social Security?

8. "It is worth it to take an action if the present value of benefits is greater than the present value of costs." Is this a correct statement? How would you apply it to the problem of the price-taker firm whose owners are trying to decide whether to operate or go out of business when the price is less than average total cost now (but above average variable cost) and expected to rise above average total cost in the future.

9. Suppose both suppliers and demanders of loanable funds (in figure 9-1) expected a 6 percent rate of inflation. What would this do to the height of the supply curve at every quantity (if we put the nominal interest rate i in the vertical axis)? What would it do to the height of the demand curve at every quantity? What would happen to the equilibrium rate of interest? (Hint: Suppose the original supply curve said that at a real interest rate of 3 percent, $100 would be supplied. What would the nominal rate have to be in order to generate a real rate of 3 percent and thus a quantity of $100 supplied?)

10. Consider figure 9-1. What would happen to the rate of interest if people's tastes changed so they were less concerned about providing for their future?

11. You want to accumulate some money over the next five years so that you can take a trip to Europe. The trip you have in mind would cost you $3000 today. Suppose there were going to be no inflation over the next five years (and you expected the price of the trip to remain at $3000) and that the interest rate in a noninflationary setting is 2 percent. (a) How much would you have to set aside if you wanted to save for the trip in five equal installments, starting one year from now? (b) Now suppose you anticipate that prices in general will increase 10 percent per year in the intervening years, and that the nominal interest rate will fully incorporate that inflation. How much would you have to accumulate in total if you expect the price of your vacation to grow as fast as prices in general? (c) If you are to set aside a constant *real* amount per year, how much must you put aside in each of the five installments? (d) Now suppose you think the interest rate will rise only to 10 percent in the face of the 10 percent inflation. How much would you have to put aside in each year in this case?

12. (a) A certain asset which promises to pay $100 per year for five years is currently selling for $379. If you paid that amount, what rate of return would you earn on your investment? (b) Suppose the normal rate of return on investments with risk similar to this one is 6 percent. Could you be said to be making an economic profit if you paid $379 for the asset? (c) If you paid $399, what rate of return would you obtain? Would you be earning an economic profit? (d) Suppose you pay $379 for the asset and at a cost of $30 are able to convince others of what you know about the asset's future revenues and risk. What price could you get for the asset? How much economic profit could you be said to have made on your purchase and resale?

13. One dealer offers you a car for $4000 cash; another offers the same car for $4200 payable in one year. Which is the better deal, if the interest rate is 10 percent?

14. You are trying to determine the cheapest method of producing zolloes. There are only two types of machines available for this purpose. The price of machine A is $10,000. After one year, the resale value would be $5000, with a maintenance and repair charge (payable at the end of the year) of $5000. Machine B sells initially for $7500. This machine may be resold for $3000 after one year. Its maintenance and repair bill (payable at the end of the year) is $6000. Assuming the outputs of the two machines are the same, and that you are only interested in producing for one year, which machine would you purchase if the interest rate is 5 percent (discount factor = 0.952)? If the interest rate is 20 percent? In each case, what is the cost of each machine?

15. Your dad is to retire at age 65, and the mortality tables show that he can expect to live for eleven years after retirement. If the interest rate is 8 percent, how much money must his company set aside before he reaches 65 so as to be able to pay your dad $1000 per month in his retirement?

16. You are considering leasing an asset for the next three years. Your projection is that it will provide net inflows of cash (after deducting expenses) of $100 at the end of the first year, $75 at the end of the second, and $125 at the end of the third year. Your lease payments will be $90 per year, payable at the end of the year. If the interest rate is 10 percent, should you take the lease? If you could have only a two-year lease, would you take it? Explain.

17. Some tenants give landlords a hard time by withholding rent and going through long legal channels to delay being evicted. Law-abiding owners will tend to be pushed around and lose rent. Tough owners will get more rent because they will forcibly evict deadbeats quickly and replace them with paying tenants. Other things equal, will the present value of an apartment building be higher for law-abiding or tough owners in the presence of aggressive renters? Would increased activism by renters tend to result in any change in the kinds of owners which apartments would have? Explain.

18. The California Water Project, through which canals were built to redistribute water to the more arid portions of California, was built at a cost of more than $1 billion. Arguments over the appropriateness of the project centered around the use of an appropriate discount rate for the project's benefits, which are estimated to last for fifty years or more. Given your answer to question 3, explain why the discount rate is so important in calculating benefits. What discount rate *should* be used?

19. You have an 8 percent mortgage of $35,000 on a house you have just bought. What is the present value of the future mortgage payments for which you have obligated yourself?

20. A piece of land which is expected to sell for $10,000 in five years currently sells for $4000. The interest rate is 10 percent. What is wrong?

21. Ace Fast Food Outlets is trying to get you to buy a franchise for their business. They say that you can earn a 20 percent return on your investment of $50,000 if you work half-time in the store. Is it a good investment?

22. Give arguments for and against the use of changes in the price of common stock as an indicator of the performance (profitability) of a company, as opposed to the net income reports made public by the company each quarter.

Adjusting Interest Rates for Inflation

This appendix discusses a few of the ways in which the existence of inflation complicates the discussion of interest rates and present values.

Suppose that on January 1, 1982, you put $100 into a savings account at 6 percent. If the rate of inflation is 8 percent, you are actually earning negative real interest. If you leave the money in the account for one year, then on January 1, 1983, you can draw out $106. But if the rate of inflation is 8 percent, it would take $108 in 1983 to buy what $100 could buy in 1982. So the $106 which you can withdraw in 1983 will not enable you to buy as many goods as $100 could have bought in 1982. This is a dramatic example of the adjustment one must make to determine the real return being earned from investments. To see how this is done in general, let us do some hypothetical calculations.

Suppose you have $100, and someone has made a contract which guarantees that if you pay her $100 today she will return to you in one year the amount of money that will be necessary at that time to buy what $104 could buy today. This is called a 4 percent real rate of interest because it tells the percentage increase in the real amount of goods you can buy if you give up your money for one year. If prices do not rise over that period, she will have to pay you only $104. But if prices rise by 6 percent over the year, she will have to pay you $104 plus six percent of $104, in order for you to have enough to buy what $104 would have bought today. That comes to $104 + (.06) (104) = 104 + 6.24 = $110.24.

In general, we can calculate the future dollar amount (A_1) that you must be paid in order for you to earn a real return of r on your initial outlay of Z as $(Z + Zr) + (Z + Zr) p = Z(1 + r) + Z(1 + r) p = A_1$ where p is the rate of inflation. Note that $Z + Zr = Z(1 + r)$ is the amount you would have to be paid if there were no price increase. It is simply the present amount plus the interest on that amount. But with an inflation rate of p, the future amount would have to be augmented by p times the amount $Z(1 + r)$. So $A_1 = Z(1 + r) + Z(1 + r) p = Z(1 + r)(1 + p)$. In our example, this turned out to be $100(1 + .04)(1 + .06) = 110.24.

The nominal rate of interest (as distinct from the *real* rate of interest) is the percentage number that is applied to the principal ($100 in the previous example) to obtain the number of dollars to be paid (or received) in the future. In our example, since $110.24 is paid in one year in exchange for $100 today, the nominal rate of interest is 10.24 percent. Because of inflation the real value of the nominal rate is only 4 percent, the real rate of interest.

What is the general formula for determining what nominal rate of interest (i) goes with any given real rate of interest (r) when the inflation rate is p? The extra dollars that are necessary because of the inflation serve two purposes: to bring the amount used to pay the principal up to the purchasing power of the initial principal amount, and to bring the amount used to pay the interest up to the purchasing power the interest payment would have if there were no inflation. In our example, the initial principal amount was $100. With a 6 percent inflation, an additional $6 must be paid one year in the future to compensate for decline of the purchasing power of the $100. In addition, with a real rate of interest of 4 percent and no inflation, the interest payment would be $4. But in order to have the same purchasing power as $4, the interest payment would have to be increased by 6 percent (that is, increased by 24¢). Then the total dollar amount of the interest payment is $p(\$100) + r(\$100) + rp(\$100) = \$6 + \$4 + \$.24 = \$10.24$. As a percent of the initial principal (that is, as i), the interest payment is

$$\frac{\$100\ (p + r + rp)}{\$100} = p + r + rp.$$

No matter what the initial principal amount is, it appears in both the numerator and the denominator; so, in general, $i = p + r + rp$. If r and p are small, rp is very small; therefore, we usually ignore rp, and write $i = r + p$. Often we rewrite it as $r = i - p$.

After the fact, this relationship is an *identity*. It *must* be true (neglecting the r p term) that the real rate of interest earned equals the nominal rate paid minus the rate of inflation experienced. If we are (as is usually the case) paid a certain nominal rate of interest i and we experience a certain rate of inflation p, we simply subtract the latter from the former to figure what we *really* earned. As our first example showed, the sad news in recent times has been that often the real return on savings accounts has been negative. Thus, if a person holds his wealth in that form, its real purchasing power *shrinks* over time. This does not mean that people are irrational to hold their wealth in this form. If that is the best return they can get, they might still prefer to forego some consumption today so that they can consume more than otherwise in the future. Nevertheless, it should be clear that such a state of affairs does not provide much inducement to save.

While the relationship $r = i - p$ is an identity after the fact, that does not mean that the numbers in the equation are always correctly anticipated by borrowers or lenders. Transactors often misestimate how fast prices will rise. If savers systematically underestimate how fast prices will rise, then the nominal interest rate they will require to attract their savings will be lower than if they had correctly guessed the inflation rate. If a saver thought he could get a real return of 4 percent from borrower X, and that inflation would be 6 percent, he would require (approximately) a 10 percent nominal rate from borrower Y in order to lend to him. If he lends to Y and gets 10 percent, but the inflation rate is 8 percent (instead of 6 percent he expected) then his *real* return is only 2 percent. This was in part what was happening in the 1970s. Savers seemed systematically to underestimate inflation, so that in retrospect the real rates they obtained after subtracting the inflation rate from the nominal rates they received were less than the real rates which had prevailed in earlier years. In fact, as we saw, in some cases the nominal interest rates were less than the rate of inflation, so that real rates of interest were negative.

INFLATION AND PRESENT VALUE CALCULATIONS

How should we adjust our present value calculations to take account of inflation? There are two ways which look different but turn out to be equivalent. The first method involves no apparent change in the standard procedure. In this approach we merely use the nominal rate of interest as our discount rate and the higher dollar values which inflation will bring as our future amounts. For example, suppose that in the absence of inflation, the revenue one can expect from a certain asset in one year is $100, and in the absence of inflation, the interest rate would be 4 percent. Then the present value of that future amount would be $96.15. Now suppose that an inflation rate of 6 percent is anticipated, and that the nominal interest rate rises to 10.24 percent, as in our earlier example. With the inflation rate of 6 percent, we can expect the revenue from the asset to rise to $106. Now the present value is 106/1 + 0.1024, which again equals $96.15. (Of course, if the future amount rose faster or slower than prices in general, or if the nominal interest rate more than or less than fully reflected the 6 percent inflation, the answer would have changed.)

Now consider the second method of handling inflation. In this method we deflate the future nominal amounts so that $1 worth of a future (deflated) payment will buy the same amount as $1 would buy today. Thus the $106 which we expect in the future would be deflated by dividing by $(1 + p) = 1.06$, giving $100 in real dollars. Then we use the *real* rate of interest to discount all future flows. In our example, the future amount (in real dollars) is $100, and discounting at the real rate of interest of 4 percent gives us 100/1 + 0.04 = 96.15, just as before. This should not be surprising, because in the first case (using the nominal interest rate and the nominal future flow) we got

$$PV = \frac{A_1(1+p)}{1 + i} = \frac{A_1(1 + p)}{(1+r)(1+p)} = \frac{A_1}{1 + r},$$

and in the second case we used

$$\frac{\left(\dfrac{A_1 (1 + p)}{(1 + p)}\right)}{1 + r} = \frac{A_1}{1 + r}.$$

So as long as we make the same assumptions in both methods, we get the same answers. But the reader can easily see that the answers one gets depend crucially on the assumptions one makes about (1) whether the future amount A will increase by more or less than the rate of inflation, and (2) whether and to what extent the nominal interest rate will incorporate that rate of inflation. In principle, inflation causes no problems, but in practice it is very troublesome.

INFLATION AND RETIREMENT PLANNING

Deciding how much to save for retirement gets more complicated when one anticipates inflation. For example, if the person in our earlier example in the section, "Saving for Retirement," wanted to accumulate by age 65 a nest egg which would buy what $79,212 could buy today, she would have to accumulate much more than $79,212. If she anticipates a 4 percent annual inflation over the thirty-year period, she would have to accumulate (3.24) (79,212) = $256,647, because if prices rise at 4 percent per year, she will (according to table 9-2) need $3.24 in thirty years to buy what $1 would buy today; so if she wants an amount that would enable her to buy what $79,212 would buy today, she will need $256,647. If the interest rate she would earn were still 6 percent, then she would have to put away $3240 per year instead of $1000 per year in order to accumulate that amount.[5]

But this neglects two factors. First, if the inflation is generally anticipated, the interest rate will rise to reflect this. If the nominal interest rate fully reflects the anticipation of 4 percent inflation, then it will rise to 10.24 percent, as in our earlier nominal interest rate example. The amount one would have to deposit annually at 10 percent (use this approximation because it is available in the tables) in order to accumulate $256,647 is only $1564. (Work this out for yourself, using tables 9-2 and 9-3 and a 10 percent rate of interest.) But we are neglecting one more factor, namely, the fact that with a 4 percent inflation rate, if I want to put away in twenty years an amount equivalent in purchasing power to $1000 today, that future amount must be greater than $1000. With an inflation rate of 4 percent,

5. This can be seen as follows. We obtained the $79,212 by multiplying our $1000 annual deposit by 13.8 (the present value of a thirty-year annuity) and by 5.74 (the future compounded amount to which $1 would grow in thirty years). (Check on this to make sure you see why we did this.) Thus $D(13.8)(5.74) = F$, where D is the deposit and F is the future accumulated value. Now to find the annual deposit necessary to accumulate $256,647, we solve that equation for D. (In other words, we solve for $D = A/(13.8)(5.74)$.) When $F = \$256,674$, $D = \$3240$.

it should be $2,190. (We get this by looking at the entry for twenty years and 4 percent in table 9-2.) Thus, if we wanted to put away the same amount in *real* terms, we would have to put away increasing amounts as time passed ($1480 in the tenth year, $1800 in the fifteenth year, and so on). Then the problem becomes one of determining the *real* amount to be deposited (with each year's actual money deposit adjusted upward for the rate of inflation) such that $256,-647 could be accumulated in thirty years.

Unfortunately, it is not easy to do this using our tables, because the annual amount would no longer be uniform in dollar terms. But we can see what is happening if we look at the algebra a little closer. Recall that our initial problem involved putting aside $1000 per year for thirty years at 6 percent interest. We accumulated $79,212. We could restate the problem by asking what is the annual deposit I would have to make in order to be able to accumulate $79,212 in thirty years, if the interest rate is 6 percent. The answer is $1000. We stated this algebraically as

$$A(1 + r)^{29} + A(1 + r)^{28} + \ldots + A(1 + r) + A = F. \tag{5}$$

If F is $79,212 and r is 0.06, then the A which makes the equation hold is $1000. Now we want to set up a new equation which enables us to find the *real* amount A, which would have to be deposited in order to accumulate a nest egg with the same purchasing power that $79,212 would have today (where the dollar amount deposited would have to be adjusted upward each year to account for inflation). We said that if inflation is 4 percent per year, the nest egg would have to be $256,657, or $F(1 + p)^{30}$ in general. And the amount which would have to be deposited each year would be $A(1 + p)^t$, where $t = 1$ for the first payment (one year from now) and $t = 20$ for the twentieth payment (twenty years from now). If

the inflation rate is built into the interest rate, then the nominal interest rate i will be such that $(1 + r)(1 + p) = (1 + i)$. Then the equation becomes

$$A(1 + p)(1 + i)^{29} + A(1 + p)^2(1 + i)^{28} + \ldots + A(1 + p)^{29}(1 + i) + A(1 + p)^{30} = F(1 + p)^{30}.$$

But since

$$(1 + i) = (1 + r)(1 + p),$$

this becomes

$$A(1 + p)[(1 + r)(1 + p)]^{29} + A(1 + p)^2[(1 + r)(1 + p)]^{28} + \ldots + A(1 + p)^{29}[(1 + r)(1 + p)] + A(1 + p)^{30} = F(1 + p)^{30}. \tag{6}$$

The interesting thing is that the solution to equation (6) is the same as the solution to equation (5). This is true because if we divide both sides of equation (6) by $(1 + p)^{30}$, we get equation (5).

The significance of this result is that if we want to make plans to accumulate a nest egg with a certain real purchasing power, we can come up with a plan to accumulate it without a great deal of difficulty, even if we are unsure about what inflation rates will be over the intervening years. The first step is to decide on the size of the nest egg we would want in the absence of inflation. Then we solve the problem of equation (5) by means of the methods we used above. It is crucial to remember to use the *real* rate of interest. It is difficult to know just what this will be in the future, but a rate of 2 or 3 percent would not be unreasonably low. (In fact, as we noted, the real rates earned on many bonds have been lower—even negative—in the last few years.) Having calculated the annual amount that would have to be deposited in the absence of inflation, we need only adjust that amount upward each year by the rate of inflation, and we should accumulate an amount equal to $F(1 + p)^{30}$, which will have the same purchasing power as F would have if there were no inflation.

chapter 10

Restrictions on Markets

Not all firms are arms-length rivals nor are they always totally independent entities. Not all markets are open to whoever wants to try his luck. In short, transactors are not always free to exchange goods and services at mutually agreeable prices. We shall encounter these issues in the discussion of collusion and cartels, restriction on entry, and labor unions in this chapter.

COLLUSION AND CARTELS

In most cases there are gains to be made by sellers if they can agree to restrict the ways they compete with each other. The term used to describe such restrictive agreements is _collusion_. The dictionary defines a _cartel_ as a "voluntary combination of independent private enterprises . . . that agree to limit their competitive activities" in various ways. In other words, a group of firms which collude can be called a cartel. What is the source of gain from collusion? We shall illustrate the gain by examining collusion on price, but a similar analysis applies to other types of collusion.

Let's consider a dramatic example of the effects of successful collusion on the profits of the colluders. Suppose we have a price-taker's industry which is in equilibrium, in the sense that (1) the price clears the market without a surplus or shortage, and (2) firms in the industry are making neither profits nor losses so that there is no tendency for firms to enter or

FIGURE 10-1
THE GAINS FROM COLLUSION

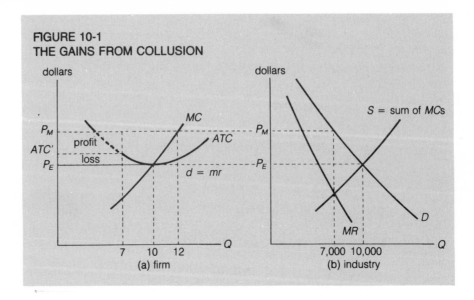

(a) firm

(b) industry

leave. (These conditions describe what we referred to as long-run equilibrium in chapter 7.) We illustrate the situation graphically in figure 10-1.

Figure 10-1 (a) shows the position of a representative firm, and 10-1 (b) shows the corresponding industry supply and demand. As discussed in chapter 7, the price tends to be at P_E where the demand and supply (sum of individual firm *marginal costs*) curves intersect. If the price were higher than P_E (when firms are acting independently), there would be a surplus (the amount firms would want to supply would be greater than the amount consumers would want to buy). If the price were lower than P_E, there would be a shortage.

Each firm acting independently finds its best position to be at a point like that shown in (a), namely, where $MC = mr = P_E$. If any one firm decided to cut its output by, say, 30 percent, it would have only a very slight effect on the price, and the firm would lose money. This loss is represented by the diagonally lined region (labelled "loss") with height of ATC' minus P_E, and width of seven. The loss arises because *average total cost* rises when output falls below $q = 10$, while the single firm acting independently cannot affect the price.

But if *all* firms decided to cut back their output by 30 percent, the price would rise so much (up to P_M) that every firm makes a profit. This profit is represented by the vertically lined region (labelled "profit"), with height of P_M minus ATC', and width of seven. The profit occurs in spite of the fact that cost per unit rises to ATC', because when *all* firms reduce their output by 30 percent, the *total* output falls by 30 percent, resulting in a noticeable rise in price (to P_M). What is happening?

When all the firms act as a unit, they are able to internalize the benefit (to them) of the higher price and are thus induced to take account of it. If one firm reduces its output, it provides a benefit to all the other firms in the form of a very slightly higher price. The benefit to any one firm is small, and of course the benefit to the reducing firm is not worth giving up 30 percent of sales for. But if *all* firms cut back, each firm is getting the benefit of the reduction in output and increased price from (in this case) 999 *other* firms. If in return one firm gives up 30 percent of its output, it could still be better off. Another way of looking at this is to note that when all the firms act as a unit, they in effect face the industry's demand curve as their "firm's" demand. Since that demand is downward-sloping, its *MR* curve lies below it, and the profit-maximizing output for the *group* (as a unit) is where that *marginal revenue* equals *marginal cost* (sum of *marginal costs* or *supply*) [shown in figure 10-1 (b)]. That will *always* be at an output less than the intersection of demand and supply. (Why?)

So this is the source of the gains from collusion: when acting as a unit, the firms in an industry are able to internalize the external benefit any firm grants the others when it competes less (by selling less, or raising its price, or reducing the quantity of its output). Activities which are not profitable when done on an individual level often are profitable when many or all of the firms in the industry carry them out simultaneously.

THE INSTABILITY OF COLLUSIVE AGREEMENTS (CARTELS)

To show that there are gains from collusive behavior does not prove that collusion will always be carried out successfully. There are inherent problems with any voluntary collusive agreement. The first is that, once the agreement is made, it is in the separate individual interest of every member to break it secretly. Look again at figure 10-1. At the new price P_M, each firm views itself as being unable individually to affect the price (just as it did when the industry was competitive). At a price of P_M, the optimal output of each firm is *not* seven, the amount which will generate the joint profit maximum, but twelve. If everyone else holds at seven and I increase to twelve, I can get an *even bigger* profit. Of course if everyone increases output to twelve, we shall all lose money; but then there is nothing I can do to keep the others from increasing, so why should I cooperate by holding back output? This dilemma faces every member of every cartel, and the larger the number of members in the cartel, the more serious it is. So a cartel has problems right from the start. These are sufficient to make a purely voluntary cartel, with no methods of enforcing the agreement, a lost cause when the number of firms is reasonably large.

What if some method of enforcement can be worked out? Are the cartel's problems over? Not necessarily. If it is possible for new firms to enter, this can be a problem. Recall that, when every firm produces the restricted output, economic profits are generated. These profits are a signal for new firms to enter the business, and in the absence of restrictions they will do so. Once new firms enter the business, the cartel can either ignore them or include them. The best strategy is to include them, because if they are ignored, they will tend to produce more (twelve units in this example), whereas if they are included in the agreement they will produce less output and hurt the other cartel members less. The trouble is that as new entrants appear, the output of each firm must be reduced still further, resulting in higher average total cost, while the optimal cartel price falls. This squeeze will eventually result in the elimination of all cartel profits. The price is higher than in the competitive (price-taker) solution, but because the output per firm is smaller, each firm's average total cost is commensurately higher, resulting in zero profits.

The above indicates that any cartel which is to succeed in the long run must have restrictions on entry. The effects of such restrictions will be discussed in more detail. Even without the problems of entry, however, there are other difficulties. One problem is that not all firms are the same size or, more importantly, have the same costs. A simple thing like this can cause dissention within the cartel. Another problem is that the cartel must be careful to control all the methods of competition. If only price and quantity are controlled, competition will tend to occur in quality.

EXAMPLES OF COLLUSION AND CARTELS

In the spring of 1975, some farmers in Iowa spent some time traveling around the state trying to persuade their fellow farmers to plant 10 percent less corn than planned. The campaign was based on the fact that a 10 percent reduction in corn output would raise corn prices by about 50 percent. All those contacted agreed, but they did not take part in the plan, largely because it was voluntary, and in that situation, no individual farmer had an interest in reducing his output without a corresponding pledge of reduction by everyone else.

Some programs of the U.S. Department of Agriculture have been more effective, notably the soil bank and acreage allotment programs, which have acted more directly to induce farmers to produce less.

Also more successful for a time was a series of collusions among equipment manufacturers. In various episodes between the end of World War II and the early 1960s, these manufacturers agreed to divide customers among themselves so as to avoid having to make legitimately competing bids on contracts to provide electrical equipment.

Several features of the collusions are interesting. First, the most successful collusions involved a relatively small number of firms. (In the case of the circuit breaker conspiracy, there were four, and then five, firms.) Our earlier analysis of cartels suggested that the smaller the number of firms, the greater the likelihood of success. Second, there were several periods when the collusion broke down. In spite of the small numbers, the collusion was not always able to be successful. Third, the methods used to collude were rather crude—for example, using a system of rotation to decide which company would get the bid. Since not all bids were equally lucrative, and since the firm with the lowest cost did not always get a given contract, the cartel was less profitable than one might at first think. Also, these profit-reducing bureaucratic arrangements led to disagreements which were the source of some breakdowns in the collusion. Fourth, the collusive agreements were not immune to entry of new firms. Our theory predicts that to the extent the collusion is profitable, it sets up an added inducement for new entry to occur. The entry, by causing existing firms to cut back on their output still further, puts added strain on the agreement. The fifth point we wish to raise about this series of collusions is that the most successful ones and the longest-lasting ones involved sales to government agencies (or government-owned public utilities). This last feature is apparently due to the fact that government officials who are soliciting contracts are prevented from seeking secret concessions from colluders (which would undermine the collusive agreement) and have a smaller inducement than would private firms to encourage new entrants into the business.

This particular series of collusions was apparently brought to an end by a series of well-publicized antitrust cases brought by the Justice Department in the early 1960s.[1]

Airline industry regulation under the Civil Aeronautics Board (CAB) prior to 1979 provides an example of the problems in controlling nonprice competition in a cartel. From its inception in 1938 until the late 1970s, the CAB's actions could best be described as those of a cartel organizer and enforcer. Economic studies done in the early 1970s indicated that CAB-regulated fares were 20–95 percent higher than they would have been in the absence of regulation.[2] The evidence is consistent with the hypothesis that airlines agreed on fares to be charged and then used the CAB to enforce the price agreements and prevent entry into markets. It is clear that entry into the business was restricted. Big news stories resulted whenever an airline was allowed to enter a market which had earlier been closed to it. Permission to operate on a lucrative route was a valuable asset, and airlines went to great lengths (including making large contributions to presidential candidates) to increase their chances of obtaining entry to certain markets.

In spite of these severe restrictions, and in spite of the CAB rules which prohibited firms from charging *less than* the official price, competition was not prevented. It merely changed form. One of the ways firms competed was by offering more flights. Once a firm was able to gain access to a certain route, it could offer as many flights as it wished. By offering

---

1. For more on this case, see "Collusion among Electrical Equipment Manufacturers," *Wall Street Journal*, 10 and 12 January, 1962. (Reprinted in Edwin Mansfield, ed., *Monopoly Power and Economic Performance*, 3rd ed. (New York: Norton, 1974); and A. A. Alchian, "Electrical Equipment Collusion: Why and How," *Economic Forces at Work* (Indianapolis, IN: Liberty Press, 1977).

2. See Theodore E. Keeler, "Airline Regulation and Market Performance," *Bell Journal of Economics 3* (Autumn 1972): 399–424.

more frequent flights, an airline could attract customers from its competitors. Airlines were induced to do this, even though it meant a smaller percentage of its seats would be filled, because with the high CAB-enforced fares, they could still cover their costs even with many empty seats. Thus, frequency of flights was an important method of nonprice competition. Other forms of competition included increasing the space per passenger ("first class legroom"), increasing the quality of meals, lounges, entertainment, and free drinks.

With the passage of the Airline Deregulation Act in October 1978, things began to change. Airlines are now able to enter and leave markets much more easily than before and have much more flexibility (especially in the downward direction) in changing their fares without CAB approval. The result has been that airline fares have (as of 1980) fallen in real terms (they rose only half as fast as prices in general) in spite of the fact that fuel costs doubled in 1979. Instead of competing solely on the basis of frequency of flights and other quality variables, airlines have been adjusting the price and quality mix that they offer in an attempt to discover what tradeoffs customers are willing to make between quality and price. The industry is still sorting itself out in the face of these new rules, but one can expect a certain pattern to emerge. When airlines are allowed to vary all the terms of sale, it will probably turn out that some customers will prefer to have better service and pay a higher price, while others will prefer to forego frills in return for a lower price. On heavily travelled routes it can be expected that both kinds of service (and possibly others in between) will exist.

This probable development under deregulation points up the inefficiency in the old system. The old higher CAB-enforced prices forced everyone to consume a higher quality product. If a customer had to pay the higher price anyway, he preferred (and was served by) the nonprice competition which provided him with the higher quality product. But some customers would have preferred even more to have a lower price and lower quality. (The higher quality was not worth it to them.) The closing off of this option to customers was the inefficiency of the artificially high price.

OPEC AND THE PRICE OF OIL

The OPEC oil cartel is the best known and most successful cartel in the world. Since 1973, when OPEC came into prominence, the price of crude oil has risen from around $2 to over $30 per barrel. Even after adjusting for inflation, the price is five to eight times as high as in 1973.

To understand the role of OPEC, we should start with some background on the world oil situation. For the first time in modern history, a major product comes chiefly from a region in which the U.S. and the other Western countries have little influence—the Middle East. The rapid increase in the wealth of the area is causing huge changes in the societies involved, and the rapid pace of these changes often leads to political turbulence. This in turn can cause interruptions in the supply from the area. Since two thirds of the oil that moves in international trade originates in the Middle East, when political upheavals occur there, they can temporarily have enormous effects on the economies of the rich consuming countries.

Partly because holding inventories is very costly, oil companies in the consuming countries hold relatively small stocks of crude oil and refined products—only enough to last three to six months. In addition, in the short run, refineries are not able, at reasonable cost, to substitute one kind of crude for another (for example, high sulphur Alaskan for low sulphur Iranian).

The result of these factors is that in the short run the demand for crude oil is very inelastic. If the amount of a particular grade decreases unexpectedly, the price necessary to clear the market in the short run can rise tremendously. It might have occurred to you that a smart oil company would, in the presence of increased risk of disruption, want to hold larger inventories so that when the disruptions and consequent big price increases came, it would be in a position to make a lot of money. The possibility of making that money would compensate for the high storage costs, so that bigger inventories would be worthwhile. Of course, if many companies held bigger inventories and drew them down during crises, the crisis-induced price increases would be less drastic. But there are at least two factors in the U.S. economy which reduce the inducement to hold these inventories. The first is that in any period of disruption price controls on oil or its products have been (and are likely in the future to be) imposed. Secondly, even in the absence of price controls, the windfall profits tax has the same effect. Thus, because of governmental controls, firms have been induced to hold smaller inventories than they might otherwise hold, and price adjustments have been bigger than they would otherwise have been.

One of the outstanding characteristics of the OPEC era has been that nine tenths of the huge price increases occurred during and after two major disruptions: the Arab embargo of 1973–74 and the Iranian cutoff of 1979. Once the price increases occurred, the difficult job of holding onto those increases began for OPEC.

As with all cartels, the success of OPEC depends on its being able to reduce its members' outputs below what they would otherwise be at such high prices. Certain key members of OPEC, such as Saudi Arabia, have been willing to produce much less than they could in order to keep total industry output low enough to support the price. This is particularly the case following a major disruption of supply and an ensuing big jump in price. If the price of oil rises substantially, the quantity demanded falls below what it would otherwise be. To make the higher price stick, someone has to produce less. Otherwise a surplus would develop, tending to lower the price. Consider the sizable increases in price in both 1973–74 and 1979 which were initially induced by huge supply disruptions. These price hikes were accompanied by numerous reports of governments of producing countries (for example, Saudi Arabia) ordering reduced shipments to prevent a glut. Not all oil-producing countries cut back. Some increased their output in response to the higher price. But the largest producers, especially those in the Persian Gulf, have greatly restrained their output. For example, Saudi Arabia, which was producing 9 million barrels per day (bpd) in early 1980, could increase its output to 12 million bpd with virtually no new equipment. And it could easily produce 18 million bpd by drilling more wells and installing more pipelines, degasification plants, and so on. The forbearance of the key members of OPEC, such as Saudi Arabia, accounts for much of the cartel's continued success.

The big increases in crude oil prices have had the expected impact on non-OPEC suppliers. Mexico's oil deposits have been developed much faster than they would have if the price had remained at the 1973 level. Alaskan oil would probably not have continued to flow in much volume had the price stayed low. Similarly, much of the new onshore and offshore drilling that is happening today in the U.S. would have been uneconomic at prices of $3 to $6 per barrel. Research into coal gasification and development of oil shale and tar sands would have been put on the back burner had prices remained low. The cutbacks required by the key (mostly Persian Gulf) countries have had to be bigger than they would have been if non-OPEC suppliers had not increased output in response to the higher prices.

Anticipations of the Future

A key fact which must be kept in mind when considering OPEC is that petroleum is a nonrenewable resource. This means that if the owner takes a barrel out of the ground today he incurs an implicit cost (in addition to the cost of drilling and pumping) because the barrel which is sold today cannot be sold in the future. The present value of the best future price represents the implicit cost of selling oil today. Suppose, for example, one expects to be able to get $100 per barrel ten years from now, and the interest rate is 10 percent. Then the present value of that future amount is $38.50 (see table 9-1). An owner who thought prices would be that high in the future and could not get more than $38.50 today would be better off leaving the oil in the ground. If he could only get $35 today, and could invest that at 10 percent, then the $35 would grow to $2.59 \times \$35 = \$90.65$ in ten years (see table 9-2), which is less than the owner could get by waiting ten years to sell the oil. What this means is that anyone (today it is mainly the OPEC governments) who owns oil (and any group of oil sellers) must constantly make forecasts about what the future price of oil will be in order to decide how much to sell today. The higher an owner thinks the future price will be, the less he will want to sell today, and the higher the price will be today.

What factors influence expectations of the future price of oil? An important component is the demand for energy. In the era when energy

FIGURE 10-2
ESTIMATION OF FUTURE ENERGY PRICES

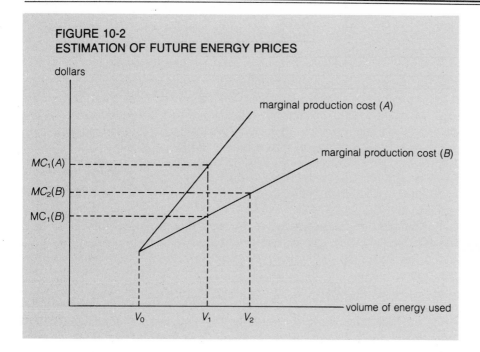

prices were about constant, the consumption of energy grew about 5 percent per year. So the demand curve was shifting to the right about 5 percent
per year. This happened because things which use a lot of energy are
normal goods, so the demand for them—and thus for energy—rose as
income rose. If there is a hierarchy of costs such as we described in chapter
7, so that only limited volumes of energy are obtainable at each production
cost level, we can expect the price at some future time to be higher than
it is today.

How high that future price will be depends on the amounts of energy
which can be produced at each cost level and on how much is consumed
in the intervening period. The more we consume, and the steeper the curve
indicating the volumes of energy available at any production cost, the
higher that price will be. This is shown in figure 10-2. If we have up to now
used volume V_0, and if by the future time in question we will have used
volume V_1, then the price in the future will have to be higher if we are faced
with curve A than if we are faced with curve B. Similarly, given that we
are faced with curve B, the price in the future will have to be higher if we
have used volume V_2 by that time than if we have used only V_1 by that
time.

The shape that transactors attribute to the marginal production cost
curves—and thus the level of future prices—depends on beliefs about the
level of price necessary to call forth other sources of energy. Curve B
reflects a more optimistic outlook regarding the availability of various
energy sources than does curve A. Thus, if a transactor believed B were
the correct curve, he would anticipate a lower future price than if he

thought A were correct. <u>The lower the price is expected to be in the future, the lower the implicit cost an oil owner bears in selling oil now. The lower that implicit cost, the greater the amount supplied today at any given price, and the lower the price will be today.</u> Thus if people come to believe that a great breakthrough (such as cheap fusion power) will come in twenty years, that will tend through the mechanism just described to lower oil prices *today*. The reverse is also true. If we (and particularly owners of oil) come to believe that fusion will *not* be available, and that shale oil, coal gasification, and nuclear energy will be less available at any price than we formerly thought, that will increase the expected future price of oil and the implicit cost of using it today, thus leading to less production and a higher price today.

What has happened during recent years of oil turbulence has been that expectations about future availability of alternative sources have become much less optimistic. Practically without exception, every piece of new information about the prospects for alternative energy sources (fusion, fission, coal gasification and liquification, shale oil, tar sands, solar power, and so on) has made us less optimistic than we were previously about the price at which they would be available. This enormous change in anticipations about the amounts of various energy sources available at various prices would have led, even in the absence of OPEC, to substantial increases in the prices of energy in general and oil in particular. The price is higher today than it would be without OPEC, but it is not five to eight times as high, as some believe.

Supply and Demand and OPEC

The kind of response which OPEC has made to the bad news about future alternative energy sources is similar to the response that would have been made by a competitive oil market. <u>Every time more bad news about the future comes out, that increases the OPEC members' implicit cost of selling oil today and increases the cartel's profit-maximizing price.</u> Not surprisingly, this kind of reasoning is surfacing in OPEC countries like Saudi Arabia. There is political pressure to cut current output. For example, proponents argue in public that the proceeds of oil sales at $11 a barrel in 1974, if invested at prevailing interest rates in the U.S. and other major economies, would have grown to $18 by 1980. But Saudi oil fetched $28 in that year. Hence, the argument that oil should be left in the ground. The effect of a change in beliefs is illustrated in figure 10-3, where we show the demand faced by OPEC. Given the initial beliefs about the future, the marginal cost (including the implicit cost) of producing OPEC oil is shown as ΣMC^0_{OPEC}. The cartel maximizes profit where $MR = MC$, at Q_0, with a price of P_0.

If a piece of bad news about future availability comes along, this causes owners to expect a higher price in the future and raises the implicit cost of selling oil today. Thus, the cartel's *MC* curve shifts to ΣMC^1_{OPEC} *and higher prices (and smaller quantity) are the result.*

FIGURE 10-3
IMPORTANCE OF BELIEFS
ABOUT THE FUTURE

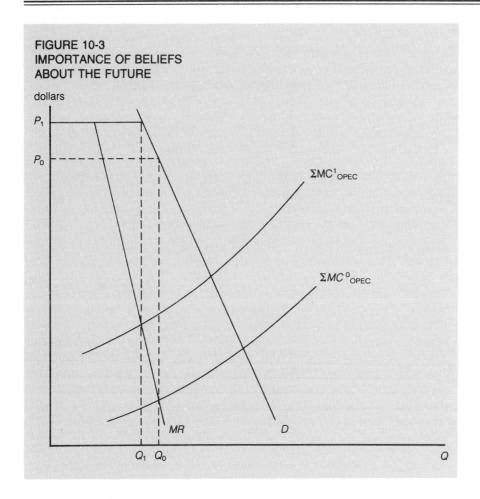

RESTRICTIONS ON ENTRY

In the presence of collusion, restrictions on entry often are essential in preserving the cartel profit gains. But even in the absence of collusive behavior by those within the industry, restrictions on entry can often be useful. For example, a restriction on the entry of taxicabs or doctors could benefit those already in the industry, even if the industry were characterized by no collusive behavior at all.

   Restrictions on the entry of resources into an industry have three kinds of effects which bring them under fire. The first is that they tend to result in a higher price. A restriction on entry acts like a reduction in supply (shift to the left of the supply curve). It reduces the amount supplied at any price, resulting in a higher price. Does the higher price mean that anyone who is in the industry is making economic profits (or a higher than normal rate of return)? Not necessarily.

Take the case of liquor licenses. In every state there are restrictions on how many establishments can sell liquor. This restriction lowers the amount supplied and raises the price of liquor. Suppose you have an opportunity to obtain a liquor license. After subtracting the rental cost of your building, labor, and other costs, you will be able to make a very good return. Suppose that after subtracting all these costs, you expect to have $5000 left over every year, as a sort of bonus for being lucky enough to be in a restricted market. (If there were no restrictions on entry, the price you could get for liquor would be so low that the $5000 would disappear.) The *present value* of a perpetuity of $5000 is $50,000, if the interest rate is 10 percent. Thus if you were given a liquor license, that is like being given $50,000. Furthermore, if you did not *own* a license, you would be willing to pay up to $50,000 to get one. More importantly, other people can do what you can do, and *they* would be willing to pay for the license also. So if licenses are transferable, you would probably have to pay an amount near $50,000 for one. Do you then make a higher-than-normal return? No. Every year, you are incurring an implicit (foregone interest) cost of $5000 on the $50,000 you paid for the license. If you add that $5000 (implicit opportunity cost) to your other costs, you are just breaking even. This is a strange result. But on closer examination, it is reasonable. The person who owns the license at the time the restrictions are imposed makes a profit. The future higher-than-normal earnings are capitalized into the selling price of the license, and any future buyer, having paid the present value of the future extra net revenue, earns only a normal return. Any right which many people recognize to be valuable will command a price. And if there is competition among buyers, the price will be such that the buyer earns only a normal rate of return.

What would happen if owners of liquor licenses could not sell them? This would not mean that the right was not valuable, but it would tend to result in inefficient operation of liquor stores. Under unrestricted sale of licenses, if I am a lower-cost (more efficient) operator of a liquor store than the current owner, the value I will place on the license will be greater than the value she places on it. Why? Because the value I place on it is the present value of the difference between revenue and cost for me. If my cost is lower, that difference (and my present value) will be higher. Thus under unrestricted exchange, there is a tendency for the lowest-cost producer to end up with the license. But if resale is barred (say one merely *forfeits* the license if one wants to get out), then the owner will *not* tend to get out, and I will not get the license. So a second result of restrictions on entry, if the rights are not resalable, is that the lowest-cost producers do not necessarily end up in the business.

The third feature of restricted entry which is condemned has been alluded to earlier. It helps to facilitate the cartelizing of the industry. We stated that restricted entry *need not* be accompanied by cartelizing, but remember that one of the problems that any cartel has is the appearance of new entrants in response to the profits the cartel's policies generate. Restricted entry reduces this problem and therefore increases the incentive of the firms in the industry to form a cartel.

FURTHER EXAMPLES OF RESTRICTIONS ON ENTRY

Tobacco Allotments

Any person who wants to grow tobacco in the United States must own or lease a *tobacco allotment*, which is a permit from the U.S. Department of Agriculture (USDA) saying the owner can grow tobacco on a certain number of acres of land.[3] This program restricts land devoted to tobacco growing and restricts tobacco output to levels below what they would be in a free market. In addition, the USDA guarantees a support price for tobacco which is widely regarded as being substantially higher than the free market price. As a result, it is estimated that in parts of North Carolina (where two thirds of the flue-cured tobacco—the kind used in cigarettes—is grown) land with a tobacco allotment sells for $5000 per acre more than land without the allotment. Although tobacco is grown on only 0.5 percent of North Carolina's farmland, it generates one third of the state's total farm income.

Taxi Medallions in San Francisco

An interesting example of licensing and the problems that accompany it is provided by the city of San Francisco. That city has long licensed taxi cabs. For each taxi cab a firm puts into service it must have a permit (called a *medallion*). Since the city issues few medallions relative to the number wanted, they command a price. Until 1978 they could be bought and sold like any other asset, and in the mid 1970s some sold for as much as $30,000. Since the price of medallions rose rapidly in that period, some in the city became disgruntled over alleged "speculation" in medallions. In 1978 the voters passed a law which prohibited the resale of taxi medallions. The law states that when the owner dies, the medallion must be returned to the city. It can then be sold (by the city) to a new owner for $7500. The new owner must be a natural person (not a corporation) and at the time of purchase must have been a taxi driver for at least one year. In spite of these restrictions, a long list of prospective buyers has formed, in anticipation of the reissuance of deceased owners' permits.

Since an owner cannot sell his medallion, there is no implicit (foregone interest) cost to his holding onto it. He will continue to use the permit as long as he can get revenue from operating his taxi which is greater than his other costs. Thus another potential owner who could earn more (because she works harder or because she is more courteous and can earn bigger tips) will not be able to buy the medallion from an old owner, as she could if medallions were resalable. Since the people who would work hardest and provide the most service do not necessarily end up owning

3. Based on Blaine Hardin, "Tobacco Farmers and the 'Salvation' Law," *San Francisco Chronicle*, 13 May 1980.

medallions, the amount of taxi service that is provided, given any number of medallions, is smaller than it would be if medallions could be resold.

THE POLITICAL ECONOMY
OF MARKET CLOSURE

The examples of market closure which we have shown lead one to wonder why such programs are in existence. The *justifications* given for the programs vary widely (from the "protection from quacks" argument for physician licensing, to the argument that tobacco farmers would have to be on welfare if they were not protected). But regardless of whether one accepts those justifications, the *ability* of groups to obtain legal restrictions on entry comes from the fact that the beneficiaries are a relatively small group who stand to gain a great deal from the restriction, whereas individuals in the general public stand to lose relatively little *per person* (but a great deal in total) from the entry restrictions. Thus, the beneficiaries find it worth their while to engage in lobbying and other political activities to obtain the restrictions, whereas the diffuse public victims find that it is not worth their while individually to lobby or otherwise work to prevent the restrictions. As a result, legislation providing such benefits at the expense of consumers is often passed.

PROFESSIONAL
LICENSING AND
CONSUMER BEHAVIOR

We have argued that licensing results in a reduced supply (shift to the left in the supply curve) of the product or service produced by the licensees. Using standard supply and demand analysis, we can see that this results in a higher price and a smaller quantity. (Draw the diagram and see that this is true.) As part of this adjustment, consumers move up their demand curves in response to the higher price. This movement may reflect a reduction in the consumption of the good or service, or it may mean that the consumers are resorting to other sources of supply. For example, if we are discussing electrical work, the licensing of electricians could be expected to shift the supply of their services to the left and raise its price. One way consumers adjust to the higher price is by engaging in more do-it-yourself electrical work. One unfortunate consequence of this response is that accidental electrocutions increase. In fact, the stricter the licensing requirements for electricians, the higher the death rate from electrical accidents.[4]

4. This finding was made by R. J. Gaston and S. L. Carroll, and was reported in "How Licensing Hurts Consumers," *Business Week*, 28 November 1977.

CONCENTRATION AND COLLUSION

We noted previously that voluntary collusion is likely to be more successful, the smaller the number of colluders. This is because, with small numbers, cheating on the agreement is likely to be more easily detected. Since this is so, a small number of colluders would be less likely to violate any agreement they might make. The higher the concentration ratio, the more likely it is that a small number of firms will control enough of the output to be able to collude successfully. (Recall that the four-firm concentration ratio for an industry is equal to the sum of the output produced by the four largest firms, divided by the total output of the industry.) Thus highly concentrated industries are generally more suspect in regard to collusion than are unconcentrated industries.

Building on this analysis, some observers have concluded that concentrated industries pose a collusion problem which can best be solved by reducing their concentration. For example, Senator Philip Hart of Michigan for many years introduced a bill which would have required the breakup of the largest firms in any industry in which the five largest firms accounted for more than 50 percent of the industry's sales any one year. As noted, stating that collusion is *more likely* with concentrated industries is not the same as saying that it will occur. Thus Senator Hart's bill would surely break up some industries in which no collusion was occurring and which were very competitive in the sense of active rivalry among firms. In addition, there is a good deal of evidence that the reason for the high concentration of some industries (the predominance of a few large firms) is that, in those industries, large firms are able to produce at lower cost per unit of output. Thus, whether collusion were occurring in concentrated industries or not, there probably would be an efficiency loss (due to higher cost of production) if the breakup policy were followed. Coming up with a policy prescription with regard to concentrated industries (beyond a ban on collusion) is not as easy as it may at first appear.

BRIBERY AND CORRUPTION

In recent years considerable attention has been paid to the fact that governmental officials are often bribed or paid off to act illegally. The cases involve everything from police scandals (as graphically reported in the movie *Serpico*) to alleged bribes to obtain bank charters, and alleged payoffs by defense contractors to foreign countries for favored treatment. All of the widely reported scandals had one thing in common—government power was involved. It is not accidental that this sort of scandal is not reported in dealings between private firms. The power of the government to seize property, prevent entry into a market, prevent exchanges, award contracts, and engage in arbitrary delays of due process are important reasons for the existence of corruption.

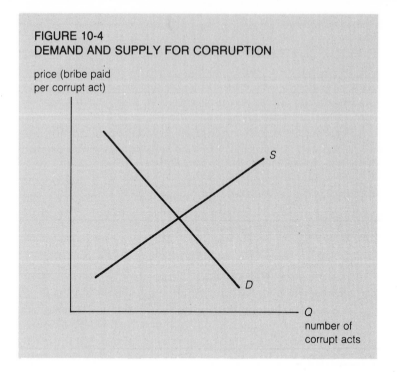

FIGURE 10-4
DEMAND AND SUPPLY FOR CORRUPTION

price (bribe paid
per corrupt act)

S

D

Q
number of
corrupt acts

It is often useful to cast problems into the framework of supply and demand analysis in order to get a clearer picture of the factors which affect the amount of an activity. In the case of corruption, we can think of business firms or private citizens as the demanders of corrupt acts and government officials as the suppliers. The price of obtaining the corrupt act is represented by the size of the bribe required. (This is illustrated in figure 10-4, which shows the hypothetical demand curve and supply curve for corrupt acts.) As indicated, the value to a private citizen of obtaining a corrupt act (the demand for corruption) depends on the government's power over economic affairs. Some examples follow.

If the government has the power (as in some Latin American countries) to expropriate a firm and nationalize it—in other words, acquire it for less than its market value—then the demand for corruption will be greater (farther to the right) than if the government has no such power. We should therefore expect corruption to be more prevalent in such countries, other things being equal.

If the government has the right to outlaw certain types of exchanges which the transactors find mutually beneficial (such as gambling, prostitution, and hard drugs), a demand for corruption is created. The exchange process creates gains for both the seller and buyer. If the exchange is outlawed, the transactors would be willing to pay up to the amount of those gains to obtain exemption from the law. The greater those gains from trade, the greater the demand for corruption and the more we would expect to see. The scale of corruption of police forces increases as the desire to engage in illegal activities increases.

If the government has the power to establish a price above (or below) the market price, a demand is created on the part of the potentially affected persons and firms to influence the price setting. The greater that power, the greater the demand for corruption and the more we would expect to see. If the government did not have the power to set the price of milk, there would have been no milk price scandal.

If the government has the power to restrict entry into a business or profession, the demand for corruption will be higher within that business or profession. The right to become a bank is restricted in most states. This sets up a situation similar to the taxicab and liquor licenses. But if the number of bank charters can be increased by government action, bribery of a government official is an alternative to buying out a bank that is already on the market. The greater the government's power in this regard, the greater the demand for corruption by potential bankers. (In 1976 Arch Moore, Governor of West Virginia, was accused of accepting a $25,000 bribe to facilitate the entry of a new bank in that state.)

When the government lets contracts to private firms to do jobs for the government, an avenue for corruption is opened up. To the extent that the officials making the choice have some leeway in deciding who gets the contract (for example, if they are not required to accept the lowest bid), this gives the officials power which creates a demand for corruption. The greater the leeway, the greater the demand for corruption, and the more we would expect to see. If government employees have the power to cause arbitrary delay in giving approval to ordinary business transactions (as, for example, when a customs official can delay the importation of a commodity through unnecessary red tape), this increases the demand for corruption. The greater the power to obstruct, the greater the demand for corruption.

The amount a person is willing to pay to corrupt an official also depends on the likelihood of being caught and the severity of punishment, as well as on the structure of business ethics. The stricter the enforcement and the higher the level of ethics, the lower the demand (as viewed by the potential recipients of bribes) for corruption and the less we would expect to see.

So far we have discussed only the demand and the factors expected to increase demand. (Recall from chapter 7 that an increase in demand results in both a larger quantity and a higher price. In this context it would be reflected in a larger number of corrupt acts by officials and a higher bribe per corrupt act.) What are the factors which would affect the location of the *supply* of corrupt acts? One factor is the general moral climate. If there is general moral approval of lying and cheating, the supply would be greater (the supply curve would be farther to the right), and the amount of corruption would be greater, with a lower bribe per occurrence. Similarly, the more lax the enforcement of the laws and the more costly it is for outsiders (such as newspapermen and reform politicians) to get the information about the corruption, the greater the supply.

This section illustrates that the fundamental economic concepts of demand and supply can be of use in increasing our understanding (in the spirit of *positive analysis*) of the phenomenon of corruption. To the extent that we think corruption and bribery are bad, we are better served by understanding those factors which increase or decrease the amount of corruption.

LABOR UNIONS

As voluntary organizations, unions could provide many useful services to their members, from group insurance policies to information about the job market. But it is not through these activities (which any club could perform) that unions have attained their current importance in the economy.

Two Principles of Modern Unionism in the United States

Under the 1935 Wagner Act (which, as amended subsequently, is now known as the National Labor Relations Act), unions may become *exclusive bargaining agents* and they also may negotiate *union security* agreements with employers. Because of these two features of modern unionism, many people claim that labor unions cannot be regarded as voluntary associations of workers. Let's examine exclusive representation and union security in turn.

Exclusive Representation. Section 9(a) of the National Labor Relations Act specifies that if a majority of workers in a particular firm vote, in a representation election, to be represented by union A, then union A gets the privilege of representing *all* the workers in that firm. Workers who prefer to be presented by some other union, as well as workers who prefer to be represented by no union, *must* accept the representation services of union A.

The principle of exclusive representation is often justified by an analogy with congressional representation elections. The winning candidate for Congress in a congressional district represents all the voters in the district, whether they voted for the winning candidate or not. Therefore, the argument goes, the same should be the case in union representation elections. This argument is based on the idea that there are no significant differences between the nature of a union representation election and the nature of a congressional representation election. Are unions governments?

Union Security. The National Labor Relations Act specifies that (except where state law forbids it) a union which is the exclusive bargaining agent of the employees in a firm may negotiate with the management of the firm for either a *union shop* or an *agency shop*. A union shop is an agreement between the exclusive bargaining agent and management that all workers in the firm must, after an initial probationary period, join the union as a condition for continued employment. An agency shop is an agreement between the exclusive bargaining agent and management that all workers, whether union members or not, must pay fees to the union, which is the exclusive bargaining agent as a condition for continued employment.

These union security arrangements protect the exclusive bargaining agent against workers, whom the union *must* represent under the principle of exclusive representation, who may try to receive the benefits of union representation without paying for them. If workers were not compelled to contribute to the support of the exclusive bargaining agent, some workers might become *free riders*—that is, they get the benefits of union representation for free. Of course, in the absence of the exclusive representation privilege, there could be no free riders. If unions represented only workers who voluntarily became union members, nonmembers could not receive any benefits for free.

Methods Used by Unions to Raise Wages

There are three main methods of action utilized by unions to increase the wages paid to workers they represent: restriction on entry, increased demand, and direct action.

Restriction of Entry. This is a very popular method used by such professions as physicians, attorneys, plumbers, and CPAs, to name a few. When most effective, the restriction is a matter of law, with a state-granted license being required. The licensing method usually exempts all those practicing in the field at the time the licensing law was passed, then imposes stricter standards on all future entrants. The restrictions have the effect of raising the cost of entering. The First Law of Demand says that, with a higher cost of getting into the profession, fewer will choose to enter. Less delicate unions use extralegal means to force employers to use only union members, then directly restrict entrance into the union.

Increased Demand. An alternative, related tactic is to *increase demand*. A union can raise the wages of its members by simply advertising that union-made goods are superior, or by arguing that it is more patriotic to buy American-made goods. Another way to increase demand for union labor is to lobby for laws which make substitutes more expensive to use. Recall from chapter 4 that an increase in the price of good A increases the demand for substitutes of A. This principle helps explain the efforts of northern textile workers' unions to get minimum wage laws passed in the South. Many textile workers in the South were earning much less than their northern counterparts, and thereby providing competition for northern goods. Requiring southern mills to pay higher wages made southern labor relatively less desirable and increased the demand for northern workers.

The same principle can operate when there is prejudice. Suppose employers are prejudiced against women workers (justly or unjustly). Then it may be in the interest of men to have an equal pay for equal work law. Why? Because men and women are substitutes for the same jobs. Managers would overcome their prejudice against women workers and hire them, if they could be hired for a wage sufficiently lower than the wage for men, but if there is an equal pay for equal work clause, this pay differential would be illegal. Thus employers would choose men rather than women. The higher wage for women increases the demand for men.

Direct Action. The third and least delicate strategy is *direct action.* By this we refer to the *strike.* Most strikes do not involve the mere withholding of services by the strikers but also restrictions on the employer's right to hire replacements (*scabs*), and on the right to work of those who do not wish to strike. Without the right to strike as we know it, unions would still be an important, and useful, institution in our economy. But they would not be nearly as powerful as they now are.

There are similarities between a union and a cartel. Without the right to strike, the union is more akin to a trade association, which may involve the pooling of market-relevant information and perhaps the cajoling of members to agree on a selling price. But the problems of a voluntary collusive agreement would also beset a voluntary union. There would be the problem of breaking the agreed-on asking wage. Suppose a union is able to obtain a wage agreement (by merely withholding services voluntarily) above the one characterizing the intersection of demand and supply curves. The First Law of Demand says that there will be fewer labor-hours demanded at the higher wage. Suppose this means each worker reduces his labor by a few hours or that some workers are let go. In either case some workers will see that they can gain by slight undercutting of the agreed-on wage, gaining extra income by increased employment. This feature would make the agreement somewhat fragile. Perhaps more important is the fact the higher wage would attract newcomers to the profession. Here is where restrictions on entry come in: they can keep this from causing the breakdown of the wage agreement.

Unions and Employment Patterns

The advent of an effective union can change the character of the labor force in an occupation. Before unionization, grocery stores hired large numbers of teenagers and retired persons as part-time help. They had the option of paying wages that were high enough to attract a more productive work force, but apparently they didn't feel the extra productivity was worth the expense. With union-won wage levels now high enough to attract head-of-household workers, the character of the labor force has changed. Naturally the teenagers and retired persons would be happy to work at the higher wages, but since other, more desirable workers also present themselves, employers have gradually shifted toward a young adult, full-time work force. Formerly, many jobs at the grocery paid so little that few employees considered them as prospects for their life's work. With wages at current levels, more do.

McDonald's hamburger chain is an example of a firm which specializes in hiring low-wage teenagers (in large numbers) to serve its customers. It is a nonunion establishment. If McDonald's were forced to unionize, we would expect three major results: (1) McDonald's would decline relative to other fast food outlets; (2) within a McDonald's, there would be fewer employees; (3) those employees would be older.

McDonald's would decline relative to other fast food outlets because with higher marginal costs, their best price would be higher. But if McDonald's price went up relative to other fast food, customers would buy somewhat less McDonald's food and more food from other firms.

There would be fewer employees at McDonald's both because of the decline in total sales and because McDonald's would adjust to the higher relative price of labor by using more machinery and less labor, and by allowing the waiting time of customers to be somewhat longer.

The employees would be older because a head-of-household type of employee would generally be more productive and/or reliable than a teenager. With McDonald's required to pay the higher wages mandated by the union contract, the more productive workers would be relatively more attractive than they were when teenagers could be hired for lower wages.

Summarizing, if McDonald's were unionized and wages rose substantially, teenage employment at McDonald's would fall substantially. More adults would be employed there than formerly, but the total employment in McDonald's would fall, both because of decline in McDonald's share of the market and because machinery and waiting customers would be substituted for labor.

SUMMARY

This chapter has discussed several types of restrictions on markets. A result which often (always?) follows from such restrictions is a decrease in the efficiency of operation of the economy. It is easy for economists to take the next logical step and condemn the restrictions, because one of the economists' value judgments is that efficiency is good. However, you should realize that this step involves a switch from positive to normative economics. If you do not agree with the value judgment, or hold that some other value outweighs it, then you need not agree with that assessment of these practices. Indeed, one could even argue (and some have) that when viewed in a more complete framework, the restrictions are not inefficient at all, but rather promote efficiency. This chapter was not meant to be the last word on the subject but rather to give it an economist's perspective.

LOOKING AHEAD

The next chapter focuses on two related issues of current interest—consumerism (and attempts by government to legislate changes which benefit the consumer) and advertising. We shall try to understand some of the economic issues involved and to discover what the effects of various governmental actions might be.

POINTS TO REMEMBER

1. Firms which compete against each other can gain by agreeing to restrict the ways in which they compete.

2. If all firms agree to cut back their output below the equilibrium level which results from independent action, the price will rise and profits will go up, up to a point.

3. Cartels are unstable because it is in the interest of every member to secretly break the agreement. This problem calls for a method of enforcing the cartel agreement.

4. Even if enforcement is effective, the cartel's profits will tend to be dissipated in the long run by the entry of new firms attracted by the profits.

5. Restrictions on entry are important because they make it easier for a cartel to work.

6. Restrictions on entry (such as taxi medallions and liquor licenses) often result in artificially high prices for goods and services (even in the absence of collusion), and in positive prices being generated for the right to be a firm in the industry.

7. Highly concentrated industries are more likely to be collusive than unconcentrated industries, but not all highly concentrated industries engage in collusion; and breaking up the largest firms in an industry would probably result in efficiency losses (due to higher costs), even if they were colluding before the breakup.

8. Bribery and corruption of government officials is more likely, the more power the government has to expropriate property, to outlaw exchanges, to fix prices, to restrict entry into a profession or business, the more leeway government officials have to obstruct business transactions through import controls, and so on. The more permissive the moral climate and the more lax the enforcement of laws, the greater the supply of corruption.

9. Unions obtain their results by (1) restricting entry, (2) increasing demand for unionmade goods, and (3) strikes.

10. There are similarities between unions and cartels.

KEY TERMS

Agency shop: A union security arrangement whereby all the workers on a particular job, if they choose not to join the union that is the exclusive bargaining agent, must nevertheless pay fees to the union as a condition of maintaining employment.

Cartel: A group of colluding firms. A voluntary combination of independent private enterprises that agree to limit their competitive activities in various ways.

Collusion: Agreement by transactors concerning the quality or terms of trade at which they will sell or buy goods.

Exclusive representation: The arrangement whereby a union that gets a majority vote in a representation election among workers on a particular job gets the privilege of representing all the workers on the job, including those who want to be represented by another union and those who want to represent themselves. A union with this privilege is called the *exclusive bargaining agent*.

Nonprice competition: Competition by means of quality or service improvements rather than by lowering prices.

Union shop: A union security arrangement whereby all the workers on a particular job must join the union that is the exclusive bargaining agent as a condition of maintaining employment.

REVIEW QUESTIONS

1. When OPEC considers raising the official price for crude oil, why can't it simply set the higher price and let every country sell as much as it did at the lower price (or wants to sell at the higher price)?

2. (a) Referring to figure 10-1, when the individual firm reduces its output from ten to seven, how much cost does it save? Can you show how big the saving is, utilizing only the *MC* curve? (b) How much revenue does the firm lose due to not selling the three units of output? (Show in figure 10-1.) How much more does the firm lose in revenue on those three units than it saves in cost? (Call this area A.) To what area in figure 10-1 does this magnitude correspond? (c) If all other firms agree to reduce their output as well, how much more revenue does the firm get on the seven units it sells. (Call this area B.) What is the interpretation of (B − A)? Explain.

3. (a) At the equilibrium output and price of a price-taker industry, what is the relationship between the price that each firm receives and the marginal cost that it incurs in producing the last unit of output? Explain briefly. (b) For the industry as a whole, what is the relationship between the price that prevails in the price-taker equilibrium and the marginal revenue that the *industry* receives from increasing industry output? Explain. (c) Therefore, what is the relationshop between the marginal cost that any firm is incurring and the marginal revenue to the industry at the price-taker equilibrium point? (d) Given that relationship, what would happen to industry profits if the industry output were reduced below the price-taker equilibrium level?

4. How big a profit could the firm in figure 10-1 get if it produced an output of twelve, while all other firms produced seven? Show graphically, using the method described in figure 10-1 and using the method described in question 2.

5. A reduction in airline service when carried out by cnly one airline would cost it a lot of customers (say 20 percent) and would be unprofitable. But the same reduction in quality, if carried out by all, might reduce sales by only 3 percent. Why? Is it possible that it would be unprofitable to cut back individually, but profitable to do it as a group? Explain the relevance of this notion to the discussion of figure 10-1.

6. Do you think the Three Mile Island accident had any effect on OPEC's profit-maximizing price for oil? Explain.

7. What do you think would be the effect on the current OPEC price if a breakthrough were found which would permit, in ten years, low cost *in situ* (underground) development of the vast oil shale deposits in Colorado? Explain.

8. We argued that the prohibition on the sale of taxi medallions in San Francisco will tend to reduce the amount of taxi service supplied given any number of medallions outstanding. Do you think that will have any effect on the degree of resistance to future increases in taxi fares? Explain.

9. If you were a taxi medallion owner in San Francisco and wanted to retire, how could you do so without letting your medallion go to waste?

10. The number of tourists visiting San Francisco increased rapidly during the 1970s. Do you think there is any connection between this fact and the rapid rise in the price of taxi medallions in San Francisco?

11. A particular farmer in North Carolina reportedly makes $60,000 per year farming eighty-seven acres of tobacco. Suppose the tobacco allotment is worth $5000 per acre, and the farmer could get a 12 percent return in his best alternative investment. How much could this farmer make per year if he simply sold the allotment and invested the proceeds? Is he making an above-normal return by farming the tobacco land?

12. What does it mean to say that some farm land has a comparative advantage in growing a certain crop (such as tobacco) relative to other crops and relative to other land? If tobacco allotments are resalable (or leasable), is there a tendency for land with a comparative advantage in tobacco growing to be used for that? Explain.

13. Young farmers in North Carolina are reportedly upset because they must pay high lease prices to owners of tobacco allotments for the use of their allotments so they can grow tobacco. They are upset because the owners make a living by doing nothing more than leasing out their government-bestowed right to grow tobacco. Would all young farmers fare better if there were a free market in tobacco? What if they simply eliminated the allotment but kept the price supports?

14. If you were a banker in North Carolina, would you favor ending the tobacco allotment program? How might you lose if it were abolished? (Hint: Do you think any loans were made to North Carolina farmers using tobacco-growing land or other tobacco-related assets as collateral? What would happen to the market value of those assets if the tobacco allotment program were eliminated?)

15. Under federal milk price support laws, milk which is to be sold fresh to the consumer is sold for a substantially higher price to processors than is milk which is to be used for such things as cheese, ice cream, and dry milk. What is the reason for the price difference?

16. Many states have laws regulating liquor prices. Liquor stores are not permitted to charge prices *below* those specified by the state and the manufacturer. (These laws are in addition to those which restrict the number of licenses to sell liquor.) Would elimination of price floors be expected to reduce the premiums paid for liquor licenses? Would the premiums disappear altogether?

17. In the early 1970s the state of Indiana created a new category of barber's license—men's hair stylist. Specific standards were set up for obtaining the license. These standards apply to all applicants after a certain date. Up to that time any licensed barber who wanted a hair stylist license could obtain one by merely filling out a form and paying a nominal fee. Why did the state not apply the same standards to all those who wanted a hair stylist license?

18. When sports events (such as the Olympics, baseball, basketball, and football games) are telecast, the league, teams, or promoters involved invariably negotiate an exclusive contract with one station or network to telecast the event. Why? Is this any different from the way cars, tires, or Kentucky Fried Chicken are sold?

19. The California Egg Program, administered by the state, provides that after a vote by the egg producers, a certain percentage of the state's egg output may be diverted to uses other than fresh egg sales in California. (For example, they may be sold to food processors or out of the state.) Who do you suspect lobbied for the bill establishing the program? Why is there not a California Concrete Program?

20. Comment on the following: "There is no right way to handle licensing of the right to produce or sell a good. If the license is resalable, only the original holder of the license makes any profit from the scheme. But if the licenses are not resalable, then the businesses tend to be operated inefficiently."

21. The market for a certain product is competitive, that is, the firms act as price-takers. There are a thousand identical firms in the industry. Currently the industry is in long-run competitive equilibrium. This means that each firm is producing where price equals marginal cost, but all the firms are just breaking even. There is no incentive to enter or leave the industry.

The following two lists give the demand curve (and marginal revenue) for the *industry as a whole* and the cost for the individual firm.

Industry Demand				Firm's Cost	
Q	P	MR	q	ATC	MC
5000	7.50	5.00	1	25.25	.50
5500	7.25	4.50	2	13.00	1.00
6000	7.00	4.00	3	9.08	1.50
6500	6.75	3.50	4	7.25	2.00
7000	6.50	3.00	5	6.25	2.50
7500	6.25	2.50	6	5.67	3.00
8000	6.00	2.00	7	5.30	3.50
8500	5.75	1.50	8	5.13	4.00
9000	5.50	1.00	9	5.03	4.50
9500	5.25	0.50	10	5.00	5.00
10000	5.00	0.00	11	5.02	5.50
10500	4.75	−.50	12	5.08	6.00
11000	4.50	−1.00			

(a) Using these two tables, find the price that is being charged in the initial situation and the quantity produced by each firm. Now suppose the firms get together and form a cartel. The cartel has the power to enforce compliance to whatever agreement on production is reached by the firms. (b) If all firms must produce the same quantity of output, what output would be voted for by the firms? (c) If all the firms produced this amount, what would the price be? At the new lower output and higher price, economic profits would be earned. This gives a signal to new firms to enter the business. Suppose that in the first year, 200 additional firms (for a total of 1200) enter the industry. (d) With 1200 firms in the industry, what would be the best price and quantity? Since there are still economic profits being earned at this point, still more firms would want to enter. Suppose 300 more enter, giving a total of 1500 firms. (e) What are the best price and quantity under this circumstance? (f) At this equilibrium, what profits are being earned by the firms?

22. In the discussion of CAB regulation, we argued that the high prices which the CAB promoted were inefficient because they forced many consumers to consume a higher quality product than they wanted. Could the same argument be made about licensing of physicians? Explain.

23. Why do you think it is the case that government contracts are almost always decided by sealed bids, whereas private contracts hardly ever (never?) are?

chapter 11

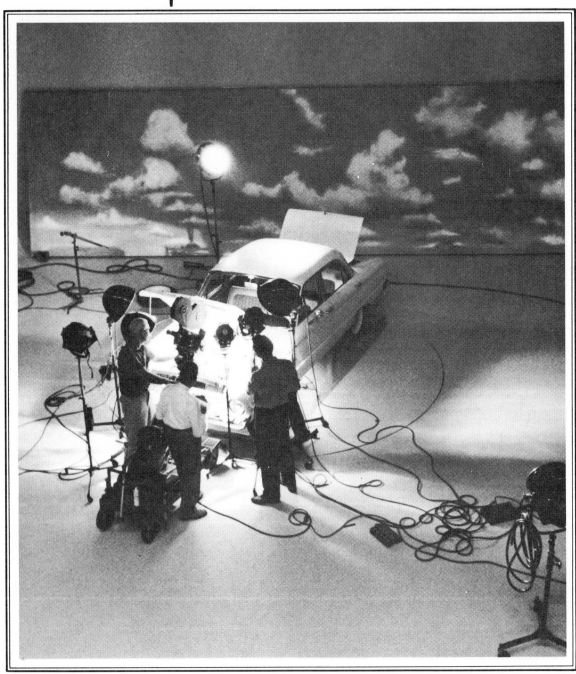

Consumerism and Advertising

The late 1960s and early 1970s saw the rise of what can loosely be called the *consumer movement*. It arose out of a conviction by some that, unless restrained, business tends to take advantage of consumers. The movement has not focused primarily on such anticonsumer phenomena as cartels and other collusive agreements (although in recent years there has been *some* attention paid to this aspect of the problem). Rather the contention has been that business firms have some *inherent advantage* over consumers (which will not be redressed by competition from other sellers) and that this advantage permits them to sell shoddier goods or charge higher prices than they should.

This chapter addresses some of these issues by discussing several problems and phenomena which arise because information about products is costly for consumers to obtain. Without such costs, there would be no consumer movement, no brand names, and no advertising. What we want to see in each case is how the costs of acquiring information change the way firms and consumers behave and lead to the institutions we observe. The chapter also attempts to use economic analysis to illuminate some of the policy questions which surround the issues of quality assurance and advertising.

292   BRAND NAMES

The first institution we shall discuss is that of brand names. When we use the term *brand name* we can have either of two notions in mind. First, brand name may refer to the *trade name* stamped on the product in question. This name identifies the manufacturer (or seller) of the product. The term *brand name* may also refer to the *reputation* which the trade name has. By this we mean that having the trade name on the product gives the potential buyer a clearer idea of the quality of the product than if the trade name were not present.

Several questions arise in regard to trade names and their reputations: Why are trade names used on some commodities and not on others? Why does a trade name sometimes develop a valuable reputation? What is the source of the valuable reputation?

Brand names emerge when information is costly. They are the market's response to the quality assurance problems which arise when information is costly. They will be observed more frequently and be more important to firms when products are complicated and designed for long life than when they are simple and short-lived. Complicated and long-lived goods reveal their characteristics only over time. Because of this, consumers are willing to pay to acquire more knowledge about just what characteristics a product will have. What would happen if producers of complicated, long-lived products (such as cars) were *prohibited* from identifying in any way who the producer was? Firms would be only weakly rewarded for producing high quality cars and weakly punished for producing low quality cars. If any firm lowered the quality of its cars, buyers would have no way to blame it. The existence of poor cars would cause buyers to distrust all cars, and so the total demand for cars would decline somewhat. But the decline in demand would not be focused on the culprit. Since firms would bear only part of the cost of depreciating the quality of their product (and, by a similar argument, reap only part of the gain from improving the quality), they would tend to produce a lower quality product than consumers want and are willing to pay for.

If instead we allow firms to identify (with exclusive trademarks) who the producer of a given product is, then brand names will develop.

In the presence of high information costs about the qualities of products, a firm which establishes a reputation for producing a product of a certain *uniform* (not necessarily the highest) quality enables customers to save some costs of search and investigation into the quality of the product. Whatever the quality of the product is, the fact that consumers can rely on it means that they will be willing to pay more for it because buying it saves search costs. The benefits of establishing a definite uniform quality are focused on the firm by the use of the exclusive trademark. The extra value which consumers place on knowing the quality of the product with greater accuracy depends on the costs to consumers of getting a quality of product which they do not want. When these costs are high, then consumers will value quality assurance more highly.

To make money from this demand for quality assurance, the producer sets a standard of quality and lives up to it over time. Then the reports of satisfied customers enable him to charge a higher price than his competitors as well as a higher price than his cost. This return is his reward for abstaining from adulteration. Consumers will pay a premium for the brand's assurance of continued superior quality. Another firm, whose product has *on the average* the same quality as our firm, but sometimes higher and sometimes lower, will not be able to charge as much for its product because of the lack of assurance of quality.

Trade name reputations are costly to develop. The firm has to incur costs to ensure that the quality level which it seeks to produce is maintained and to bring the existence of this uniform quality level to the attention of consumers. Given the value that consumers place on the greater accuracy of knowledge, the higher the cost of developing the brand name, the less likely it is to be developed. There are, in a sense, a supply and demand for brand names. We put all the things which determine the value consumers place on quality assurance (such as benefits from avoiding injury due to a poor product or a closer fit with one's preferences) in the category of demand. Those factors which influence the cost of providing quality assurance (such as quality control costs and costs of disseminating the information about the characteristics of the product and getting people to believe it) go in the category of supply. If there were an increase in the demand for quality assurance (because consumers perceived a greater potential cost from using an inadequate product) with no change in the supply of quality assurance, the result would be more use of brand names and a higher premium in price for those whose brand names were well developed.

There is some inertia in consumer behavior. Once a firm has established a valuable trade name reputation it could, for a time, decrease the quality (or increase the variation in quality) of its product and not lose sales. This is because once the reputation is established, consumers use the trade name as a substitute for search and thorough prepurchase investigation of the product. Only after the disappointment of lower-than-expected quality will consumers foresake the product. This may take a long time in the case of some long-lived products. But once the reputation of the trade name has been damaged, it will take a long time for the firm to build it back up again because those same consumers will now be reluctant, without further investigation (or a price discount) to purchase commodities with the damaged name.

These same considerations suggest that it will sometimes be hard for new products of unknown firms to break into a market. Until they have established a track record and a trade name reputation, they will sell at a discount relative to other products with established reputations, even though their quality might be just as high and just as uniform as those of the established products. This is a *cost* of entry, just as buying a machine is. The firm must invest in its brand name by incurring the costs of quality assurance without getting any immediate benefit.

There are various ways of getting around the *time* problem in developing a track record (that is, the problem that, with long-lived goods, some experience with the products over their whole lifetime is required to establish a reputation). One way is through linking. In this procedure, the new product is linked to other products which have a good reputation by using the established product's trade name. For example, suppose a firm is producing a new household appliance. If it already has a good brand name in similar products, it can reduce consumer skepticism and shorten the time required to attain consumer acceptance by using the old established product's name on the new one. The reason this works is that, by linking the new product to the other well-established ones, the firm is putting the reputation which it has developed via the other products in jeopardy. If the new product is not as good as the older ones, the names of *all* the products carrying that trade name will be tarnished. This would be a big penalty for the firm to pay, so consumers can be fairly sure that a firm with well-established brand names in other products will try to maintain the same quality standards in the new product which shares the name. Thus linking may be expected to be observed when the ordinary gestation period for trade name reputations is long.

This line of reasoning suggests that the economics of information and trade name reputations provides a basis for economies of large firm size— large in the sense of many products. Because of the linking phenomenon, a single firm producing many products may have lower costs than if all those products were produced by separate firms.

CAVEAT EMPTOR

The process of brand name development we have been describing will be observed in a regime of <u>caveat emptor</u>, which is a Latin expression for "<u>let the buyer beware</u>." The notion is that the buyer of the product is responsible for seeing to it that she gets the kind of merchandise she wants. If the consumer has no recourse in the event she buys faulty merchandise, then she will be more likely to place a high value on a well-established brand name product. She will tend to rely heavily on the reputations which firms have developed for their products over time. Thus those products which have a good reputation will sell at a substantial premium over other products which, either because they are new or because they have not been reliable in the past, do not have as good a reputation.

Another institution which would be expected to emerge in a *caveat emptor* environment is the private consumer research organization, such as Consumer's Union (publishers of *Consumer Reports*). Organizations such as this can take advantage of the economies of centralized information collection. Thus consumers can purchase at a low price information which can help them decide when it is a good bet to buy a cheaper product rather than pay the premium price for the product with the well-established brand name.

If there are no restrictions on what consumers and firms can do, there will be those who do not want to pay for the information from consumer research organizations. Some will pay the premium which a good with a well-developed brand name develops. Others will take their chances and buy the cheaper products without seeking advice on which ones are worth buying. Some of that latter group will be right—they will get a good buy, because the cheaper product will be better relative to the brand name product than the price differential suggests. Others will be wrong—they will get products which are so much inferior to the brand name items that the price discount does not compensate them for the low quality.

Furthermore, there will sometimes be deliberate deception. Because it is costly for consumers to obtain information, it will sometimes pay firms to pretend that their product is something it isn't. Our theory says that when consumers know this kind of activity is occurring, brand name items will carry an even bigger premium, and this tends to make production of shoddy goods less profitable, relative to producing good ones. But not all consumers will make the right choice, and firms will occasionally be able to make money through deception. If the deception involves a substantial amount of money, it may pay consumers to seek redress through the courts under the civil laws which prohibit fraud. But in the case of more modest deceptions, the only remedies under *caveat emptor* are reliance on brand names and use of consumer research organizations.

THE CONSUMER MOVEMENT AND GOVERNMENT REGULATION

It is often argued that the institutions which evolve under the rule of *caveat emptor* are insufficient to handle the problems of quality assurance. The consumer movement is based on this premise. The argument is that the mechanism described under *caveat emptor* produces too many defective, low quality, or unsafe products. A related assertion is that the low quality products are being sold at much higher prices than they should be.

The remedy usually sought by those in the consumer movement has been regulation. The regulations are generally of two types. The first is laws which require provision of certain types of information. Truth-in-lending and truth-in-labelling laws fall into this category. The second is laws which regulate the types of products which can be marketed. This is typified by the Food and Drug Administration (FDA), the Consumer Product Safety Commission (CPSC), the National Transportation Safety Administration (NTSA), and the Occupational Safety and Health Administration (OSHA).

The informative and restrictive types of regulation seem to be based on different theories of regulation. The information-providing type is based on the idea that, for some reason, the market provides too little information to enable the consumer to make an intelligent choice. A government requirement that certain information be provided then permits the consumer to make a more intelligent choice with a smaller expenditure of resources in acquiring information. In the case of a product which is suspected of being dangerous (for example, a carcinogen), this approach would require the manufacturer to state evidence. Then the consumer would be allowed to choose for herself whether to buy the product.

The restrictive approach would set standards as to what sorts of products could be sold. The argument for this could be either that the consumer would arrive at the same standards if she had all the information the government agency does, or that the consumer does not know what is good for her. The latter rationale, if it is used, is clearly paternalistic, whereas the former is really an extension of the informative approach. (The regulator can save even more information costs by going ahead and selecting the appropriate product. If that is the product the consumer would have chosen anyway, she can be saved all those information and decision costs by having the decision made for her.)[1]

BENEFITS AND COSTS
OF REGULATION

What are the benefits of regulation? First let us look at purely informational regulation. The government's requirement that firms provide information affects the way consumers make choices about which goods to purchase. It makes it relatively cheaper for a consumer to look directly at the characteristics of products rather than rely on the brand name process we described earlier. It may as a result make the process of brand name development (the culling of successful from unsuccessful products) work itself through more quickly than it otherwise would because consumers would be able to recognize more cheaply the products that fit their preferences.

The form of regulation that restricts the kinds of products that can be sold tends to supplant the whole process of brand name development. For that process is substituted a procedure whereby taxpayers incur the costs of having government employees discover the characteristics of products and decide the value to be placed on various characteristics of products. Then the sorts of products that are perceived by the government employees to provide benefits that are greater than the costs are allowed to be sold. The benefits take the form that the information gathering and decision-making costs are incurred only once (by the taxpayers through the government agency) instead of millions of times by consumers. The more similar the preferences of consumers are to each other and to those of government employees, the more likely this procedure is to be an acceptable one. In

---

1. There is one type of situation in which provision of information is not enough even for those who are generally willing to allow consumers to choose for themselves. That is the situation in which the use of the good by one person causes harm to another. Many regulations are designed to address this problem. It is discussed in more detail in chapter 12.

a very homogeneous society in terms of income and cultural background, it is likely that the public would acquiesce to more government regulation than in a heterogeneous one.

Clearly, one consideration in evaluating both types of regulation is the taste the public has for being coerced. There may be some individuals who are made much worse off simply by the knowledge that they were prevented from making their own choice, even though they would have chosen the same goods that the government did. Others, of course, may not be concerned about having someone else make the decision for them. But if it is a government decision, people do not get to choose individually whether the government will make it for them or not. All must live with the same outcome.

What are the costs of government regulation? The costs fall into two basic categories. First there are the observable uses of resources in the regulatory process. Those resources have prices that represent their value in alternative uses, and we can add these up to obtain a portion of the costs of regulation. The other category of costs of regulation includes a series of distortions in the way markets operate. These too represent foregone benefits, but they are harder to measure.

In the area of resource costs we have agency budgets and compliance costs. The regulatory agencies (such as the Department of Energy (DOE), the Environmental Protection Agency (EPA), FDA, CPSC, NTSA, and OSHA) have many employees and use numerous other resources. These costs are reported annually in the budgetary statistics of government. For the year 1977 budgetary costs of regulation at all levels of government was estimated to be $5.1 billion.[2] (This would be much bigger today because the budget of the DOE alone was over $10 billion in 1980.) This figure is dwarfed, however, by the costs firms incur in complying with the regulation. In 1977 these were estimated to be $84.8 billion. These compliance costs can in turn be broken down into paperwork costs ($25 billion) and the costs of the extra resources firms require to carry out their business in accordance with the regulations ($59.8 billion).

All of the costs we have mentioned so far are relatively easy to measure. The remaining costs are much more difficult to measure, although we think they exist. First, one difficulty (which may lead, at least temporarily, to inappropriate consumer choices) is that it is impossible for the government to require manufacturers to provide all the information which might be relevant to an informed choice. Consumers may be led to put undue weight on the information that is provided while neglecting other relevant information which is not provided. For example, if appliance manufacturers are required to put estimates of annual energy consumption on their products, this may cause consumers to shop by comparing energy consumption, while neglecting the fact that designing appliances for reduced energy consumption can shorten their useful lives. If consumers would really rather use more energy and get a longer-lived appliance, this will

2. Source for all the estimates in this section: Chase Manhattan Bank Economics Group.

eventually happen, but only gradually as people learn to ignore the energy use numbers. When this problem occurs, the long-run effect is that people ignore the information which is provided and rely again on the evolution of brand names. But then the provision of the (misleading) information is worse than useless.

Another difficulty with regulation, which limits the available product assortment, is that regulators cannot represent all consumers. We mentioned earlier that this type of regulation is most likely to be acceptable if consumers are homogeneous in their preferences and if there is little inequality of income. If these conditions are not met, then the standards which are set are likely not to conform to the choices that at least some consumers would have made. For example, in the safety area non-flammability standards for mattresses make them more expensive to produce and result in higher prices. Smokers (especially those who smoke in bed) may very well find that the reduced risk of fire from a smoldering cigarette is worth the extra cost, but it is likely that many nonsmokers would place no value on this feature. Similarly, lawnmower safety standards make lawnmowers more expensive while reducing the chance that a careless user will harm himself. Careless users may find this tradeoff to be worthwhile, but some careful users will not. This line of reasoning suggests that an important feature of this type of regulation is that it causes redistributions of net well-being among consumers.

A well-documented negative aspect of restrictive regulation is that it reduces the amount of innovation. This type of regulation inevitably increases the cost of marketing a product with new characteristics or design. Such changes make life difficult for regulators and they will tend to impose the costs of discovering whether the new product is consistent with the standards on the manufacturers. A dramatic example of this phenomenon is found in the case of pharmaceuticals. The 1962 amendments to the Food, Drug, and Cosmetic Act made two important changes in the law. The first was that it required the maker of a new drug to prove its efficacy. (Proof of safety was already required in the earlier version of the law.) The second change was that it eliminated the requirement that the FDA had to either approve or disapprove of the new drug within 180 days of its submission for consideration. Under the new law, the FDA could take as long as it wished to decide whether a new drug should be put on the market. These two changes in the law seem reasonable enough. But their effect was to increase greatly the cost and time involved in marketing a new drug. In the late 1950s and early 1960s, it cost about one half million dollars and took about twenty-five months to develop and market a new drug. By 1978 the typical cost had risen to $54 million and the time necessary to market a new drug had stretched to eight years.[3] Since the general price level doubled over that period, the cost of drug development

3. W. M. Wardell & L. Lasagna, *Regulation and Drug Development (Washington, D.C.: American Enterprise Institute, 1975)*, p. 46; and L. Lasagna, "The Uncertain Future of Drug Development," *Drug Intelligence and Clinical Pharmacy* 13 (April 1979): 193. Cited in M. Friedman and R. Friedman, *Free to Choose* (New York: Harcourt Brace Jovanovich, 1980).

was "only" fifty times as high as before, while taking four times as long. One would expect this to slow significantly the flow of new drugs onto the market, and this has been confirmed by numerous studies.[4]

A related problem caused by standard-setting regulation is that it tends to increase the optimal size of firms. This happens because in some cases the product development and other compliance costs tend to be about the same magnitude for all firms. If that is true, then the regulatory cost acts like a fixed cost—one that does not increase as the amount of output produced increases. We can see the effect this has by examining figure 11-1. In the absence of regulation, the cost per unit of output is $20 when output is 100 and again when output is 200. The output at which average total cost is lowest is 150 in this example. If we now impose a cost of compliance of $1000 on any firm wanting to produce this good, then the regulatory cost per unit of output is $10 per unit when output is 100, making the average total cost including regulatory cost $30 put unit. But when output is 200 units, the regulatory cost per unit of output is only $5 for a new average total cost of $25.

Suppose firm A was originally producing 100 units, while firm B was producing 200. Then they would have the same cost per unit of output, in the absence of regulation. But with the regulatory compliance cost of $1000, firm B now has a lower cost per unit than A ($25 versus $30). The effects of this are that large firms will fare better than small firms; small firms will be more likely to lose money than large firms, and they will tend either to grow larger or get out of the business. But if the market for the product has not increased, the only way we can have a larger average size of firm is to have *fewer* firms. Thus, one effect we can predict is that the industry's concentration ratio (see chapter 6) will increase, and either firms will drop out or entry will be retarded.

This phenomenon appears to be part of what has happened in the automobile industry, where safety, pollution, and mileage regulations apparently placed a larger relative burden on Chrysler than on Ford and GM, because the regulatory compliance costs were approximately equal for all firms, resulting in a bigger cost increase per unit of output for the small firm than for the larger ones.[5]

One last cost of regulation is that, when regulatory agencies have the power to impose huge costs on firms, it is in the interest of the firms to develop ways of influencing the regulators. This could conceivably be through bribery. At the local level, this is often observed. To our knowledge, explicit bribery has not been a problem with the major federal regulatory agencies. Rather, the response of corporations to the regulatory deluge of the last fifteen years has been to change their structures (including the type of person who is appointed president) so that they can deal more effectively with government. In addition to spending huge sums on lobby-

---

4. The earliest study to document this effect is Sam Peltzman, *Regulation of Pharmaceutical Innovation* (Washington, D.C.: American Enterprise Institute, 1974).
5. See K. W. Clarkson, C. W. Kadlec, and A. B. Laffer, "Regulating Chrysler out of Business?" *Regulation*, vol.3, no.5 (Sept./Oct. 1979): 45–50.

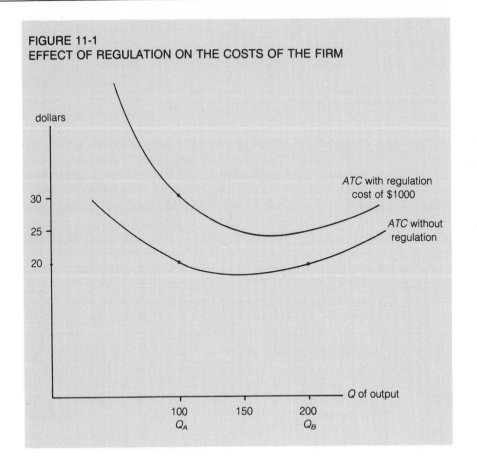

FIGURE 11-1
EFFECT OF REGULATION ON THE COSTS OF THE FIRM

ists whose job it is to influence the way regulatory legislation is written, companies now spend a great deal of effort consulting with the regulators so that the regulations that come out will be less damaging than they might otherwise be. The presidents of many large corporations now have backgrounds in law and government rather than in the actual production of the goods which the firm sells. This change in the way firms do business is a hidden cost of compliance with the regulations.

REGULATION OF THE QUALITY OF GOODS AND THE BEHAVIOR OF FIRMS

An additional feature of the phenomenon of regulation is that it changes the incentives of firms. With a regime of pure *caveat emptor*, the only guarantee of quality that consumers have is the development of brand names by firms. Accordingly, firms have an incentive to maintain the quality of their products to the extent that there is easy brand identification. When the government introduces regulation of any kind, whether it be standards of quality or provision of information, the government is in effect standing behind the information or the quality of the product. In other words, it is establishing a government brand name. When this happens, there is a change in the firms' incentives. To the extent that the government seal of approval supercedes the private brand name, the firm is one of a group of firms, all sharing the same brand name (provided by the government). In this situation, it is in the interest of each firm to depreciate secretly the quality of its good, since the results will tend to be spread among all the firms sharing the government's approval. So to the extent that the brand name is collectivized, each firm takes less care in protecting it. That role now falls to the provider of the brand name—the government. An implication of this analysis is that after the introduction of regulatory standards, the government will be faced with the problem of having to spend more to enforce the regulations which firms have an incentive to break. Thus the budget invariably ends up being much larger than the one set when the regulation is passed.

Does this mean that regulation is never economically justified? Hardly. However, a prudent taxpayer and consumer would be interested in knowing the full costs of a proposed regulatory program as well as its benefits, before deciding that the program is worth it.

The proper role of government in consumer affairs is not a settled issue. We have merely presented some of the important issues involved in this area of public discussion.

ADVERTISING

Why is there advertising? This may seem like a silly question, but if we are to understand the economics of advertising, it is important to know what makes advertising profitable. Advertising would not exist if information were not costly. If all the information consumers ever wanted to know could be obtained at no cost, advertising would be superfluous. But of course we know that information (about prices, about what products exist, and about the characteristics of products, for example) is not free, so we listen to and read ads.

Of course, the main trouble with ads is that, since they are put out by the firms they are intended to benefit, we can't always trust them to be truthful. How should we act on this fact? To say that advertising is sometimes false and misleading is not the same thing as saying that it makes the information problems worse. Advertising is a symptom of an imperfectly informed market—not the cause. It is very difficult to discover what (if anything) should be done to limit or control the kinds or amounts of advertising. There are many questions of fact which must be answered before any policy prescriptions can be proposed. What kind of information does advertising provide? What are some of the economics of controlling deception? Does advertising encourage or hinder entry? What is the effect of advertising on the level and dispersion of prices? Not all the answers to these questions are known, but some results are available.

Advertising and Information

It is clear that advertising steps in to help fill the vacuum provided by a lack of consumer information.[6] What kinds of information does advertising provide? What kinds of goods tend to be advertised? We can divide advertised goods into two categories—those whose characteristics can be identified cheaply by the consumer *before* consumption, and those which can be evaluated clearly only *after* consumption. We call the former *inspection* goods, and the latter *experience* goods.

What goods fall into which categories? Probably most goods are experience goods because even goods which we think we know may not be what they appear to be. But for practical purposes, we can put some goods such as articles of clothing and food into the inspection goods category—once you see them you know what they are and what they will do for you.

Suppose the producer or seller of an inspection good is considering advertising. Would it pay him to lie about the product? No, because it is too easy for the consumer to detect such falsehoods before purchase. Furthermore, the consumer would then know that the advertiser was a liar and not believe him in the future. What about experience goods? Because the consumer cannot determine the truth until he has consumed the product, the seller has a larger incentive to give false information but not about all aspects. For example, it will not pay the producer of shaving cream to say that he is selling dessert topping, because consumers would very quickly and easily detect such a discrepancy and the advertising expense would be wasted. However, information about how well (relative to other products) a product performs its function is much less easy to test and therefore much more suspect. The wary consumer will not take such information too seriously.

Are consumers totally at the mercy of producers in the case of experience goods? No, because of the repeat purchase phenomenon. An advertiser generally does not look for only a single purchase from a consumer. Advertising usually does not pay if it evokes only single purchases. Rather, advertising will usually pay only if it results in multiple future purchases once the consumer has been introduced to the product. As a consequence, we have the following rule of thumb on which consumers can rationally act: "It pays to advertise a winner." Thus the mere fact that a firm advertises a product is evidence that it thinks it has a product which consumers will return to for repeat purchases—a good product. It is this *indirect* information which is important for experience goods, rather than direct

6. The analysis of this section relies heavily on that used by Philip Nelson in "The Economic Value of Advertising," in *Advertising and Society* (New York: New York University Press, 1974).

information about characteristics of the product. On the contrary, indirect information is not particularly valuable for a buyer of an inspection good, so most advertising about them is direct. Repeat ads are important for experience goods, because they help to convey the message that the brand is heavily advertised, increasing the likelihood of its being reputable. Repetitious direct information ads about inspection goods are not profitable, because once the factual information is obtained, repetitions are superfluous. Consequently, we would expect experience goods to be much more heavily advertised than inspection goods, and they are (about three times as heavily).

Deception

We have already said that although there is some incentive to engage in deceptive advertising, consumers have power because of their ability to avoid a second purchase of an unsatisfactory good. That this power keeps false advertising somewhat in check is undeniable. Nevertheless, there is deception. Of course, because it is known that advertisers may be deceptive, consumers are appropriately distrustful of advertising claims, and this may be the source of some inefficiency. It may be that an advertiser has a truly fine product whose special characteristics she would like to bring to the attention of potential customers. The trouble is that no one believes her claims (even though they are true). If ads were generally more truthful, a truthful ad would be better believed. Thus some advertisers might favor restrictions which would ensure truth in advertising, because it would increase viewer receptiveness.

This argument provides a possible rationale for such things as FTC regulation of advertising. But there are some problems with the approach the FTC has taken. First, when the agency announces as its goal the elimination of false and misleading advertising, there is bound to be some confusion among consumers about just what the agency is actually doing. Some consumers may mistakenly think that all ads can now be trusted. Beforehand, they were appropriately distrustful. Now they may be deceived.

Another problem relates to the fact that so much advertising conveys only *indirect* (not particularly factual) information. The content is not so important as its memorableness, which is enhanced by such techniques as hyperbole or humor (such as Joe Namath modeling panty hose). Strict regulation of the content of indirectly informative ads is unnecessary and probably counterproductive, since by becoming more factual, ads are less memorable and perform their function less satisfactorily.

Rather than regulating *all* ads, an alternative (suggested by economist Philip Nelson of the State University of New York) is to have two categories. Type I ads would be factual. The advertiser would speak a key phrase to the effect that all information in the ad is verifiable, and if found to be false, the advertiser could be sued or fined. This would provide a forum for the truly informative ads about characteristics of experience goods. Type II ads would be unrestricted. The advertiser could say anything he wanted to provide an outlet for the indirectly informative ads which are so important for experience goods. This proposal may not be the answer, but it is worth discussing as an alternative to current FTC practice.

Advertising and Entry

Does the ability to advertise impede or stimulate entry into an industry? In the jargon of economics, is advertising a barrier to entry? The question has been the subject of some controversy. It is possible to look at both direct and indirect evidence on the subject. For any given degree of advertising done by already established firms, a new entrant will like it better if she is able to advertise more. But suppose *all* advertising is banned in an industry. Would new entrants prefer this to an absence of restrictions on advertising? Probably not. With unrestricted advertising, a newcomer has a weapon with which it can overcome the brand loyalty which established firms have built up. By means of advertising, a newcomer can reach its potential in the market much more rapidly.

We can get another perspective by looking at the industries which advertise most heavily and comparing the brand switching that takes place there with the switching that takes place in less heavily advertised sectors. One study found that brand shares were more stable in food products than in toiletries, even though toiletries advertise more heavily.[7]

There is some controversy concerning the examination of some *indirect* evidence on the question. If advertising provided an effective barrier to entry, any above-normal returns which were earned in an industry would not be dissipated through the process of entry by new firms. Thus, we should expect to see a higher rate of return on investment, on average, in the industries which advertise heavily. There is some disagreement about whether this differential actually exists. The first scholars to check found that the rate of return was higher when the ratio of advertising expenditures to sales was higher. Later scholars have disputed this finding, saying that the rates of return were incorrectly calculated. The argument of the revisionists is as follows. Advertising expenditures are an investment. The investment acts like a capital asset in that it yields a return, depreciates, and requires maintenance. (This explains why new products are more heavily advertised than old ones. The new products are building up capital by advertising a lot at the outset.) But in spite of the fact that advertising creates a stock of capital much like any other capital, it is not considered as one of the firm's assets by the accountants. Thus the size of any firm's capital stock is *understated* due to leaving out advertising capital. If the size of the firm's capital stock is understated, the rate of return calculated will be *larger* than the true rate of return. The revisionists have recalculated rates of return for heavy advertisers, after adjusting their capital stock upward to account for the advertising capital. The result is

---

7. See L. G. Telser, "Advertising and Competition," *Journal of Political Economy* 72 (December, 1964): 537–62.

that rates of return in the heavily advertised sector are no different from those in other sectors.

Advertising and Prices

There are two ways in which advertising could affect prices. It could affect the *level* or the *dispersion* (differences among sellers) of prices. The effect of advertising on the *level* of prices probably differs from case to case. This may seem odd. At first glance it seems obvious that advertising would have to raise prices, because advertising is a cost and it must be covered by revenue in the long run. This is true as far as it goes, but it leaves out an important possibility—the increased advertising might result in a lowering of *other* costs that is sufficient to offset the cost of the advertising. This could happen if there were significant economies of scale. If large firms have lower average costs than smaller firms, and if advertising permitted larger firms to obtain more customers, average cost *could fall* as a result of the advertising. (See figure 11-2.)

Without advertising, average total cost is the same as average production cost (the curve labeled APC). Suppose that with no advertising the firm can sell Q_1 units of output. The total cost per unit would be $ATC_1 = APC_1$. Now suppose the firm engages in some advertising. The advertising cost can be viewed as a fixed cost, so advertising cost per unit (AAC) gets smaller and smaller as quantity increases. Suppose that with advertising the firm can sell Q_2 units. What has happened to total cost per unit? Total cost per unit is now the sum of production cost per unit and advertising cost per unit ($ATC = APC + AAC$). In this example, we see that the total

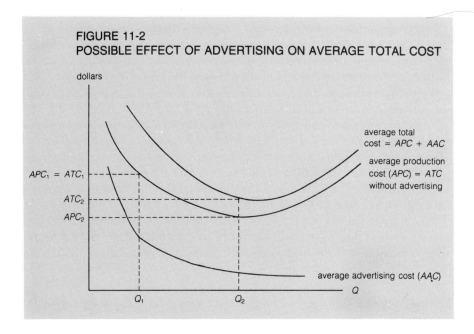

FIGURE 11-2
POSSIBLE EFFECT OF ADVERTISING ON AVERAGE TOTAL COST

cost per unit is lower at Q_2 (with advertising) than it was at Q_1 (without advertising). This need not happen, but it can happen, and it does apparently happen in many cases.

In the case of prescription eyeglasses, it was found that the average price was *lower* in those states which permitted advertising. The explanation is apparently that there are economies of scale in the dispensing of eyeglasses, and that advertising resulted in fewer, larger firms who were able to exploit those economies of scale.

Another way in which advertising can lower prices consumers pay is by lowering what is called the *distribution margin*—the difference between the price the manufacturer charges (to the retailer) and the price the retailer charges (to the consumer) as a percentage of the former. (This is also sometimes called *retail markup*.) Even if the price the manufacturer receives goes up, the price consumers pay can go down if the distribution margin falls enough. How could this happen? The first way is that by increasing the rate of sales, advertising results in greater turnover at the retail level. If a heavily advertised good stays on the shelf only a short time, the retailer's cost of handling it is lower and he might be induced to lower his markup. The second way advertising can lower the distribution margin is by creating product identification. With heavy advertising, consumers become aware of the exact name and manufacturer of the product. This facilitates price comparisons by consumers and encourages retailers to engage in price advertising—retailers are more likely to advertise a price cut if there will be a big response to it, and the response to it will be bigger for a better known product. This kind of phenomenon has apparently occurred with the television advertising of toys.[8]

If there are no economies at either the production or distribution level, advertising will result in higher prices—if it survives as a competitive tool.

If consumers are willing to pay a higher price for a heavily advertised brand than for a similar unadvertised brand, this suggests that buyers are getting some benefit from the advertising that makes the product worth the higher price. Our earlier discussion of the information components of advertising indicated that a consumer's knowledge that a good is heavily advertised indicates to him that the product is likely to be a good one. This saves the consumer the cost of further investigating the properties of various products. Thus, even if the heavily advertised brand sells for a higher *price* than the unadvertised brand, the cost to a consumer (price plus the information costs he must incur in discovering whether the product is appropriate) will be *lower* for the advertised brand, if the consumer finds it worthwhile to buy it instead of the unadvertised brand.

If consumers do not find that their total costs (including price and information gathering) of purchase are lower with the advertised brand, they will not buy it. They will prefer instead the lower-priced unaderver-

8. See R. L. Steiner, "Does Consumer Advertising Lower Prices?" *Journal of Marketing* 37, (October 1973): 19–26.

tised brand. If enough consumers feel this way, advertising will not pay for that product.

Sometimes when a new type of product is introduced, it is heavily advertised by most brands. But once the product becomes well known, unadvertised brands begin to do better, relative to the heavy advertisers. An example is frozen orange juice concentrate. When the product was first introduced in the late 1940s, most brands were heavily advertised. As the years went by, consumers, having learned what the new product was, began to shift toward less advertised (and lower-priced) brands.

While the effect of advertising on the *level* of prices appears to depend on circumstances, the effect on the *dispersion* of prices for a given product seems clear. When advertising about prices is permitted, prices for a given product become more nearly uniform. This is a clear case of advertising's role as a disseminator of information. In the absence of price advertising, it is costly to obtain information about what the best available price is. Consequently, some firms will be able to survive even though they are charging much higher prices than other firms. With advertising, the very high prices will no longer be viable, because consumers will be more likely to know about lower-priced outlets and patronize them.

An example of this phenomenon is the pricing of prescription drugs. As of 1976, thirty-three states restricted the advertising of prescription drugs. What would one expect to be the results of that policy? In the states where advertising is banned, there have been instances where the identical item (same brand) varied in price by hundreds of percent among sellers. The dispersion of prices would be smaller in states where price advertising was allowed.

This much is subject to very little controversy among economists. It would be more surprising if one found that prices were, on average, lower where advertising was allowed. As noted, the effect of advertising on the average price is unclear from a theoretical point of view. There is evidence, however, that in the states where price advertising is allowed, drug prices are lower, on average, than in the advertising restricted states.[9] The result is similar to the results found in regard to the prices of eyeglasses—in states where advertising of price was allowed, the average price was lower than in states where price advertising was banned.[10]

Advertising and Artificial Want Creation

As a postscript to our discussion of advertising, it may be worthwhile to discuss the relation of advertising to the issue of artificial demands. It can hardly be denied that because of advertising we buy things we would not otherwise buy. The question is, what can we infer from this presumption? One possible conclusion we could come to is that these products are not

---

9. John F. Cady, *Restricted Advertising and Consumption—The Case of Retail Drugs* (Washington, D.C.: American Enterprise Institute, 1976).
10. L. Benhan, "The Effects of Advertising on the Price of Eyeglasses," *Journal of Law and Economics* 15 (October 1972): 337–52.

really useful and are scarce only in the most artificial sense. One well-known economist has concluded as much.[11] One might even conclude that advertising, the villain in the piece, should be banned, or at least carefully controlled so as to prevent such abuses.

On closer inspection, the implications are not so clear. First of all, advertising is merely a low-cost way of conveying the manufacturer's pitch to the potential consumer. Advertising does not create the product. It only permits the manufacturer to put it before the consumer.

But the issue of want creation is still there. It is still true that we would not be consuming certain products (deodorant is an example) if some firm hadn't produced them and figured out a way to convince us to use them. This is quite different, however, from saying that we should not consume these products or that their scarcity is artificial. Saying that there is not an innate desire to use deodorant is not so different from saying that there is not an innate desire to hear Beethoven or read Shakespeare. Nevertheless, most of us would be reluctant to say that the demands for these products are tainted because they were culturally induced.[12]

The issue of want creation, and the related issue of advertising as the tool which facilitates it, are not simple to resolve. But pointing out the existence of the phenomenon is not sufficient to permit condemnation.

LOOKING AHEAD

The main purpose of this chapter has been to show that the emotion-charged areas of consumerism and advertising can be analyzed fruitfully by means of the tools of economics. Although the issues are often complex, economics offers some useful insights and enables us to approach these subjects in a systematic manner. The next chapter applies economic analysis to another emotion-charged area, that of externalities, property rights, and public goods.

POINTS TO REMEMBER

1. Brand names evolve under a system of *caveat emptor* because they permit consumers to economize on the costs of evaluating products.

2. If the use of trade names were prohibited, the quality of products would decrease.

3. Brand names will be more valuable and more frequently observed, the higher the costs to a consumer of determining directly the characteristics of products.

11. J. K. Galbraith, *The Affluent Society* (Boston: Houghton-Mifflin, 1958).
12. F.A. Hayek, "The Non-Sequitur of the Dependence Effect," *Southern Economic Journal* 27 (April, 1961): 280–85.

4. The argument in favor of a policy of *caveat emptor* is that consumers under such a policy have a strong self-interest motivation to be careful about the purchases they make.

5. The economic argument in favor of government regulation is that information concerning the characteristics of goods can be obtained by the consumer more cheaply by having some central agency (the government) collect and disseminate it.

6. The noneconomic argument for government control is that, even when they have sufficient information, consumers often make incorrect decisions.

7. The costs of regulation include the direct budgetary costs of the agency involved, as well as the cost of the resources used by firms to comply with the law, the fact that regulators do not make the same decision all consumers would have made, the tendency to be less innovative, and the greater likelihood of corruption.

8. When product quality is regulated, the firms involved have a reduced incentive to be careful about their own private brand name.

9. Advertising exists because information about the characteristics and terms of sale of commodities is costly for consumers to obtain.

10. Most advertising concerns experience goods.

11. Advertising about the ability of experience goods to perform their functions is least likely to be truthful.

12. Much information in ads concerning experience goods is indirect and based on the principle that it pays to advertise a winner.

13. There is some controversy over whether advertising acts as a barrier to the entry of new firms.

14. Permitting advertising could raise or lower the average price paid by consumers, depending on whether there are sufficient economies of scale in production and distribution of the good.

15. Permitting advertising of prices can be expected to reduce the dispersion prices.

KEY TERMS

Average advertising cost: Advertising cost per unit of output produced. (Advertising cost divided by the amount of output produced.)

Brand Name: The trade name which a product carries, or the *reputation* which a product's trade name possesses.

Caveat emptor: Literally, "let the buyer beware." The policy that the consumer purchases at his own risk, with the seller having no legal responsibility for defects in products.

Experience good: A good whose characteristics cannot be completely known until it is purchased and consumed.

Government brand name: The phenomenon which occurs when government specifies a certain quality level of product and puts its seal of approval on the product.

Indirect information: With respect to experience goods, information which does not specify the characteristics of the good directly, but rather conveys the information that the advertiser thinks enough of the good to advertise it.

Inspection good: A good whose characteristics can be obtained by inspection by the consumer before purchase.

Price dispersion: The degree to which prices for a given commodity differ among sellers. A ban on price advertising tends to increase price dispersion.

REVIEW QUESTIONS

1. Some goods (such as many food items) are bought frequently and repeatedly by consumers. Consumers can thus quickly punish a producer of a bad product by refusing to buy further. But other goods (such as meals eaten by tourists, aluminum siding, and some long-lived appliances for the home) are not subject to this kind of discipline from consumers. (a) Would you expect the proportion of bad products to be greater in the former or the latter case? (b) Would a consumer be more wary of a product which had been on the market for six months in the former case or the latter case? (c) Would a new product's chances of success be greater if it were the first type or the second type of product? (d) Does your answer change if the product is introduced by a large, well-established firm?

2. "The existence of trademarks which cannot be copied or infringed on acts to prevent other firms from producing a product exactly like that of a given firm. This is a restriction on entry and is thus inefficient." True or false? If true, is there any mitigating benefit of trademarks which might make them worthwhile?

3. "The higher the cost to the consumer of making an intelligent decision, the greater the likelihood that he will delegate decision-making authority to someone else." Do you think this is true? Can you cite any evidence?

4. Should the Consumer Product Safety Commission try to ensure that all products on the market are foolproof, so that even a person who carelessly misuses the product cannot hurt himself? Who would gain and who would lose from such a policy?

5. An FDA regulator can make two kinds of mistakes in deciding whether to approve a new drug for sale: (a) She could approve an unsafe drug for sale, or (b) she could keep a safe and effective drug off the market. If you try to minimize the chance of making a type a error, you increase the chance of making a type b error, and vice versa. If you were charged with deciding whether to permit a new drug on the market, which kind of error would you be most careful to avoid? Why?

6. A contraceptive device known as the cervical cap was being test-marketed in Europe in 1980. As of that time no U. S. pharmaceutical companies had applied to the FDA for permission to market the item in this country. Leaders of some women's organizations complained that no U.S. companies were interested in the product because it was so cheap and effective that it would take away business from other, higher-priced devices. What do you think of the women's groups' reasoning? Why has the device already been marketed in Europe? Can you think of any other reason the marketing would be slower here than in Europe?

7. Suppose total regulation compliance costs are equal for all firms in an industry. If all firms were originally earning zero economic profits, and if the existence of the regulations does not increase the total *demand* for the product, what will happen to the profitability of the firms that were originally in the business. If some drop out, what will happen to the price of the product and the quantity sold?

8. Make a list of some goods which you consider to be predominantly inspection goods. Make another list of experience goods. Could a good ever be an inspection good to one person and an experience good to another?

9. "You can get consumers to buy almost anything if you spend enough advertising it. But that doesn't mean it pays to put a bad product on the market." Why?

10. "If a product were really good, it would never need to be advertised." Comment.

11. Are highly advertised brands always better than less advertised ones? Does that mean that advertising is wasteful and misleading?

12. Advertisers claim that changes in the amount spent advertising a new product will have very little effect on the number of customers who choose to buy a product for the second time (repeat purchasers). What does this say about the ability of advertising to make a bad product sell?

13. In 1980, some marketing specialists calculated that $10 million or more was needed to successfully introduce a new packaged food or a household or personal-care product on television. This number was significantly lower in earlier years. Is this increase because of higher prices for a given amount of commercial time or because more commercial time must be purchased to overcome entrenched brands? Would the policy implications be different if the first explanation were the reason, rather than the second? Explain.

14. In 1980, the *Wall Street Journal* reported that "One major advertiser recently stopped all advertising of a household product.[13] 'We're just waiting for it to die,' says a marketing executive there. Another of the company's products, once a major name in the category, is faltering because its $3 million TV ad budget pales in the face of competitors that spend four to eight times as much." Do you think the company spends only $3 million in advertising its product because it cannot raise more money? If this is not so, why does it not spend more?

15. Some brand names appear to be insubstantial—that is, they do not relate to the physical characteristics of the product but rather to the image which allows consumers to get vicarious benefits. (Examples would be the "Marlboro man" for cigarettes, and the "hard working man" image of Miller beer.) Is this a legitimate role for advertising? If not, how would you control it? What is your criterion for legitimacy?

16. Approximately $28 billion is spent each year by firms to advertise their products. About 20 percent of that amount goes to advertising agencies and for such things as direct-mail advertising. The rest is paid to TV and radio stations, newspapers, and magazines. It in effect pays for the production of these other goods (TV, radio, newspapers, and magazines). Would your position on any public issues concerning advertising be changed if those percentages were reversed?

17. It has been suggested that consumers would be better served if some of that $28 billion were spent on improving the product rather than advertising. How would you bring this about? Would you rely on the social responsibility of business? Would you simply require every firm to cut back on advertising by (say) 25 percent? How would you make sure that the extra money went for higher quality production? What do you do about new firms or products?

18. Some observers have proposed that the $28 billion spent on advertising be used instead to disperse information of the type found in *Consumer Reports* magazine or some independent quasigovernment testing laboratory. Evaluate this proposal. What would be its benefits? Its costs? How would you decide how the money is raised and on what products it is spent? Would you ban advertising along with this?

19. Has the big increase in advertising of dry breakfast cereals in the last twenty-five years resulted in higher or lower prices of those cereals (relative to all other prices)? The cereal manufacturers claim that such advertising has lowered prices by shortening the amount of time cereals sit on store shelves and by smoothing out sales over the year. Whether their conclusion is true or not, is the explanation consistent with that given in the chapter for the possibility of lower prices with advertising?

13. *Wall Street Journal*, 4 April 1980.

chapter 12

Property Rights,
Externalities, and
Public Goods

THE MEANING OF
PROPERTY RIGHTS

Property rights are the rights of persons to decide the uses to which resources will be put. It is worth emphasizing that property rights are not the rights of property, but rather the rights of *people* concerning property. As such they are one of many *human* rights. *Private* property rights are the rights of a person (or firm) to decide what happens to a resource. It includes the right to sell the rights if the owner so chooses.

What is the role of property rights in an economy? Most fundamentally, the institution of private property enables one person to bring his wants and desires effectively to bear on another person. How does this happen? Suppose I would like to have some milk. I could buy a cow, let it graze in my back yard, and perhaps supply my own milk. But there is another person who is better at supplying my daily requirements of milk without going to all that trouble. The question is, how do I get it from him? One way is to just walk off with it. But the farmer is unlikely to make milk available if he suspects that other people will steal it. On the other hand, if we say that the farmer has a private property right to all the milk his cows produce, then he will gladly market milk because with his property right to the milk he can collect a fee when he markets it. Property rights and markets are thus a very effective way of harnessing the power of self-interest and encouraging people to do what we want them to do. Property

315

rights may not have been designed in heaven, but they are an effective way of operating with imperfect people.

THE MEANING OF EXTERNALITY

An externality exists whenever a decision maker takes an action which has costs or benefits which are not fully brought to bear on him. Externalities exist everywhere. Some are trivial, such as the flowers that grow in my front yard. The fact that they make the front of my house look prettier provides a benefit (a more esthetically pleasing view) to passersby. I am unable to collect payment for that benefit, so it is an externality. (A seller of milk does not have that problem. Since he can keep people from consuming his milk unless they pay, he does not provide benefits for which he is not compensated.) Other externalities, such as the smoke from a coal-fired electricity generating plant in the middle of a large city, have nontrivial consequences. The generating plant imposes costs on people by depriving them of clean air and increasing the risk of disease, without getting their permission or compensating them.

When an externality imposes costs (as in the case of the generating plant), we call it a *negative externality* or an *external diseconomy*. When the externality confers benefits (as in the case of the flowers), we call it a *positive externality* or an *external economy*.

WHY DO EXTERNALITIES OCCUR?

Why are there externalities? The meaning of the term suggests the answer. There is a failure in the mechanism by which the preferences of other people are transmitted to the decision maker. In the case of the dairy farmer, the property rights to the milk were clearly defined and easily exchanged. Buyers can make their wishes (that he market more milk) known by offering to buy milk at a certain price. He decides whether the buyers' benefit (the value they place on the milk) is enough to compensate him for his additional cost of marketing more milk. If their benefit (value offered) is great enough, we can be sure that his self-interest will lead him to market more milk, which is the efficient thing to have happen because the extra benefits are greater than the extra costs.

Are all the benefits and costs of the actions of the generating plant effectively brought to bear on decision makers through market prices? When the firm buys labor, it is presumably paying the cost. It is paying an amount sufficient to induce the workers to work there rather than for another employer. The same holds true when the firm purchases most other inputs. But what about the air? The atmosphere is an input to the production process. The electric company uses the air as a receptacle for the smoke. What price does the firm pay for this input? Zero. What is the cost of using it? Clearly not zero. As with all other resources, the cost of using it is the value of the best foregone alternative. One alternative use is to leave the air unspoiled for the enjoyment of the populace. Presumably the people concerned place some value on this use (they would be willing to pay something to have it), so a cost is incurred when the air is fouled. If someone owned the air, he could decide who got to use it just as a landowner decides who gets to use his land according to who will pay the most for it—who places the highest value on it. Clearly the breathers of air place some value on having clean air. But just as clearly, the electric company would be willing to pay something to use it as a receptacle for smoke. Note, though, that if the electric company had to pay for the use of the air it would use less (pollute less). This is simply an application of the First Law of Demand, which says that the higher the price one must pay to do something, the less he will do.

The fact that no one owns the air (no property rights are defined) is the reason for the pollution—the external diseconomy. We refer to a situation in which, for one reason or another, property rights and markets are not operative, as a case of *market failure*.

When we encounter a market failure, resulting in externalities, it often helps in arriving at a policy prescription to inquire into why there are no property rights or market. In many cases, the reason is that the costs of defining, enforcing, and exchanging property rights are so high that it is not worthwhile to engage in those activities. Operation of a costless market might result in a gain of $100,000 due to putting the resource to a higher-valued use. (For example, the steel plant might cut back its pollution at an expense of $40,000, resulting in cleaner air worth $140,000 to residents.) But if the operation of the market would cost $200,000, none of it would happen. In that case it is better to leave it alone than to have private property rights and a market in air. (If you think about it, property rights in air seem to be a hopeless case. It is hard to even imagine a system which is at all comparable to property rights in other goods, such as land. Air is just too fleeting and hard to control.)

GOVERNMENT CONTROL OF EXTERNALITIES

In such cases there is another alternative—government control. The approach which governments generally take is to specify standards for each firm—"Firm A shall not emit more than Q^* pounds of pollutant X per day." But there are other alternatives, including exchange of pollution rights and taxation of pollution, which may be more efficient.

The Polluting Firm
In order to understand the efficiency aspects of various policies we must first take a closer look at why a firm can benefit from polluting. Figure 12-1

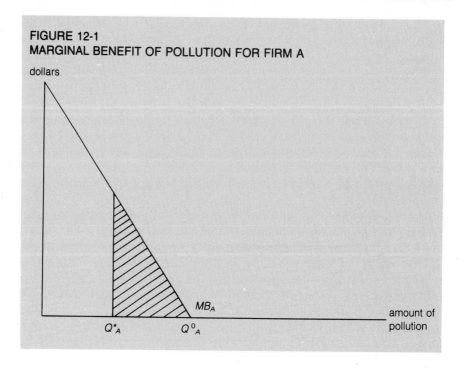

FIGURE 12-1
MARGINAL BENEFIT OF POLLUTION FOR FIRM A

shows firm A's "marginal benefit of polluting" for various levels of pollution. The height of the curve at any quantity tells the number of dollars the
firm would gain if it were allowed to emit one more unit (say pound) of
pollutant. The source of the gain is the saving in the use of other inputs.
Perhaps if it is allowed to emit the smoke, the firm can save the cost of a
scrubber or some other pollution-reducing device. This saving is a marginal benefit of being allowed to emit more smoke. The smaller the amount
of pollution the firm is emitting, the higher the marginal benefit from being
permitted to emit one more unit. This is because the amount of additional
other inputs the firm must employ to reduce pollution by one unit increases as the firm reduces its emission. If the firm is emitting one hundred
units per day, a relatively minor modification might enable it to reduce
that emission to ninety-nine units per day. But if it is emitting only ten
units per day, a much more substantial adjustment would be required to
reduce emissions to nine units per day. Thus, when the firm's emission
level is low, the marginal benefit of pollution is high, and as the emission level increases, the marginal benefit falls. Beyond a certain point,
the marginal benefit of pollution is zero. There is no further saving in
other resource costs which the firm can obtain by emitting more pollution. In figure 12-1 this occurs at quantity Q^0_A. If the firm were allowed to
emit as much pollution as it wanted with no charge or penalty, it would
emit Q^0_A.

Direct Control

If the pollution control authority sets a standard of Q^*_A units of pollution, firm A will incur a cost equal to the diagonally lined area in figure 12-1. The cost takes the form of employing successively more expensive devices for preventing escape of emissions, until the emission level has been reduced to Q^*_A.

Pollution Tax

Alternatively, the pollution control authority could induce the firm to emit Q^*_A by specifying a tax or price of T_A for polluting. This is shown in figure 12-2, which shows the same marginal benefit of polluting curve as figure 12-1. With a tax of T_A per unit of pollution, the firm would again choose to emit Q^*_A units of pollutant. If the firm continued to emit Q^0_A units, it would incur a tax liability of $(T_A)(Q^0_A)$. In reducing emissions to level Q^*_A, it finds that the resource cost of each unit's reduction (which is equal to the height of the MB_A curve at that quantity) is less than the extra tax that would have to be paid if that unit of pollutant were emitted. But if the firm reduced the emission level below Q^*_A, the extra pollution reduction costs it would have to incur would be greater than the tax saving it would obtain.

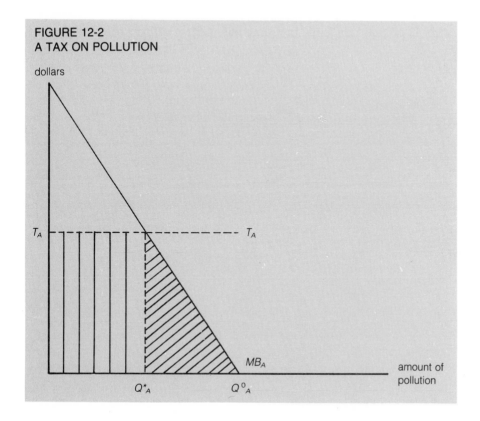

FIGURE 12-2
A TAX ON POLLUTION

Thus, the firm emits Q^*_A. It incurs a pollution-reduction cost equal to the diagonally lined area, just as with direct control. In addition, it pays a tax of $(T_A)(Q^*_A)$ for the Q^*_A units of pollutant it emits.

More than One Emitter

Suppose there are two emitters, each emitting a certain amount in the absence of any restrictions. This is shown in figure 12-3. MB_A has been moved from figure 12-1, but to aid in exposition we have reversed the quantity axis so that an increase in A's emission is shown by a move to the *left* from the point labelled 0. The "marginal benefit of polluting" curve for firm B is drawn in the usual way, with a move to the right indicating an increase in B's emission of pollutant.

In the absence of any restriction, A emits Q^0_A and B emits Q^0_B, for a total of Q^0_T (not shown). Suppose the pollution control authority knows the initial amounts being emitted and wants to reduce the total to level Q^*_T (not shown). As we shall see, there are higher and lower cost ways of obtaining this result, but in order for the authorities to identify the lowest-cost method, they must know the pollution reduction costs of both firms. It is unlikely that they will know these costs in detail. As a result, the pollution control authority is likely to order rather arbitrary reductions in emissions so that the total amount emitted is Q^*_T. For example, it may order that both firms reduce emissions by the same amount or same percentage, or that they emit the same quantity. Whatever rule is chosen, it

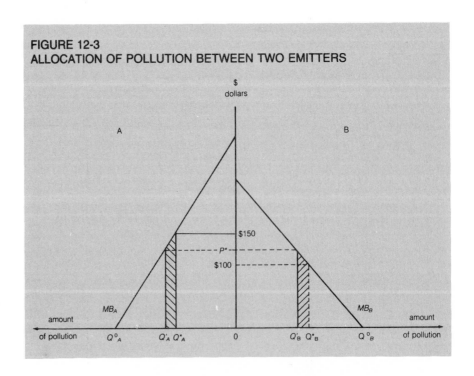

FIGURE 12-3
ALLOCATION OF POLLUTION BETWEEN TWO EMITTERS

is likely that the marginal benefit of pollution for firm A at its assigned amount will not equal the marginal benefit of pollution for firm B at its assigned amount. For example, suppose A and B are told to emit equal amounts $(Q^*_A = Q^*_B)$ where $Q^*_A + Q^*_B = Q^*_T$ and that at that point MB_A = \$150, while MB_B = \$100. (This is shown in figure 12-3.) Since the marginal benefits differ, it is possible for firms A and B to engage in a mutually beneficial exchange which keeps the total amount of pollution at Q^*_T. Firm A is willing to pay up to \$150 to be allowed to emit one more unit of pollutant. This is because it could thereby save \$150 in pollution control costs. Firm B would be willing to reduce its emissions by one more unit if it were paid anything over \$100, because that is the extra pollution control cost it would have to incur in order to bring about that reduction. If firm A paid firm B an amount between \$100 and \$150, both firms could gain by having A emit one more unit and B emit one less unit of pollutant (and the total pollution control costs incurred to achieve emission level Q^*_T would be \$50 less than if A and B had not exchanged). In fact, if exchange were permitted (and were not too costly), they could continue to benefit by exchanging pollution rights (that is, having A buy the right to emit units of pollution from B) until $MB_A = MB_B$. (MB_A is A's maximum offer price for the right to emit another unit of pollutant, and MB_B is B's minimum asking price required to get it to emit one less unit of pollutant. As long as MB_A is greater than MB_B, they can make more mutually beneficial exchanges.) The total amount of pollution emitted would be the same as under controls, but the total cost of compliance would be less than it was when A emitted Q^*_A and B emitted Q^*_B. In figure 12-3, exchange proceeds until B is emitting Q'_B and A is emitting Q'_A (where $Q'_A + Q'_B = Q^*_T$) and the common marginal benefit of pollution is P^*. Firm A's saving in pollution control cost is the lined trapezoid with width of $Q'_A - Q^*_A$ and height ranging from P^* to \$150. Firm B's extra pollution control cost is the lined trapezoid with width of $Q^*_B - Q'_B$ (equal to $Q'_A - Q^*_A$) and height ranging from \$100 to P^*. Since A's saving is greater than B's increase, there is a net reduction of pollution control costs if A and B can costlessly exchange pollution rights. There will always be a potential gain of this sort if the marginal benefits of firms differ at the emission level which is imposed on them and if transaction costs are sufficiently low.

The firms will exchange until their marginal benefits of pollution (which correspond to their marginal costs of controlling pollution) are equal. Once that allocation of pollution rights has been attained, there is no way to reduce aggregate pollution control costs any further by reallocation of pollution rights. If A increased its emissions beyond Q'_A, it would save an amount *less than* P^*, and if B reduced its emissions below Q'_B, it would incur an additional cost *greater than* P^*. Thus, the sum of their pollution control costs would increase. Similarly, if A emitted less than Q'_A, it would incur an extra cost greater than P^*, while B would save an amount less than P^* if it emitted more than Q'_B. Thus any change in the allocation of pollution (from Q'_A and Q'_B) would increase total pollution control costs. This means the allocation Q'_A and Q'_B, where $MB_A = MB_B$, must be the lowest-cost (efficient) allocation.

Another way of improving on the direct control outcome is to impose pollution taxes. We saw earlier that we can induce a firm to emit any specified amount of pollution by imposing the right level of pollution tax. We can now see that it is possible to use pollution taxes to achieve the same minimum aggregate level of pollution control costs which we obtained via exchange of pollution rights. In our example, a pollution tax of P^* per unit emitted would induce firms A and B to emit Q'_A and Q'_B, respectively, just as under the exchange system. Firm A would cut back to Q'_A because, up to that point, the saving in taxes due to cutting back is greater than the increase in pollution control costs. At Q'_A the MB_A (which is the marginal pollution control cost) equals P^*. Similarly, firm B will be induced to cut back to Q'_B, where MB_B equals P^*. As we noted before, that allocation, at which A and B have equal marginal pollution control costs, is the allocation which minimizes the cost of attaining a total of Q^*_T of pollution from the two firms.

How would the authority arrive at the tax level P^*? If it knew the marginal benefit schedules, it could simply find that price such that the amount emitted by A plus the amount emitted by B totalled Q^*_T. Of course, if we knew the marginal benefit schedules that completely, we could simply assign Q'_A to A and Q'_B to B and forget the tax. The trouble is that no one knows what all those schedules look like. Each individual firm may have a good idea of its schedule, but no central authority knows it. Thus, the authorities could not simply specify the efficient allocation. If it used the tax system, the tax P^* would have to be arrived at by trial and error. If it announced a tax higher than P^*, it would find that less than Q^*_T would be emitted. If it announced a tax rate less than P^*, it would find that more than Q^*_T would be emitted. The tax rate might be adjusted annually, and it might take several years for the equilibrium level of taxes to be reached, but it is at least possible for the least costly allocation of pollution rights to be discovered in this manner.

Actions of the EPA

The actual policies of the Environmental Protection Agency (EPA) and local environmental agencies have been largely confined to direct controls. The agency sets emission standards which are, as far as possible, uniform for all firms. There have been some cases where standards have been relaxed for certain firms because the costs of compliance were judged to be too high, but there has been no systematic attempt to allocate pollution rights according to the costs of pollution control by means of either taxes or exchange of pollution rights. While the EPA and other regulators have generally continued to set uniform standards, there has been some limited encouragement of the exchange of pollution rights. In the late 1970s, Standard Oil of Ohio was encouraged to make arrangements whereby it would install pollution control equipment in some Los Angeles area businesses in return for being allowed to emit some fumes into the air in the process of putting crude oil into a pipeline in Long Beach. Because of a variety of difficulties, this arrangement was never worked out, but it suggests the possibility of future cost-saving arrangements. A second case in 1979 was more successful. The San Francisco Bay Area Air Quality Management District allowed a firm to install pollution control equipment in some dry cleaning plants in return for being allowed to build a gasoline storage facility. It is too early to tell if this sort of exchange will be commonplace in the future.

Another change in the EPA's policy which also allows for more flexibility is the concept of the *bubble*, introduced in 1980. Under the bubble concept, a firm is allowed to increase its emission of some pollutants in return for decreasing its output of others. For example, a firm might be allowed to increase its output of sulphur in return for decreasing its output of hydrocarbons. One area of difficulty is that the EPA must decide how much sulphur can be traded for a pound of hydrocarbons. This involves trying to estimate the relative damages which various pollutants cause—not an easy task. But the early estimates are that, due to the bubble policy, some corporations may be able to meet pollution standards at 60 percent less cost than they are now incurring.

THE OPTIMAL AMOUNT OF POLLUTION

In our earlier example, the pollution control authorities specified a total allowable pollution level of Q^*_T. But how do we know that is the appropriate amount? How does one determine the *optimal* level of pollution? The mere mention of the idea of an optimal level (other than zero) of pollution makes some people cringe. But by now you can probably see what the argument for such a concept would be. We have already seen that those who pollute have a demand for pollution and place a value on the use of the environment as a waste receptacle because of their costs of reducing pollution. Is this really a legitimate demand? Should the corporations' costs enter into our calculations? We believe so. First of all, the costs are real. Secondly, the demand to pollute is derived from the demand for the final product. It is because we want steel that the steel mill finds it in its interests to pollute. When the steel companies (or other polluters) don't have to pay the full cost of all their resources, this means that more steel is produced at a lower price. When the corporations are forced to pay the full cost, the reverse occurs—a reduced output and higher price.

Once we incorporate the idea that there is a demand for pollution, by way of the demand for the products whose production entails pollution, it is a small step to see that an efficient allocation of resources involves a comparison of the extra benefits from additional pollution control with the extra costs (in the form of increased cost of production and lower consumption of the goods produced by the polluting methods). Ultimately it comes down to a question of how much of *other goods* we are willing to give up to get more of a clean environment. We can illustrate this choice by means of a simple diagram. (See figure 12-4.)

The optimal amount of pollution occurs when the benefits of an extra

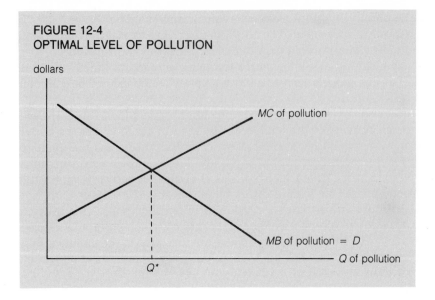

FIGURE 12-4
OPTIMAL LEVEL OF POLLUTION

dollars

MC of pollution

MB of pollution = *D*

Q of pollution

*Q**

unit of pollution are just offset by the costs of that extra pollution. The benefits take the form of reduced expenditure on pollution control devices and increases in the consumption of goods whose production generates pollution. The costs take the forms of lost benefits because of impaired health, reduced agricultural output, and reduced enjoyment of the environment, among others. Although we know these costs exist, it is very difficult to measure them because no complete market for environmental attributes exists. A market for pollution rights is beginning to emerge, and this may enable us to get a better idea of the shape and location of marginal benefits of pollution curves, but there is no prospect of having a market whereby a prospective polluter buys the right to pollute from victims. As we pointed out earlier, the movements of the air are such that it is not usually possible to *identify* all those affected by a given infusion of pollutants, let alone negotiate with them. Thus, the best we can hope for now is to identify the marginal benefits schedule and make some very crude estimates about the marginal costs of pollution.

POLLUTION IN URBAN
AND UNDEVELOPED
AREAS

Is the optimal amount of pollution greater in urban or in open areas? At first glance it might seem obvious that the cities should have more pollution. But that is not necessarily the case. By formulating the problem in terms of marginal benefits and marginal costs, we can see that it could go either way. What determines the height of the *marginal costs* of pollution

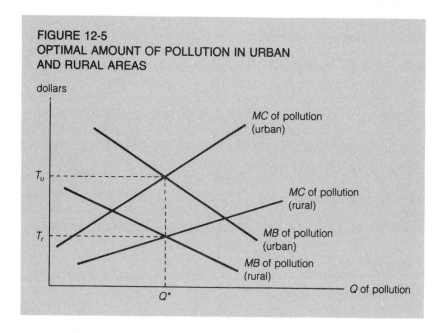

FIGURE 12-5
OPTIMAL AMOUNT OF POLLUTION IN URBAN
AND RURAL AREAS

curve? Basically, it is the number of people in the area and their demand for a clean environment. Also, since a clean environment is probably a normal good, the *marginal costs* of pollution schedule would be higher when per capita income is higher. For both of these reasons, the *marginal costs* of pollution curve would be higher in urban than in rural areas. What about the demand for pollution or *marginal benefits* of pollution curve? The demand to pollute will be higher in urban areas because of the desire of polluting firms to be near their markets. Also, in the case of cars, the demand to pollute would be directly related to the number of people and per capita income. So both the *marginal benefits* and *marginal costs* of pollution schedules would be higher in urban than in relatively un-populated areas (see figure 12-5).

Figure 12-5 illustrates a case in which the optimal amount of pollution is the same in both areas. Of course, the optimal amount could have been larger or smaller in the urban than in the undeveloped area. But notice, there is a tendency for the effects which urbanization has on the demands and costs of pollution to be offsetting. The higher demand (*marginal benefits*) for pollution would tend to *increase* the optimal amount of pollu-tion in the cities and increase the optimal "pollution tax." But the higher *marginal costs* of pollution tends to *decrease* the optimal level of pollution in the cities and increase the optimal pollution tax. The effects on the *quantity* of pollution are offsetting, while the effects on the tax are reinforc-ing—the optimal pollution tax will clearly be higher in the cities than in the outlying areas. These implications seem to go contrary to the direction the Environmental Protection Agency (EPA) is moving. The EPA appears to favor uniform pollution taxes (or their equivalent) over the whole country and tougher standards (lower pollution levels) in unpopulated areas than in urban areas.[1]

HAS THE QUALITY OF THE ENVIRONMENT WORSENED?

Has the quality of the environment deteriorated so badly over time that the human race is rapidly approaching extinction? Is pollution much worse today than in earlier times? Such does not appear to be the case. A look at conditions fifty or one hundred years ago would reveal lower water and air quality than we now have. Sewers and sewage treatment as a means of improving water quality are not all that old. The smoke from factories in earlier days was quite toxic and in many ways more dangerous than today's smog. The health hazards from the very large amount of horse manure which preautomobile transportation generated should not be overlooked. In short, a strong case could be made that pollution today is less than fifty or one hundred years ago. This is not terribly surprising. A clean environment is probably a normal good—the demand for it increases as income increases. In our optimal level of pollution diagram, this would be reflected in a higher *marginal cost* of pollution schedule for a rich society than for a poor society. This tends to result in a smaller amount of pollution because of stricter governmental sactions against pollution which a richer society would tend to vote on itself.

The above argument suggests that since a clean environment is a normal good, richer societies would be expected to bring more political pressure to bear to clean up the environment through tougher laws. The evidence is consistent with this view. But in addition to this *collective* action, many *private* actions of people in a richer society serve to provide a cleaner environment as a by-product. For example, the substitution of natural gas and oil for coal as a heating fuel, which has resulted in greatly reduced air pollution for a given amount of heat, was due primarily to the voluntary decisions of individuals (reflecting the fact that natural gas and oil are easier to handle and make less mess, advantages which would be more valuable as members of the society become richer). Thus in certain cases, a cleaner environment may be a natural by-product of private decisions which society makes as it gets richer.

Nevertheless, in some cases (such as pollution of the oceans), conditions are probably worse now than they were one hundred years ago. The increase in world population and income has *not* led to that happy circumstance in which people's private actions have incidentally reduced ocean pollution. Increased income and wealth have, if anything, increased the propensity of people to foul the oceans. Furthermore, there has not been

1. For a more detailed discussion along the lines of this section, the reader is referred to S. Peltzman and T. N. Tideman, "Local vs. National Pollution Control: Note," *American Economic Review* 62 (December 1972): 959-64.

a great deal of progress in the area of voluntary agreements or supranational control of dumping into the oceans. The oceans are an important example of a common property resource (absence of private property rights), and we have not been rescued from this situation by the good fortune of having (as in the case of natural gas and air pollution) privately beneficial developments which coincidentally reduced the pollution level.

THE PRISONER'S DILEMMA

Cases where externalities are present (where the decision maker does not bear all the costs or receive all the benefits of her decision) can often be usefully analyzed by means of a construction known as the prisoners' dilemma game. A *game* for our purpose is an interactive process whereby the rewards or punishments that a person receives depend on the actions of other people as well as on her own actions. Obviously a very wide variety of social interactions fit into the category of games as defined here. Some of these interactions have patterns which occur in many different settings. The regularities can sometimes be isolated and the resulting abstract model of behavior is analyzed as a game.

The Game

The particular features of the prisoner's dilemma game can best be seen by means of the example from which the game gets its name. Two prisoners (A and B) have been arrested. The authorities know that they committed a rather minor crime for which they can be convicted. The authorities also suspect that they have committed a much more serious crime, but they can't be convicted of this unless one of the two turns state's evidence or confesses. To elicit a confession, the authorities put the prisoners in separate interrogation rooms and present them with the following choices. Prisoner A is told, "If you confess and B does not, you go free and he gets twenty years. If you both confess to the more serious crime, you'll each get five years. If he confesses and you don't, you get twenty years and he gets off. If neither of you confesses, you each get one year." The information is summarized in a matrix in figure 12-6.

The matrix shows prison terms for both A and B, based on various combinations of actions. A's penalty is always shown to the left of the slash and B's to the right. There are four outcomes. For example, the outcome when A confesses and B doesn't is shown in the lower left, where A gets zero years and B gets twenty years.

One feature of the prisoner's dilemma is that the two players are better off if they cooperate with each other (by *not* confessing, in this case), than if neither cooperates with the other (they confess). The upper left corner always has a better payoff than the lower right. The other key feature is that the strategy confess (don't cooperate) dominates. That is, regardless of what B does, A is better off confessing. If B does not confess, A gets zero

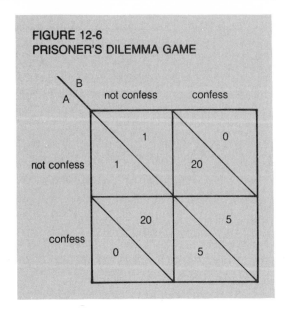

FIGURE 12-6
PRISONER'S DILEMMA GAME

versus one year by confessing (figure 12-6). If B confesses, A is better off confessing, because he gets only five years instead of twenty. So A should, on this basis, confess. The same is true for B. (Check the matrix to make sure.) The trouble with this is that it leads both of them to confess, and they are worse off than if neither confessed. This paradox is the essence of the prisoners' dilemma.

Prisoner's Dilemma and Externalities

What does this have to do with externalities? We often find ourselves in situations which have the same characteristics as the prisoner's dilemma game; a few are almost exactly the same. For example, the problem of nuclear disarmament in the United States and the USSR, where cooperation would be disarming (analogous to not confessing in the above example) and noncooperation would be not disarming. If both countries disarm, they still have parity, but they save all the resources poured into defense. But if the United States disarms and the USSR does not, the United States loses due to USSR dominance (and vice versa if they disarm and the United States does not). If neither disarms, neither country has a gain in security, but the expense continues to increase.

In most situations where the prisoner's dilemma applies, the interaction of a large number of people is involved. Some examples are: air pollution by cars, litter, highway congestion and car pools, cutback of fuel consumption, whale overkill, and the use of the directory assistance operator at the telephone company. In fact any case in which we are imposing external costs on *each other* can be usefully described by the prisoner's dilemma.

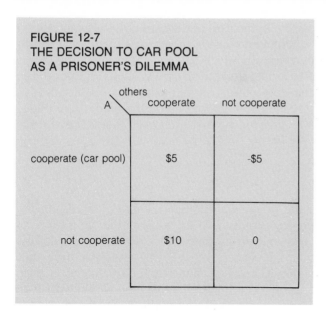

FIGURE 12-7
THE DECISION TO CAR POOL
AS A PRISONER'S DILEMMA

	others	
A	cooperate	not cooperate
cooperate (car pool)	$5	-$5
not cooperate	$10	0

Highway Congestion and Car Pools

Let's look at automobile congestion. These days it is trite to talk about commuting cars coming into big cities with only one person in them. Congestion could be reduced by increased use of car pools. In fact, if every driver joined a car pool, the reduced congestion would permit significantly faster trips for everyone. So why don't more people join car pools? Because they are in the prisoner's dilemma—there are mutual externalities involved. Suppose we can put dollar amounts on the gains or losses that occur with car pooling. The accompanying matrix (figure 12-7) shows the payoffs to a typical person, depending on what he and others do.

Taking part in a car pool is inconvenient. You may have to rearrange your schedule. There is extra driving to get to your rider's house. You have to find a rider. Nevertheless, if a large portion of the populace takes part, you might be better off taking part than if *no one* does. Suppose your weekly gain is $5 if you, and everyone else, participate. But with everyone else car pooling, you are even better off by *not* car pooling, because you get the reduced congestion without the car pool hassle. Suppose no one else is cooperating. Then if you cooperate, you get the hassle without the reduced congestion, so you are doubly bad off. (Negative $5 gain.) If no one car pools, there is neither gain nor loss, because that is the *status quo*. Again notice that we would all be better off if everyone were in a car pool (the upper lefthand corner). But we are strongly driven to the lower right-hand corner, where no one cooperates—a prisoner's dilemma.

The Source of the Problem

What is the source of the prisoner's dilemma? It always involves a failure of the players to take account of a cost or benefit they are conferring on other players—an externality. In the case of the car pool, the external cost is the cost of congestion. When one more car gets on a freeway, it causes all other cars to slow down very slightly. While the cost is small to any *one* of those drivers (maybe 1¢ of lost time), if there are several hundred cars involved, the total external cost which I am imposing on other drivers can be quite large. Since everyone has a right to be on the road, I don't have to compensate the other drivers for the cost I impose. That is why I drive as much as I do.

Solutions?

What is the way out of the prisoner's dilemma? There are two types of solutions. One is the *coercive* solution. Since we could all gain from car pooling, we could pass a law requiring everyone to be in a car pool. This would put us in the upper left corner. But this presents three problems. First, contrary to the example, probably not everyone would gain from universal car pooling. Second, even if one *did* gain, she would gain even more by violating the agreement, so she is not really out of the prisoner's dilemma. Third, the temptation to break the agreement results in enforcement costs.

The second solution is to change the payoffs for various actions so that everyone is induced to cooperate *in her own self-interest*. How could this be done? One way might be to charge a fee for the use of the road or, more dramatically, to charge those drivers who are not car pooling. In this example, if the weekly charge for road use to non–car poolers were more than $5, it would be sufficient to induce the representative individual to take part. (A $6 charge would make the bottom row payoffs $4 and −$6, both inferior to the upper row counterparts.) Thus, if there is a sufficient charge for the use of the resource, each person is brought out of the prisoner's dilemma and into a straightforward cooperative game.

You may have noticed that the latter solution has a lot in common with the property rights discussion earlier in the chapter. In fact the points raised are very similar. The existence of private property rights which are easy to exchange and enforce brings transactors automatically out of the prisoner's dilemma by making cooperative behavior in their own self-interest, just as charging for road use brings the users out of the prisoner's dilemma.

OTHER ECONOMIC ISSUES INVOLVING EXTERNALITIES

Traffic Safety

Issues of traffic safety are often involved with externalities. By having backup lights on my car, I reduce the chance of other cars running into me when I am backing up. This act on my part confers external benefits on those who might collide with me. They would, presumably, even be willing to pay me a small amount to ensure that I have backup lights, but since the costs of negotiating with each interested person are so high, I get no offers. A workable alternative is to have mandatory installation of backup lights. Other safety measures, from standardized bumper heights to brake inspections, have a similar justification. Of course, the mere existence of an external benefit doesn't mean the action is worth the cost. Some comparison of the gains from increased safety with the costs of the devices and of enforcement is necessary.

Another consideration is resistance to coercion. There may be a demand for freedom by the citizens. This says that citizens might be willing to give up some of other goods (or efficiency) in return for being able to make their own decisions. If their behavior is coerced, this imposes a cost on them (in the form of a reduced amount of the good being able to make their own decisions). This cost must be added to the cost of the devices and the cost of enforcement, and then compared to the benefits in order to find out if the law is worth it. But these measures do have a clear basis in the economics of externalities.

Of a different character are those devices, such as the seat belts, air bags, and the padded dash, which help the occupants of a particular car but provide no benefit to other motorists. There is no obvious externality here, and laws requiring installation must be based on some other argument, such as the paternalistic one that people don't know what's good for them.

Pesticides

Another example of a group of products which may result in externalities is pesticides. Substances such as DDT can impose external effects in two ways. First, they are chemically very stable; they do not break down into simpler (nontoxic) compounds very quickly. As a result, they may retain their toxicity long after rain has washed them away from the area where they were used. Also, they may continue to be toxic even as they move through the food chain from simple organisms up through large animals. It is very difficult to trace the path of a given dose of DDT, so it would be virtually impossible for those who are damaged to sue users to claim compensation for damages.

The prescription for this problem is complicated by the fact that DDT and related compounds have been very helpful in combatting certain pests, especially malaria-carrying mosquitoes. Since there are externalities both in the combatting of the pests and in the dispersal of the pesticides, resulting from a lack of markets in both cases, the discovery of the best policy is likely to be very difficult. If a benevolent government official could know everything about all the benefits and costs on both sides, he could improve on the market outcome by deciding whether and in what amounts to allow particular pesticides to be used. Unfortunately, government officials are only human. They not only cannot possibly have complete knowledge, but they are subject to severe pressures both from users of the pesticides and from environmentalists, and their decisions will probably not be ideal.

Another externality problem associated with pesticides is the problem of pesticide-resistant strains of pests. Heavy use of pesticides can result in the evolution of strains of pests which are resistant to standard pesticides. The result is a higher cost of controlling pests. The problem is that the costs imposed by any one person's use of a pesticide are borne mostly by others. Again, we can imagine a policy which would cause users to take into account all the costs of their actions, but actually carrying out that policy is very difficult in view of the very great informational problems of this case.

PUBLIC GOODS
(AND BADS)

Many cases of externalities involve what are called public (or collective) goods (or bads). When I put a pollution control device on my car, the reduction in pollution is enjoyed jointly by everyone in the area. In fact, adding additional consumers of the cleaner air does not reduce its consumption by anyone else. Furthermore, it is not possible to exclude anyone from consuming the improved air quality. Consequently, air pollution control is a public good (or, air pollution is a public bad). As the above example illustrates, public goods are characterized by joint consumption (zero cost of adding extra consumers) and high cost of excluding nonpayers.

Joint consumption means that it is no more costly to have many people consume the good than it is to have one consume it. Once the good is produced, adding more consumers does not add any more cost. High exclusion cost means that with a public good, it is very costly to keep additional people from consuming the good once it is produced. Thus public goods not only *may* be but *are* consumed by many people at once.

Not all goods with the property of joint consumption have high exclusion costs. For example, a television signal possesses the joint consumption property because additional viewers can watch any show merely by turning on their TVs (and they do not keep anyone else from using the same signal). But the technology exists for cheaply excluding nonpayers from watching the program (by means of scrambling devices), so it is not a public good in the same sense that national defense is. In the case of national defense, not only do we jointly consume the benefits, but if it were paid for by voluntary contributions, it would be prohibitively expensive to exclude those who did not contribute.

By contrast, a *private good*, such as an apple, can only be consumed by one person; additional people can consume apples only if more are produced; and it is possible to exclude people from consuming your apple.

What are the economic implications of public goods? The first interesting point is that if we want to know whether it is efficient to produce another unit of a public good, we have to know the *sum* of the amounts which all people affected by it would be willing to pay. For example, suppose a lowering of the ozone count in the Los Angeles basin by an average of 0.05 part per million would cost $5 million. Is it worth it? To find out, we would have to know how much each person in the area would be willing to pay. If the *sum* of those amounts were greater than $5 million, then it would be worthwhile. By contrast, to know whether it is worthwhile to produce another apple, we have to know whether any *one* person is willing to pay the price, since only one person will benefit from the additional apple.

The second interesting point is that there will be underproduction of public goods (as long as they remain truly public) in the absence of some coercive collective arrangement. We have already seen this point in relation to air pollution. If potential beneficiaries cannot be excluded if they do not pay, then no voluntary arrangement will provide for the optimal amount of the good, since it is in the interest of every individual to attempt to obtain benefits without paying for them (the prisoner's dilemma again).

This is not to say that government provision will necessarily result in the efficient amount of a public good. Economic theories of government are not very well developed, and we shall not delve into them in this book. But we should, nevertheless, acknowledge that those theories which we do have do not allow us to conclude that the government will produce the proper amount of a public good. It is efficient to produce more of a public good as long as (and only as long as) the sum of the marginal benefits of doing so is greater than the marginal cost. Sometimes government action may result in too much or not enough of a public good, but we cannot tell how it will come out in any case. Markets can sometimes fail because of externalities; but so, too, can government. There are simply no grounds for believing that government intervention in markets always makes things better rather than worse.

There is probably no example of a *purely* public good, in which every consumer consumes *exactly* the same amount, for which the marginal cost of additional consumers is literally *zero*, and for which it is *impossible* to exclude nonpayers. But many are close enough to be analyzed by the public good model. Air pollution abatement falls into that category. Other public goods are national defense, ideas, theories, and melodies.

SHOULD PUBLIC GOODS BE PUBLIC?

What this seemingly silly question asks is, should public goods be provided by a public agency? Granted that purely voluntary arrangements are inadequate for public goods, we still do not have to argue for direct public provision. An interesting example is education. Suppose that education through high school benefits others besides the person being educated, and that the educated person is not paid for the benefit she confers. Perhaps the skills of reading, writing, and mathematics will make a person a better citizen, one more likely to vote intelligently, and less likely to be a criminal. These benefits are public good externalities.[2] All citizens can consume them at once, and it is not possible to exclude anyone from consuming them. Since they have public good characteristics, no student would be able to sell her good citizenship traits—that is, receive payment from all those who benefit from her education. Thus *some* students will tend to invest in education less than would be efficient—that is, they would (if they had to pay the cost of their own schooling) stop educating themselves at a point where the *social* benefit (their own private benefit *plus* the external benefits) was greater than the additional cost of going to school for another year. Why would this happen? With purely private arrangements, the student's family would purchase more education up to the point where the additional *private* benefit (including increased earnings and increased nonmonetary benefits) equalled the additional cost of another year of schooling.

The situation is illustrated in figure 12-8. The student (and her family) are assumed to have a demand for education (labelled marginal *private* benefit, *MPB*). The height of the demand curve at any point represents the marginal private (pecuniary and nonpecuniary) benefit from having one more year of schooling. (As usual we assume their marginal private benefit falls as more education is consumed.) As long as this marginal private benefit is greater than the marginal cost, it is worthwhile to go on. Thus in this example, with marginal cost of MC_o, the student would choose Q_p of education.

But remember that we are assuming that there are *external* benefits flowing from the education. They are represented by the curve labelled marginal *external* benefit (*MEB*). Note that the *marginal external benefit* falls as more education is consumed. The additional benefits that other members of society get from a child's completion of the sixth grade are not as great as the additional benefits from the fact that the child completed the first grade. At quantity Q_p, the *marginal external benefit* is still positive, which means that other people would obtain further benefits from (and would be willing to pay for) having the child get more schooling. It is the fact that this marginal *external* benefit is positive at Q_p which tells us that the student would consume too little schooling if she and her family had to pay the full cost. This is because the optimal (best) amount of education is where the marginal *social* benefit (the sum of marginal external benefit and marginal private benefit of further schooling equals its marginal cost. If $MPB = MC$ (as it does at Q_p), then marginal social benefit is *greater* than marginal costs, since marginal external benefit is positive. Thus more education should be consumed, up to the point where $MSB = MC$. This occurs at Q_o in figure 12-8, where the MSB curve (which is the vertical sum of the MPB and MEB curves) intersects MC. As we noted above, the student will not voluntarily consume Q_o if she has to pay the

2. There are some who would argue that education does not reduce criminality—only the risk of being caught. If this is true, then there is no external benefit, but rather, perhaps, an external cost from increased education.

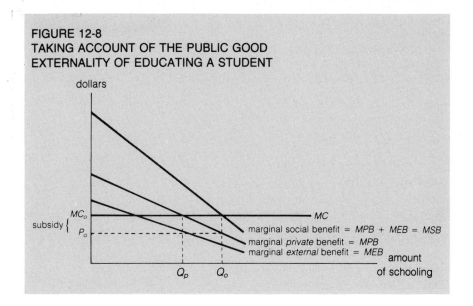

FIGURE 12-8
TAKING ACCOUNT OF THE PUBLIC GOOD
EXTERNALITY OF EDUCATING A STUDENT

dollars

MC_o

subsidy { P_o

MC

marginal social benefit = MPB + MEB = MSB
marginal *private* benefit = MPB
marginal *external* benefit = MEB

amount
of schooling

Q_p Q_o

full cost (MC_o per unit). In order to induce the student to consume Q_o, the price to the student must be reduced (somehow) to P_o, at which price she would demand Q_o. The desirability of some sort of subsidy to education is implied.

How is the subsidy to be carried out? One way is to have all of the direct costs paid by the government via public schools. The direct costs include teachers' salaries, buildings, materials, and administrative costs, but do *not* include the opportunity cost of the student's time. As the student proceeds, this opportunity cost component looms larger in the decision. Another method would be to have publicly owned schools, but charge tuition appropriate for the particular student. The tuition charged would be such that the student's family would choose quantity Q_o. In figure 12-6, this would entail a price to the student of P_o. The size of the optimal subsidy would depend on the private demand for schooling (the marginal private benefit schedule). The higher the private demand, the lower the optimal subsidy. If there were a higher private demand, the optimal quantity would be larger but the optimal subsidy would be smaller.

Marginal and Inframarginal External Benefits

If the private demand (*marginal private benefits*) were such that it intersected *marginal cost* at a quantity larger than where marginal external benefit equals zero, the optimal subsidy would be zero. This case is illustrated in figure 12-9, where, for the sake of argument, we have assumed that the *MEB* curve is the same as for the previous case. (The marginal

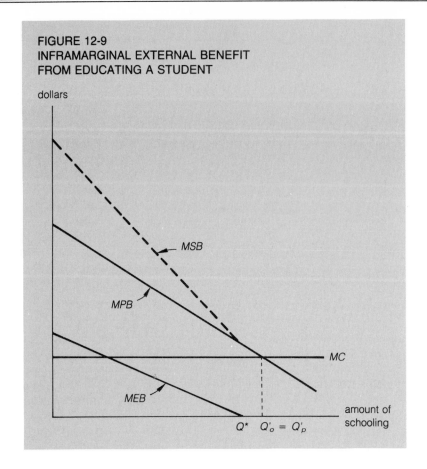

FIGURE 12-9
INFRAMARGINAL EXTERNAL BENEFIT
FROM EDUCATING A STUDENT

external benefits from any level of education could reasonably be supposed to be the same for all people educated.) The MSB curve is again the vertical sum of MPB and MEB But note that MEB is zero at Q^*, meaning that, if the student gets more education than Q^*, the rest of the society gets no more benefit than they did when she obtained Q^* of education. Since her own private benefits would induce her to consume $Q'_o = Q'_p$, there is no efficiency argument for subsidizing this student's education. At the margin of decision ($Q'_o = Q'_p$, where the student would stop on her own), there is no one who would be willing to pay any more to have her get additional education. This is reflected in the fact that MEB is zero at Q'_o. If *marginal external benefit* is zero at the privately optimal point, then no subsidy is called for on efficiency grounds. The externality is *inframarginal* (within the margin or to the left of the margin).

This point applies to many other situations. The existence of an externality is not interesting in the sense of calling for action unless it is marginal. We provide many uncompensated benefits to other people by various actions in our daily lives. (Civilization could be thought of as a mass of beneficial externalities.) But the question for policy purposes is whether *at the margin* we are conferring external benefits or imposing external costs on others. If not, then there is no problem.

An Alternate Strategy—Vouchers

These two basic types of subsidy—full payment of direct costs by the government and partial payment of direct costs depending on the private demand for schooling—do *not* depend for their implementation on state ownership and operation of schools. Rather than having government ownership, we could have direct government subsidies to the students, much as we have now with the GI Bill. The subsidy could be in the form of a *voucher*, which would be redeemable only for schooling. The voucher scheme could be either for uniform amounts for all students or for larger amounts for those with a presumed lower demand for schooling. In either case, we get the benefit of encouraging the creation of the public good externality from education without having public schools. What advantages do vouchers have? One is that with private, independent schools, there would be more *competition* among schools to attract students. This competition would be expected to encourage innovation and generally result in schools which are more nearly tailored to the desires of the students and their parents. There is also some reason to believe that it would result in lower costs of operation.

Vouchers are a complicated issue, and we have only introduced the concept. But the point is that determining that there is a public goods aspect to a problem does not ensure that *direct public provision* is warranted, although public *support* is usually implied.

LOOKING AHEAD

This chapter has touched on several aspects of the externality problem in economics. The existence of externalities is evidence of a market failure—the failure of an effective market (voluntary exchange mechanism) to develop. Often this failure implies that some sort of government action can be efficient. This action may take the form of taxing or subsidizing the activity in question, or of public provision. Economics can help in the analysis of these alternatives.

An issue of great interest is the distribution of income and wealth and their determinants. Here too the government plays a role. Chapter 13 will deal with this important topic.

POINTS TO REMEMBER

1. Property rights are a method of causing people to take account of the wishes of other people through offers to buy and sell.

2. Externalities occur when property rights are imperfectly defined or enforced, or difficult to exchange.

3. When externalities are too costly to remedy through market channels, government regulation may be called for.

4. The three basic approaches to pollution control are (1) establishment of emission standards without the possibility of exchange of pollution rights among firms; (2) establishment of standards while allowing exchange of pollution rights among firms; and (3) use of pollution taxes.

5. The exchange of pollution rights approach and the taxation approach can be shown to be more efficient than strict use of standards, in the absence of transactions and administrative costs.

6. The optimal amount of pollution is such that the cost of a slightly greater reduction is just offset by the benefits obtained from that reduction.

7. The optimal amount of pollution may be the same in developed and undeveloped regions of the country, because both the demand for and the cost of pollution are greater in the heavily populated areas.

8. The prisoner's dilemma game illustrates the kind of social interaction involved in such phenomena as pollution, litter, and other mutual externalities.

9. Government regulation is often the way to resolve the prisoners' dilemma, if property rights cannot be established.

10. Government regulation of externalities is often called for when the exchanges which might otherwise occur between the interested parties are too costly to transact.

11. Public goods tend to be underproduced in the absence of collective-coercive arrangements.

12. Activities which have public good attributes are not necessarily more appropriately produced by public enterprises than by private firms with subsidies to the consumers.

13. The existence of external benefits (costs) from an activity may not justify any subsidy (tax) or government action, if the externality is infra-marginal.

KEY TERMS

External diseconomy: A negative externality.

External economy: A positive externality.

Externality: An interaction between people in which a decision maker causes costs to be borne involuntarily by others (negative externality), or provides benefits to others for which she does not receive payment (positive externality).

Inframarginal externality: An externality which would *not* increase in size or amount if the activity generating it were to increase in size or amount. Inframarginal externalities do not create any efficiency problems.

Marginal externality: An externality which would increase in size or amount if the activity generating it were to increase in size or amount.

Market failure: A failure of the exchange process to act in such a way as to result in payment by decision makers to those on whom they impose costs, or payments to decision makers for benefits they provide to others.

Pollution: The creation of a negative externality (usually as a by-product of some other activity).

Prisoner's dilemma: A social interaction (or game) in which the participants could all gain by engaging in some specified cooperative behavior, but in which each player is individually rewarded for not cooperating. The typical result is that none cooperates and all are worse off than if all had cooperated. The game often describes the behavior of people when each person is imposing an externality on the others.

Private property rights: Rights of individuals or firms to decide how their property is used. These include the right to refuse others permission to use the property and the right to sell it, as well as the rights to the goods which the property produces.

Property rights: Rights of people concerning the use of property.

Public good: A collective good. A good which is characterized by being jointly consumed by many persons at once and by the great difficulty (or impossibility) of preventing non-paying people from consuming it.

Voucher: A method of subsidizing a particular activity. The voucher is a grant of money which can be used by the recipient only for the specified activity.

REVIEW QUESTIONS

1. Explain the following phenomena by means of the prisoner's dilemma model (use a matrix to specify realistic values for the costs and benefits of cooperation): litter, air pollution by cars, cutback on fuel consumption, whale overkill, use of directory assistance operator.

2. Imagine you are living in Los Angeles in the year 1960. Smog is a severe problem, and it is widely believed that most of the smog is caused by automobiles. Furthermore, suppose it is the case that, if all car owners installed a pollution control device, each car owner could obtain an annual benefit of $50. The annual cost of the device is (let us say) $20. Using the prisoner's dilemma model, explain what would happen if installation of the device were voluntary.

3. For every case of a free-rider problem (the name sometimes given to the prisoner's dilemma because each participant, by not cooperating, is attempting to get a free ride from the other participants) there is also a forced-rider problem. The forced rider is one who would not gain even if everyone cooperated in the specified way. If a coercive-collective solution to the problem at hand is undertaken, he would be worse off. Find circumstances in which there might be a forced rider in the following: air pollution caused by cars, car pooling, directory assistance on the telephone, cutback on fuel consumption.

4. Suppose firm X's marginal benefit of pollution schedule is as follows:

Emission	Marginal Benefit
1	7
2	6
3	5
4	4
5	3
6	2
7	1
8	0

(a) How many units of pollutant would firm X emit if there were no controls on its behavior? How much cost would firm X incur if it were ordered to reduce emissions to four units? Explain. (b) How many units would firm X emit if it were taxed at the rate of $3.50 per unit emitted? Explain. (c) What would be firm X's total (tax plus pollution reduction) cost of compliance in the tax case? (d) Which system of regulation would firm X prefer?

5. Suppose firm Y's marginal benefit of pollution schedule is as follows:

Emission	Marginal Benefit
1	40
2	35
3	30
4	25
5	20
6	15
7	4
8	0

(a) Suppose both firm X (in question 4) and firm Y have been ordered to reduce emissions from eight to four. How much cost would each firm incur in complying with the order? (b) What would happen if X and Y were permitted to exchange pollution rights, with the understanding that total emissions (X's plus Y's) would still be eight? What would be the saving in total pollution control costs at the new allocation? (c) How much would each firm emit if instead there were a tax of $5.50 per unit of pollutant emitted? Would either firm prefer the tax system to the control-with-exchange system? Explain. (d) Would either firm prefer the tax system to the control-without-exchange system? Explain. (e) Would your answer to (d) change if under control without exchange, firm X were allocated six units and firm Y two units of allowable pollution? Explain.

6. Refer to questions 4 and 5. Suppose the pollution control authorities have determined that firms X and Y must emit no more than ten units of pollutant Z between them. X is now emitting six units, and Y is emitting four units. The marginal benefit to X of being allowed to emit a seventh unit is $1. What is the marginal cost, if X and Y are to remain in compliance with the law?

7. Which method of controlling pollution (taxes or specification of standards) do you think would be more likely to be subject to lobbying efforts by firms for special exceptions? Why?

8. Would specification of standards be more or less likely than imposition of pollution taxes to induce firms to find ways of reducing their output of pollutants? Why?

9. Suppose you are the owner of a firm which has been emitting substantial amounts of pollution in the absence of governmental controls. It is now clear that you will be subject to pollution emission regulations. Rank the three methods discussed in the chapter (direct controls without exchange, direct controls with exchange, and pollution taxes) in order of your most preferred to least preferred option. Explain your ranking.

10. How would you go about estimating the benefits of a reduction of 0.05 part per million in the average ozone count in Los Angeles?

11. "The instability of cartels is a prisoner's dilemma." Show by means of the prisoner's dilemma matrix.

12. "No locality in the country would voluntarily increase its pollution level without getting something in return." Is it possible that some parts of the country might accept more pollution if compensated sufficiently? Examine the following two situations and see if they meet the above condition. (a) The Los Angeles Department of Water and Power, in conjunction with some electric utilities, attempts to build a coal-fired power plant in the "Four Corners" area (where Arizona, New Mexico, Utah, and Colorado join). (b) The City of Chicago buys some land in central Illinois to which it pumps sludge, the residue from sewage treatment plants.

If you decided either of these cases did not meet the condition for mutually beneficial exchange, how could the transactions be changed so as to ensure that they were mutually beneficial?

13. The Pacific Gas and Electric Company (PG&E) operates an electric generating plant at Moss Landing, California. The utility is now required to burn fuel oil instead of natural gas about half the time. As a result, an ash composed of iron oxides and sulfuric acid builds up and is occasionally blown out of the smoke stacks. The ash forms a corrosive film on cars and fishing boats in the area. The boat owners do not complain to the local Pollution Control District because PG&E reimburses them for the considerable costs (as much as $8000 per year) of keeping their boats clean. It is estimated that it would cost between $20 million and $50 million to develop a system to prevent the emission of the ash. Is it efficient for PG&E to emit the ash? Explain.

14. The *Wall Street Journal* reported that there was a struggle in Ohio regarding implementation of the EPA's sulfur-dioxide standards for electricity generation.[3] One method would be to import more low-sulfur coal from neighboring states and use about one third less high sulfur Ohio coal. This would result in fewer coal mining jobs in Ohio. An alternative would be to install scrubbers (flue-gas desulfurization equipment) on the utilities' smoke stacks. This could cost as much as $1 billion per year. If you could decide this problem, what criteria would you use? Would you consider the redistribution of wealth in your considerations? Why?

15. Several years ago many household products were packaged in aerosol cans, using chloro-fluorocarbon propellants. Some scientists discovered evidence which suggested that these aerosol propellants were causing damage to the earth's protective ozone layer. This damage would, it was believed, lead to increased incidence of skin cancer and other skin ailments as more of the sun's damaging rays were allowed to penetrate to earth. Suppose these scientists turned out to be correct. Would government requirement that products containing fluorocarbons be so labelled be expected to solve this problem? Explain.

16. In the next few years it will be possible for cable TV companies to charge their subscribers for individual events, such as a boxing match. Then a boxing match with only five hundred thousand viewers may be televised on cable TV (at a charge of, say $2), whereas the same match would not be worth televising on the commercial channels. Will this increase or decrease the number of boxing matches put on? Is it more efficient to have boxing matches televised on free (commercial) TV or on pay TV?

17. Consider the following two quotations: (a) "Television shows should be shown free of charge because once a TV show is produced, there is no cost to allowing more people to use it. Thus any positive price will inefficiently exclude some viewers." (b) "Television shows should be sold to

---

3. *Wall Street Journal,* 15 February 1979.

viewers rather than given away, because otherwise there is no adequate mechanism for deciding whether the value that consumers place on the show is greater than the cost." Is there any way of resolving the conflict between these two positions?

18. The improper use of penicillin can cause penicillin-resistant strains of bacteria to develop. Who gains and who loses from such an eventuality? Is there any inefficiency here? Explain. If so, how could it be dealt with?

19. Suppose my neighbors would be willing to pay a total of $20 per month to have me mow my lawn regularly, another $10 per month if I keep my hedges trimmed, and another $5 per month if I plant ten flowers. They would not be willing to pay anything to see more than ten flowers in my garden. Suppose I mow my lawn, trim my hedges, and plant fifteen flowers with no compensation. Am I imposing an externality on my neighbors? Is it marginal or inframarginal? Could my neighbors and I benefit from an exchange whereby they pay me to grow flowers, mow my lawn, or trim my hedges? Why or why not?

20. Lighthouses have often been used as an example of a public good, because there is no cost to allowing more ships to use it and because it is very difficult to exclude ships from using the light once it is operating. Can you think of any way of excluding people who do not pay for the use of a lighthouse?

21. "Even if all current and future users of our freeways engaged in car pooling, it would not reduce congestion permanently, because the reduced current congestion would merely encourage others (who had been deterred by the congestion) to use the roads and increase congestion again." Comment.

chapter 13

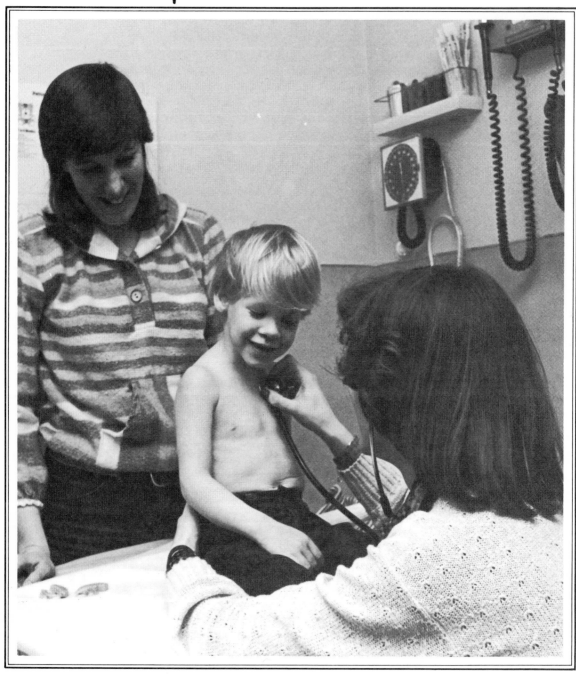

Income
Distribution

Income or wealth distribution relates to the third question in chapter 1—who gets what? It is difficult to analyze because problems of efficiency and fairness are wrapped up in the questions that arise. We shall discuss in this chapter the determinants of income and wealth, the effects of government policies on that distribution, and some economics of voluntary redistribution through charity.

INCOME VERSUS WEALTH

In an economy, distribution usually refers to *income* distribution, but another useful concept is *wealth* distribution. Wealth, as usually measured, incorporates the holdings of nonhuman assets, such as stocks and bonds and real estate. Income is usually regarded as the amount a person could consume without reducing her wealth. Suppose you are a retired person living entirely on your nonhuman wealth, which is in the form of $100,000 in bonds earning 8 percent. Your income is $8000 per year, because if you spent only $8000 per year, you would never have to touch the $100,000 principal. But you could take your $100,000 and buy an annuity from an insurance company. If your expected remaining years of life were ten years, then you could get an annuity of $14,900 per year at an interest rate of 8 percent. (To check this, refer to table 9-3, the 8 percent column, under ten years.) The table entry is 6.71. This means that the present value of $1 per year for ten years is $6.71. In other words, if you put away $6.71 at 8 percent interest, and withdrew $1 at the end of each year, you would be able to do it for exactly ten years, at which point you would have no more money left. Suppose you put away $100,000. How much could you withdraw every year for ten years? If $6.71 invested at 8 percent gives you $1 per year for ten years, then $100,000 invested at 8 percent would give you ($100,000/6.71) times $1, or $14,900 per year. If you spent $14,900 per year you would be spending more than your income, because you would be using up some of your wealth—the initial $100,000—each year in addition to the interest from the $100,000. Many older people with small incomes have a larger command over resources than their incomes suggest. Consider home ownership by elderly people. Many elderly people have a small income, but they own a home with a high value. They are actually comparatively rich, but they can't utilize the wealth unless they sell the house, which they are often unwilling to do.

HUMAN VERSUS NONHUMAN WEALTH

In the previous section we said that wealth, as usually measured, includes holdings of nonhuman assets. A true measure of a person's wealth would be the sum of the values of her human and nonhuman assets. Human assets are the skills and knowledge which the person has, and which enable her to earn wages or a salary. Conceptually, human wealth would be the present (discounted) value of the future wages and salaries a person will be able to make over her lifetime. Using this concept, we could say that a struggling medical student, while she may have a very low current income, and have a small nonhuman wealth, is very wealthy because her *human* wealth (the present value of her future earnings as a doctor) is very high.

While human wealth is interesting and important, it is difficult to measure. If we knew exactly what a person would be able to earn over her lifetime, we could calculate human wealth by merely discounting the earnings. But obviously we cannot know these earnings streams in advance with any great accuracy, thus the difficulty in measuring human wealth.

Because human wealth is difficult to measure, there are no statistical studies showing the distribution of wealth with the human component included. All the statistical studies we have include only nonhuman wealth. The distribution of human wealth is probably more nearly equal than the distribution of nonhuman wealth, so statistics on the distribution of nonhuman wealth overstate the extent to which total wealth is unevenly distributed.

MONEY INCOME VERSUS NONMONEY INCOME

When we talk about income distribution, we almost invariably refer to the amount of *money* a person earns. This practice is misleading in two ways. First, it ignores the fact that people place a positive value on their leisure time. This means that the person who works three quarters of a year and makes $9000 is not necessarily worse off than the person who works all year and makes $12,000. And that person is not necessarily worse off than the person who works fifteen hours of overtime per week and makes $18,000. In other words, a lot of the differences between incomes is voluntary. It reflects differing preferences for leisure as opposed to the goods which can be bought with money.

Second, the use of money income to measure income distribution is misleading because it doesn't take into account the control over resources which comes from political power. There may be no money millionaires in the People's Republic of China, but there are certainly political millionaires, people who live in a style and have a control over what is done, which could be obtained only with a large money income in other countries. To live as the president of the United States does would require several million dollars per year in income for a private citizen. The nonmonetary income of U.S. senators is similarly very large. The point is not that these nonmonetary incomes are unjust, but merely that the measured income which appears in statistics should be handled with care.

DETERMINANTS OF INCOME DISTRIBUTION— DEMAND AND SUPPLY

A person's wealth and income depend on the amount of human and nonhuman resources which he owns, and on the prices at which he can sell or rent out those resources. What determines the prices and amounts of resources owned?

As with all prices, the demand and supply conditions determine the prices of resources. As mentioned in chapter 3, the demand for an input, such as labor services, depends on the price that can be obtained for the output it helps to produce and on how much extra output could be produced by using one more unit of the resource in question (the marginal product of the input). Thus the price a person receives for the resources he sells or rents depends on the demand and supply for the resources; and the demand for the resources in turn depends on the demand and supply of the final products that the resources are able to help produce, as well as on the productivity of the resource in producing those final products.

The demand and supply of the resources are made up of the individual demands and supplies of the separate buyers and sellers of the resources.

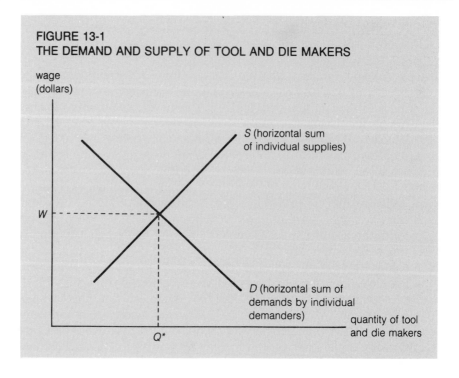

FIGURE 13-1
THE DEMAND AND SUPPLY OF TOOL AND DIE MAKERS

The amount of a resource demanded at any price is the sum of the amounts demanded by all potential buyers of the resource. The amount supplied at any price is the sum of the amounts supplied by all potential suppliers of the resource. Figure 13-1 shows the total demand and supply for a particular type of labor, in this case, tool and die makers. This approach gives some clues as to why some people make more than others. Those who make a lot are those who own resources for which the demand is great or the supply is small, or both. Demand and supply are the basic categories into which we can put the factors which determine prices.

Demand and Supply of Doctors' Services

To get a clearer picture of the process at work, examine the case of doctors. Why do doctors make so much money? The basic reason is that the value of the extra output that one more doctor would be able to produce is very high.

Demand. Figure 13-2 shows the demand for doctors' services. As usual, the demand curve is downward-sloping, indicating that at a lower price, more doctors' services would be demanded. How do we get the income of doctors out of this? First, note that given any number of doctors available, there is a total amount of doctors' services which can be provided. Say that amount is Q^*. (Q^* is obtained by simply adding the amounts of doctors' services provided by all doctors practicing. These amounts may differ,

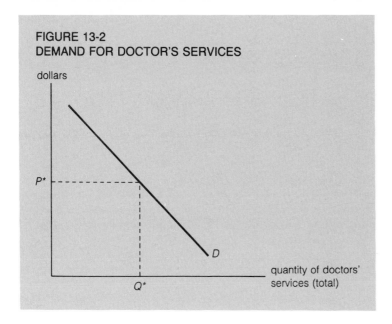

FIGURE 13-2
DEMAND FOR DOCTOR'S SERVICES

depending on the skill or time worked by various doctors.) Then the price per unit of doctors' services would be P*. How much would any given doctor make, then? To see this we merely multiply the price per unit of services times the amount of services that the doctor in question would produce.

Marginal Products. We can see several things here. First, the amount a doctor makes is equal to the value of the extra output that is produced when she works. Thus doctors' salaries are equal to the value of their marginal products. The more productive a doctor is, the more she will make. But even if a doctor were very productive in terms of the amount of services she could produce, her income would not be high if the price of doctors' services were low.

Supply. What determines the price? The location of the demand curve for doctors' services plays a role. The richer people are, the higher that demand will be. Also, the demand will be higher if the government is paying the bills than if people are paying their own bills. (Thus we can see that national health insurance would tend to increase the demand for doctors' services and the salaries of doctors.) The other factor determining the price is the amount of doctors' services supplied. In our example so far, we have merely assumed that there is a certain amount supplied. But the amount of services supplied depends on the number of doctors, and the number of doctors in turn depends on the income that a prospective doctor can expect to earn. In other words, there is a supply curve of doctors, and the higher the expected income (resulting from a higher price of doctors'

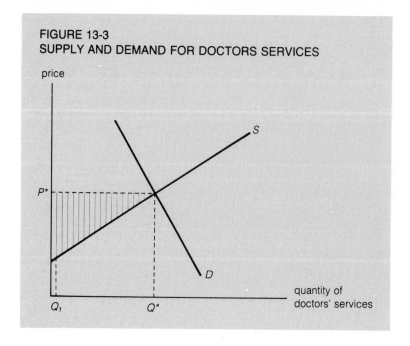

FIGURE 13-3
SUPPLY AND DEMAND FOR DOCTORS SERVICES

services), the more doctors would become available and the more doctors' services would be supplied.

This feature of the market is illustrated in figure 13-3, where both the demand and supply of doctors' services are shown. The supply curve is upward-sloping to show that in order to get more doctors' services, a higher price must be paid.

Increasing Supply Price. This is true because, in order to draw more people into medicine, the additional people must be bid away from better alternatives. The first few units of doctors' services that are produced (represented by the distance from 0 to Q_1) would not require a very high price to cause them to be supplied. This is because there are some people who are (a) very good at providing doctors' services and/or (b) not very good at other things. Feature (a) means that the price per unit of doctors' services would not have to be very high in order for doctors to make a lot, since they can produce so much. Feature (b) means that their alternatives are not very good, so their income as doctors would not have to be very high to induce them to be doctors and supply those services. These are, in other words, people who have a very low *cost* of providing doctors' services. They would have a comparative advantage in being doctors even at very low prices for doctors' services.

As we try to attract more doctors' services, we find that we have to rely on people who are (a) less productive at being doctors and/or (b) have better alternatives. The price of doctors' services would have to be higher to attract such people, because the amount they can produce is smaller (so the price per unit of services would have to be higher in order to generate any particular income); and the income they can earn elsewhere is higher, so the income they could earn in medicine would have to be higher to attract them from those alternative occupations. Thus, as we try to attract a larger quantity of doctors' services, the price per unit must be higher.

Location of Supply. What determines the *position* of the supply curve? One thing which would affect it is the natural distribution of talent. If a lot of people are born with a natural inclination toward that type of work, the supply curve will be lower and farther to the right, and the price of doctors' services will be lower. The more expensive it is, in terms of time (years of foregoing income) and outlays to become trained as a doctor, the farther to the left and the higher the supply curve will be. The better the alternatives of persons with an inclination toward medicine, the farther to the left and higher the supply curve will be, implying a higher price of doctors' services.

For example, an increase in the demand for scientists (such as biologists and chemists) will shift the supply of doctors to the left.

We might mention in passing here that a toughening of admissions and graduation standards at medical schools (caused perhaps by a tightening of licensing requirements for doctors) would also shift the supply curve to the left, resulting in a smaller amount of doctors' services and a higher price.

So the intersection of the supply and demand curves illustrates the determination of the price of doctors' services and doctors' incomes. A similar procedure could be used to analyze the income of any group. If we find a group with very high incomes, it will always be the case that either the supply curve is very far to the left or the demand curve is very far to the right. In the case of doctors, we may find that there is an artificial stimulus to demand or an artificial restriction on supply resulting in a different (higher in this case) income. Cases of very low incomes can be traced to either very low demand or very great supply, or both. There are occasionally cases (where training costs are subsidized, for example) in which the supply curve has been artificially shifted to the right, resulting in lower incomes.

Economic Rent

In discussing figure 13-3, we pointed out that some doctors would be willing to supply their services even if the price of those services were much lower than it is today. (Those doctors are located on the first portion of the supply curve.) Suppose such a doctor would be willing to supply her services even is she received as little as $5 per unit of services, whereas the current price is $20 per unit. That extra $15 per unit is unnecessary to get this person to be a doctor. Economists call that difference *economic rent* (the difference between the smallest amount a resource would be willing to accept to do what it is doing and what it actually receives). The amount of economic rent which any resource earns is thus the difference between its supply price and the price it actually receives. In figure 13-3 we show almost all suppliers of doctors' services receiving economic rent. The total amount of rent being received is the vertically lined area, obtained by adding the amount for each doctor.

Most members of every occupation receive some economic rent. Only the supplier with a supply price exactly equal to P^* did not receive some in figure 13-3. Economic rent is very similar to consumer surplus, discussed in chapter 3. They both represent a gain from being able to trade in the market (for buyers, the price is lower than the maximum that some would be willing to pay for some units, and for sellers, it is higher than the minimum for which some would be willing to sell).

DETERMINANTS OF INCOME DISTRIBUTION— QUANTITY OF RESOURCES OWNED

As we mentioned before, a person's income depends both on the price he can obtain by selling or renting out his resources and on the quantity of resources he owns. That quantity depends on several factors.

Past Earnings. In part, what people own today depends on what they could sell their resources for in the past. Owners of empty oil wells may be rich today if they were able to obtain a good price in the past for selling the oil.

Saving. Two persons who earn the same income over a certain period may have different wealth and income in the future if they save different amounts. The sad truth is that, in the absence of unforeseen events, it is not possible to increase one's wealth without saving. Some differences in current income reflect past differences in saving.

It may be worthwhile to elaborate on this point a bit. Suppose you have $100,000 which you have invested in tax-exempt municipal bonds. If the coupon rate is 6 percent your income from the bonds is $6000. If you save that income (reinvest it) your wealth will grow by $6000, while if you spend all of it your wealth will be unchanged. Saving makes your wealth grow. The only other way your wealth can grow is if the market value of the assets you own increases because of unforeseen changes in supply and demand conditions.

Work-Leisure Choices. As mentioned before, decisions about how much to work can affect the distribution of income expressed in money terms, as well as cause the distribution of money income to give a misleading picture.

Inheritance. The inheritance of both human and nonhuman assets plays an important role in determining the distribution of income and wealth. The emphasis is usually on the inheritance of nonhuman wealth, but the inheritance of talents and capabilities and the benefits provided by one's environment are of tremendous importance also. We shall have more to say about this shortly.

SOME GENERAL THOUGHTS ABOUT INCOME DISTRIBUTION

Who, then, gets what under a voluntary exchange system? Very broadly, those persons who own commodities which consumers happen to place a high value on will do well. The assets which people control can be of either the human or nonhuman variety.

Consider human assets—mental and physical abilities from which are derived labor services. What determines how rich a person will be from his human assets? Certainly absolute productivity counts. A fast typist will earn more than a slow typist, other things equal. But a person may be very productive at pursuits which "don't pay well"—a nice way of saying that consumers don't place a high value on the commodity produced. The value of the commodity a person produces depends on consumers' tastes, on how plentiful it is, and on how plentiful and close its substitutes are. A person may be tremendously knowledgeable about ancient Roman poetry. But if few people are willing to pay for his capability, he will not get rich from selling his knowledge. On the other hand, a singer may be barely able to carry a tune; but if the sound she and her group put out catches the public's ear, she can be very rich indeed. Jimmy Connors is very rich because he happens to be able to do things with a tennis racquet which very few others can do as well. Since there is a large demand, relative to the number of people with his skills, he commands a high price. If there were five thousand people on the tennis courts with the skills of Conners, he (and they) would each command a much smaller income than he does now.

The same kind of considerations apply to the remunerations from nonhuman commodities. You may own a beautiful factory, but if it specializes in producing tire tubes for automobile tires, it won't produce much income. The income you recieve from your wheat farm depends in part on the condition of the Russian harvest.

Apparently the distribution of talent is not very equal. Not only do people appear to have innate aptitudes for different things, but some people seem to have an aptitude for many things, while others appear to have no aptitude for anything. But as mentioned in chapter 4, everyone has a *comparative* advantage in *something*. The trouble is that this may be simply the best of all the bad alternatives available. One person's comparative advantage may be in a $3000 per year "job," while another's may be in a $100,000, per year "position."

While aptitudes certainly play a role in determining the amount for which a person can sell his skills, other factors obtrude. A person with great inherent ability but little schooling may not develop those aptitudes and will, as a result, be able to command less in the marketplace. The degree to which a person is conditioned to achieve has an effect on earnings. Two persons with equal native ability and schooling may earn drastically different amounts, depending on the amount of effort they put out.

Finally, a very important determinant of income distribution is luck. Some people just seem to be in the right place when rewards are handed out. The existence of luck is a manifestation of the fact that we cannot see the future clearly—that there is uncertainty. Since that is the case, there will be unexpected occurrences in the economic world. There will be times when owning a resource will prove to be a wise move—as today, when owners of petroleum resources are wealthier than they were five years ago. At other times, events show that certain goods were not valuable —as in recent years when the demand for large, gas-guzzling cars fell, and those who specialized in producing them were made poorer.

EFFICIENCY AND INCOME DISTRIBUTION

What does efficiency have to do with income distribution? We are so accustomed to talking about the *fairness* aspect of the problem—"it's fair for doctors to have high incomes because they go to school so long" or "it's not fair for the Beatles to be millionaires because they don't know as much music as a member of the London Symphony"—that we often overlook the role which resource prices, and therefore income distribution, play in directing resources to the uses which have the greatest value to consumers. When a person is able to earn an inordinately high price for his resources (high income), that is a signal that consumers have a large demand for the good produced by those resources, and that close substitutes are not in great supply. The high price serves two purposes. It encourages consumers to economize on their use of the good involved, and it encourages others to get themselves into a position to produce the good. If the price of the resource is kept low, then both the consumers and other potential producers are given a distorted signal: that the resource in question is not particularly scarce or valuable; it need not be conserved, nor should anyone be induced to produce more. If "excess" income is merely taxed away, then the owners do not have as large an incentive to find those willing to offer the highest price for the resource; and again the incentive for new entrants to appear is dulled. Since resources are not preordained as to their uses and do respond in part to the relative rewards in various uses, this efficiency aspect of income distribution is significant.

But what about the luck aspect? When luck plays a large role in the determination of a person's rewards, is there anything other than a fairness consideration? One important consideration is the extent to which a person can choose what risks to bear. A private property exchange economy permits some selectivity in risk bearing. If one wishes to bear some of the risk of a bad wheat harvest in the Soviet Union, she can do so by investing in the commodities market. Likewise one can, for the most part, avoid such risks by staying out of commodities. By way of contrast, a socialist organization involves *less* selectivity in risk bearing. The government guarantee of loans to Chrysler in effect means that all taxpayers are sharing the risk of future changes in the profitability of Chrysler. When steel companies or railroads are nationalized (as in the case of Conrail in the Northeast) the risk of changes in the demand and supply conditions in those industries is spread over all taxpayers, rather than borne by a relatively small group who voluntarily choose to be owners.

Another feature of the "luck" aspect is that it is often impossible to disentangle "luck," "foresight," and "good management." We know that there *is* luck, but we don't always know when a return (high or low) to a resource owner is due to luck and when it is due to one or both of the other two. Thus, attempts to mitigate by taxes the effects of unexpected changes in supply and demand run the risk of dulling the incentives which the price system provides to produce in accordance with consumers' wishes.

HOW IS MONEY INCOME DISTRIBUTED IN THE UNITED STATES?

We have talked a good deal about the factors which determine the distribution of money income.[1] But what *is* the distribution? Look at the percentage income shares (before taxes) earned by the various segments of the society. Table 13-1 lists those shares for selected years between 1947 and 1973. To obtain these numbers, families are divided into fifths, or *quintiles*. For 1973 the first entry shows that the poorest 20 percent of families earned 5.5 percent of all income earned by families, while the richest 20 percent earned 41.1 percent of all income earned by all families (before taxes).

An interesting feature in table 13-1 is that the relative shares of the various quintiles have remained very stable over the period considered, with only a very slight upward trend for the lowest four quintiles and a slight drop for the highest.

Another perspective can be obtained by examining table 13-2, which shows the percentage distribution of families by money income level for the same years. For 1973 the table shows that 5.9 percent of the families had incomes of less than $3000, while 9.3 percent had incomes above $25,000. The table gives the entries in terms of the prices prevailing at the time. It shows that, over the period shown, nominal incomes (measured in terms of current dollars) rose dramatically. Median income approximately quadrupled, from $3048 to $12,073. Over the same period, of

---

1. This section draws heavily on the data presented by Edgar K. Browning, *Redistribution and the Welfare System* (Washington, D.C.: American Enterprise Institute, 1975).

TABLE 13-1
PERCENTAGE INCOME SHARES FOR FAMILIES BEFORE
DIRECT TAXES FOE SELECTED YEARS

| Income Group | Percentage Share | | | |
	1973	1966	1960	1947
Lowest quintile	5.5	5.6	4.8	5.1
Second quintile	11.9	12.4	12.2	11.8
Third quintile	17.5	17.8	17.8	16.7
Fourth quintile	24.0	23.8	24.0	23.2
Highest quintile	41.0	40.5	41.3	43.3

Source: U.S. Bureau of the Census. Cited in E. K. Browning, *Redistribution and the Welfare System* (Washington, D. C. American Enterprise Institute, 1975), p.9.

TABLE 13-2
PERCENTAGE DISTRIBUTION OF FAMILIES BY MONEY INCOME LEVEL
FOR SELECTED YEARS

| Income Class | Percentage of All Families Falling in the Class Shown | | | |
	1973	1966	1960	1947
Less than $3000	5.9	14.3	21.6	48.9
$3000 – $4999	13.2	22.3	33.2	39.3
$5000 – $9999	19.7	33.7	30.9	9.0
$10,000 – $14,999	25.6	20.4	10.6	
$15,000 – $20,000	26.2	7.5	2.8	2.8
More than $25,000	9.3	1.7	.9	
Median income (dollars)	12,073	7,447	5,631	3,048
Median income (constant 1973 dollars)	12,073	10,269	8,436	6,032

Source: U.S. Bureau of the Census. Cited in E. K. Browning, *Redistribution and the Welfare System* (American Enterprise Institute, 1975), p. 8.

course, prices rose. In fact, they approximately doubled. If the numbers for the previous years are expressed in terms of 1973 dollars (if, for example, the 1947 median family income of $3048 were expressed as the number of dollars one would have to have in 1973 in order to buy what $3048 could buy in 1947), we can see that prices approximately doubled over the period, implying that median income in real terms (in other words, in terms of the amounts of goods that one could buy if one had the median income) approximately doubled over the period. The trend suggested is that, on the average, families at all levels of income had their incomes doubled in real terms over the period shown. The incomes shown in table 13-2 include social security income, unemployment insurance benefits, and cash payments of public assistance.

While table 13-2 shows a dramatic increase in the real level of median income, there were still about 22 million people in 1973 who lived in families with incomes below the federally established poverty line ($4540 per year for a family of four in 1973). In view of the spectacular increase in social welfare expenditures, especially in the last decade, these numbers are rather disturbing. With all that spending, one would expect fewer poor people.

However, a study by Edgar K. Browning of the University of Virginia points out that the statistics we have cited do not count transfers of income *in kind* (that is, gifts which lower the price to the purchaser of goods, such as food stamps, medicaid, and public housing). If in-kind transfers are counted, then the per capita income of the lowest quartile of the population was $1812 per year, yielding $7248 income per year for a family of four in 1973. Of course, some of those in the lowest quartile are not receiving as many government benefits as others; this refers to the *average* of all those in the lowest quartile, so not all families of four in the poorest quartile had an income of $7248. But inclusion of these transfers would tend to make the income distribution figures shown in tables 13-1 and 13-2 appear more equal.

Other evidence that suggests the same conclusion is provided in a 1977 study by the congressional Budget Office. When in-kind transfers were included, the study estimated that, in 1976, only 6.4 percent of the population had incomes below the officially established poverty level. Other studies have estimated the proportion to be as low as 3 percent. This contrasts with the Census Bureau's estimate of 12.3 percent, which was obtained by excluding in-kind transfers.[2]

THE NEGATIVE INCOME TAX

While the available evidence indicates that the war on poverty has, for the most part, been won, since only about 5 percent of the population has an income below the poverty level (when in-kind benefits are counted), there are severe problems with the current system. First there are heavy administrative costs in many of the programs. Since the programs are designed to help only those with certain disabilities or others who are deemed unable to earn income, considerable administrative time must be devoted to ensuring that only those who are supposed to get the benefits do so. Furthermore, this effort necessarily involves some intrusion into the privacy of those who receive benefits. When an applicant is forced to show that he or she is in a sufficiently bad situation to justify receiving the benefits, he or she inevitably suffers a loss of dignity. Secondly, there is a rather severe penalty, under the current system, for earning income while receiving welfare benefits. Since the benefits one can receive are almost always

2. See Martin Anderson, *Welfare—The Political Economy of Welfare Reform in the United States* (Palo Alto, CA: Hoover Institution/Stanford University, 1978), pp. 17–24.

related to the income one earns, when a recipient earns extra income, his benefits fall. One scholar has estimated that in the range from zero to $10,000 income, the typical beneficiary loses approximately 70¢ to 80¢ in benefits for every extra dollar earned. Thus recipients of welfare are currently paying a very high marginal tax rate on earned income. This provides a powerful disincentive to work.

In 1962, Milton Friedman proposed an alternative to all existing welfare programs and other attempts to help poor people (such as minimum wage laws and controls on the prices of key commodities).[3] Friedman called his plan a *negative income tax*. Its main distinctive features would be reduced administrative cost (including reduced intrusion on people's private lives), smaller penalties for earning income, and reduced intervention in markets.

The present personal income tax law specifies that a person or a family must pay some percentage of its *taxable income* to the federal government each year. Taxable income is defined as earnings minus personal exemptions and minus deductible expenses such as mortgage interest and medical expenditures. In 1979 the personal exemption was $1000 per person, so for a family of four the personal exemptions would amount to $4000. The standard deduction for a married couple, filing a joint return, was $3400. So for a family of four taking the standard deduction, its taxable income would be its earnings minus $7400. (The $7400 is the sum of the personal exemptions and the $3400 standard deduction.) If this family earned $10,000, it would be taxed on only $2600 (its earnings minus $7400); if it earned $9000 its taxable income would be $1600; and if it earned $7400 its taxable income would be zero—it would pay no tax at all. If the family earned $5000 its taxable income would still be zero. Under present tax laws negative values of taxable income are not allowed.[4] The lowest amount of taxable income allowed is zero. Thus under present law, if a family earns zero or $7400, or anything in between, its taxable income is zero.

Friedman's proposal is simply to allow negative values of taxable income and to apply a special tax rate to negative taxable incomes. If taxable income is defined as earnings minus $7400, and if a family earned zero during the year, its taxable income would be −$7400. If the tax rate applied to negative taxable incomes were 60 percent (Friedman actually proposed 50 percent), the family's tax would be 0.6 (−$7400), or −$4400. A negative tax of $4400 means that instead of the family sending a check to the Internal Revenue Service (IRS), the IRS would send a check for $4400 to the family. If the family earned $2000, its taxable income would be $2000 minus $7400, or −$5400. Its tax would be 0.6 (−$5400), or −$3240. The IRS would send a check to the family for $3240, and the

---

3. Milton Friedman, *Capitalism and Freedom* (Chicago: University of Chicago Press, 1962), chap. 12.
4. This discussion ignores the "earned income credit," which allows for a very modest (maximum $500) credit to those who earn between zero and $10,000.

TABLE 13-3
NEGATIVE TAXABLE INCOME

Earnings	Taxable Income (earnings − $7400)	Tax (.6 × taxable income)	Disposable Income (earnings + negative tax)
$ 0	$ − 7400	$ − 4440	$4440
1000	− 6400	− 3840	4840
2000	− 5400	− 3240	5240
3000	− 4400	− 2640	5640
4000	− 3400	− 2040	6040
5000	− 2400	− 1440	6440
6000	− 1400	− 840	6840
7000	− 400	− 240	7240
7400	− 0	0	7400

family would have this plus the $2000 it earned, to spend. Its spendable (or disposable) income would be $5420.

Table 13-3 shows a family's taxable income, its tax, and its disposable income for earnings between zero and $7400. Note that for every dollar increase in earnings the check from the IRS decreases by 60¢. In effect the family gets to keep 40¢ of each additional dollar earned, up to $7400. When the family earns $7400 it neither pays the IRS nor receives a check from the IRS. The family would pay positive tax on all earnings above $7400, just as it now does.

While the negative income tax would impose a rather severe penalty for working (a 60 percent marginal tax rate in our example), that penalty is still milder than the 70 to 80 percent marginal tax recipients pay under the current system. Furthermore, since the level of benefits would be based strictly on income level, and not on marital status or other lifestyle characteristics, there would be less intrusion on people's private lives and lower costs of administration. Of course, each family would have to be convinced that after the negative tax and its earnings were spent there would be absolutely no more tax money coming in. Poor families can make their own decisions once they know for sure what their spendable income will be. Those who make bad decisions will have to rely on voluntary charity.

The negative income tax plan would ensure that each family has a minimally acceptable amount of purchasing power with which to participate in the market process. If it were implemented in the place of all existing welfare and income maintenance schemes, we never again would have to prevent markets from working on the grounds that the poor cannot participate in the market processes. Of course, Milton Friedman does not advocate adding the negative income tax to the welter of existing welfare and income maintenance programs. He proposes the negative income tax *as a substitute* for *all* existing schemes. In 1970, President Nixon proposed a negative income tax plan to Congress. He called it a Family Assistance

Plan (FAP). Friedman opposed FAP because Nixon proposed it in *addition* to existing programs.

The main reason Friedman and many other advocates of limited government favor the negative income tax is that there does seem to be a political consensus in the United States that it is inappropriate to make unfortunate people depend entirely on voluntary charity. Since it seems inevitable that there will be some form of coerced charity in the United States, advocates of limited government want that coerced charity to take a form that interferes with individual liberties in the least undesirable way possible. They offer the negative income tax as a way to accomplish that goal.

A particularly striking example of the side effects of trying to help unfortunate people by directly interfering in a market was afforded by the gasoline crisis of early 1974. At the beginning of 1974, people had to wait in long lines (in Baltimore up to ten hours) to purchase gasoline because government bureaucrats forced the price of gasoline below the level that would make the quantity of gasoline wanted equal the (sharply reduced) amount available. The excuse given was that the poor could not afford to pay the market clearing price (which was estimated to be 60¢ per gallon of regular). Senator Henry Jackson accused the oil companies of making "obscene" profits. But the poor as well as the nonpoor ended up having to pay a truly obscene price for gasoline. The costs of the many hours wasted standing in line, the costs of the uncertainty about when gasoline could be purchased, and the costs of frustration and anger added to the money cost at the pump came to a truly astronomical price per gallon of gasoline.

TAXING INHERITANCE

Many persons who are willing to go along with the outcome of the market process of voluntary exchange in many respects draw the line at inheritance. Many questions involved in the issue of whether or how much inherited wealth should be allowed are issues of equity or fairness and, as such, are not particularly amenable to economic analysis. But there are some issues on which economic analysis can shed some light. The first is the cost of controlling intergenerational transfers of wealth. The solution is not as simple as passing a law.

First, the donor will tend to give her wealth away *before* death, which gives rise to gift taxes, and the cost of enforcing these is not negligible. Second, the effect of the inheritance tax rate on the amount of inheritance tax collected must be considered. One response to an inheritance tax might be for the donor to put large amounts of her wealth in the form of *annuities*, payable as long as she lives. Under this approach, the rich donor has a very small estate when she dies, because so much wealth has been converted to annuities. The result may be such a large reduction in taxable inheritance that inheritance tax receipts fall.

This is basically a question of the elasticity of inheritance with respect to tax rate. If a 10 percent increase in the tax rate (from 20 to 22 percent, say) causes a 20 percent reduction in the amount of taxable inheritance, then tax receipts from inheritance tax will fall. If we define the tax rate elasticity of inheritance as the percentage change in inheritance divided by the percentage change in the tax rate (percent change in inheritance/ percent change in the tax rate), then tax receipts (the tax rate times the amount of inheritance) are maximized when the elasticity is one. Those who feel no warmth for inheritance may nevertheless argue in favor of a less-than-confiscatory tax, because they wish to milk the inheritors for as much tax as possible.

Another feature of the inheritance question is related to the general point on incentives to perform the tasks consumers want performed. Donors choose to leave wealth to inheritors because they find that to be preferable to buying more consumer goods in order to dispose of their wealth. A law which taxes or confiscates inheritance in effect says that if you get rich, you are not going to be able to get as much utility out of wealth as you otherwise could. What this means is that there will be some reduced incentive to create wealth. How important is this factor? We do not know.

ECONOMICS OF VOLUNTARY REDISTRIBUTION— CHARITY

What is charity? One definition is the giving away of wealth. It is tempting to refer to giving without receiving anything in return, but this is a slippery idea. When a benefactor gives a million dollars to a college and has a building named for her, is she really getting nothing in return for her gift? The only pure charity is a case in which the donation is anonymous. The rest have aspects of an ordinary exchange.

Is Pure Charity Irrational?

Of course not. *Rationality* merely means that one makes consistent choices. If a person likes to give away wealth (or gifts in kind), there is nothing in economics to say that this is silly or irrational. Under what circumstances would pure charity (or mixed charity and exchange) occur? It would occur if the utility from the charitable act exceeds the utility the donor would get from the best alternative use of the resource (whether money or services). If the benefit I get from *your* having one more dollar is greater than the benefit I get from *my* having it, then I will give you the dollar (if it doesn't cost me anything to find you). It's hard to argue with this statement. There is no way in which it could be shown to be false. It is true *by definition*. We are merely saying that one of the goods people consume is the knowledge that they give resources to others.

There are some meaningful propositions which can be developed from it, however. First, assume that the benefit I get from giving you something increases as the ratio of my wealth to your wealth increases. The richer I am, relative to you, the more benefit I get from giving goods to you, so the more likely I am to give to you. On the societal level, we should expect charity to be more prevalent among those in the higher income categories, because their income is larger relative to that of potential recipients. Another implication is that since charitable giving is a good, it obeys the First Law of Demand: the lower the price, the more a person will consume; that is, the lower the cost to the giver of giving charity, the more charity will be given. So having a tax deduction for charitable contributions increases charity. A related implication is that the greater the benefit received by the giver, the more that will be given. This means that if there were a law requiring all charity to be anonymous, the amount would be reduced; some potential donors would find the transaction less beneficial and engage in less of it. These are all applications of the First Law of Demand to the concept of charity.

Who Gains What from a Gift?

Most of the time charity does not involve a simple transfer of purchasing power. The reason is apparently that the giver gets more benefit if he can direct the use of the resources. An implication of this is that if there were a law requiring that all gifts be in the form that the *recipient* wanted, less would be given.

The result of having the donor specify the way in which the gift can be used is that the value of the gift to the recipient is less than it would be if he could choose its form. As an example, consider the food stamp program, which enables low income persons to buy food more cheaply (sometimes free of charge). Suppose that a family is given $200 worth of food stamps for a month and that they otherwise would have spent $120 per month for food. They are getting a gift worth $200, but if they had a choice, they would prefer $200 in cash, because then they could purchase a different consumption pattern if they chose. In fact, they might be indifferent between $200 worth of food stamps and $170 in cash.

The $200 expenditure on food by taxpayers frees $120 of the recipient's money (which would have been spent on food) to be spent in other consumer markets. The other $80 worth of food is a gift in kind, which is worth only $50 to the consumer. (We know it is only worth $50 because the whole $200 bundle of food, which is equivalent to $120 in cash and $80 in food, is worth only $170. So the in-kind part must be worth only $50.) The gift of food stamps is thus inefficient from the point of view of the recipient, but the donors (taxpayers) may get more benefit from giving $200 worth of food stamps than from giving $170 in cash.

There is another wrinkle to this problem. It costs more to administer a food stamp program than a cash transfer program. Thus we might have to collect $250 in taxes to give a family $200 worth of food stamps (worth

$170 to the family), while it might require only $180 of taxes to give a transfer of $170. If the differential in administrative costs is high enough, the taxpayers might choose to go to direct payments, even though they would prefer to guide the expenditures.

The Charity Business

Much of the charity in this country is handled through large organizations, such as the Red Cross, the Cancer Society, and the United Fund. Such organizations perform a service for both the recipients and the donors. They bring to the attention of donors the existence of worthy recipients and coordinate the funneling of resources to such recipients. They are in fact performing a middleman's function by arranging for mutually beneficial exchanges, one-sided though they may be.

Charitable organizations have administrative expenses which result in the spread between what donors give and recipients receive. There has been some controversy about the size of this spread; some charities have an administrative cost of up to 50 percent of the amount donated. Some localities now require charity solicitors to state what their cut is as part of their pitch. Should we be concerned with the size of the cut? Certainly if there were a way to provide exactly the same product at a lower cost, we would all favor it. The question, though, is whether we should always prefer an organization with a lower cut to one with a higher cut. To answer this we need to know how the administrative costs arise. For our purposes, there are two important areas of these costs. The first is the cost of deciding who should receive the gifts. This may seem very easy, but in fact it is costly to arrange. The giver probably would not want a charitable organization to minimize its distribution costs. The way to do that presumably would be to give out the money at random or by some other inappropriate scheme. Givers would be more willing to give if the organization were more careful in its dispensing. But since that care is expensive, there is a point beyond which that extra care is not worth the extra "cut." So there is an *optimal* distribution expense, but it would not in general be the *minimum*.

The other main administrative cost is the cost of *attracting* donors. This is analogous to advertising in other areas. Advertising is a sign of the lack of information (on the part of potential donors) on the opportunities available. A donor who knows all about the operation may still prefer to have the agency advertise if it results in a net increase in the amount given to the final recipients.

Why are most (all?) charitable organizations nonprofit firms? One reason is tax treatment. Gifts to profit-seeking enterprises are not deductible. This makes profit-seeking enterprises less attractive, because for any given cost, they will be able to provide less benefit per dollar given. It may also be that donors don't trust profit-seeking firms to operate in their interests. If this is true, then we should explain why this is not also the case for other types of industries.

Efficiency in Giving

Occasionally, when we encounter a situation which seems to require some charitable action, we have the problem of choosing the most appropriate method for achieving the goal. A current example is the case of the starving millions of the world. Clearly charity could be of some help in this area. But what is the most appropriate method? One approach is based on the fact that many pounds of grain are required to produce one pound of beef. If we could reduce our consumption of beef, we could have grain available to send abroad. Exactly what the mechanism for collecting and sending the grain should be is not clear. One way would be for all who wish to, to consciously cut back on their consumption of beef by one pound per week (say), and donate the money saved to an organization which would buy the grain and send it abroad.

What are the economic implications of the plan? If less beef is consumed, less grain will be used to feed cattle. However, there would probably be a net *increase* in the demand for grain because each dollar saved by consuming less beef can buy one dollar's worth of grain, while much less than one dollar's worth of grain is embodied in one dollar's worth of beef. (Meat producers have costs to pay other than feed costs.) On the other hand, not all of each dollar contributed will be spent on grain. The organization that administers the program will have to use some of the donations to pay its costs. It is hard to say what the net effect on demand will be. If there is no change in the total demand for grain, there will still be a lowering of beef prices due to the reduced demand for beef. Higher-cost beef producers will leave the industry. This will increase beef consumption by those not participating in the program.

However these conflicting forces work out, the question is, is this an efficient (low-cost) way to give? The answer is probably no. There are lower-cost (and less painful) ways to give grain to needy countries. Instead of cutting back only on beef consumption, the donors could simply donate an amount of money equal to the price of one pound of beef per week and consume whatever amount of beef they want. Thus they would reduce their consumption of *all* goods somewhat. What would be the effect on prices?

We can see what would happen by examining figure 13-4. Figure 13-4(a) shows the demand and supply of beef. The contribution of an amount of money equal to the price of one pound of beef would shift the demand for beef to the left only slightly, because the reduced amount of money available means that there will be a slight decrease in the consumption of *all normal* goods, at any price.

This decrease in the demand for beef would also cause a slight decrease in the demand for grain (from D to D'). More than offsetting this would be the relatively large increase in demand for grain due to the actions of the charitable organization (from D' to D''). The higher price of grain would cause the supply of beef to shift to the left [from S to S' in (a)]. The result would be a reduction in beef consumption and a higher price of beef. The effect of the net increase in the demand for grain would be a higher price and a larger amount produced.

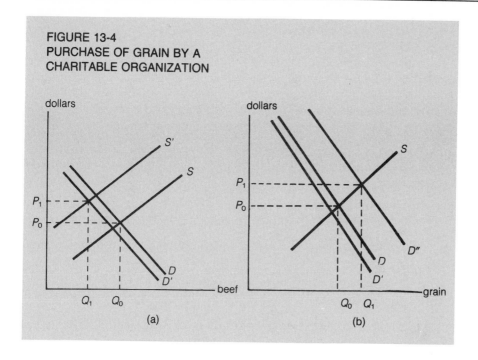

FIGURE 13-4
PURCHASE OF GRAIN BY A
CHARITABLE ORGANIZATION

One effect of the second approach, in contrast to the first, is that beef and grain prices rise, impinging on the consumption plans of other consumers. Whether the donors would choose the second plan or the first would depend in part on whether they are made worse off to a greater degree by concentrating their donation in beef or by knowing that other consumers are paying higher prices.

CONCLUSION

This chapter has examined the distribution of wealth from two different angles. First, we sketched the distribution which emerges from the operation of a private property exchange system, and how that distribution is related to the basic way in which such a system answers the fundamental economic questions of what, how, and for whom. The second half discussed some economic questions involved in the voluntary redistribution of wealth through charity. It is fitting to end the book with a discussion of the economics of charity, for it emphasizes that economics can be used to help us to understand things that are usually thought not to be economic. Actually, economics is an inquiry into the implications of choices that people make. All choices are economic, and all action based on those choices can be usefully analyzed using the tools of economics. We hope that at this stage you can see why that is true.

POINTS TO REMEMBER

1. Income is somewhat misleading as an indicator of the control over resources because it neglects the concepts of human and nonhuman wealth and does not take account of nonmoney income in the form of leisure and amenities or of nonmoney income in the form of (political) power.

2. A person's income and wealth are determined by the amount of resources a person owns and by the prices for which the services from those resources sell.

3. The amount of resources a person owns depends on inheritance (human and nonhuman) and on past income and saving patterns.

4. The prices of resources depend on the demand and supply for those resources.

5. Most persons earn some economic rent in the amount which they are paid.

6. Luck (a manifestation of uncertainty) is an important determinant of income, but it is hard to distinguish from foresight and good management.

7. Inequalities of income can play a role in causing the economy to function more efficiently.

8. Pure charity is not irrational, and much of what goes by the name of charity has aspects of ordinary exchange in it.

9. The recipient of a gift would generally prefer to have a gift in money rather than in kind, because money is easier to convert into what the recipient wants.

10. The cut which charitable organizations take out of the gifts they collect before arriving at the amount distributed is analogous to the middleman's cut and is not necessarily waste.

KEY TERMS

Economic rent: The difference between the minimum amount a resource would be willing to accept in return for doing what it is doing and the amount it actually receives. The difference between a resource's remuneration and its supply price (the latter subtracted from the former).

Income: The amount which could be consumed without reducing wealth. The flow of goods and services which wealth provides.

Marginal product: The amount of extra output produced when one more unit of an input is used, holding other inputs constant.

Negative Income Tax: A form of welfare program in which families which earn less than a designated amount of income receive as a cash payment a certain percentage of the difference between what they earn and the designated amount.

Saving: That portion of income which is not consumed. Saving gives rise to investment, which is the creation of additional wealth or capital.

Value of marginal product: The price of the output in question multiplied by the marginal product of the input in question.

Wealth: A person's (or group's) holdings of assets (both human and non-human). Human wealth is the skills and earning power embodied in people. Nonhuman wealth includes land, buildings, machinery, and financial assets.

REVIEW QUESTIONS

1. Al and Billie are equally skilled at their jobs of training lions for the circus, but Billie is also a fine computer programmer, while Al cannot do anything else. Who has the higher cost of being a lion-tamer? Who has the higher supply price of being a lion-tamer? Will Billie earn more as a lion-tamer? Who will obtain more economic rent?

2. Janet and Tom are accountants. Tom struggled and strained to pass his courses and finally, after several years of trying, obtained his Certified Public Accountant's (CPA) certificate. Janet breezed through and passed the CPA exams on the first try. Since Tom had to work harder, does he get paid more for being a CPA? Suppose Janet loves her work, while Tom hates it. Will Tom be able to charge more because the disutility of the work is so great?

3. Is it fair for a garbage collector to receive higher pay than a school teacher? What do you mean by fair?

4. Suppose your job is to establish the proper salary for streetsweepers in San Francisco. How would you know whether you had come up with the correct amount? Suppose you set as your criterion that you should adjust the salary until the number of people who wanted the job equalled the number of jobs available (quantity supplied equals the quantity demanded). Does McDonald's use that criterion in setting salaries for store managers? Does GM use it to set the compensation of its president? One problem that arises is that of qualifications of the applicants. There may be thousands of people who want to be president of GM (at least for a while) at the salary offered, but GM may not consider them qualified. The same could be said of streetsweepers. For any wage rate, the number of "qualified" persons applying can be reduced by raising the qualifications required for the job. How would you decide the proper qualifications of a streetsweeper? Might you expect any difference in the process by which this is accomplished in the private versus public sector? Are you more likely to be rewarded for making a correct personnel decision (or punished for making an incorrect one) in a for profit private firm or in a nonprofit firm or government agency?

5. Imagine a society with five persons. Their incomes (per year) are as follows in three different years, in constant year 3 dollars.

Person	Year 1	Year 2	Year 3
1	$ 2,300	$ 3,000	$ 4,500
2	4,500	6,100	9,000
3	6,400	8,600	12,750
4	9,400	12,500	18,750
5	15,000	20,000	30,000

In year 1 what percent of income is accounted for by the lowest quintile of the population? The second? The third? The fourth? The highest? What are the percentages for years 2 and 3? What is the median income in year 1? Year 2? Year 3? By what percentage did each person's income increase between years 1 and 2? Between years 2 and 3? Between years 1 and 3?

This would appear to be roughly what the U.S. data (expressed in constant, 1973 dollars) are like, with each person representing the average income of his quintile (ignoring transfers of income in kind).

6. Suppose I am given certificates entitling me to $100 worth of the foods of my choice, as long as I spend it this month. (I usually spend $150 per month on food.) Would I prefer to have this gift or a gift of $100 cash? Would your answer be different if I normally spent only $75 per month on food?

7. Suppose a voucher program is instituted to support education. Consider a person who was previously sending a child to a private school and paid the full cost with no subsidy. If the voucher is for $800, would you expect this person to spend $800 more per year on her child's schooling?

8. Suppose you are going to subsidize a given activity. For any given outlay that you make, will the total amount of the activity be greater if you give a lump sum subsidy which you designate must be used on the activity or if you offer a payment to the consumer for every unit he buys? Which of the two categories would the educational voucher mentioned above fall into? Into which would a food stamp program whereby a consumer is permitted to use $100 of stamps for every $20 he pays?

9. Moslem law requires that all charity be anonymous. Nevertheless, the amount given is larger as a fraction of income than in Christian countries. Does this mean that a change in Christian precepts to require that all gifts be anonymous would increase giving in Christian countries? If not, what *does* it mean?

10. In this chapter we referred to the fact that charitable organizations, such as the United Way and the Cancer Society, are performing a middle-man's function. In chapters 2 and 3 we argued that with ordinary exchange, the middleman's cut tends to be no larger than the cost of performing the function. Can we make a similar statement about the cut of charitable organizations? Why might we not be able to do so?

11. Using table 13-1 we can construct a graphical representation of the degree of inequality of money income. On the horizontal axis, mark off 0, 20, 40, 60, 80, and 100 percent from left to right. Label the axis "cumulative percentage of aggregate families ranked from poor to rich." Do likewise on the vertical axis, moving from top to bottom. Label this axis "cumulative percentage of money income." For the year 1973, the lowest 20 percent (quintile) of the population received 5.5 percent of the income (before taxes). Go to the right to 20 percent on the horizontal axis and up to 5.5 percent on the vertical axis, and place a dot that is 20 percent to the right of zero and 5.5 percent above zero. The second quintile received 11.9 percent of the income, so the two lowest quintiles received a total of 5.5 + 11.9 = 17.4 percent of the income. Accordingly, find the point which is 40 percent to the right of zero and 17.4 percent above zero and place a dot there. Continue the procedure for the third, fourth, and highest quintiles. Then connect the dots starting at the origin. Now construct similar curves for 1966, 1960, and 1947. These curves are called *Lorenz* curves. What would the Lorenz curve be if income were completely equally distributed?

12. Suppose 5000 new physicians are graduating from medical school. Will they be the 5000 people of that age group who are absolutely the best at learning how to be doctors? Explain. Should they be? Why or why not?

13. In figure 4-1, we stated that the lined area under the supply price line was the economic cost of obtaining 100,000 paratroopers through a voluntary scheme. What is that amount of money represented by that area? The budgetary cost was $800 million. What is the difference between the budgetary cost and the economic cost and what do we call it?

14. What would be the effect on the distribution of income if a given quality of military force were obtained by means of a draft instead of a volunteer army? Whose taxes would be reduced and whose would be increased?

Glossary

Absolute advantage: Greater productive capacity. A person has an absolute advantage, relative to another person, in producing a good if she can produce more of it.

Accounting cost: The costs that accountants are permitted to consider. These differ from economic costs in that they do not include implicit costs, and they include depreciation in arbitrary ways.

Accounting profit: The difference between the total revenue a firm obtains and accounting cost.

Acquisition cost: The difference between the purchase price of an asset and its immediate resale price.

Administered price doctrine: The assertion that some firms can and do act arbitrarily to raise prices (as in cases where demand for their product and/or costs fall).

Agency shop: A union security arrangement whereby all the workers on a particular job, if they choose not to join the union that is the exclusive bargaining agent, must nevertheless pay fees to the union as a condition of maintaining employment.

Annuity: A series of uniform annual payments.

Autarky: Self-sufficiency. A system whereby a person or society produces all that it consumes (with no trade).

Automation: The substitution of machinery for labor in a production process.

Average advertising cost: Advertising cost per unit of output produced. (Advertising cost divided by the amount of output produced.)

Average fixed cost: Fixed cost per unit of output. Fixed cost divided by the quantity produced.

Average total cost: Total cost per unit of output. Total cost divided by the quantity produced.

Average variable cost: Variable cost per unit of output. Variable cost divided by the quantity produced.

Brand name: The trade name which a product carries, or the *reputation* which a product's trade name possesses.

Capital good: A good which provides benefits over time.

Cartel: A group of colluding firms. A voluntary combination of independent private enterprises that agree to limit their competitive activities in various ways.

Caveat emptor: Literally, "let the buyer beware." The policy that the consumer purchases at his own risk, with the seller having no legal responsibility for defects in products.

Ceteris paribus: A Latin expression meaning "other things the same." It is what is provisionally assumed in order to talk about such things as the demand curve. In that case, the other things which are held constant are income, prices of other goods, expected future prices, and tastes.

Change in demand: A shift in the location of a demand curve due to a change in income, prices of other goods, expected future prices, or tastes.

Collusion: Agreement by transactors concerning the quality or terms of trade at which they will sell or buy goods.

Comparative advantage: Lower cost. A person (or firm or country) has a comparative advantage in a given activity, relative to another person (or firm or country), if she can produce the activity at a lower cost.

Competition: A market structure characterized by having a sufficiently large number of firms producing sufficiently similar products to produce a situation in which the consumers pay the lowest possible price consistent with cost. A process of rivalry among firms which produces these results.

Complements: Goods which are related in such a way that an increase (decrease) in the price of one causes the demand for the other to decrease (increase). Such goods usually are used together to perform a given service.

Concentration ratio: The ratio of the total amount of output (or assets) accounted for by a particular number of the largest firms in an industry (often four) to the total amount of output (or assets) in the industry.

Consumer surplus: The difference between the maximum total amount which a consumer would be willing to pay to have the quantity of a given good he has (rather than do without it entirely) and the actual total amount he pays for that quantity of the good.

Corporation: A firm with more than one owner, characterized by the owners' having liability only up to the amount of money they have invested in the firm.

Cost: The most highly valued sacrifice incurred when an action is undertaken.

Demand curve: A diagrammatic representation of the relationship between the quantity of a good which is demanded and its price (*ceteris paribus*).

Demand schedule: A tabular representation of the relationship between the amount of a good which is demanded and its price (*ceteris paribus*).

Derived demand: The notion that the demand for such things as inputs into the production process depends on (is derived from) the demand for the final product and the prices of other inputs.

Discount factor: The number by which an amount (or amounts) to be paid in the future is multiplied to obtain the present value of the future amount (or amounts). In the case of a single future amount coming in t years, the discount factor is $1/(1 + r)^t$.

Discount rate: The interest rate (r) which is used in calculating a present value.

Economic profit: A rate of return in excess of the normal rate of return. Revenues greater than the sum of all costs.

Economic rent: The difference between the minimum amount a resource would be willing to accept in return for doing what it is doing and the amount it actually receives. The difference between a resource's remuneration and its supply price (the latter subtracted from the former).

Economies of scale: A situation whereby the cost per unit of output produced by a firm falls as the firm increases in size.

Efficient action: An action for which the benefit is greater than the cost.

Efficient allocation: A situation such that the cost of any further action will be greater than its benefit.

Efficient method of production: A method which provides a given benefit at the lowest possible cost or which provides the most benefit for a given cost.

Elastic: Characteristic of a demand curve in the range where its elasticity is greater than one.

Elasticity of demand: (price elasticity of demand.) A measure of the responsiveness of the quantity demanded to changes in price. It is calculated by taking the ratio of the percentage change in quantity to the percentage change in price which caused that change in quantity.

Elasticity of supply: The ratio of the percentage change in the quantity supplied to the percentage change in the price of the product.

Entrepreneur: A person whose comparative advantage is in seeing discrepancies between the value of a resource in a certain use and its cost to that use (value elsewhere).

Exchange: The activity whereby one person gives some of one good to another person, in return for which the second person gives some of another good to the first person.

Exclusive representation: The arrangement whereby a union that gets a majority vote in a representation election among workers on a particular job gets the privilege of representing all the workers on the job, including those who want to be represented by another union and those who want to represent themselves. A union with this privilege is called the *exclusive bargaining agent*.

Experience good: A good whose characteristics cannot be completely known until it is purchased and consumed.

Explicit cost: A cost which entails the outlay of money.

External diseconomy: A negative externality.

External economy: A positive externality.

Externality: An interaction between people in which a decision maker causes costs to be borne involuntarily by others (negative externality), or provides benefits to others for which she does not receive payment (positive externality).

Firm: An organization of people engaged in production, characterized by having: (1) owners (residual claimants) who are sometimes managers, (2) joint production (teamlike production), and (3) a monitor or monitors whose job it is to reduce shirking by the team members.

First Law of Demand: The assertion that the relationship between the price of a good and the quantity demanded is negative, that is, that demand curves are downward-sloping.

First Law of Supply: The assertion that the higher the price, the more that will be supplied. The assertion that supply curves are upward-sloping.

Fixed cost: Cost which does not vary with output and which, for certain decisions (such as changes in output while remaining in business) cannot be avoided. For the already set up firm, fixed cost corresponds to possession cost.

Good: Something which someone wants some of rather than none of.

Government brand name: The phenomenon which occurs when government specifies a certain quality level of product and puts its seal of approval on the product.

Implicit cost: A cost which does not involve an outlay of money, but rather the foregoing of an inflow of money or benefit.

Income: The amount which could be consumed without reducing wealth. The flow of goods and services which wealth provides.

Incremental cost: The change in total cost when the decision maker takes some action (such as increasing the quantity of output produced).

Indifference curve: A locus of points representing combinations of goods between which a transactor is indifferent.

Indirect information: With respect to experience goods, information which does not specify the characteristics of the good directly, but rather conveys the information that the advertiser thinks enough of the good to advertise it.

Industry supply curve: The horizontal sum of the individual firm supply curves.

Inefficiency of natural monopolists: The price which the firm charges is greater than the marginal cost of producing additional output.

Inelastic: Characteristic of a demand curve in the range where its elasticity is less than one.

Inferior good: A good for which the demand decreases (increases) as income increases (decreases).

Inframarginal externality: An externality which would *not* increase in size or amount if the activity generating it were to increase in size or amount. Inframarginal externalities do not create any efficiency problems.

Inspection good: A good whose characteristics can be obtained by inspection by the consumer before purchase.

Investment: The creation of capital goods. Transforming resources into sources of future rather than present consumption.

Long-run equilibrium: A situation in which the firm is maximizing profits, but at which zero economic profit is being earned. In a price-taker industry it is characterized by having quantity demanded equal quantity supplied, but with zero economic profits. There is no tendency for firms to enter or leave an industry which is in long-run equilibrium.

Marginal analysis: Analysis of the effects of small changes in decision variables. Specifically, an analysis of the change of benefit and/or the change of cost when there is a one-unit change in something.

Marginal cost: The change in total cost (or change in variable cost, since fixed cost by definition does not change) per additional unit of output produced. The change in total cost divided by the change in output. More precisely, marginal cost is the change in total cost resulting when there is a change of one unit of output produced.

Marginal externality: An externality which would increase in size or amount if the activity generating it were to increase in size or amount.

Marginal product: The amount of extra output produced when one more unit of an input is used, holding other inputs constant.

Marginal value of a good: The maximum amount of another good a person would be willing to give up to obtain one more unit of the good in question. (If she gave up more than this amount she would be worse off after the transaction.) Alternatively, the marginal value of a good is the minimum amount of another good the person would be willing to accept in return for giving up one unit of the good in question. (If she received less than this amount, she would be worse off after the transaction.)

Market failure: A failure of the exchange process to act in such a way as to result in payment by decision makers to those on whom they impose costs, or payments to decision makers for benefits they provide to others.

Markup: The difference between the price of output and the wholesale price of some key input.

Methodological individualism: An approach which takes the individual as the starting point of analysis. It is a denial of the idea of collective values or preferences, other than as an amalgamation of individual values and preferences.

Microeconomics: The study of the behavior of individual transactors under scarcity, and the coordination of their actions by mechanisms such as prices.

Middleman: A transactor who buys a good from one transactor for reselling to another transactor. Firms are middlemen.

Minimum wage law: A law which specifies that, in certain industries, no employed person may legally be paid less than a certain amount, called the minimum wage. Of course, an unemployed person receives a zero wage.

Model: A simplified (abstract) representation of some real-world process.

Monopoly: A firm which is (a) a single seller of the product it produces, or (b) operating in a market where entry is restricted, or (c) a price-searcher firm.

Multipart pricing: A pricing policy whereby the seller sells different units of the same commodity for different prices to the same buyer. Multipart pricing can only be carried out by a price-searcher who is able to prevent resale of the commodity.

Natural monopoly: An industry in which the natural result of the competitive process is the survival of only one firm. The usual reason for natural monopoly is extreme economies of scale.

Negative income tax: A form of welfare program in which families which earn less than a designated amount of income receive, as a cash payment, a certain percentage of the difference between what they earn and the designated amount.

Nonprice competition: Competition by means of quality or service improvements rather than by lowering prices.

Normal good: A good for which the demand increases (decreases) as income increases (decreases).

Normal rate of return: The rate of return which prospective investors would require to get them to invest in any particular industry. It is equal to the rate of return which could be earned in the best alternative industry with equivalent risk.

Normative statement: A statement based, at least in part, on opinion about what ought to be (or ought to have been, or ought to be in the future). It cannot be shown to be true or false.

Oligopoly: A market setting in which there are few enough sellers for the sellers to take into account the reactions of their rivals to their actions.

Operating cost: Cost other than acquisition and possession cost. This cost is incurred only if the asset is used during the period in question.

Partnership: A firm with more than one owner, all of whom bear unlimited liability for the debts of the firm.

Perpetuity: A perpetual annuity.

Pollution: The creation of a negative externality (usually as a by-product to some other activity).

Positive statement: A statement which can be tested (at least in principle) and shown to be true or false. A statement about the way things are, or were, or will be.

Possession cost: The decrease in the resale price of the asset over the period in question, plus the amount of interest which could be earned on the initial resale price, plus any taxes and insurance.

Present value: The amount which one would be willing to pay today to obtain the right to a certain amount or series of amounts in the future.

Price: The amount of other goods (often money) which a transactor must pay in order to obtain one unit of a good in exchange.

Price discrimination: Selling the same commodity for different prices to different customers, or selling different products at prices which do not accurately reflect the differences in marginal costs. It can only be carried out by a price-searcher who is able to prevent resale of the commodity.

Price dispersion: The degree to which prices for a given commodity differ among sellers. A ban on price advertising tends to increase price dispersion.

Price-searcher firm: A firm with market power—that is, power to influence the price of the good it sells. A firm which faces a downward-sloping demand curve.

Price-taker firm's supply curve: The MC curve in the range where it lies above the AVC curve.

Price-taker market: A market characterized by having a sufficiently large number of sellers of substantially the same product that each firm takes the price of the product as given. A certain type of competitive market.

Prisoner's dilemma: A social interaction (or game) in which the participants could all gain by engaging in some specified cooperative behavior, but in which each player is individually rewarded by not cooperating. The typical result is that none cooperate and all are worse off than if all had cooperated. The game often describes the behavior of people when each person is imposing an externality on the others.

Private property rights: Rights of individuals or firms to decide how their property is used. These include the right to refuse others permission to use the property and the right to sell it, as well as the rights to the goods which the property produces.

Production possibilities curve (PPC): A curve showing the various combinations of goods which can be produced, given the limited resources at the disposal of a person, firm, or economy.

Profit: (or economic profit) The difference between the total revenue the firm obtains and its total costs.

Profit contribution: The difference between the revenue that a firm receives and its variable (operating) cost. It is available to defray fixed (continued possession) cost, and any left over after paying these costs is economic profit.

Profit-maximizing output: The output at which the extra revenue a firm earns by selling one more unit of output is just offset by the extra cost which must be incurred to produce that extra output ($MR = MC$). For a price-taker, this means that $P = MC$, since $P = MR$ for the price-taker.

Property rights: Rights of people concerning the use of property.

Proprietorship: A firm with a single owner who bears unlimited liability for the debts of the firm.

Public good: A collective good. A good which is characterized by being jointly consumed by many persons at once and by the great difficulty (or impossibility) of preventing non-paying people from consuming it.

Rate of return: The discount rate at which the present value of the benefits of an investment project equals the investment required.

Saving: That portion of income which is not consumed. Saving gives rise to investment, which is the creation of additional wealth or capital.

Scarcity: A situation in which not everyone can have as much of everything as he wants.

Second Law of Demand: The assertion that demand curves are more elastic in the long run than in the short run.

Second Law of Supply: The assertion that supply curves are more elastic in the long run than in the short run.

Separation of ownership from control: The phenomenon that occurs when the owners of the firm are not directly involved in its management. This gives rise to problems for the owners in getting the managers to do what the owners want.

Shortage: A situation in which the amount of a good wanted at the actual existing price exceeds the amount made available at that price.

Specialization: Producing more of a good than one consumes.

Substitutes: Goods which are related in such a way that an increase (decrease) in the price of one causes the demand for the other to increase (decrease). Such goods usually can be used somewhat interchangeably to perform the same services.

Sunk cost: Cost which has already been incurred and cannot be avoided by taking any further action. Unavoidable cost.

Surplus: A situation in which the amount of a good wanted is less than the amount made available at that price.

Total cost: The sum of fixed and variable costs.

Transactor: An individual decision-making unit in the economy, such as a household, firm, or government agency.

Union shop: A union security arrangement whereby all the workers on a particular job must join the union that is the exclusive bargaining agent as a condition of maintaining employment.

Unitary elastic: Characteristic of a demand curve in the range where its elasticity equals one.

Utility: A word used to denote the preference for one good or bundle of goods. "Bundle A has more utility for me than bundle B" means "I prefer bundle A to bundle B."

Value of marginal product: The price of the output in question multiplied by the marginal product of the input in question.

Variable cost: Cost which varies with output. For a setup firm of a given size, this corresponds to operating cost.

Voucher: A method of subsidizing a particular activity. The voucher is a grant of money which can be used by the recipient only for the specified activity.

Wealth: A person's (or group's) holdings of assets (both human and nonhuman). Human wealth is the skills and earning power embodied in people. Nonhuman wealth includes land, buildings, machinery, and financial assets.

Index

379

384

†